REMBRANDT

REMBRANDT

CHRISTIAN TÜMPEL
Professor at the Institute of Art History
of the Catholic University of Nijmegen
including chapters by
ASTRID TÜMPEL
Director of the Steintormuseum at Goch

FONDS MERCATOR-ANTWERP

The chapters about Pieter Lastman and about the HUNDRED GUILDER PRINT are by Astrid Tümpel.

Documentation and typewriting:
Günther Nordmeyer, Martin Dierker, Claudia Müller-Ebeling, Ursula Sdunnus, Heike Ferslev, Judith van Gent, Erika Hamann, Petra van Burk.

Proofreading:
Dr. Ingewert Groh, Arie Hartog, Peter van der Coelen, Ron Manheim.
I owe much to Dr. Helmuth Leppien for his reading of the German text.

Translation: Dr. Edmund Jephcott
in collaboration with Dr. Alfred and Mrs. Isabel Bader.
Edited by Jackson Mac Low.

Some of the chapters of this book have been published earlier by Rowohlt in the series 'rowohlts bildmonographien' vol. 251. These texts were adapted for present book, and 28 chapters were added, along with an extensive section of notes, an alphabetic bibliography and faithful colour illustrations of all available Rembrandt paintings.
In the near future this book will moreover be completed with a catalogue raisonné of Rembrandt's paintings which is now being prepared by the author.

In the captions the name of the artist — or the attribution — has only been adopted when it is not one of Rembrandt's works. Furthermore the captions contain, besides the usual information, also the number of the painting in the forthcoming œuvre-catalogue (Cat. ...) and the corresponding number in Bredius 's catalogue. (or, if the work is not mentioned by Bredius, its number with the RRP).
The paintings having a normal number are generally considered by the author to be of Rembrandt's own hand. If he has serious doubts, however, this is indicated by 'Rembrandt (?)'. Using a K-number, for instance Cat. K1, means that the author considers these paintings to be copies. Paintings with an A-number are allegedly attributions. Paintings made by pupils or assistants in Rembrandt's workshop under his supervision are also listed as attributions.
The numbers in the margin refer to the page on which the painting is to be found.

D/1986/703/13
ISBN 90 6153 168 3

FOR DR. ALFRED AND MRS. ISABEL BADER.

Cover:
BATHSHEBA WITH KING DAVID'S LETTER. Detail.
Signed 'Rembrandt f. 1654'.
Canvas 142 × 142 cm
Paris, Louvre.
Cat. 24/Bredius 521.

Frontispiece:
SELF-PORTRAIT. About 1661. Detail.
Canvas 114.3 × 94 cm.
London, Kenwood House, The Iveagh Bequest.
Cat. 174/Bredius 52.

CONTENTS

FOREWORD

The better known an artist is and the longer he remains at the centre of cultural interest, the more legends grow up around his life and work. These are passed on from one generation to the next, obstructing new interpretations. So Rembrandt is still regarded as the genius of the Protestant faith, who sought inspiration for his biblical works solely in the Scriptures. The undue importance attached to chiaroscuro has had an almost ruinous effect on the judgement of his art. Many critics believe that Rembrandt's chief aim was to develop this one artistic device, which caused him to lose sight of his subject as he created. For this reason, most critical works accept the view that even in his most famous painting, the allegedly enigmatic NIGHT WATCH, he emphasised some guardsmen by illumination and relegated others to the shadowy background only for the sake of chiaroscuro, so forfeiting the good-will of his patrons and of the upper class of Amsterdam. Yet many documents, remarks by Rembrandt himself, and a careful study of his works lead us to an entirely different view.

The difficulty, indeed, the near hopelessness of drawing a definitive picture of Rembrandt is aptly expressed by the well-known art historian Julius Held:

> Earlier generations pointed primarily to his technique.... Others, depending on their personal interest, have stressed his religious views, his humanity, his feeling for nature, and his psychological subtlety. Art historians have rightly drawn attention to the astonishing development of his art as a manifestation of his unparalleled capacity for self-education and a progressive enlarging and deepening of feeling and experience. I believe we see one thing clearly: Rembrandt's art is so rich and complex that to seek a single formula which could provide us with a complete explanation is futile.[1]

It is certainly not possible within the framework of this monograph to cover all the aspects of Rembrandt's extraordinarily diverse art. So, in the following account of the various stages of Rembrandt's life, we shall pursue one central theme — the methods he used to give form and expression to his subjects. Though unusual for his time and still fascinating today, these methods have not so far received the attention they deserve; an understanding of them can contribute decisively to a new and more precise evaluation of Rembrandt's art.

SELF-PORTRAIT. About 1657.
Signed: 'Rembrandt f'.
Wood 49.2 × 41 cm.
Vienna, Kunsthistorisches Museum.
Cat. 171 / Bredius 49.

GETHSEMANE. About 1652.
Pen and bistre, white heightening. 184 × 301 mm.
Hamburg, Kunsthalle.
Benesch 899.

REMBRANDT'S YOUTH IN LEYDEN AND HIS TRAINING AS A PAINTER

When Rembrandt Harmenszoon van Rijn was born in Leyden on 15 July 1606, the Netherlands were engaged in a protracted war (1568-1648) in which they were beginning to free themselves from the economic and religious domination of Catholic Spain.

Philip II of Spain had been regent of the Netherlands since 1555. Opposition to the unbearable oppression of his government and its persecution of the Protestant minority was led by William, Prince of Nassau-Orange. After his murder by a fanatical follower of Philip II, leadership in the war of liberation passed to his son Maurice. In 1579 the seven northern provinces seceded from Spain and founded the Eternal Union of Utrecht. In 1609, three years after Rembrandt's birth, a truce began which was to last twelve years. Prince Maurice's successor, the chief executive officer of the United Provinces, Stadholder Prince Frederick Hendrick, then renewed the war against Spain with such success that fighting was confined to the borders and the high seas. The independence of the Republic was achieved in 1648.

The history of Rembrandt's native town is intimately connected with this struggle for independence. The city succeeded in withstanding a Spanish siege in 1573/74. A year later, William of Orange founded the University of Leyden, which soon became the most prominent Protestant centre of higher education. During the twelve-year truce (1609-21) — while Rembrandt was growing up — many Protestant weavers left Flanders for reasons of faith and settled in Leyden, the city becoming in consequence one of the most important textile centres in Europe. The economic structure had features of early capitalism; child labour was permitted, and a large portion of the population belonged to the impoverished proletariat.

This political development fostered economic and cultural growth, and Rembrandt was the most important representative of this artistic flowering.

His parents belonged to the upper-middle class. His 13 father, Harmen Gerritsz, was part-owner of a mill located on the outskirts of Leyden near the old Rhine. It is for this reason that Rembrandt later added to his name the designation 'van Rijn', which in his generation became the family name. Later biographers have been inclined to belittle Rembrandt's origins, referring condescendingly to 'the miller's son.' There is no reason for this: his father came from an old Leyden family. Four generations had been millers, and many members had held important positions in the city 12 government. His mother, Neeltje (the diminutive of Cornelia) van Suijttbroeck, came from a patrician family of

REMBRANDT'S MOTHER AS THE PROPHETESS HANNAH PRAYING.
Signed: 'R 1630'.
Copper 15.5 × 12.2 cm.
Salzburg, Residenzgalerie.
Cat. 75 / Bredius 63.

MUSIC-MAKERS IN BIBLICAL COSTUME.
Signed: 'RHL 1626'.
Wood 63.4 × 47.6 cm.
Amsterdam, Rijksmuseum.
Cat. 118 / Bredius 632.

REMBRANDT'S MOTHER. About 1631.
Etching 145 × 129 mm. 2nd state.
Bartsch 348.

Leyden, even though her father had been a baker.[2]

The grain business was a very profitable one. There were recurrent famines in the late 16th and early 17th centuries, and the Dutch, particularly the citizens of Amsterdam, took advantage of grain shortages in the interior and the plight of the armies. They bought up corn from all over Europe in years of good harvests, stored it in huge granaries, and sold it at inflated prices during the years of famine. Rembrandt's parents belonged to the group of burghers and lesser nobility who, after the Reformation in Holland, grew rich as Calvinists and aspired to greater power. Rembrandt's father and mother had grown up in Catholic families, but had been converted to Calvinism and were married in the Reformed St. Peter's Church at Leyden.

The family probably lived in a house on the Weddesteeg, diagonally across from the mill. Presumably Rembrandt was born there, the eighth of nine children. His first name was, and is, very uncommon. We know today that to have such an unusual name can be a burden to a child, but in exceptional circumstances it can also act as a spur to outstanding achievements. (Rembrandt was later able to sign his paintings with this first name alone, because there was no danger that he might be confused with any other painter of the same name.)

His parents had all their other sons apprenticed as craftsmen and tradesmen. The eldest, Adriaan, learned his father's trade and later inherited the mill; Willem became a baker like his maternal grandfather. However, they planned greater things for Rembrandt. 'His parents sent him to school to learn Latin at an early age; he was then sent to the university so that, with his knowledge, he could serve the city and the community to the best of his ability,' writes the burgomaster, Jan J. Orlers, in the second edition of his *Descriptions of the City of Leyden* (1641), which contains the earliest biography of Rembrandt.[3]

The Latin school was built in 1600 as a Calvinist educational institution. An inscription above the entrance announced that the pupils were to be taught languages, liberal arts, and above all, the fear of God. A school syllabus giving a definite curriculum was not published until after Rembrandt had left the school,[4] but as we can assume that this was merely a written confirmation of existing practice, we can learn from it something of the subjects taught as well as the spirit of the education provided. The study of Latin — reading, writing, and speaking — was considered of prime importance, as the name of the institution shows. Latin authors such as Cicero, Terence, Ovid, Virgil, and many others were read as a basis for the study of grammar rather than for their content. Some Greek was also taught, in accordance with Humanist ideas of education. The aim of this education was a very superficial one; it was intended solely to teach the student an elegant mode of life and a stylish manner of expression. Moral education was limited to the learning of Latin epigrams by heart. The young Rem-

Rembrandt's entrance form to the Leyden University, 1620. Leyden, University.

Rembrandus Hermanni Leydensis Studiosus Litterarum annor: 14 apud parentes

brandt is not likely to have been particularly attracted by this dry study of Latin, and his work is little influenced by the shallow manner of interpretation taught at school. As a painter he later entered more directly and naively into the stories of poets and the Bible and grasped more correctly their real historical and moral meaning than did the humanists who tried to force them into an alien mould.

The frequent lessons in religion were intended to give the students a knowledge of the Bible and of Calvinist doctrine and to train them to debate on questions of dogma. The children read the Gospels in Greek and learned the Lord's Prayer by heart. A chapter of the Bible was read every morning. The senior classes sang psalms, the hymns of the Calvinists. They had to go to church twice on Sundays, in the morning and again in the afternoon, and were tested in school on what they could remember of the sermons. This was asking a good deal, for the sermons usually lasted more than an hour. In the sixth year they discussed the differences between various Christian denominations and studied the Heidelberg catechism, which dealt with matters of dogma. The upper grade learned how to criticise heretical views, as was customary in all sermons of the time.

Such was the school to which his parents sent Rembrandt at the age of seven. To begin school at this age was in keeping with the educational ideas of the Humanist Erasmus of Rotterdam, who said that seven years of play should be followed by seven years in Latin school and a further seven years at university. Accordingly Rembrandt left the Latin school at the age of 14 to continue his education as a scholar at the university, which was also based on Calvinist princi- (12) ples. His entrance form to the university reads: *Rembrandt Harmensz., from Leyden, student in the Faculty of Philosophy, 14 years old, living with his parents.*[5]

It was the dream of all ambitious students of the arts in Europe to attend Leyden University because much outstanding work was done there, particularly in the field of language and philosophy. Stadholder Maurice of Nassau who, as head of the army, was interested in the ancient arts of war, together with the general assembly of the provinces, the States General, invited a French Huguenot, Joseph Justus Scaliger, to Leyden. Scaliger was a famous classical philologist who attracted the ablest scholars. That the university sought to wrest the leadership in classical scholarship from the Italian universities reflects a growing pride and sense of national identity. Despite their interest in the ancient writers, Daniel Heinsius and Scriverius wrote in their mother tongue, and compared classical with Batavian antiquities. This intense interest in the precise study of languages manifested itself in the official Dutch translation of the Bible, the 'Staatenbijbel', produced in Leyden between 1626 and 1637. It is a masterpiece of language and scholarship and was acknowledged as such by other religious denominations. Here theology and classical philology complemented one another. Since these scholars with their Humanist training interpreted the stories of the Old Testament in moral and typological terms, they could draw connections between events in antiquity and those in the Bible, either relating classical and Old Testament stories to events in the New Testament or finding parallel moral teachings in both.

Rembrandt grew up in this intellectual climate against this

REMBRANDT'S FATHER. About 1630.
Chalk and wash drawing. 189 × 240 mm.
Oxford, Ashmolean Museum. Benesch 56.

Jan Jacob BYLAERT.
THE LATIN SCHOOL IN LEYDEN.
Pen drawing, coloured. 180 × 105 mm.
Leyden, Municipal Archive.

background of university aspirations. His attempt to develop from earlier Dutch art a new style, which adopted the achievements of Italian painting while preserving national characteristics and aims, forms an analogy with the choice made by poets to write in Dutch rather than Latin.

We do not know how long Rembrandt attended the university. J. J. Orlers states only that 'he had no desire or inclination whatsoever in this direction, because his natural impulse was towards the art of painting and drawing. Therefore his parents were compelled to take him out of school and, according to his wish, they apprenticed him to a painter from whom he would learn the basic and principal rules of art. As a result of this decision, they took him to be taught by the excellent painter Jacob Isaacz. van Swanenburgh. He stayed with him for about three years, during which time his progress was such that art lovers were most amazed, for it was evident that he would one day become an exceptional painter'.[6]

Jacob Isaacz. van Swanenburgh belonged to one of the city's most respected families, which had remained Catholic and retained its ties with Italy. That Rembrandt's parents were not narrow minded in religious matters and attached importance to a broad training is indicated by this choice of teacher. Swanenburgh was influenced by Roman artists of the circle of Federico Zuccari, and like them he painted views

Jacob Isaacsz. VAN SWANENBURGH.
HELL.
Wood 93.5 × 124 cm.
Leyden, Stedelijk Museum 'De Lakenhal'.

of Italian cities with small, colourfully dressed figures. However, his works were chiefly characterized by scenes 14 showing hell and witches, which brought him into conflict with the Inquisition in Naples. Although no thematic influence of Swanenburgh is discernible in his works, it is likely that Rembrandt learned more than just the technical aspects of painting in these three years. In his fantastic hell scenes, influenced by Hieronymus Bosch and Pieter Breughel the Elder, Swanenburgh represents the horror and panic of the damned in many stages, ranging from terror to resignation. The depiction of such reactions later became one of Rembrandt's most important artistic aims. Moreover, Swanenburgh's scenes of hell and witches are night pieces; the figures are accentuated by the use of light. It was here that Rembrandt first learned that in the play of light and dark important elements can be emphasised while the less important are left in obscurity. He was also influenced by the smallness of his teacher's paintings, which accommodated an abundance of figures and actions. Within the narrowest confines Swanenburgh handled themes which had previously been treated in monumental altar paintings. Although Rembrandt later took an entirely different approach to 'histories' and chose quite different subjects, it is likely that the small format characteristic of his early work was adopted from his first teacher.

Pieter BAST.
PLAN OF THE CITY OF LEYDEN. 1600.
Engraving 374 × 440 mm.
Leyden, Municipal Archive.

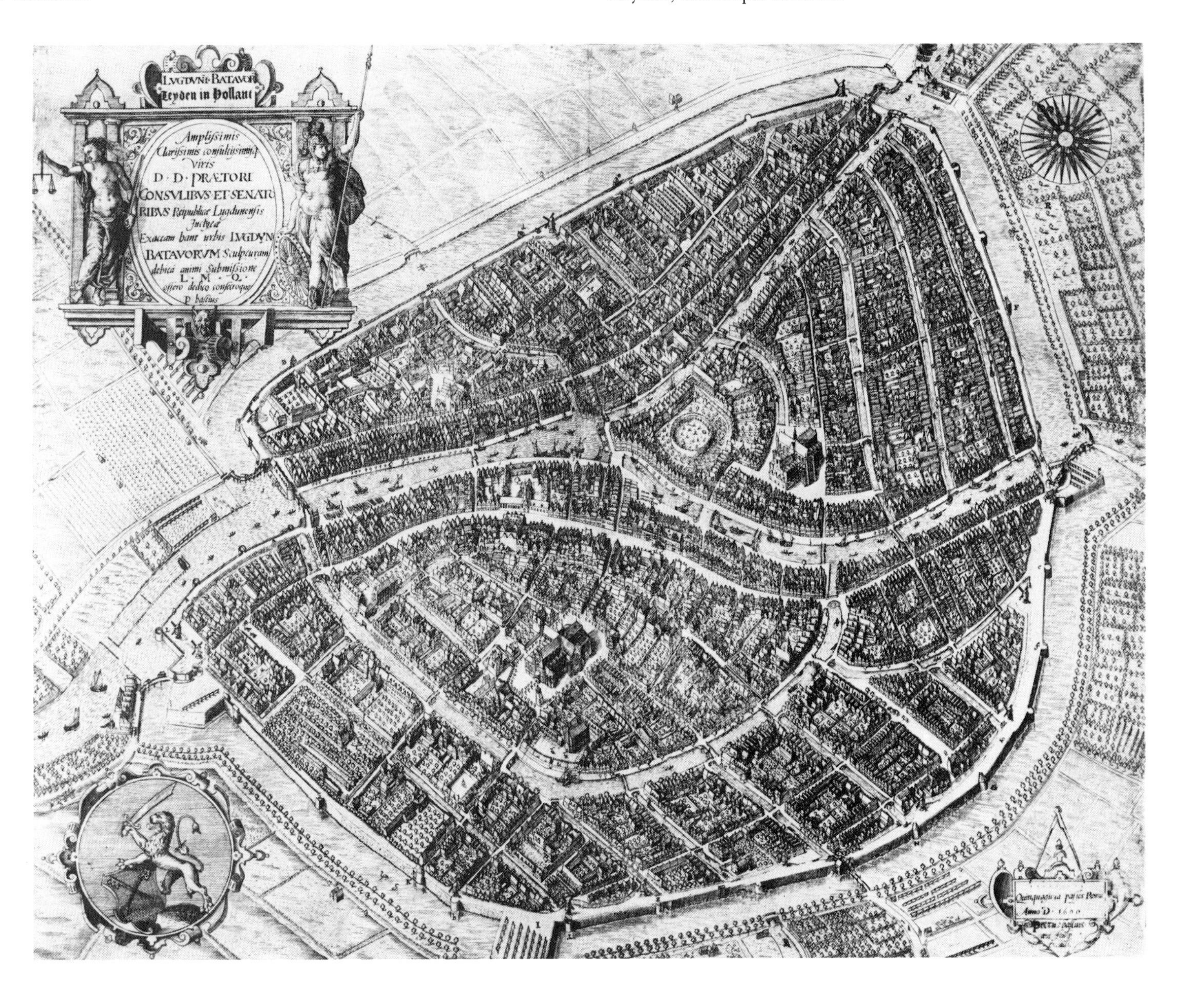

REMBRANDT STUDIES UNDER PIETER LASTMAN

Rembrandt found his true master in Pieter Lastman, the Amsterdam painter of 'histories' (by which were meant scenes from the Old and New Testaments and mythology as well as from history).[7] Jan Lievens, with whom Rembrandt worked closely after his return from Amsterdam, had studied with Lastman after being taught by Joris van Schooten. We know that Rembrandt, on his father's wish, likewise went to Lastman in Amsterdam, J. J. Orlers tells us: 'His father considered it appropriate to spend more money and take him to the famous P. Lastman, who lived in Amsterdam, so that he might be better taught and instructed.'[8] Even though, according to Orlers, this period of study lasted only six months, it made a decisive impression on Rembrandt. At a time when painters were beginning to specialise in a single subject — landscape, still life, flower paintings, genre, or portraits — the most important painter of histories in Amsterdam was Lastman. The great Dutch poet Joost van den Vondel compared him with Rubens and wondered which would surpass the other in fame.

Pieter Lastman, a Catholic like Swanenburgh and probably born in Amsterdam about 1583, was a pupil of the Mannerist Gerrit Pietersz. Sweelink, whose style influenced his early works. However, during a trip to Italy undertaken about 1603, he found new models. The painters he met in Venice and Rome had a lasting influence on his work. At first Hans Rottenhammer seems to have impressed him most; later, through intensive study of the works of Adam Elsheimer, Michelangelo da Caravaggio, and the Carracci brothers, he evolved a style of history painting which was entirely his own. He combined the monumental style of Paolo Veronese with the concentrated, cabinet-size works of Elsheimer, in which history and landscape are convincingly combined. When Lastman returned to Amsterdam, not later than 1607, he soon became one of the most influential painters there.

While his early works still mix Venetian and Roman elements, juxtaposing them like pieces of scenery seen from different perspectives, after 1611 the pictures achieve formal unity. Lastman now shows the main figures at close quarters in the foreground; the powerful figures stand out plastically in a light that detaches them from their surroundings. In the 19 Rotterdam FLIGHT TO EGYPT (1608) he succeeds in harmonising figures and landscape. Branches and roots in the dark foreground provide a decorative framework for the main group of the fleeing Holy Family. Lastman stresses the close bond between Mary and the child Jesus. Joseph is depicted as a robust carpenter striding vigorously onwards. To the

Pieter LASTMAN.
THE BAPTISM OF THE CHAMBERLAIN.
Monogrammed and dated 1623.
Wood 85 × 115 cm.
Karlsruhe, Staatliche Museen.

THE BAPTISM OF THE CHAMBERLAIN.
Signed: 'RH 1626'.
Wood 63.5 × 48 cm.
Utrecht, Rijksmuseum Het Catharijneconvent.
Cat. 35 / Bredius — / RRP A5.

Pieter LASTMAN.
JOSEPH SELLING CORN IN EGYPT.
Signed and dated 1612.
Wood 62 × 91 cm.
Dublin, National Gallery of Ireland.

right there is a view of a waterfall and a castle.

After 1612 the figures become still more vivid and plastic. They are placed in a foreground which is itself brightly lit. In 1612, Lastman produced the imposing history painting THE DEPARTURE OF HAGAR.[9] It depicts the conflict of the patriarch Abraham, who was first urged by his wife Sarah, who had remained infertile despite God's repeated promises, to sire a child by another woman, Hagar, but then had to drive her out when his wife gave birth to an heir, Isaac. Abraham lays his right hand in blessing on the head of his weeping son Ishmael and with his left hand touches the arm of Hagar, who, bathed in tears, gazes into his eyes. In the background Abraham's palace is seen to the left; from the gateway Sarah looks on with Isaac on her arm, a detached spectator. To the right spreads a mountainous landscape crossed by a river in a deep valley, with an old Roman bridge. This fragment of landscape is painted in cool green tones, while Abraham's palace, placed in shadow, is in strong brownish-greens. The main figures in the foreground are set off from the background by clear colours, by the illumination, by their separation from the landscape behind them, and by perspective. We see the faces from slightly below, which gives the picture a monumental quality.[10] Lastman's pictures are entirely based on the history, even when poetic licence allows

JOSEPH SELLING CORN IN EGYPT. About 1637.
Signed: 'Rembrandt ft.'
Black chalk. Drawn on two sheets glued together.
317 × 404 mm.
Vienna, Graphische Sammlung Albertina. Benesch 446.

him to add numerous decorative motifs. This is clear from a 20 consideration of only one of the works which Rembrandt knew and later, at about thirty, copied.

Lastman not only composed histories comprising a few figures; he also portrayed crowd scenes with a skill that Rembrandt admired throughout his life. A good example 20 from 1612 is JOSEPH SELLING CORN IN EGYPT. The subject had already been treated in Bible illustrations, but Lastman conceived it quite differently, depicting it in its context in a wholly new way, based on an exact knowledge of real events. Joseph had interpreted a dream for Pharoah: after seven abundant harvests would come seven lean ones. For this prediction he was made the ruler's deputy and immediately ordered the building of granaries for the good harvests. When famine subsequently broke out, the Egyptians offered him all of their possessions. Lastman shows them selling silver, cattle, and even their freedom for corn. So Egypt fell into bondage. In early capitalist Amsterdam, which grew rich like Pharoah by storing grain, the point was understood. In the middle ground of his picture, Lastman shows Joseph looking down on a despairing couple with their child and cattle. This scene is the focal point of the action. But Lastman is not only concerned with the organizational side of the transaction. He shows people crushing together in their need; everyone wants to be first; a sack of corn has opened, spilling its precious contents; this is gathered up by a kneeling woman while a child stills its hunger. It is all told in a discursive, almost anecdotal way; yet despite the epic breadth, the details never distract attention from the main theme.

Two years later, in 1614, Lastman painted PAUL AND BARNABAS IN LYSTRA, which Rembrandt copied in his thirties and which the great Dutch poet Joost van Vondel thought a miraculous work.[11] The crux of the story depicted here is that the apostles Paul and Barnabas are not recognised in the heathen town of Lystra as messengers of Christ; they are worshipped by the crowd as Mercury and Jupiter in human shape, because they have healed a lame man. The two apostles despairingly ward off the false adoration. Lastman puts them on a stage with the healed man below to the left, showing bystanders the crutches lying on the ground. With unsurpassed variety, an abundance of motifs, and knowledge of ancient customs and topography, Lastman paints the immense sacrificial procession approaching in the distance. Into this painting Lastman has put his whole knowledge of the ancient world.

In the pictures painted after 1615, Lastman normally places the horizon low. This enables him, in the painting THE ANGEL LEAVING THE FAMILY OF TOBIAS, to depict the whole caravan in the background, kneeling before the angel.[12] Lastman is concerned to emphasise the apparition of the angel before the pious father and his loyal son, but at the same time to show the whole herd that the son has brought back from his journey, half of which he offers to the angel. It is noteworthy too that Lastman corrects an older tradition in painting; the narrative does not take place in front of the house but to one side of it. Whereas the earlier tradition sought to depict the parting from the family by showing the house, which in biblical language is often equated with the family, Lastman, adhering to the text, makes it clear that the

Pieter LASTMAN.
THE FLIGHT INTO EGYPT.
Monogrammed and dated 1608.
Wood 28 × 25 cm.
Rotterdam, Museum Boymans - van Beuningen.

Rembrandt's workshop.
THE FLIGHT INTO EGYPT.
Signed: 'RH 16(27)'. Wood 26.4 × 24.2 cm.
Tours, Musée des Beaux-Arts.
Cat. A4/Bredius 532A.

THE DISMISSAL OF HAGAR (after Pieter Lastman). About 1637.
Black chalk. 192 × 150 mm.
Vienna, Graphische Sammlung Albertina.
Benesch 447.

Pieter LASTMAN.
DAVID AND URIAH.
Signed: 'Lastman fecit 1619'.
Wood 42 × 63 cm.
Groningen, Groninger Museum voor Stad en Lande.

unknown wanderer (who has miraculously protected the young Tobias on his perilous travels) has led the young and the old Tobias a short distance from the house and revealed himself to them as an angel. Unlike the painters before him, Lastman is interested in the apparition of the angel, with old Tobias bowing reverently and young Tobias receiving the angel's blessing with outspread arms. It was scenes of apparition that particularly interested Lastman.

In his late works the patterns of composition worked out previously are retained, and the only significant changes are in the rendering of detail. Folds of drapery are ampler and heavier, covering the bodies opulently and descending in thick, doughy convolutions. The foreground is richly painted, forms are plastic in vivid light. In the background the painting grows flatter and looser, particularly in the twenties. The paintings produced in 1622/23 influenced Rembrandt during the period he spent working with Pieter Lastman, as well as the work from the early phase around 1614. He certainly knew the painting BALAAM AND THE ASS, in 21 which the stylistic elements just mentioned are to be found.[13] In it Lastman depicts a little known story from the Old Testament. On their journey to the Promised Land of Canaan after the flight from Egypt, the Israelites had camped in the territory of the Moabites. Fearing the Israelites, the Moabite king, Barak, summoned the prophet Balaam to pronounce a curse on them. However, God commanded Balaam to go to Barak, but to do only what He would tell him. On his way to the king he was approached by an angel with a sword. Balaam's ass saw the angel and stood still. But the prophet — who did not see the angel — drove the ass on with blows. Suddenly it began to speak, and Balaam's eyes were opened; he recognised the angel. Lastman portrays the moment when the ass sinks to its knees and begins to speak. The model for the painting was probably a drawing by Dirk Vellert of which only a fragment has survived; it shows Balaam trying to drive the ass forward. Lastman follows the drawing in the composition of the group, with Balaam and the ass. But he distinguishes more clearly than Vellert between the main figures, which are emphasised by lighting, and the secondary ones.

In Lastman's paintings almost all the motifs relating to the story provide explanation rather than psychological interpretation. In two paintings on the theme of DAVID AND URIAH, 20 Lastman made decisive changes from the traditional treatment: he chose a later moment in which the terrible decision is still reverberating.[14] David had committed adultery with Uriah's wife; to keep it secret Uriah was to return from the war and sleep with Bathsheba. But he refused to leave the holy war in contravention of the law. After twice vainly demanding that Uriah sleep at home, David summoned him and gave him a letter to the army commander ordering that Uriah be sent to the most advanced point of the front. This happened and Uriah was killed. In contrast to tradition, Lastman did not depict one of the earlier meetings, but chose as his subject the handing over of the letter, with the scribe also present. This accessory to the crime looks up in silence at David. In this way we become witnesses. Like Uriah we look up at David, who is shown from below, seeing Christ's progenitor from Uriah's perspective as a sinner. The Bible does not mention that the letter was sealed — this motif, which is quite central to the picture, was taken by the learned artist from *The Antiquities of the Jews* by Flavius Josephus.[15]

In 1623, shortly before Rembrandt joined his workshop, 17 Pieter Lastman painted THE BAPTISM OF THE CHAMBERLAIN. He painted this scene four times during his life. Rembrandt was to emulate him in this, producing an etching and three 16 paintings on the theme.[16]

An African chamberlain returning home from Jerusalem meets the apostle Philip. Philip interprets Isaiah to him in Christian terms, showing him that Jesus is the Son of God promised by the Scriptures. Thereupon the chamberlain allows himself to be baptised in a river. Everything in the picture is bright, clear, and firmly painted. The coach from which the chamberlain and the apostle have alighted to perform the baptism seems palpably present, as do the two main figures by the river.

In front of the coach stands a Moorish boy holding the Bible from which the chamberlain and Philip have been reading and which has led to the conversion and the baptism. The colours here have a mild brightness without violent contrasts. In the main figures, the servant, and the coach, warm colours predominate. So the scene in the foreground stands out strongly from the cool green tones of the rocky, tree-grown mountain in the background. The whole composition is orientated towards the onlooker. The chamberlain kneels well in the foreground, his arms crossed reverently on his breast. He looks towards the onlooker. Behind him is Philip, a broad, powerful figure; with his left hand he draws back his ochre cloak while holding his right hand over the chamberlain's head to baptise him. The coachman, the man in the coach, and the Moorish boy with the Bible witness the holy event and are moved by it. To ornament the foreground, a brown and white dog stands in the road. He represents the creaturely world uncomprehending of the sacred happening, and herb-like vegetation proliferates along the river bank.

Around Pieter Lastman had formed a circle of artists who imitated his style: his own brother Nicolaes, Jan Tengnagel (a nephew of Rubens), the brothers Jan and Jacob Pynas, François Venant, and Claes Moeyaert.[17] Adriaan van Nieulandt and Pieter Isaacsz. were stylistically close to them for a time. Some of them were related by marriage: Tengnagel had married the sister of the Pynas brothers, and Venant had married Lastman's sister. Pieter Lastman, the Pynas brothers, and Tengnagel had been in Italy in the first decade of the century, where they had experienced the new discoveries in the painting of landscape and histories. On their return the others fell increasingly under the sway of Pieter Lastman's powerful compositions; in the second decade of the century he emerged as the most inventive and erudite history painter in Amsterdam. This circle of older painters was later joined by the younger painters Adriaen van Nieulandt and François Venant, who had both been apprenticed to Pieter Isaacsz., and later to Claes Moeyaert. Pieter Isaacsz. was the son of the agent of the States General in Elsinore, Denmark. His brother was the historiographer Johannes Isacius Pontanus, who wrote an informative history of Amsterdam. He received his training from the leading Mannerists Johann van Aken and Cornelis Ketel. From 1590 on, he lived in Amsterdam

Pieter LASTMAN.
BALAAM AND THE ASS.
Signed: 'Lastman fecit 1622'.
Wood 41.3 × 60.3 cm.
New York, Mr. and Mrs. Richard L. Feigen.

THE PROPHET BALAAM AND THE ASS.
Signed: 'RH 1626'.
Wood 63.2 × 46.5 cm.
Paris, Musée Cognacq-Jay.
Cat. 1 / Bredius 487.

Jan TENGNAGEL.
CHRIST ENTERING JERUSALEM.
Signed and dated 1623.
Canvas 170 × 270 cm.
Hamburg, Katholisches Dekanat.

Claes MOEYAERT.
GOD APPEARING BEFORE ABRAHAM IN SICHEM. Before 1624.
Monogrammed.
Wood 35 × 46.3 cm.
Amsterdam, William Russell Collection.

and soon gained a good reputation as a portrait painter. In 1630 he built his house in the recently opened St. Anthonisbreestraat, proudly calling it 'The Cronenburgh' after the castle of his lord, the Danish king. In 1608, Pieter Lastman's mother bought a house in this street, and Lastman moved there with his brother Nicolaes. Other painters followed. Next door to Pieter Lastman lived the successful portrait painter Cornelis van der Voort. So the well-to-do area gradually became a colony of artists, who mostly came from wealthy or prominent families. They were trying to make their names as painters. They were tolerant towards each other, although belonging to different faiths. Pieter Lastman and Claes Moeyaert were from Catholic families who had lost their influence and connections in Amsterdam through the transfer of political offices to Protestants. Jan Tengnagel and François Venant were Protestants, but part of the group of moderate Calvinists called Remonstrants. Venant was later to take up the cause of the Remonstrants' freedom, and in the same years that Rembrandt was studying under Lastman, Tengnagel, in his high political office as the ruler's representative, was ensuring that the Calvinists in the guilds did not intolerantly impose obedience on all those of other persuasions and so provoke a new revolution. The tolerance existing between the artists is clear from the marriage between the Remonstrant Venant and Lastman's sister, who was and remained a Catholic. If a number of the Catholics among them came from families which had previously held offices, the Protestants were partly from the families to which power had been transferred.

The artists used to pass on or even mutually exchange commissions. When for instance, in 1610, Pieter Isaacsz. received commission to paint 22 pictures on copper for the king of Denmark, Christian IV, he did not only share this work with his pupil Adriaen van Nieulandt but also with Pieter Lastman and other friends.[18]

Pieter Lastman had a great influence on the history painters of this circle. They produced variations on his compositions, used them for new subjects, and imitated them. Rembrandt therefore came into contact with a large group of artists who were much influenced by his teacher. They imitated his style to such an extent that many of their pictures were until recently regarded as painted by their great model. Although they gradually freed themselves from this excessive influence — in the period when Rembrandt was apprenticed to Lastman — the solutions they found were rarely better than those they had derived from their master. Jan Pynas, probably the oldest of them, used Lastman's compositions as a starting point in many of his works.[19] In them everything is indicated rather than executed, lacking the rich substance, the colourful and plastic density, of Lastman. In contrast to the latter's work, Jan Pynas's JOSEPH DISTRIBUTING CORN IN EGYPT makes limited use of narrative motifs and depicts everything in a simpler, calmer, flatter, less ornamental manner. He has taken over from his model the Egyptian family desperately begging for bread, but reduced the ornamentation in order to make the Egyptians' plea clearer. The man in the foreground carrying bread illustrates how Joseph gives the Egyptians bread in exchange for their sheep, horses, cattle, and asses. The simplification and enlargement of the figures is striking; in his later works

Jan Pynas took this tendency still further. The figures fill large areas of the foreground and the landscape element recedes.

According to Houbraken, Rembrandt went to study under Jacob Pynas after his period of work with Pieter Lastman and learned sepia painting from him.[20] This seems merely an attempt by Houbraken to find an art-historical origin for a stylistic peculiarity of Rembrandt in the thirties. It is doubtful whether Rembrandt got to know Jacob Pynas in Amsterdam, since the latter was living in Delft and only there developed the sepia-painting technique. But there was a large number of his paintings in Amsterdam, many of which were regarded until very recently as masterpieces by Elsheimer. These calm, idyllic landscapes, composed of dark and light zones layered one behind the other, with rounded mountains and hills and small historical scenes embedded among them, were thought characteristic of Elsheimer; in fact, they are much closer to Paulus Bril. Apart from these landscapes with historical detail, he produced history paintings influenced by Pieter Lastman; some of them were until recently thought to be works of the master. In PAUL AND BARNABAS IN LYSTRA, which Jacob Pynas is likely to have painted shortly before Rembrandt's arrival in Amsterdam, he takes over Lastman's composition but inverts it.[21] The foreground figures are larger, cutting abruptly across each other; lightness and depth are lacking. Without proper regard for distance, they appear from behind each other or a fold in the ground; being themselves flat, in colourful garments with coarse folds, they merge with the colours of the darkened foreground.

In 1623 Jan Tengnagel painted CHRIST ENTERING JERUSALEM. The monumental picture clearly reveals his late style. He continues his earlier use of large figures and takes their already powerful gestures to excess. The followers welcoming Christ seem almost to be dancing. This overemphasis represents a return to Mannerist modes. He gives one of the spectators his own features, thus making himself one of the witnesses who direct the onlooker's attention towards Jerusalem.

François Venant and Claes Moeyaert were about ten years younger than Tengnagel and Jan Pynas. Venant transforms Lastman's DAVID AND JONATHAN, painted in 1620, into a calm, Classicist composition.[22] He changes the viewpoint of the figures and alters the gestures. Jonathan is seen from directly in front; the three-quarter view of David in Lastman's painting is converted into a strict profile. Finally, in that year Claes Moeyaert painted THE VISION OF ABRAHAM.[23] Compared to Lastman's powerful figures, Moeyaert's look consumptive. The main and subsidiary figures are not clearly distinguished. From the CORIOLANUS painting Moeyaert has taken over the horseman in shadow, but has also included a further secondary figure in the foreground, distracting from the main scene.

The comparison with these imitators and followers probably made the superiority of his own master clear to the young Rembrandt. The way others made variations on his teacher's compositions stimulated and impressed him — he too later produced his own variations on Lastman. But the solutions found by these artists did not satisfy him. No one equalled the control Lastman had over his pictures, his ability to manage large groups. None could match his erudition. The exchange of ideas with these painters must have been more important to Rembrandt than their history pieces. He saw how some of them created large group portraits, making use of the knowledge they had gained through history painting.

François VENANT.
DAVID AND JONATHAN.
Monogrammed.
Wood 30.5 × 47 cm.
Paris, Institut néerlandais, Fritz Lugt Collection.

Influenced by the cult of genius, critics have long believed that it was only Lievens who learned from Rembrandt, who was one year his senior, and that Lievens was at once eclipsed and consumed by Rembrandt's sun. They ought to have been more cautious, for the two biographers, Orlers and Huygens, both tell us more about Lievens than about Rembrandt and point to the long, successful activity of Lievens, who was a child prodigy.[24]

The burgomaster of Leyden, Jan Jansz. Orlers, appended a detailed biography of Lievens to the second edition of his history of Leyden of 1641. It is many times longer than the description of Rembrandt's life. This is not surprising, for Orlers greatly admired the young artist; eight of his paintings were owned by his family, whereas he had bought nothing by Rembrandt.

Lievens, he writes, was apprenticed at the age of eight to Joris van Schooten, an able painter of histories and portraits. When he was about ten (that is, probably in 1617) his father took him to the famous history painter Pieter Lastman in Amsterdam, where he developed rapidly. After that, from the age of eleven or twelve, the boy worked independently in his parents' home. According to Orlers, Lievens at that time was quite obsessed with his work. When, on 4 October 1618, there was a clash between Remonstrant citizens and the Calvinists, he neither interrupted his work nor noticed what was happening. He was just then engaged in copying engravings by Willem Buytewech (who was similarly oblivious of earthly matters). The boy, who had not yet found his own style, looked round for works by the great masters, copied and assimilated them. So he produced a copy of the painting HERACLITUS AND DEMOCRITUS by his famous Haarlem colleague Cornelis Ketel. It was said of this inspired and somewhat extravagant artist that he had created enchanting paintings with his fingers and his feet. No wonder the ambitious boy copied him. But he also created, Orlers tells us, works following his own composition and ideas and based directly on life. Here Orlers indirectly indicates that Jan Lievens had broken away from Lastman's themes and joined the trend of modern specialist painting. He painted still lifes, figures, portraits, and also, though not primarily, histories. Stylistically Lievens broke with Lastman and aligned himself with the most modern tendencies in Dutch painting, the Caravaggisti in Utrecht and the Haarlem Classicists. The Utrecht Caravaggisti, among whom Honthorst and Hendrick Terbrugghen were pre-eminent, brought Caravaggio's style to Holland in their own interpretation. They produced realistic religious history paintings, but also genre pieces in

116

THE OLD TOBIAS AND HIS WIFE.
Signed: 'RH 1626'.
Wood 40.1 × 29.9 cm.
Amsterdam, Rijksmuseum.
Cat. 2 / Bredius 486.

Jan LIEVENS.
FIRE. (From a series of the Four Elements).
Wood 83.5 × 60 cm.
The Hague, S. Nystad Oude Kunst B.V.

Jan LIEVENS.
PILATE WASHING HIS HANDS IN INNOCENCE.
Wood 83.8 × 105 cm.
Leyden, Stedelijk Museum 'De Lakenhal'.

which the scene is reduced to one or more life-size figures and space and milieu are given only sketchily.[25] The whole emphasis is on the figures, their physiognomies, and their expressive, rhetorical gestures. The scenes are interpreted through the light. Since illumination is the artistic means of giving form, the artists are able more than ever before to depict biblical scenes in interiors, as well as night scenes. In 1614 the most gifted of the Utrecht painters, Hendrick Terbrugghen, had returned from Italy. In 1616/17 he became a member of the painters' guild. His figures are often placed before a sunlit wall. The whole picture space is filled with a delicately rendered luminous atmosphere. In 1620 the most successful Utrecht painter, Gerard van Honthorst, returned to his native town. At about 20, in 1610, he had gone to Rome. There he was nicknamed 'Gherardo della Notte' on account of his night scenes. The plasticity and vigour of Caravaggio's paintings give place in Honthorst to renderings in pale light, with gentle, refined figures and a smooth surface. Terbrugghen and Honthorst had a great influence on Lievens and later on Rembrandt. But whereas Terbrugghen remained largely unknown, Honthorst had a brilliant career. Even in Rome he worked for the Roman nobility, the high clergy, and the Grand Duke of Tuscany; in Utrecht commissions came from all sides. He painted numerous likenesses of citizens and nobles, officers and princes. He instructed the children of the exiled Bohemian king Frederick. He spent almost the whole of 1628 at the English court, where he painted many portraits and the allegory APOLLO AND DIANA. Later he became court painter to the stadholder. He became the great model for the stylistically adaptable Lievens. In 1632 Lievens even attempted to make a career like Honthorst at the English court.

Above all, the Utrecht painters' genre scenes, the depictions of drinkers and musicians, young people playing with fire, gamblers and horse-dealers, made an impression on Lievens. So, in his painting FIRE, one of his series THE FOUR ELEMENTS, he took Honthorst's THE SOLDIER AND THE GIRL as his point of departure.[26] In it a girl holds a glowing coal with a pair of tongs to light a candle. The symbolic meaning of her action is clear from the behaviour of the man. He looks amorously at her, embraces her, clasps her bosom. The light brings the girl's face and bosom out of the darkness. This theme is very common in Dutch literature. The burning coal is a metaphor for the dangers of love. In an emblem the popular poet Cats has a gallant say about marriage that woman is like a coal, she either burns or soils. In a somewhat more temperate metaphor the coal motif has survived until today in the verse: 'No fire, no coal can burn as hot as secret love'. In a similar way Terbrugghen shows a girl lighting a candle; point of view and lighting largely coincide. Lievens adopted this kind of composition. In contrast to Honthorst's unambiguous representations that are construed at first sight, he prefers the isolated figure engaged in playing with fire. Yet the scene has an erotic character; the youth is 'unbuttoned', his shoulder exposed, as in the case of wanton shepherds.

In these early paintings, which Lievens painted before Rembrandt's return to Leyden, he renders softly modeled figures monumentally, with strong light-and-shadow effects. If no Caravaggesque models are available to him — as in the case of the rest of the paintings in the FOUR ELEMENTS series — his representation remains much more strongly attached to the antiquated style of the late Goltzius and his student Joris van Schooten. He depicts strong, muscular figures in heavy, billowing fabrics.

Jan Lievens's THE FIVE SENSES is also marked by the Utrecht models, even though Haarlem influence is discernible in the bright, colourful execution and detailed characterisation of the subjects.[27] The five senses are not depicted by special attributes or heavily symbolic actions, but by rhetorical actions. The drinker symbolises taste by his raised glass; sight is conveyed by the old man peering through his lorgnette; the youth fondling the girl represents feeling, the smoker scent, and the musician hearing. The various figures are assembled into a loosely knit society, bound together by a common action. Orlers was struck by the novelty of his approach. Traditionally the five senses had been presented on different panels; here he represents the five senses on one panel. The spatial relations are not clear in this arrangement. The figures jostle together on an extremely shallow stage. The head of the seated musician is at the same level as those of the standing figures.

Lievens also imitates the Utrecht painters in his history paintings. The composition of the painting PILATE WASHING HIS HANDS IN INNOCENCE is based on a picture produced by Hendrick Terbrugghen in 1621, as Nicolson has observed.[28] However, Lievens moves the main figure more prominently into the centre and involves the onlooker in the action by pointedly turning Pilate towards him. Lievens's brushwork and bright colours recall the early pictures of the Haarlem painter Salomon de Bray, of whom the figure looking frontally out of the picture is also typical.

26

When Rembrandt returned to Leyden in 1625, the two young artists clearly exchanged ideas, as they had done with the Amsterdam history painters and portraitists. There is an ineradicable legend, found over and again in art histories, that they opened a studio together. It originates in the fact that the two young artists were compared as a pair by Huygens and Orlers in accordance with the rules of classical rhetoric, so that their lives and work might be better distinguished.[29] We shall take leave of this legend and pursue the mutual influence of the two painters.

Rembrandt had brought back copies of the most recent as well as of earlier compositions by Lastman from Amsterdam; Lievens had enlarged his substantial output of head studies and biblical histories into Caravaggesque half-length figure pictures, series, and pendants. By the range of his subjects, his modern Utrecht–Haarlem style, and the scale of his work, Lievens obviously impressed Rembrandt. In so doing, he drew Rembrandt's attention to the Utrecht painters. Evidence of this is his early painting CHRIST DRIVING THE MONEY-CHANGERS FROM THE TEMPLE (1626), based on Lievens's early, undated painting THE BACKGAMMON-PLAYERS. The history painter Rembrandt does not present, like Lievens, a genre scene centring on the ruinous and transitory game, but chooses for his composition the very unusual form of the half-length figure to present a biblical scene which also shows how people (money-changers) give themselves up to the pursuit of money. However, in Rembrandt's early work this half-length figure picture is an exception, for he stayed true to what he had learned from Lastman. But he tried to combine this with the stimulus coming from Lievens, that is, to unite history painting in the tradition of Adam Elsheimer with Caravaggesque painting. Others had begun to do so before him. But Rembrandt went beyond them by not treating the picture space as a narrow arena plunged in obscurity with brightly lit figures acting in front of this dark foil. His figures appeared in strongly foreshortened interiors or exteriors. By contrast, Lievens first adhered to the half-length figure form of picture, with a preference for monumental, life-size figures. He only made use quite early of the type of composition that Rembrandt had brought from Lastman in a few drawings. His drawing MUCIUS SCAEVOLA AND PORSENNA, for example, is based on Lastman's CORIOLANUS, a painting of 1622; he also uses Vorsterman's engraving after Rubens's ADORATION OF THE MAGI.[30] He schooled his drawing style on that of engravers, working with cross-hatching. He covered in shadow areas. The drawing has more spatial depth than his other works, but a relief-like manner remains typical of him. While in Rubens the procession is cut across by the middle ground, where figures lean forward to catch sight of what is happening, Lievens blocks the view with lances. What is typical of him is the arresting dramatisation of the scene.

34

48

Rembrandt made use of both of the models followed by Lievens in constructing the groups of figures in his painting DAVID WITH THE HEAD OF GOLIATH BEFORE SAUL. The artistic exchange between the two young painters was sometimes so close that they worked from the same models. But in general, Lastman's history paintings were of no great importance to Lievens. What influenced him more, as we have seen, was Utrecht and Haarlem painting. This he transmitted to Rembrandt.

49

The exchange of impressions with Lievens was undoubtedly important for Rembrandt. However, Rembrandt, older by a year, soon took the lead, although Lievens had had longer practical experience. Lievens's tendency towards one-sidedness and extreme positions benefited them both, for it confirmed them in their resolve to go their own way. Though their teachers' generation had gone to Italy to study perspective and the use of colour from the originals, the two young artists had a different goal in view. They wanted to surpass their mentor Lastman in the depiction of mood through facial expression and gesture. Italian painting in about 1620 could provide no real stimulus here. But did they not thereby lay claim to freeing themselves from the classical rules of Italian art? If so, it was not only painters who were trying to break free from old bonds — theologians, philologists, and even medical men were throwing off these fetters. The theologians were starting to doubt the interpretations of the Church Fathers and reformers. Surgeons called the doctrines passed down from antiquity into question and sought to explore and describe human anatomy. And the great humanists of Leyden, who truly knew the classical sources and spoke the classical languages fluently, liberated themselves from their normative power and dared to compose their works in Dutch.

Rembrandt and Lievens, too, went their own way, building on what they had learned, but on the lookout for new impulses. Understandably, the impression which Lastman had made on Rembrandt was still fresh; his first task was to come to terms with these compositions. His earliest known painting, THE MARTYRDOM OF ST. STEPHEN of 1625, is at first sight so reminiscent of Lastman that it was only recognised as his own work a few years ago. Anyone who looks at it more closely, however, will already find Rembrandt's personal handwriting in every detail. His starting-point was a composition of his teacher's (produced in 1619) on the same subject. Although the painting has been lost, its content is preserved in a drawing by an unknown artist which has survived.[31] Lastman presents the main scene in the right half of the picture: Stephen is stoned by three youths. Boys pass them large stones. Above the group are seen representatives of the Roman occupying force. In the left half of the picture, Lastman presents the Pharisee Saul, who is looking after the stoners' clothes and so has only a walk-on part, far too prominently in the middle ground. Rembrandt corrects this; he moves Saul and his fellow-believers into the background as spectators and brings the Roman militia to the front, for it was their task to supervise the execution. But as they are not

53

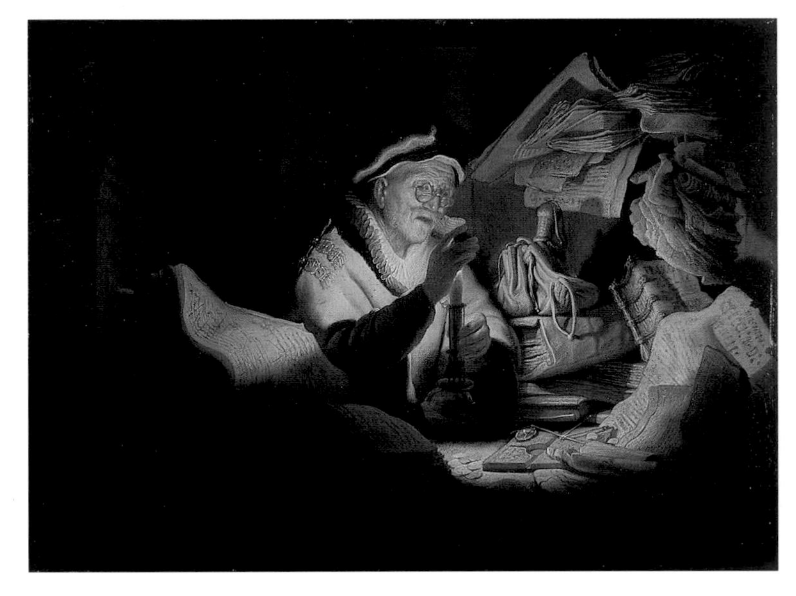

THE RICH FARMER.
Signed: 'RH 1627'.
Wood 31.7 × 42.5 cm.
Berlin-Dahlem, Staatliche Museen Preussischer Kulturbesitz, Gemäldegalerie.
Cat. 36 / Bredius 420.

THE PROPHET JEREMIAH MOURNING THE DESTRUCTION OF JERUSALEM.
Signed: 'RHL 1630'.
Wood 58.3 × 46.6 cm.
Amsterdam, Rijksmuseum.
Cat. 6 / Bredius 604.

the motivating force, he places them in shadow, while the real puppet-masters in the background, the Pharisees and Elders, are brightly lit. So the young artist here masters for the first time the possibility of distinguishing between important and unimportant elements within the picture, not by spatial stratification, but solely by illumination. This was to open the whole picture space as a stage for action. The violence of the action and the brutality of the persecutors is not expressed in Lastman's work. By contrast, Rembrandt dramatises the scene: five youths have set upon Stephen, whose swollen face already shows clear signs of martyrdom. The faces of the tormentors and witnesses are distorted; their features express human baseness. The strong contrast between light and dark heightens the pathos and harshness of the scene. Although Rembrandt starts from tradition and borrows some figures from an Italian print, the New announces itself everywhere in this early work.

In 1626, a year later, Rembrandt took up a new theme in his CHRIST DRIVING THE MONEY-CHANGERS FROM THE TEMPLE. His conception is unusually bold. He depicts the story, which had traditionally been treated as a crowd scene, by means of a few persons in a half-length figure picture, using a monumental form of composition that was used by the Caravaggesque painters in Utrecht primarily for life-size pictures. The wrath of Jesus and the avarice and fear of the dealers are expressed only by gesture and facial expression. The colours are strong, the brushwork coarse, which heightens the drama of the scene.

34

During 1627 and 1628, Rembrandt abandons all-too-obtrusive colour and structural effects and evolves a more monochrome tonality from which the chiaroscuro is to develop further. Concentration on the essential enables him to express a maximum of spiritual tension by a minimum of action. Earlier art had characterised biblical and mythological heroes by an explanatory scene, often in the background, showing an important episode in their lives. Rembrandt, by contrast, presents the historical figures in the midst of a historical situation and in a historical space, characterising them only through gesture and facial expression and dispensing with the explanatory scene.

This is to be seen in pictures as early as the small ANDROMEDA in the Hague, dating from 1627. Usually, with this subject, the fight of Perseus with the dragon was indicated in the background. (The Ethiopian Queen Cassiopeia had boasted of being more beautiful than all the Nereids, bringing on herself the anger of the gods. The land was visited by floods and a monster. As Zeus would only free it from the plague if the King's daughter Andromeda was thrown to the monster, her father had her fettered to a rock and promised her to the man who would kill the beast. Perseus succeeded in vanquishing the dragon and received Andromeda as his wife.) Rembrandt shows only Andromeda fettered to the rock. Her saviour is not visible, which makes her despair particularly affecting. Such isolation of the main figure was used in medieval art to heighten the emotive content, especially in devotional pictures. Rembrandt took over this device.

43

Lastman had presented almost all his histories in a

Early Leyden follower of Rembrandt.
THE THREE SINGERS (HEARING). About 1626/27.
Wood 31.6 × 25 cm. Originally 21.6 × 17.8 cm.
The Hague, Galerie Cramer.
Cat. A27 / Bredius 421.

Early Leyden pupil of Rembrandt.
THE SPECTACLES-SELLER (SIGHT) About 1629.
Wood 32.8 × 25.3 cm. Originally 21 × 17.8 cm.
St. Martins, Guernsey, Daan Cevat Collection.
Cat. A29 / Bredius — / RRP B3.

Early Leyden follower of Rembrandt.
THE OPERATION (FEELING). About 1626/27.
Wood 31.7 × 25.3 cm. Originally 21.5 × 17.7 cm.
The Hague, Galerie Cramer.
Cat. A28 / Bredius 421A.

landscape. In illustrations in the Bible and in books as well as in other graphic works, Rembrandt found numerous histories that took place in an interior. His predecessors had mostly avoided such scenes. They suited Rembrandt perfectly, for as chiaroscuro became an important means for him, he could use the light sources in a room to interpret the events. He therefore made use of many subjects that had not previously featured in painting. Among them was THE RICH 29 FARMER, a picture that has up to now been misunderstood as a genre scene. The subject is a parable from the 12th Chapter of Luke. A rich man resolves to demolish his old barns and build new ones in which to hoard provisions from which he can live at ease. But God says to him: 'Thou fool, this night thy soul shall be required of thee: then whose shall those things be which thou hast stored?' The parable closes with the maxim: 'So it is for him who lays up treasure for himself, and is not rich in God.' In earlier versions Death is to be seen in allegorical form as a skeleton, or in the background the rich man's wish to build a barn has already been put into effect. Rembrandt leaves all this aside and concentrates on the rich man, showing him — as the parable does — trapped by the things of this world. Here, too, Rembrandt goes beyond Lastman: the treasures, books, and papers surrounding the farmer testify not only to commerce. In Leyden painting they were used as symbols of transience. By surrounding the rich man with these things and showing him looking at a coin, Rembrandt makes clear his dependence on transitory possessions. The Hebrew characters remind the onlooker here as in other histories that a biblical theme is being presented, actualised by contemporary objects and dress. In this picture Rembrandt has removed the scene from its context. He was the first to conceive it as an isolated scene without allegorical or simultaneous additions.

In other works he placed persons who until then had usually been presented in isolation in a situation characteristic of them, instead of relegating the action to the background. The apostle Paul, for example, he shows in prison, writing his epistles. 'Thrown into gaol and writing nevertheless — so his endurance and struggle are shown; the barred cell in the old prison and the religious champion writing, fully prepared for action.'[32] The picture lives on the contradiction between the prison situation and the mental vigour of the apostle, and exactly this is conveyed by the letters written by Paul from prison. All the models used by the artist for THE APOSTLE PAUL IN PRISON show Paul in a landscape. Rem- 34 brandt was the first to discover the interior as a place of action. The figures, too, he did not derive, as earlier painters had done, from imagination or from the works of greater or lesser masters. When Rembrandt took up the theme of PETER AND PAUL IN DISCUSSION, which Lucas van Leyden had 32 treated before him in a memorial altar and an etching, he did 33, 32 not simply take the figures from this model; he made his own studies from life. The thick folds of the garment worn by the 34 apostle are carefully rendered. The old man who served as the model for both Peter and Paul had a long head and a flowing, forked beard, as the study shows. In the painting Rembrandt had to change this, for Peter was traditionally shown with a square, compact head.

PETER AND PAUL IN CONVERSATION.
Signed: 'RHL 1628'.
Wood 72.4 × 59.7 cm.
Melbourne, National Gallery of Victoria.
Cat. 38 / Bredius 423.

The subject of PETER AND PAUL IN DISCUSSION had developed, as far as the tradition of pictorial representation is concerned, from typical images of the two chief apostles, always characterised by their attributes, the key and the sword. Rembrandt conceived the conversation as a scene, and in all the scenes with several figures showing Peter and Paul, he never included the attributes. He eliminated them here, too, and tried to make the history recognisable by the depiction of place. He asked himself which was the place appropriate to this conversation and portrayed the apostles in a study, surrounded by all the paraphernalia of learning. The globe makes it clear that theirs is a world mission. Rembrandt undoubtedly found the stimulus for this presentation of the story in the biblical text. In the Epistle to the Galatians, Paul reports that after three years of missionary activity he has returned to Jerusalem from Arabia to meet Peter and has spent fifteen days with him (Gal. 1 : 18). As the context shows, he wanted to reconcile his views on the Gospel with those of Peter. Rembrandt therefore shows the two men in a theological discussion; Paul is pointing to a passage in the Bible.

Rembrandt therefore begins his artistic career as a painter of histories. Fascinated by Lastman, he occupies himself primarily with this type of subject, which was regarded by art theoreticians as the most difficult and the highest. Like Lastman he treated almost as many Old Testament as New Testament scenes. He seldom concerned himself with scenes from mythology or church history. Nor did he find much inspiration in contemporary poetry. It is the old, time-honoured stories that capture his imagination.

Our picture of Rembrandt as an illustrator of Bible stories is still determined by critical views from the turn of the century. In highly imaginative terms they describe him as growing up in an almost idyllic atmosphere with the Bible. A well-known cultural historian writes:

> He was fond of painting his mother, the miller's wife, and other women, reading the Bible. We can picture the winter evenings when, by the dim light of a single candle, an old woman reads to the solemn men the beautiful stories of the Jews, in which the scene is so vividly present before us and each sentence is as palpable as in Homer. As the candle-light shone on the aged heads and on the great printed leaves of the Book, Rembrandt devoured the reader and the read with eyes and ears, and often may have said to himself: 'I shall paint that later.' And he kept his word.[33]

Art is here naively interpreted as a reflection of biography: Rembrandt's chiaroscuro is explained by the inadequate lighting in his parents' home.

But the critics went further, postulating that his religious denomination, too, was reflected in Rembrandt's creative process. While the Catholic artists made use of pictorial tradition, the argument ran, Rembrandt as a Protestant artist took his subject solely from the biblical text. The

Lucas VAN LEYDEN.
PETER AND PAUL IN CONVERSATION.
Monogrammed and dated 1527.
Engraving 100 × 144 mm.

Lucas VAN LEYDEN. ►
PETER AND PAUL.
Two wings of the triptych of the Last Judgement.
Wood, 264 × 76 cm each.
Leyden, Stedelijk Museum 'De Lakenhal'.

PRELIMINARY STUDY FOR PETER. About 1628.
Red and black chalk, heightened in white. 295 × 210 mm.
Berlin-Dahlem, Staatliche Museen Preussischer Kulturbesitz, Kupferstichkabinett.
Benesch 7.

CHRIST DRIVING THE MONEY-CHANGERS FROM THE TEMPLE.
Signed: 'R f 1626'.
Wood 43.1 × 32 cm.
Moscow, Pushkin Museum.
Cat. 34 / Bredius 532.

THE APOSTLE PAUL IN PRISON.
Monogrammed: 'R (H or L) 1627'. Additionally signed on the open book: 'Rembrandt fecit'.
Wood 72.8 × 60.2 cm.
Stuttgart, Staatsgalerie.
Cat. 37 / Bredius 601.

Rembrandt critic Werner Weisbach, for example, writes: 'Since, as a Protestant, he could refer directly to the biblical texts, they became his main source of inspiration'.[34] He is supposed not only to have broken radically with tradition, but to have discovered through his reading many new subjects which he was the first artist to sketch. As the biographers of Rembrandt permit themselves what they never allow to the genius himself — to make use of the works of predecessors and contemporaries and uncritically to borrow whole passages from them — this dogma still has a determining influence on Rembrandt criticism today.

We shall have to take leave of this legend too. It is a product of the religious and national tendencies of the 19th century. The Protestant republican Dutchman Rembrandt was opposed to the Catholic royalist Fleming Rubens. In the 17th century, however, there was no great difference between the confessions in the interpretation of most biblical and mythological histories, as regards their literal or moral meaning.[35] The dispute concerned dogmatic or liturgical topics and church history. Both Catholic and Protestant painters drew on the Bible and on earlier tradition. In their search for knowledge they also made use of medieval legends and *The Antiquities of the Jews* of Flavius Josephus when treating stories from Holy Scripture.[36] In this erudite tendency, painters of the different denominations were of one mind. More radical than they, Rembrandt seeks pictorial solutions. He does not want simply to tell a didactic story, but to create an emotional effect through telling the story.

UNINTERPRETED HISTORY.
Signed: 'Rf 16(26)'.
Wood 89.8 × 121 cm.
Leyden, Stedelijk Museum 'De Lakenhal'.
Cat. 117 / Bredius 460.

JUDAS RETURNING THE THIRTY PIECES OF SILVER.
Signed: 'RL 1629'.
Wood 79 × 102.3 cm.
England, private collection.
Cat. 40 / Bredius 539A.

CONSTANTIN HUYGENS DISCOVERS REMBRANDT AND JAN LIEVENS

Jan LIEVENS.
PORTRAIT OF CONSTANTIN HUYGENS (1596-1687).
Wood 99 × 84 cm.
Amsterdam, Rijksmuseum (on loan from Musée de la Chartreuse, Douai).

In 1628, Rembrandt was already a well-known painter in Leyden. His work was widely praised, so that a Utrecht lawyer interested in artistic matters, Arent van Buchel, noted in Latin: 'The Leyden miller's son has great ability, but is before his time'.[37] In November of the same year Constantin Huygens, secretary to Stadholder Prince Frederick Hendrick and father of the famous physicist Christian Huygens, came to Leyden.[38] He clearly took the opportunity to visit Rembrandt and Jan Lievens in their studio, for a few days later, Lievens went to The Hague to make the first sketches for a 37 portrait of Huygens. Constantin Huygens was enthusiastic about the work of both the young artists — Rembrandt was 22 and Lievens 21 — and discussed their artistic ideas and plans with them, giving them well-intentioned advice.

Constantin Huygens was an unusual personality. As secretary he had to accompany the stadholder to battlefields and undertake diplomatic missions.[39] He received the highest honours, including numerous gold chains. King Louis XIII made him a knight of the French Order of St. Michael and decorated him with the Bourbon coat of arms. Despite his cosmopolitan outlook (Huygens composed poetry in Dutch, Latin, and French), he was patriotic and attentively followed cultural events throughout the Netherlands. His poetry, in which he describes the life of ordinary people in the Netherlands, is among the best in Dutch literature of the time. His library contained almost 3,000 books, mainly theological, legal, and Humanist. He owned books by the great writers and thinkers and corresponded with Descartes, among others. In his autobiography, written between 1629 and 1631, which deals with the period from 1596 to 1614, he tells of his ancestors and the careful education he received. After an account of how he was taught to draw by Hendrick Hondius, he makes observations about painting in his time and mentions the two young artists in Leyden.[40] He writes that even as a child he was interested in painting, but was allowed by his father to learn only drawing, which at that time formed part of the general education of rich children. When he wanted to paint, he had to do it in secret, so that his father did not notice that he was neglecting other studies in favour of this hobby. In fact, painting was and remained his real love. He watched its development in Holland and Flanders, which he correctly considered as historically one, judging contemporary artists with a highly developed feeling for their talent and quality. Although holding Mannerist painters in high esteem, he was fascinated by the works of the younger generation. He admired the young masters who were advancing Dutch landscape painting, certain that they would surpass their teachers. But he too valued history painting above all other branches of art. His autobiography mentions the history painters Pieter Isaacsz., Pieter Lastman, and Jan Pynas in Amsterdam; Abraham Bloemaert, Gerard van Honthorst, Hendrick Terbrugghen, and Dirck van Baburen in Utrecht; and Everhard van der Maes at The Hague, as well as Abraham Janssens and Anthony van Dyck, and particularly praises the work of Rubens. He then turns to the two young artists Rembrandt and Lievens. He considered them to be geniuses endowed by nature with uncommon talent that would develop by itself. In his opinion they were the equals of their contemporaries and would soon surpass them. Nowadays opinion is vigorously opposed to the cult of genius; it is rightly pointed out that the spiritual ancestors of the great were frequently very minor artists, and that important painters can owe a great deal to unimportant predecessors. (Rembrandt, too, took over much more from his predecessors than has hitherto been realized.) However, it is incorrect to say that the concept of genius as we know it today did not yet exist in the 17th century. It can be seen quite clearly in Huygens' description. Huygens believed that lack of money often led parents to find quite ordinary teachers for their sons; if these teachers could see their students later, they would be just as ashamed as the teachers of many of the greatest poets, thinkers, and scientists.

SAMSON BETRAYED BY DELILAH. About 1629/30.
Monogrammed: 'RHL 1628'.
Wood 61.4 × 50 cm.
Berlin-Dahlem, Staatliche Museen Preussischer Kulturbesitz, Gemäldegalerie.
Cat. 4 / Bredius 489.

Basically, these artists owe nothing to their teachers and everything to their own talent; they would have gone just as far without any teachers at all. In his opinion, the artistic genius of Rembrandt and Lievens was so strong that it became evident in their early youth. 'Both are mere striplings, and to judge by their figures or their faces, they seem children rather than youths.'[41] Clearly Huygens is so dazzled by the new art that he fails to see its connection with older work, and describes it in terms which became customary in the biographies of artists during the Romantic period.

Unfortunately, Rembrandt and Lievens did not follow the far-sighted suggestion that Huygens had previously made to Rubens: that both artists compile a list of their works. Such a register would have saved later generations the decades of work necessary to separate Rembrandt's work from the many student works and fakes which generations of dealers and collectors have sold under his name. This list, which was either never made or has not survived, would contain about 400 paintings, almost half of which are now lost, and eliminate some 200 works by students, and fakes. A catalogue of his etchings would be only slightly larger than present ones, would contain a few unknown originals which have not survived, and would omit a number of students' works. Above all, there would be a major discrepancy in the number of drawings. It is here that the largest losses have probably occurred, as it is likely that about half the drawings now attributed to Rembrandt would have to be deleted. With his excellent perspective on the art of his time and his interest in all its innovations, Huygens understood exactly what the two artists were aiming at. His extraordinary linguistic ability enabled him to express these aims with great subtlety. Undoubtedly, the two friends themselves would never have been able to describe their goals with such precision and detachment. The following comparison between the two artists, which hardly differs from present-day judgements, is of particular value:

> I shall venture to pass a superficial judgement on each, and to assert that Rembrandt surpasses Lievens in taste and depth of feeling, but that the latter excels him by a certain amplitude of invention and the boldness of his themes and figures. If, in his young heart, Lievens strives after all that is noble and sublime, he paints the forms that he sees in his mind's eye life-size or even larger. Rembrandt, wholly immersed in his work, seeks to encompass his ideas in a smaller scope, and to attain in compressed form an effect that one looks for in vain in the colossal pictures of others. In his history pieces, as we call them, Lievens is admirable, but he will not easily match Rembrandt's vivid imagination.[42]

The accuracy of Huygens's judgement is confirmed by a comparison of Rembrandt's early work SAMSON AND DELILAH, 38 a masterly composition depicting a great variety of emotions, with Lievens's solemn yet somewhat comical life-size treat- 39 ment of the same subject. Huygens advised Lievens to concentrate on painting portraits. (As a result, Lievens may have persuaded him to sit as a subject.) On the other hand, Huygens was so impressed by Rembrandt's histories that he describes in detail the painting JUDAS RETURNING THE THIRTY 36 PIECES OF SILVER, which Rembrandt had just finished in

1629. He stresses how the despair and remorse of the treacherous disciple are shown through facial expression, gestures, and even clothing. This painting caused a sensation at the time, as is shown not only by the many copies and etchings by Jan Joris van Vliet, in which only the figure of Judas is depicted, but also by Huygens's words:

> I should like to take the picture of the repentant Judas, who brings back the reward for betraying his innocent master to the high priest, as an example of all his work. Let it be compared to the whole of Italian painting and the most impressive works left behind by early antiquity. The attitude of this despairing Judas — not to mention the many other admirable figures in this one picture — this ranting, whining Judas begging forgiveness without hoping for it, while his features yet tell of this hope; Judas with his ravaged face, his torn hair and garment, the arms grappling, the hands painfully clasped as he throws himself on his knees in a blind transport of emotion, his body racked with violent pain: I hold this figure up beside any work of art produced by the centuries; and I should like it to be seen by those ignorant persons who are forever asserting — I have taken issue with them elsewhere — that nothing can be done or said today that has not already been done or said in antiquity. I contend that no Protogenes, Apelles, or Parrhasios ever imagined, or would imagine, if they returned to earth today, the diverse emotions which — I say this in astonishment myself — a young, beardless, Dutch miller has concentrated and expressed as a unity. Bravo, Rembrandt![43]

Huygens's artistic sympathies were, however, divided. Although he rightly saw that this uncompromising work expressed a reality which the artists of antiquity had not encompassed, he encouraged Lievens and Rembrandt to go to Italy. As an educated Humanist, he believed they should learn drawing from Raphael and human proportions, as laid down by antiquity, from Michelangelo. In this, Huygens's attitude shows the same duality as that of many other Humanists. They encouraged the new tendencies in the arts, philology, and theology, but did not dare abandon the old restrictive norms entirely. Although filled with pride to see the ancient world surpassed in their own country, they felt bound to that world. Rembrandt and Lievens knew and used ancient sources as well as works by Raphael, but the only norm for them was their own intention, which they expressed in their own artistic language. They were unable and unwilling to produce a theoretical reason for their rejection of Italy. Their teachers, after all, had all travelled there. Their reply to the urging of their patron sounds somewhat awkward. They argued that so many paintings had been collected in Holland that they could see more there then in Italy itself. Their real reason was different: both artists wanted to express their feelings in histories, whether dramatic or peaceful, which they could not learn in Italy. To do this, they needed to observe themselves and their fellow-men, to grasp the variety and ambiguity of human feelings, and to express these in natural movements. They were realistic enough to be aware that a journey to Italy, which took months in those days, would cost them much time. There were many artistic fields and techniques which they had not yet mastered (e.g., landscape and allegory) or were only painfully starting to learn (e.g., head studies, portraits, genre, and animal life). They therefore believed they could not afford to undertake such a journey at that time. They did not even allow themselves the innocent pleasures of youth. Huygens thought it desirable for them to take more care of their bodies, which were far from robust and already had suffered because of their sedentary occupation. We owe to him one of the few reports we have on Rembrandt as a person and on his attitude to his work. He was hard working and tenacious. Even those of his contemporaries who were jealous of his achievements or held different artistic principles did not deny this. The biographer Joachim von Sandrart describes Rembrandt several times as an example of the diligent painter, and one of Rembrandt's pupils gave a similar account to Filippo Baldinucci, the Italian painter and art theoretician, though he added that the master had difficulty in completing a painting quickly. This criticism was not without foundation; Rembrandt himself blamed his 'studious diligence' for a delay of at least four and probably six years in completing one commission.[44] Clearly Rembrandt and Lievens agreed that despite their great ability only indefatigable work would enable them to attain their artistic goal.

Jan LIEVENS.
SAMSON AND DELILAH.
Monogrammed 'IL' with faked signature: 'Rembrandt f. 1633'.
Canvas 131 × 111 cm.
Amsterdam, Rijksmuseum.

1630

In the first years of Rembrandt's work at Leyden, from about 1625 to 1628, the two artists seem to have followed fairly independent paths. They exchanged ideas and sometimes treated the same subjects. But they did so on very different scales, Rembrandt preferring whole figures on a small scale and Lievens large-scale half-length figure pictures.

Lievens's series THE FOUR EVANGELISTS illustrates his approach to the subject of prophets and apostles.[45] While Rembrandt, in his early work, presents the Old and New Testament figures in historicised, single-figure scenarios, 34, 42 showing Paul, for example, in prison or in his study, and enriching the portrayal with motifs taken from the Bible, Lievens depicts the four evangelists quite traditionally, with their usual attributes, as half-length figures. Since the realistic treatment of the heads makes the attributes look antiquated, the latter are shrouded in obscurity. The lion behind Mark, the bull behind Luke, and the eagle behind John appear like shadows. Lievens lights up the main figures and the objects in the foreground, but allows the motifs in the background to be almost lost in darkness. He uses the dark background as a neutral foil, giving it no depth. The foreground is congested with objects: books are piled up in front of Mark; the angel holds up the Bible before the apostle Matthew — who looks deep into the angel's eyes. Lievens's figures are enclosed in heavy, bulging garments beneath which their limbs are indiscernible. Only the hands and faces are painted naturalistically. Lievens's brushstroke follows 'the wrinkles of the skin, the dishevelled hair'. He particularly enjoys painting 'the decorative scrolls of dog-eared folios' and gives the contours of the bodies a singular vibrancy.[46]

If Rembrandt's figures are compared to these, it is evident that they are the outcome of a close observation of nature. Exemplary composition is given second place. Beneath the figures' heavy clothing, the positions of the limbs can be discerned. Even when Lievens has obviously realised the weaknesses of his own works, he begins to translate Rembrandt's small whole-length figure pictures into half-length 34 figure pictures using models. In the Bremen ST. PAUL, Rembrandt's work on the same theme done in 1627 is transposed into a large-format half-length figure study.[47] But, in a departure from Rembrandt's way of seeing, the picture space is again neutralised and the broad frontal presentation of the apostle accentuates surface rather than depth.

Lievens began only later to compete with Rembrandt in producing histories with small figures. It seems as if Lievens — a gifted painter of classical, Caravaggesque pictures —

Jan LIEVENS.
THE RAISING OF LAZARUS. About 1631/32.
Etching, 359 × 311 mm. 3rd state.
Rovinski 3.

THE ENTOMBMENT. Dated 1630.
Red chalk heightened in white, 280 × 203 mm.
London, British Museum.
Benesch 17.

THE APOSTLE PAUL AT HIS DESK. About 1629/30.
Wood 47.2 × 38.6 cm.
Nuremberg, Germanisches Nationalmuseum.
Cat. 74 / Bredius 602.

was thrown off course by the rivalry. As an adaptable and receptive talent, he did not consistently evolve his own style, preferring to show that he could express himself in the language of others. But the assimilation remained superficial. Only at the end of the Leyden period did he achieve masterpieces in Rembrandt's style. But when he lost the stimulus that came from constant contact with Rembrandt, his pictures immediately became much weaker. Joris van Vliet's etching SUSANNA AND THE ELDERS records an early painting by Jan Lievens that has been lost.[48] In this small-figure composition Lievens bases himself on Rembrandt's histories, for example, his ANDROMEDA. The comparison makes clear the difference between Rembrandt's sensitive pictorial language and Lievens's declamatory style. Rembrandt isolates Andromeda, shows her in her fear and abandonment. He dispenses with the dragon and even the rescuing hero. Lievens does not show the heroine in such isolation from her scenic context. On the contrary, he includes the two old men, showing how they seize Susanna by the hair, touch her, pull her backwards, and uncover her body. The gesture used by Lievens is inspired by previous pictures showing the rape of women. Men grasp the women, who resist but are unable to escape the brutal force. Precisely by this quotation, this language of gesture, Lievens confuses his depiction, for Susanna did not give in to the men. Rembrandt therefore later presented the scene differently. Taking a painting by Pieter Lastman as his starting-point, in the final version he softens all the coarse features and shows Susanna covering her loins and bosom with her arms, surprised but not overpowered. It is her chastity that shields her. Rembrandt therefore shows her in isolation, as a single figure. Lievens had wanted to show vividly how Susanna is threatened, but had given the scene an almost comic aspect by the too literal presentation and the disparity between verisimilitude of detail and a caricaturistic descriptive manner (the gigantic Susanna, the ugly old men who, however, remain stock figures without physical presence).

43

153

Perhaps influenced by Huygens's commendation of Rembrandt's small-scale yet monumental histories, Lievens began to paint the same scenes as Rembrandt in small-figure history pieces. Which of the artists first took up a subject is not always clear, since Lievens only dated his pictures after 1629, which makes a chronological ordering of his works difficult. No doubt Rembrandt sometimes took over and improved on Lievens's compositions in the course of this rivalry. About 1628/29 both artists produced versions of SAMSON BETRAYED BY DELILAH. Only the Berlin painting bears the doubtful dating 1628, but Lievens's small-figure sketches and large half-length figure picture (both in the Rijksmuseum, Amsterdam) must have been painted at the same time or soon after.[49]

38

39

In his fascinating *mise en scene*, which foreshadows the dramatic outcome, Rembrandt proves himself the greater artist and the superior narrator:

ANDROMEDA CHAINED TO THE ROCK. About 1629.
Wood 34.5 × 25 cm.
The Hague, Mauritshuis.
Cat. 94 / Bredius 462.

THE RAISING OF LAZARUS. About 1630/31.
Wood 96.2 × 81.5 cm.
Los Angeles, County Museum of Art.
Cat. 42 / Bredius 538.

THE RAISING OF LAZARUS. About 1630.
Etching 366 × 258 mm.
Hamburg, Kunsthalle.
Bartsch 73.

CHRIST AT EMMAUS. About 1629.
Monogrammed: 'R(HL)'.
Paper mounted on wood 37.4 × 42.3 cm.
Paris, Musée Jacquemart-André.
Cat. 41 / Bredius 539.

In Rembrandt, flickering light pervades the whole picture space, coming from far back behind the curtain and heightening the sense of danger and foreboding. In the muted scale of brown, ochre, and grey-blue tones, Samson's robe stands out most strongly as he hides his head in Delilah's lap, oblivious of what is happening around him — ('and she let him fall asleep in her lap').[50]

Delilah turns to the Philistine and points to Samson's hair — ('and called to one that he cut off seven locks of his hair'). The Philistine creeps forward, his eyes dilated with fear — Samson, after all, has killed thousands of his fellows. The scissors are already partly open. In a moment he will cut off Samson's hair with them and deprive him of his strength. Behind this Philistine another soldier is seen. He holds out his sword, reminding us that the powerless man's eyes will be put out. Everything that threatens Samson is close to him: in the background there is even a ring fixed to the wall, of the kind used for chaining prisoners in their cells. These objects that point to Samson's weakening, blinding and imprisonment make visible what is about to happen to him.

In Rembrandt's DELILAH there is a progression — motifs and lighting intermeshing — from Samson's feet past his back to Delilah, then to the man creeping up, and finally to the helmeted soldier, forming a spatial (and temporal) sequence: the figures are successive like their actions.

Lievens tried to develop this scene, which Rembrandt had ordered on a deep stage in layers corresponding to the narrative sequence, in the flat foreground of his picture. The three figures are built up in pasty, bulging forms like a relief. The group thus lacks outline, the shadows merge in dark patches, and the background is unconnected by light, action, or sequence. The weaknesses are in the spatial and dramatic presentation. Lievens's Philistine stares wide-eyed at Delilah, but the effect is unconvincing, since the foreground is brightly lit. Rembrandt places his Philistine in semi-darkness in the background. His face is in shadow, the dramatic features softened by chiaroscuro. The Philistine has to peer strenuously in the dimness.

39

In Lievens, because the scene is wrongly constructed spatially, these motifs take on a grotesque, almost comic aspect. Revealingly, he treated the subject once again in a form in which he felt more secure, the half-length figure study. Here the difficult problem of rendering space did not present itself.

About 1629 both artists worked a great deal on head studies and historical portraits. Lievens drew closer to Rembrandt's conceptions. How close the contact between the two artists was at this time is shown by a portrait which Lievens painted of Rembrandt.[51] It shows him in fancy dress with the cap, gorget, and cape known to us from his self-portraits. It differs from these, however, in that the face lacks the momentary, accidental character given by lighting and is less dramatised. But the joint work on heads and portraits benefited both. About 1630/31 Lievens visibly approaches Rembrandt's style. Their rivalry reaches a peak when they produce at least five works on THE RAISING OF LAZARUS.[52] Lastman and his circle had frequently painted this miracle, which allowed a vivid depiction of the different reactions of the onlookers.[53] The two young artists were undoubtedly stimulated by these works. In keeping with

40, 41, 44, 45

THE GLORIFICATION BY SIMEON.
Signed: 'RHL 1631'.
Wood 60.9 × 47.8 cm.
The Hague, Mauritshuis.
Cat. 43 / Bredius 543.

tradition, they present the scene in the burial cave.[54] Whereas earlier artists show Lazarus already awake and in possession of his powers, Rembrandt chooses a different moment. 44 He shows life slowly returning to the man still marked by death. Perhaps he had seen something of Caravaggio's quite different, but related, version.[55]

It appears that Rembrandt was the first of the two to 44 address the theme. The process of composition is unclear and was perhaps retrospectively obscured by Rembrandt. Christ is presented as the central figure. He stands on the grave cover, overcoming death, standing above death. His right hand is lifted in a gesture of both command and blessing. His left hand rests majestically at his side. He is surrounded by onlookers and disciples, but elevated above them as they are bending forward to see the miracle. Their attitudes express their involvement. Rembrandt has grouped them in a semicircle around Lazarus. In the left foreground we see one of Lazarus's sisters, with her back to us. Next to her is a witness. To his right stands the other sister; she holds out her arms in fear and joy at once, as if still shocked and protecting herself. Above her an old man is seen. The light falls on Christ's face and on his right hand. It shines on the faces of the most important witnesses and illuminates Lazarus, who is wrapped in a linen cloth and is painfully sitting up. It is reflected from the weapons hanging above the sarcophagus, which show him to be a knight.

The picture is painted from below.[56] The onlooker sees the event from the viewpoint of Lazarus, as if he too were called back from death to life. This accords with the rhetoric of Baroque songs about Lazarus.

Lievens is likely to have started his painting on this theme in the same year as Rembrandt.[57] The difference between the two works could not be clearer. Lievens isolates the figure of Christ, separating it from the onlookers. He is visible on a platform high above the grave. With his hands joined in prayer, he looks solemnly towards heaven. Radiance surrounds his face. Lievens arranges the spectators on a kind of stage to Christ's right. They do not appear as whole figures — they are visible only as half-length figures expressing utmost amazement. A huge shroud is pulled by one sister with a dramatic gesture from the coffin set far below her. Lazarus is lifting his hands from the grave as if calling for help.

Lievens probably produced an etching on the subject 41 during the composition of the painting.[58] In it he further reinforced the opposition between Christ and the onlookers. The space around Christ is larger. There is a bright halo around him. The solemn effect of the painting is heightened in the etching. It appears that Rembrandt was deeply impressed by his fellow-artist's composition. Perhaps he even owned the painting, for in his inventory of 1656 a raising of Lazarus is mentioned as a painting by Lievens. In a drawing 40 that he dated (wrongly?) 1630, he copied the etching.[59] He was impressed by the figure of Christ emphasised through isolation and the rendering of the action on two separate stages. He soon drew a burial of Christ, using this composition. The two theatres of action at different heights seemed to him appropriate to the burial. The disciples and followers of the dead man carry the rigid corpse, which is wrapped in a white linen cloth. Rembrandt matches Lievens's powerful

41 etching, the influence of which later travelled as far as Italy, by a composition showing his ability to open the picture space as a theatre for action.[60] He tries to surpass Lievens in boldness and — stimulated by a painting by Jacob Pynas — he presents the scene of the raising of Lazarus from the 45 viewpoint of Christ.[61] The latter is shown in the foreground from the back. His left hand, outstretched in blessing, bestows new life. Like a ruler, Christ rests his other hand on his hip. The cowed onlookers are clearly distinguished from him. We are included among them, since we see Christ somewhat from below.

47 In 1631, Lievens and Rembrandt both produced crucifixion pictures.[62] The paintings are of similar size and are both rounded at the top. Probably they both resulted from a kind of competition. Rembrandt's painting alludes to a work completed by the Amsterdam painter Claes Moeyaert in 1629. In this picture, behind the plastically rendered figure of Christ, is a landscape with women looking up at the cross. Rembrandt's Christ, by contrast, is shown in total isolation. Yet from high on the left, heavenly light breaks into the darkness, throwing into relief a body that is not beautiful and regular in appearance, but tortured. The body is twisted, the head bent. It is scored with deep furrows. The background is painted in brownish-black tones.

Lievens's impressive, brooding work, in which grey and black tones predominate, shows Christ dying on the cross, his arms stretched steeply upwards. The head is bent to one side. Bright light from the left and above falls on the emaciated body, which stands out from the dark sky like a relief. A broad stream of blood flows from the wound in his side. Rembrandt fits the horizontal beam of the cross into the upper semicircle of the picture in such a way that the arms, the beam, and the arch form a powerful tension which, like the illumination, lifts the figure upwards. There is a further motif that Lievens omitted to use to heighten the impression of suffering. In Rembrandt the upright of the cross also makes the suffering visible, since it is not a smooth beam but rough wood; low down, bark is discernible that has a similar texture to the streaming blood. The ends of the cross-beam are notched, the cross wedged into the ground with crude blocks. This expresses violence. The rough parts of the cross are illuminated. Lievens, by contrast, lets it fade into the darkness, does not particularise it in Rembrandt's special way. Instead, he shows the blood flowing from the wound in a broad stream.

It seems that Rembrandt had the better of the competition in contemporary opinion as well. For the stadholder was probably induced by Rembrandt's crucifixion picture (which had roughly the same format and the same semicircular top) to commission a Passion series from him, while Lievens received no comparable commission. So the number of commissions each artist received from the court reflects Huygens's judgement that although Lievens was admirable in his history paintings, he could not match the vigour of Rembrandt's imagination. It was clearly thought at the court that Rembrandt was the better narrator of biblical histories. Not only his rendering of emotions but also his clearly intelligible, but at the same time profound, pictorial language earned Rembrandt early success and recognition.

CHRIST ON THE CROSS.
Signed: 'RHL 1631'.
Canvas on wood 99.9 × 72.6 cm
Le Mas d'Agenais, France, parish church.
Cat. 44 / Bredius 543A.

Pieter LASTMAN.
CORIOLANUS AND THE ROMAN WOMEN.
Signed and dated 1622.
Dublin, Trinity College.

THE LANGUAGE OF THE BAROQUE

In his training and early work Rembrandt learned the language of art. No textbook taught him this. Some motifs were explained by art theorists, but most were common property, practised in the workshops, handed down through art, propagated internationally through illustrations, and applied in the political and cultural events of that time.

A history or genre scene was presented in rhetorical language. Pictures did not show what would have been seen by an eye-witness. Rather, the events, whether imagined or seen, were conveyed by formulae that were universally understood.

If Rembrandt were presenting, for example, a biblical scene that had not previously been treated in a painting and which he had himself come across in an illustration, he had to cast the story in contemporary formulae in accordance with status, protocol, and etiquette. I shall explain this with reference to one of his earliest paintings, the small sketch (49) DAVID PRESENTING THE HEAD OF GOLIATH TO SAUL. The subject had never before been treated in a painting; he had probably come across it in an etching by Maerten van Heemskerck. It shows the young David standing before Saul's throne in the army camp, holding up the head of Israel's feared opponent. At David's feet lies Goliath's gigantic sword. As a shepherd boy, David wears a pouch and carries a winnowing shovel. The text below the etching states: 'David presents Abner to Saul, carrying the head of the Philistine in his hand'. Rembrandt used a similar (35) structure in a history painting in Leyden, previously not interpreted, in which two soldiers kneel before an emperor whose sentence they listen to in fear.

Here, however, Rembrandt wanted to achieve a different solution, in both form and content. So he looked around to see what modern interpretations of the theme of 'people coming before a ruler' existed. Two paintings occurred to him: Lastman's composition of a few years earlier, entitled (48) THE ROMAN WOMEN BEG CORIOLANUS FOR PEACE, of which Rembrandt is sure to have had a copy, and Rubens's mighty altar painting THE ADORATION OF THE MAGI, the composition of which Lucas Vorsterman had reproduced in an engraving.[63]

For the arrangement and depiction of the army camp, Rembrandt used Lastman's composition. We find the horseman on the left, the gigantic tent in the background, the horseman and soldiers before it, and the motifs in shadow framing the event in the foreground. David is in the same position as the kneeling women in Lastman. Rembrandt took the king and the royal household from the engraving after

DAVID WITH THE HEAD OF GOLIATH BEFORE SAUL.
Signed: 'RH 1627'.
Wood 27.2 × 39.6 cm.
Basle, Öffentliche Kunstsammlung.
Cat. 3 / Bredius 488.

CORIOLANUS AND THE ROMAN WOMEN. About 1659/60.
Pen drawing 195 × 250 mm. Wash by a later hand.
London, British Museum.
Benesch 1045a.

AN OLD MAN ASLEEP AT THE HEARTH.
Signed: 'P (to be read as R) L ..29'.
Wood 51.9 × 40.8 cm.
Turin, Galleria Sabauda.
Cat. 119 / Bredius 428.

Rubens. In Rubens's composition one of the kings from the Orient kneels before the child, who lays his hand lovingly on the king's head. A second reverent king approaches with outstretched hand; a child carries his train, another his gifts. For the depiction of the royal household, Rembrandt took over a number of pre-existing formulae: King Saul is presented like the king whose train is carried by children. This was a court ritual that Rembrandt often made use of when depicting the meeting of a king or hero with a commoner.[64] So, to the left of the centre of the picture stands the mighty figure of Saul, dominating everything. Before him stands the small David, holding Goliath's head in his arms. And just as, in Rubens, one king bows before the Christ child, Rembrandt makes the army commander Abner bend down to the shepherd boy who, thanks to the grace bestowed by God, has saved his people as the poor and weak child Jesus brings redemption to the world. Just as court dress is emphasised by the sumptuous clothing, the heavy togas and cloaks and their glowing colours, David is characterised in the opposite way, as a poor shepherd boy. Rembrandt shows him barefoot, in shirt-sleeves.

By the quotation from Rubens's famous work, Rembrandt makes us aware not only of court etiquette, the order of precedence between shepherds and kings, but at the same time, of the theological meaning: the commander bows before the saviour who was himself to be the progenitor of the Redeemer. King Saul, however, remains unmoved, keeps his distance. It is not he who converses with David, but a general. This points to Saul's unbending disposition. Visually we are made aware that the sympathy shown by Abner is not shared by Saul, who is tormented by jealousy. The dog in the foreground expresses the reaction of his kind to unexpected visitors and events. This motif too is taken from Rubens's picture.

Finally, Rembrandt has also borrowed the order of dress from Rubens's picture. The commander Abner, like his model, the kneeling king, is shown in a fur coat; Saul, like King Balthazar, wears knee-boots; and the shepherd boy David, like his poor descendant Joseph, is barefoot.

The fur coat was at that time in the Netherlands the winter clothing of the rich. It is not known in the Bible. But as a man in fur was immediately indentifiable as rich, Rembrandt depicts important biblical personages — not only in this picture — wearing such garments: the pious Simeon in THE PRESENTATION OF JESUS IN THE TEMPLE, for example, or the covetous rich in the dramatic scene of CHRIST DRIVING THE MONEY-CHANGERS FROM THE TEMPLE, Rembrandt introduces these motifs — because only their social significance concerns him — even when they run counter to modern climatic notions, as when he shows the Chamberlain from the East wearing a fur coat under a blazing desert sun. Rembrandt's intention is to represent the high position of the black man who is converted to Christ, not the climatic conditions in the Orient. What fascinates us is the way that, even as a young artist, he does not merely assemble motifs, but finds new formulations and uncovers levels of meaning that had not previously been perceived.

51
34
16

What is immediately striking about the Chamberlain is that he is wearing a light-coloured fur coat with a white belt. In another Rembrandt painting on the same theme which has been lost, this imagery clearly made an impression on his contemporaries, for an engraving taken from it bears the inscription that the sacrament of baptism 'washes white the black man's soul, but not his skin'.[65] In biblical picture language, the just and the transfigured wear white garments. White stands for purity. The belt too has a special significance: the man of faith girds himself with a belt of virtues.

Rembrandt never used these formulae in a schematic way, but studied how to translate the biblical text into pictorial 25 language. A characteristic example is the painting TOBIAS AND ANNA. The pious Tobias had been a rich man who had been impoverished through his own generosity and blinded after a virtuous deed. His wife had to support him by spinning. Rembrandt therefore shows him in a costly but worn-out fur coat. It is ragged, patched, telling, like the disintegrating leather sandals, of past splendour. The threadbare expensive clothes are matched by the cramped room, the broken windows, the flaking plaster, and the lowly occupation of the woman. The social decline suffered by the family on account of their faith is clearly translated into pictorial language. In a similar way, Rembrandt later shows 359 the Prodigal Son in the threadbare attire of a landowner. Naturally, the Bible does not describe the clothing of either Tobias or the Prodigal Son. Rembrandt painted it in terms of the social conceptions of his time, so that the decline could be deduced from the clothes. In the 17th century a person's social status could be inferred even from his shoes. Saul, David, Jonathan, and Samson wear knee-boots, like the lieutenant in the so-called NIGHT WATCH. A rich hero like Samson must be in a compromising situation if he has taken 38 off his shoes — (SAMSON WITH DELILAH). In the Old and New Testaments, shoes have a quite different function. They are articles of use which, for example, must be removed in the temple, as is still the custom in Islam. Whereas, in the biblical account, the high priests served at the Holy of Holies barefoot, Rembrandt and his circle show the priests in the Temple wearing shoes, while Jesus and his disciples are barefoot. One might infer that in Rembrandt's conception the priests were desecrating the holy place. That this is not the case is shown by looking at other pictures: the positive heroes of the Old and New Testaments are shown wearing shoes if this reflects their status — for example, the old 51 Simeon holding the Saviour in his arms. If Rembrandt therefore shows Jesus, his disciples, the apostles, and numerous prophets barefoot, his intention is to make clear, in keeping with a widely disseminated tradition, that they belong to the common people, are poor, or have renounced riches. This observation confirms once again my contention that the language of the Baroque was stamped by the social order of the time.

The prophets find themselves in a position different from that of the disciples of Jesus. On the one hand, they are, as advisers to the princes and kings, part of the court; on the other, they are usually common people who have been called by God and who at God's command fight for the oppressed. 28 Rembrandt resolves this conflict by showing the prophet 21 Jeremiah, or Balaam, wearing fine garments trimmed or lined with fur, yet barefoot. The common people are depicted with bare arms and bare legs, and sometimes with uncovered torso.

THE GLORIFICATION BY SIMEON. About 1628.
Signed: 'Rembrandt f'.
Wood 55.4 × 43.7 cm.
Hamburg, Kunsthalle.
Cat. 39 / Bredius 535.

OLD MAN IN AN ARMCHAIR.
Monogrammed and dated 1631.
Red and black chalk, 225 × 145 mm.
Haarlem, Teylers Museum. Benesch 40.

A particularly unusual situation is indicated if this 'sartorial order' is not respected. When Balaam beats the ass in his rage and blindness, his sleeve slips up to his shoulder. The same motif is found when Christ drives the money-changers out of the Temple. Christ here has not rolled up his sleeves; they have slipped up his arms. So not only his clenched left fist is visible, but also his tensed right arm.

21

34

As we come to understand Rembrandt's pictorial language, we can no longer accept such superficial notions as that, in his early depictions of the raising of Lazarus, Rembrandt showed the cave 'with a canopy formed of tapestries to which arrows, quivers, sabres, and turbans have been attached' because this gave him an opportunity 'to indulge his addiction to still life' and to reproducing the objects collected in his studio.[66] This interpretation echoes the Classicist criticism that Rembrandt encumbered his pictures with accumulated lumber that had nothing to do with his subject. This was supposed to discredit Rembrandt as an untrained, uneducated artist. But precisely the seemingly irrelevant motifs show how Rembrandt has immersed himself in the story and expressed its peculiarities in a picture language valid for his time. He knew more about the history and its tradition than most of his predecessors. Weapons and sashes were characteristic adornments of the nobility. In the Baroque period the bearing of arms was permitted only to the civic patriciate, the nobility, and the soldiers. Rembrandt obviously knew the medieval legend which described Lazarus as a knight. Most artists would have made nothing of this information. Rembrandt depicted weapons and medals over the grave. By showing a turban, a bow, and a quiver of arrows beside the sword and the sash, he indicated that this was a story from ancient times. Rembrandt was to use these motifs analogously later in his portraits of aristocrats: classical examples are the etching of Jan Six and the figure of Frans Banning Cocq in the so-called NIGHT WATCH.

44, 45

218

In the portrayal of a history or a genre scene, facial or bodily language or, as it was called then, the depiction of human affects, emotions, desires, and passions, played a central role. Textbooks on art theory in Rembrandt's time usually devoted a special chapter to this topic. Karel van Mander writes in a didactic poem:

> No human being is so steadfast that he can completely overcome his moods, weaknesses, and inclinations, or that emotions and inner passions do not touch his heart and his senses, so that the outward limbs are affected and a visible movement of the whole figure, the face, and gestures give clear signs. Those versed in nature give these things different names: first and foremost love, then lust, joy, pain and anger, sorrow and grieving that grip the heart, and faint-heartedness and almost unconquerable fear, as well as arrogance and envious feuds. These and suchlike things are called affects. The painter should pay them serious attention, exploring their nature exactly, in order to dispose these parts of the face so as to reveal what touches the heart, and to express it by gestures of the body. But Nature shows everything that expresses the affects better than it can be described.[67]

After this theoretical introduction, and the proviso that 'everything that expresses the affects' is shown by nature better than it can be described, van Mander refers to famous works of antiquity and the Renaissance in which emotions are particularly aptly reproduced, and formulates a number of rules. He thereby makes us aware of the practice prevalent at the time. In portraying the emotions, artists schooled themselves on previous models and on nature.

Rembrandt's contemporaries, pupils, and pupils of pupils later claimed that he was particularly successful in expressing the affects, and that he discovered powerfully expressive gestures and movements for certain emotions. From the outset he tried to convey human feelings by facial expressions and body language, and thereby to convey and interpret the content of a history. If he did not agree with the expression of feelings in a model, or if he saw a different moment with a different reaction as more worthy of depiction, he sought gestures that seemed to convey the chosen moment or feelings more aptly and included them in his composition.

In his earliest known painting, THE MARTYRDOM OF ST. STEPHEN, he dramatises and illuminates the gesture of the main figure. Whereas Lastman in his painting shows Stephen in his distress with piously joined hands looking meekly

53

THE MARTYRDOM OF ST. STEPHEN.
Monogrammed 'R f' and dated 1625.
Wood 89.5 × 123.6 cm.
Lyons, Musée des Beaux-Arts.
Cat. 33 / Bredius 531A.

towards heaven, Rembrandt depicts him with outspread arms. With his left arm stretching towards the light, he looks up to heaven and sees the Vision of God (which Rembrandt conveys by light). Stephen is shown as conquering his martyrdom.

25 In the painting TOBIAS AND ANNA, produced a year later, Rembrandt corrects his model's composition. If Buytewech had shown poor Tobias scolded by his wife for his mistrust, Rembrandt shows the moment which followed: in his despair Tobias begs God for death. (He had wrongly accused his wife of stealing the kid.) Tobias wrings his hands and lifts them up in his despair. Even his blind eyes are raised to heaven. The old man's face is furrowed with pain. Rembrandt took Tobias's attitude from a model showing an entirely different story, THE REPENTANCE OF PETER. In this he shows his special genius for removing eloquent gestures from their original context and incorporating them in a composition in such a way that they seem invented for this scene. He also takes care to preserve the sequence of the story: the main personage acts or speaks, and the other people react to his words or action. They do not all speak or act simultaneously (unless this is demanded by the text); the reaction of one person is always occasioned by the words or acts of another, unless someone is so preoccupied with his own thoughts or deeds, in the background or to one side, that he is not involved in the central event. In this way Rembrandt's formulations, even when they are taken from a different context, escape becoming stereotypes. They are completely integrated into their new setting.[68]

The small painting CHRIST DRIVING THE MONEY-CHANGERS FROM THE TEMPLE, despite the half-length figure composition untypical of Rembrandt's early style, offers a particularly clear example of his pictorial language: action and reaction are here conveyed only through facial expression and movements of the upper body, particularly the arms and hands. 34

The theme of CHRIST AT EMMAUS had been treated by numerous artists before Rembrandt. The young Leyden painter surpasses them all in the boldness and naturalness of his portrayal of reactions, since he turns the story into a dramatic scene of recognition and worship. Two disciples had gone from Jerusalem to Emmaus. Jesus joined them as they walked, but they did not recognise him. In the evening 44

Lucas VAN LEYDEN.
DAVID PLAYING THE HARP BEFORE SAUL.
Engraving 254 × 183 mm.
Bartsch 27.

they pressed him to stay with them. 'And it came to pass as he sat with them at table that he took the bread, gave thanks, broke, and gave it to them. Then their eyes were opened and they recognised him. And he vanished before them'.

In a picture painted about 1628 which draws on an engraving by Goudt of a composition of Elsheimer's, JUPITER AND MERCURY WITH PHILEMON AND BAUCIS, Rembrandt elaborates with poetic freedom on the reactions of the disciples: one disciple has fallen to his knees to worship the resurrected Christ. The stool he had been sitting on has been knocked over. (Such transitory motifs are used frequently by Rembrandt in recognition scenes.) The other disciple lifts up his hands in alarm. He is so dazzled by Christ that he bends forwards to peer at him. Christ Himself is silhouetted by a light standing on a table behind him. Only the upper right part of the picture is strongly illuminated. Almost the whole of the rest is in darkness. Thereby the dramatic reaction of the disciple who has fallen to the ground is somewhat withdrawn, moderated. In the background we see the innkeeper's wife at the stove. She is too busy to notice the resurrected figure, and the light from the fire is weak beside that surrounding Christ.

Probably a year later, Rembrandt painted his small, striking picture DAVID PLAYS THE HARP BEFORE SAUL. At the feet of the grim-faced Saul, who is possessed by an evil spirit, the shepherd boy plays the harp to soften his mood. At the centre of the picture Saul's fist is visible, clenched round his spear. (The legend says that Saul threw his spear at David out of jealousy of his successful deeds.) So this fist expresses all of the anger and displeasure of the king tormented by melancholy and envy. The furrowed brow, piercing eyes, and upward thrust of the mouth betray the king's mood. By contrast, David, kneeling as a subordinate in the lower left corner, is absorbed in his playing. We really see only the body of the harp and the two hands serenely plucking the strings. 55

Rembrandt's composition is based on an engraving by Lucas van Leyden, whom he revered and imitated. It is 54 certainly no accident that he chose this work as his model, making it for the first time the subject of a painting, for Karel van Mander called it exemplary in his didactic poem: 'With his sharp and learned graver Lucas van Leyden has shown with great art how David plays the harp before Saul, sketching for us so naturally the essential being of Saul in his madness'.[69] Rembrandt attempts to surpass Lucas van Leyden. He concentrates in his painting on the gestures of the two main characters and the physiognomy of Saul. All the secondary figures shown by Lucas van Leyden are omitted. The idea of using the King's hand as the centrepiece may have been suggested by Peter Lastman's painting DAVID 20 AND URIAH, from which Rembrandt also took ideas for his composition.

Rembrandt's picture made such an impression that it was evidently copied at once, this copy being disseminated as early as 1633 in an etching by the Antwerp artist Willem de Leeuw. This etching was inscribed with Latin verse by the Amsterdam Catholic Humanist Cornelis Gijsbersz. Plemp (1574-1638). Plemp's lines exhibit the same rhetorical language that Rembrandt used: the feelings are expressed by a dramatisation of gestures. Plemp goes to excess in this and thereby makes clear to us that the greatness of Rembrandt's art also consists in his ability both to elucidate and to retract at the same time. David's face and form are in shadow; the face is only seen outlined against the harp.

In order to show the feelings involved in an inner conflict, Rembrandt (like other Baroque artists) takes as his model for inward agitation studies depicting reactions to a threat of physical violence. Judas, for example, in the famous JUDAS RETURNING THE THIRTY PIECES OF SILVER, is modelled on 36 people being executed.[70] His attitude expresses the despair of someone who stares death in the face. By the wringing of the hands and the asymmetry of the movement, Rembrandt has further heightened these traits.

Huygens, too, in his laudatory description of this figure, follows a rhetorical principle.[71] He does not mention only what he sees and what history narrates, but exaggerates Judas's bodily reaction to express the extremity of his despair. According to Huygens, Judas has torn his hair and his garment; his hands are painfully clasped, his body racked by violent pain. In the painting these movements are not to be seen: Huygens has accumulated these formulae expressing despair through bodily reactions to convey the deep impression the piteous figure has made on him.

DAVID PLAYING THE HARP BEFORE SAUL. About 1629/30. Cat. 5 / Bredius 490.
Wood 61.8 × 50.2 cm.
Frankfurt, Städelsches Kunstinstitut.

In Amsterdam Rembrandt became one of the greatest portrait painters in European art. When he was maturing as an artist in Leyden he did not imitate the important portrait painting of his contemporaries. The excellent artist David Bailly was active in Leyden, attracting notice by his delicately drawn portraits; Frans Hals was working in nearby Haarlem. Nowhere in Europe do so many portraits of individuals and groups seem to have been produced at that time as in Holland. And yet initially Rembrandt hardly attempted to paint portraits in the usual sense.[72] He observed and painted people's faces to include them as characteristic types in his histories. He shared this interest with Jan Lievens, who had succeeded, early in his career, in selling a head study to the stadholder. Huygens mentions it in his diary as 'the so-called portrait of a Turkish commander, painted after the head of some Dutchman'.[73] Models from the local people were dressed up in historical or exotic garments so that they could be used in a history painting. Sometimes the inventories record who sat as Rembrandt's models.[74] Contemporaries noticed that Rembrandt took people from his circle as models for biblical figures, heightening their expression, attitude, and appearance to biblical proportions. The figures in his pictures were not imagined but seen.

At the time of Impressionism there were sometimes imaginative speculations on how Rembrandt's head studies came into being: Rembrandt is supposed to have adorned relatives who came into his studio with objects chosen at random from his art collection, and then painted them. Such ideas have been popularised by films. How such a scene was imagined is shown by a quotation from an essay on art history which appeared in 1897:

> It may have been about the year 1650... . A magnificent helmet comes into his hands. He has already painted many helmets...but this precious piece surpasses all the weapons he has portrayed. His brother, older by ten years,...comes into his studio. Apprenticed as a cobbler, now a miller, part-owner of the mill inherited from their father. An unmistakable Rembrandt physiognomy... . The prematurely aged man has been ill treated by fate: taciturn, concealing some inner grief as he sits facing the artist, his heart burdened, seeing no solace in the future, tired and resigned... . On to his head, no little to his surprise, the artist thrusts the helmet. As if bowed by shame at this undeserved adornment, yet assenting affectionately to the painter's impetuous wish, he lowers his eyes. And as Rembrandt begins his study from this model,

HEAD OF AN OLD MAN. About 1629/30.
Monogrammed: 'RHL'.
Wood 24 × 20.3 cm.
Milwaukee, Collection of Dr. A. and Mrs. Bader.
Cat. 128 / Bredius[2] 633.

THE WARRIOR. About 1627.
Signed: 'RH. v. RIN' (?).
Wood 40 × 29.4 cm.
Switzerland, private collection.
Cat. 126 / Bredius[2] 132.

LAUGHING MAN. About 1628.
Signed: 'Rt.'
Copper 15.4 × 12.2 cm.
The Hague, Mauritshuis.
Cat. 127 / Bredius 134.

THE PROPHETESS HANNAH (REMBRANDT'S MOTHER).
Signed: 'RHL 1631'.
Wood 59.8 × 47.7 cm.
Amsterdam, Rijksmuseum.
Cat. 76 / Bredius 69.

Karel de MALLERY after Maerten de Vos.
THE PROPHETESS HANNAH.
Engraving.

it forms itself mysteriously and involuntarily into a symbol of Tragedy itself.[75]

Art critics of the time also explained the genesis of the head studies biographically, classifying them as portraits in catalogues of Rembrandt's works. They understood them as heightened portraits of the artist's father and mother, his brother Adriaen and his sister Liesbeth. Few of these opinions have proved correct. Rembrandt's brother Adriaen and his father were long dead, as documents have since shown. What were thought to be portraits of his sister Liesbeth are, for the most part, studies produced by pupils. It does appear probable from documents, however, that Rembrandt's mother was the model for head studies of an old woman, although only a single etching at one of his dealers was so described long after his death.[76] There is much in favour of this identification, as we shall see later. But apart from professional models, Rembrandt clearly also used members of his family, including his father, who, however, looked quite unlike the old man who was taken for him by earlier critics.[77]

The first Dutch painter to produce head studies was Frans Floris.[78] Karel van Mander has given a detailed account of their function and effect: Floris painted them because he allowed his pupils to execute large paintings that he first sketched in chalk on the canvas. They were then able to incorporate the head studies into the paintings. This practice was later introduced by Rubens in the large workshop he ran. Most of his head studies are from the period before 1620, when he organised his workshop in such a way that he could carry out large commissions without having to paint everything himself.[79] These works incorporated studies of his brother's children, for example, whom he used variously as putti or little angels in large compositions. It is noticeable that Rubens, too, painted certain types: bearded old men, old women, young warriors, turbaned Africans, etc. When Rubens was later able to draw on a large repertoire, he produced no more head studies. It is interesting to note also that Rembrandt starts to produce head studies when he takes his first pupils, about 1628. They serve as models and suggestions for the pupils, who quote them in their own history pieces. In Lievens's case the head studies clearly had a different function. He does not conceive his historical figures as wholes, but assembles them from details — the garments, the dramatically gesturing or immobile hands, a powerfully expressive face. He therefore created head studies that he incorporated literally into his histories.

The old lady with brightly striped dress pensively listening to the strains in Rembrandt's painting THE MUSIC-MAKERS is (10) generally taken to be his mother. This face also appears in specifically biblical histories as a heroine from the Old or the New Testament. In 1628, Rembrandt based on it the face of the despairing Anna in the Amsterdam painting ANNA (25) ACCUSED BY TOBIAS OF STEALING THE KID; he used her often for the prophetess Hannah and for the aged Rebecca. In (11, 59) Rembrandt's circle she was inserted in compositions as sybils, as Job's wife, and as the embodiment of avarice. The type of the old woman was widely applicable. Rembrandt had found it in Utrecht painting, where it served for portraying procuresses and Avaritia, but also for the aged wives of biblical figures.[80] In the 1620s and 1630s, Rembrandt several times depicted in paintings and etchings the (46, 51) theme of the presentation of the Christ child in the temple, in which the prophets Hannah and Simeon recognise him as the Lord, using the studies of his mother as models for the prophetess Hannah. This is seen from the use of the same attributes or attitudes in the different cases. As Collin Campbell has demonstrated, Rembrandt's starting-point was an engraving after Maerten de Vos, in which the prophetess sits on a chair, reading the Bible; in the background Hannah and Simeon are represented worshipping in the temple. Rembrandt characterises the prophetess as she is described in the Bible. He shows her in an Oriental robe, and (59) a detail of her curious head scarf recalls the Tallith, the prayer shawl which the Jews wear over their clothing when worshipping. The quasi-Hebrew script in the open book makes it clear that this is a Bible figure. In a different and far more impressive way than de Vos, he expresses the woman's extreme age.

By all appearances he first studied the human face in drawings which served solely as preparation for history paintings. Only later does he appear to have detached the heads, which had been given a heightened expression in the histories, from this context and presented them in isolation as head studies. So, in his earliest surviving portrait study, he shows an officer wearing a splendid hat with peacock feathers, and a gorget over his uniform, from which the hilt of a sword projects. It is not an officer of Rembrandt's time that is depicted here; this man resembles the mercenaries who appear in pictures from the Reformation period. Graphic works from that time served the painters of the 17th century as models for their biblical and mythological history pieces. We therefore find similarly dressed soldiers in the painting THE MARTYRDOM OF ST STEPHEN and in the Leyden history painting, which has not yet been interpreted.

56

53, 35

At the end of the Leyden period, in 1631, Rembrandt produced the great painting in Salzburg. In 1639, a year before her death, Rembrandt painted his mother again, in a picture now in Vienna. Bent over her stick, she appears as an old woman, again characterised by the same prayer shawl, as THE PROPHETESS HANNAH. The prophetess appears in a similar attitude in the etching THE PRESENTATION IN THE TEMPLE.[81] Only when Rembrandt painted portraits in Amsterdam, after 1631, did the portrayal of his mother begin to resemble official portraits. It is then comparable, for example, to Lievens's painting of Huygens. Rembrandt portrays his mother as a widow. She wears a black veil. Objections have been made to the interpretation of this veil as being a widow's veil on the grounds that wearing such a veil was not customary in the middle class; however, the use of veil to indicate widowhood does occur in the pictorial language of Baroque histories. As Rembrandt's father had died shortly before, Rembrandt uses this motif to characterise his mother's new status, which she had in common with the prophetess Hannah.

11

37

Rembrandt's workshop.
A YOUNG MAN WITH A GORGET.
Signed: 'RHL 1631'.
Wood 56 × 45.5 cm.
San Diego, Fine Arts Gallery.
Cat. A32 / Bredius 144.

Rembrandt's workshop.
YOUNG MAN WITH PLUMED BERET.
Signed: 'RHL 1631'.
Wood 80.3 × 64.8 cm.
Toledo, Ohio, Museum of Art.
Cat. A31 / Bredius 143.

SELF-PORTRAIT. About 1628.
Wood 22.6 × 18.7 cm.
Amsterdam, Rijksmuseum.
Cat. 153 / Bredius — / RRP A14.

Few artists have painted themselves as often as Rembrandt.[82] In his whole life he portrayed himself more than thirty times in paintings, twenty-six times in etchings, and twelve times in drawings. His pupils frequently copied these self-portraits painted in the workshop, learning from them 65 and painting themselves in a similar way. But it also became fashionable in Rembrandt's circle to portray oneself as an 63 artist like him. Rembrandt's etchings helped to spread the self-portraits to other countries. Rembrandt had first reproduced his own face in biblical and mythological histories and genre pieces. In this he was complying with art theory and continuing an old tradition. Art theorists, themselves generally painters, had repeatedly demanded that artists should identify themselves with the roles of persons depicted. Only in this way could they appropriately represent the emotions of those persons. When Rembrandt depicts himself as a 35, 53 witness of the ancient scene, as one of the youths stoning St. 10 Stephen, or as a principal figure in the historical music scene, he is thereby at one with this demand of theory. At the same time, he is following a tradition common among history painters. Thus an anonymous author (Bredero?), in the biography of Karel van Mander (appended to the latter's biographies of Dutch and German painters), describes a history painting by this artist in which he has portrayed himself:

> There is in Amsterdam...one of his last and greatest paintings, the children of Israel crossing the Jordan with the Ark of the Covenant. Here he has portrayed himself in a close likeness, although he was then ill, as one of the Levites or bearers of the Ark, and likewise the first owner of the picture...with his first wife... . Around the frame, inscribed in golden letters, are the following verses composed by himself:
>
> After long struggles in this world each Christian comes
> Unto the realm at last of sweetest joys;
> Yet the Jordan, called Death, he first must cross
> Which is the way all flesh must pass
> To overcome his final foe:
> If in this journey he succeed, he shall salvation know.[83]

The Old Testament story is related to the eschatologically determined fate of each individual human being. Karel van Mander, the artist himself, is, shortly before his death, one of those Israelites who must bear the Ark, the salvation of Israel, across the Jordan into the Promised Land. When Rembrandt was in Amsterdam, he may have admired how

SELF-PORTRAIT, STARING. 1630.
Etching 51 × 46 mm. Only one state.
Hamburg, Kunsthalle.
Bartsch 320.

THE PAINTER IN HIS STUDIO. About 1629.
Wood 24.8 × 31.7 cm.
Boston, Museum of Fine Arts.
Cat. 157 / Bredius 419.

22 Tengnagel painted himself as one of the spectators of the procession into Jerusalem. By these depictions of themselves in biblical histories the artists related the stories to themselves, translated them into the present, made the story of long ago a story of their own time (the Prodigal Son today — '*De verloren zoon hedendaagse*'). But with these self-depictions the artists also created for themselves a lasting memorial. Just as, despite all transience, their art would tell of them after their deaths, so too their image would be preserved beyond their deaths.

The Mannerist painters had often portrayed themselves in certain historical roles.[84] In a famous double portrait Ketel painted himself as the ancient philosopher Democritus, and Joos van Winghen depicted himself as Apelles, the painter of antiquity. Often these chosen historical roles are decidedly provocative, as when Hans von Aachen shows himself laughing in the company of a Madonna Venusta with a lute, or when Lodewijk Finsonius appears in a rhetorical role naked and holding a kind of fool's sceptre. Rembrandt does not develop his first portraits as analogies of these role portraits. Rather, he proceeds from the self-representations in the histories, where they are subjected to a sudden violent movement or an apparently accidental illumination. He detaches these self-portraits from their thematic contexts, studying light and shade and various emotions in his own face. It becomes his pattern for the physiognomy and the reactions of the young men he portrays in his histories. He produces a whole series of drawings, etchings, and paintings in which he portrays himself in the most diverse moods and illuminations. By isolating the self-portraits from the histories, he attains a new type of self-portrait by which he can demonstrate his own capabilities as a painter.

About 1628, Rembrandt represented himself for the first time in a portrait. The details are hardly discernible in areas of shadow. The sharp illumination falls on the left cheek and the neck; the background is brightly lit. So the head seems subordinate to the light, as if seen by chance. In these portraits Rembrandt studies the play of light on the face, so that he can insert the heads into history paintings. They look as if seen at a particular moment. But something else takes place as well. With these self-portraits Rembrandt places himself in a sequence of portraits of artists.

In the 16th and 17th centuries, series of portraits of artists had been published. The artists were shown in historical or fantastic costumes that seemed mysterious and alien, as if earlier artists had lived outside the bourgeois world. Sometimes, too, stylistic features of the artists depicted were alluded to. In this way, or through a parallel to a particular picture, the artist's portrait became a trade-mark. Rembrandt continues this tendency. He boldly displays his artistic skill, works with chiaroscuro. Light appears 'at the points most important to him, around which he artfully and deliberately held together light and shade, so that light was merged judiciously into darkness; the colour effects were luminous, with high reason in everything', as Sandrart writes of him in another context.[85] In his early self-portraits Rembrandt seeks to grasp emotions by using light to heighten expression — but in a way quite out of keeping with tradition. So he places the eyes in shade and at the same time mutes the intensified gaze by a layer of darkness. A year after his first self-portrait, in 1629, Rembrandt again painted himself, in a picture of no more than postcard size. He represents himself at a moment of great concentration and intense gazing. He looks intently at the onlooker. His mouth is slightly open. His hair is standing out in tight curls. Again only the left half of the face and the tip of the nose are illuminated, but now light falls on the chin also. The contrast between light and dark parts is less schematic. The light also falls on the white collar, which has a lace border. On the other hand, there are now areas of shadow on the wall. Rembrandt has again drawn the hair with the brush handle in the wet paint, revealing the colour tone beneath.

Probably in the same year, he produced the enchanting self-portrait in the Mauritshuis in The Hague. At that time Rembrandt was already working for the Dutch court. The role portrait expresses his increased self-confidence. He dresses himself like an officer with a typical gorget. The pink face contrasts strikingly with the deep ice-grey of the armour. As compared to the works of 1626, the picture displays a wonderful softness in its modelling. The colours merge with hardly perceptible gradations, even where bright and dark parts meet. Rembrandt here has effortless command of his

68

Rembrandt circle.
REMBRANDT ('SELF-PORTRAIT'). About 1629.
Wood 49.7 × 37.3 cm.
Atami (Japan), MOA Museum.
Cat. A62 / Bredius - / RRP A22.

Rembrandt circle.
A YOUNG MAN ('SELF-PORTRAIT'). About 1630.
Monogrammed: 'RHL'.
Wood 41.5 × 34 cm.
Amsterdam, Rijksmuseum.
Cat. A63 / Bredius 5.

SELF-PORTRAIT.
Monogrammed and dated 1629.
Wood 15.5 × 12.7 cm.
Munich, Alte Pinakothek.
Cat. 154 / Bredius 2.

SELF-PORTRAIT. About 1628.
Wood 69.7 × 57 cm.
Liverpool, Walker Art Gallery.
Cat. 159 / Bredius 12.

artistic means, manipulating light and darkness and emphasising the contrasts between hard metal and soft material, clear forms and dissolving contours.

This technical mastery and his talent as a painter enabled Rembrandt to break through class barriers. It was possible for him to escape artisan status and be admitted to the nobility. Constantin Huygens, secretary to the stadholder and a great patron of Rembrandt's, also refers to this when he writes in his diary of Rembrandt and Lievens in these years:

> When I think of the origin of these two there is no more eloquent disproof of the argument that nobility is a question of blood. On this point I should like to recall that many deserving men have been most wittily caught by the most brilliant of the Italians, Boccalinus — a modern author of great talent and percipience. He tells the story of an anatomical investigation of the corpse of a noble. When the veins had been carefully examined by the attending doctors, all denied that nobility was manifested in the blood, since this dead body was no different to that of an ordinary person or a peasant.

Constantin Huygens refers to the two young painters as 'a noble young pair from Leyden *(Nobile par adolescentum Leidensium)*'.[86] It is certainly not by chance that Rembrandt and Constantin Huygens expressed themselves at the same time on the nobility of the artist, one in painting, the other in writing.

Towards the end of the Leyden period, about 1630, Rembrandt produced two paintings and an etching showing 64, 67, 72 full-length portraits of himself. In the first painting, produced about 1629, he portrays himself in his studio. 64

> The bare workshop is shown in bright light between the shadowy parts to right and left. The cracks in the flaking whitewashed wall and the rough woodwork indicate its simplicity. The figure of Rembrandt, looking out intently in his painter's coat, dominates everything: it is his studio, his workplace. Yet in the foreground, large and distinct, stands the easel. As a motif it has a preponderance that can only be understood from older ideas on painting.[87]

Kurt Bauch, the eminent Rembrandt critic, derives the idea of the picture from emblematic sources. In the *Emblemata Politica* of Justus Reifenberg, published in 1632 in Amsterdam, the old maxim originating in Pliny, *nulla dies sine linea*, is symbolised by a painter *standing* at his easel and drawing a line. This representation departs from tradition in *not* show-

SELF-PORTRAIT. ▶
Signed: 'Rembrandt f. 1631'.
Wood 81 × 54 cm.
Paris, Musée du Petit Palais.
Cat. 160 / Bredius 16.

SELF-PORTRAIT.
Signed: 'R (HL) 1630'. Copper 15 × 12.2 cm.
Stockholm, National Museum.
Cat. 158 / Bredius 11.

SELF-PORTRAIT. About 1629.
Signed: 'RHL ..9'.
Wood 89.5 × 73.5 cm.
Boston, Isabella Stewart Gardner Museum.
Cat. 156 / Bredius 8.

SELF-PORTRAIT. About 1629.
Wood 37.9 × 28.9 cm.
The Hague, Mauritshuis.
Cat. 155 / Bredius 6.

ing the painter *seated*. Rembrandt presents himself in the same intense attitude in which he shows his apostles. The artist holds a brush in his right hand, and a maulstick, several brushes, and the palette in his left. Behind him we discern further art implements standing on the table and hanging on the wall. The light falls on the picture on the easel. It stands in full illumination and throws dark shadows on the floor and on the wall and doorway. Rembrandt stands far back from the picture. Both motifs, the light and the distance from the picture, express ideas that Rembrandt also gave voice to later: he considered that pictures ought to be hung in the correct lighting so that they glow as they should, and the onlooker ought to stand back from them — only when seen from a distance would all the parts be linked together. So the picture gives us an idea of how Rembrandt understood himself. The bareness of the studio speaks of his work discipline, from which nothing distracted him.

A biblical hero, a painter, a beggar — all these are roles that a human being can play in his short life on earth. It is in keeping with Baroque rhetoric, with its immanent knowledge of the transience of all worldly success, that Rembrandt 72 presented himself in quick succession as a freezing beggar who cries out for help, and as a wealthy Oriental potentate. 67 In 1631 he presents himself in the role of an Old Testament hero. His right hand rests self-confidently on his hip while he leans with his left on a stick. Weapons lying on a table in the background and the dog in the foreground underline the stately pose. Rembrandt's contemporaries believed that in Turkey people wore the same clothes as personages in the Bible. Biblical scenes could therefore be given a realistic turn if they were shown as analogous to life in Turkey. In such exotic pictures the encyclopaedic interest of the Dutch, which also expressed itself in the foundation of commercial centres and colonies, took special satisfaction.

It was not until 1631, when Rembrandt painted portraits of Amsterdam merchants that accorded with the elegant style originated by the *Feinmaler* (painter of fine details) 69 Miereveldt, that he produced in an etching A BOURGEOIS SELF-PORTRAIT. He thereby presents himself as a portrait painter of the patriciate. Only here does he portray himself as a citizen, with collar and mantle and even a hat. In the careful detail of the execution, recalling an engraving, something else that is new has come into being: a portrait etching. It has nothing in common with the earlier kind of engraved portraits, but is rather a painting translated into graphic form.

SELF-PORTRAIT IN A CLOAK AND WIDE-BRIMMED HAT.
Signed: 'Rembrandt f.' and dated 1631.
Etching 149 × 131 mm. 8th state.
Hamburg, Kunsthalle.
Bartsch 7.

It would be pointless to ask who was the greatest European sculptor, architect, or painter of the Renaissance and the Baroque.[88] In the course of the centuries and in the different countries of Europe different answers would always be given. But the question who the greatest etcher was could receive only one answer: Rembrandt. It was not until a century after him that there was another artist for whom etching played a similarly important role: Francisco de Goya. But Goya cannot be imagined without Rembrandt, and his aquatint technique is already marginal to etching. Rembrandt's incomparable significance in the history of etching resides in the fact that he was the first to explore the full artistic possibilities of this technique.

The process of etching relieves the artist of the time-consuming and difficult necessity of cutting the lines of a drawing directly into the copper plate with a graver, as is the case with engraving. Instead, he covers the plate with a thin, black-dyed, acid-proof varnish and can easily scratch his drawing into this layer. The plate is then immersed in acid, which eats into the copper where it has been exposed by the etching needle and so inscribes the lines of the drawing. The etcher therefore works with a freedom similar to that of a draughtsman. While the engraver has of necessity to move his cutting implement in calligraphic, unbroken lines, the etcher with his needle can scratch, use hatching, or produce violent, loose, or short lines, and in short can express his feeling in the flow of his line with much the same freedom as in drawing. In the etching process the edges of the lines are somewhat eaten into by the acid; they are less smooth, do not start or end as finely as in engraving. This makes it possible to produce decidedly painterly effects through etching, to give surfaces an animation of light and shade.

In the 16th century the possibilities of etching were very seldom recognised and exploited. Sometimes it was used merely as a means of duplicating drawings, and those who used it tried to imitate engraving, which was considered more proper. Even Jacques Callot, who was later so exemplary for Rembrandt, tried to achieve the effect of engraving in his etchings.

Among those practising the art of etching in the Netherlands between 1590 and Rembrandt's first high point as an etcher, around 1630, there was only one for whom etching was a central means of expression. This was Hercules Seghers, who attempted in his coloured etchings to achieve effects suggestive of paintings. Undoubtedly Rembrandt, above all in his late phase, was deeply influenced by him. He too tried at that time to produce colour effects with the black

SELF-PORTRAIT, SHOUTING. 1630.
Etching 73 × 62 mm. 3rd state.
Hamburg, Kunsthalle.
Bartsch 13.

NUDE WOMAN SITTING ON AN EARTH MOUND. About 1631.
Etching 176 × 160 mm.
Hamburg, Kunsthalle.
Bartsch 198.

SELF-PORTRAIT AS A BEGGAR. 1630.
Etching 116 × 69 mm. Only one state.
Hamburg, Kunsthalle.
Bartsch 174.

THE BEGGAR WITH THE CHAFING-DISH. About 1630.
Etching 77 × 48 mm. 2nd state.
Hamburg, Kunsthalle.
Bartsch 173.

etching technique, but he never coloured his etchings or made colour prints. Rembrandt produced etchings throughout almost his whole life. The earliest were done about 1625, when he returned to Leyden from Amsterdam; up to his bankruptcy in 1656 he made more than 270 etchings, but after that he etched only infrequently.

Rembrandt would sketch the scene to be etched on the copper plate and then execute the darker parts. From time to time he made trial prints, on which he frequently drew to make the emphases clearer. As soon as he had reached a state that satisfied him, he made several copies. But often he later re-worked the etching, whether by altering the background, intensifying the darkness of night pictures, for example, or by revising the whole plate and so producing a new work. For some etchings there are as many as eleven different states. The earliest etchings that have been preserved are very modest and simple. In terms of graphic quality, they are to be seen as no more than reproductions of drawings. No influence of any particular master is discernible in the technique. It is therefore probable that Rembrandt acquired the technique in collaboration with Jan Lievens and Joris van Vliet. It is all the more astonishing that after these slight beginnings Rembrandt became within five years a master of etching technique, achieving new and unfamiliar solutions through a constant study of prints by Callot and the great copper-plate etchers such as Dürer and Goltzius and the etchers of Rubens.

About 1627, Rembrandt came across Callot's series *The Beggars*, which opened a new aspect of reality to him. There were beggars in Leyden in large numbers, even in the '*Golden Age*'. But they became the subject of Rembrandt's pictures, not because he met them daily, but because of the impression

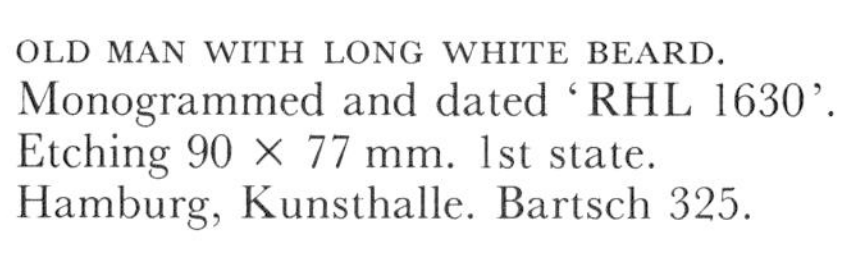

OLD MAN WITH LONG WHITE BEARD.
Monogrammed and dated 'RHL 1630'.
Etching 90 × 77 mm. 1st state.
Hamburg, Kunsthalle. Bartsch 325.

REMBRANDT'S MOTHER WITH A BLACK VEIL. About 1631.
Etching 146 × 129 mm. 3rd state.
Hamburg, Kunsthalle.
Bartsch 343.

SELF-PORTRAIT, LOOKING OVER HIS SHOULDER.
Monogrammed 'RHL' and dated 1630.
Etching 72 × 60 mm. 3rd state.
Hamburg, Kunsthalle. Bartsch 10.

REMBRANDT'S MOTHER.
Monogrammed and dated 'RHL 1628'.
Etching 65 × 63 mm. 2nd state.
Hamburg, Kunsthalle. Bartsch 354.

BEGGAR WITH A WOODEN LEG. About 1630.
Etching 113 × 65 mm. 2nd state.
Hamburg, Kunsthalle.
Bartsch 179.

Callot's drawings made on him. He produced numerous etchings based on these virtuoso works. But while Callot's beggars have a certain dignity, in Rembrandt they arouse pity. Clad in torn garments, they are marked by wretchedness. Rembrandt saw the beggar warming his hands over a brazier in a work by Callot. Bloemaert, too, took this figure from Callot's work in producing his own series. But while in the latter the beggar is made to look almost elegant by the flowing forms, in Rembrandt he is rigid and embittered. He has taken from Callot the limitations of the human figure, the pointed edges of the drooping garments, and the vertical hatching. But Rembrandt draws the figure more strongly, emphasises the irregularity and raggedness. The claw-like hands convey the shivering of the outcast — how deeply Rembrandt empathised with this role is shown by a small etching presenting HIMSELF AS A BEGGAR.

72, 74 · 72 · 72

In two etchings from 1628 his mother appears in the same emotively heightened manner as in THE PRESENTATION OF JESUS IN THE TEMPLE. Rembrandt has already succeeded, through a dense network of hatching, in showing the face in a dramatised, momentary illumination. At this time he also studies HIS OWN FACE, etching it in the most diverse moods: happy, angry, serious, surprised, fearful, or jocose. At the same time, he studies and fixes effects of light, shade, and movement. In small etchings of histories he is able to achieve the monumentality of a painting. Soon after this, he reached his first peak as an etcher, when he succeeded in producing painterly chiaroscuro effects through a complex tissue of lines. In so doing, he departs entirely from the contemporary manner of engraving, with its even contours and monotonous parallel hatching.

73 · 51 · 63, 71, 73

In the small etching THE TWELVE-YEAR-OLD JESUS IN THE TEMPLE of 1630, he emphasises the contrast between massive forms (such as the mighty columns) and the delicate boy, so that the onlooker is astonished in the same way as the scribes in the picture; Mary and Joseph in the background are still quite far from the child Jesus, and we wonder whether his parents have caught sight of him yet. Space is no longer a shallow stage for Rembrandt, but a theatre of action in which events that have just happened continue to resonate and future events are portended.

75

The etching THE SONG OF PRAISE OF SIMEON AND HANNAH separates the poor believers from the people kneeling on the steps before the high priest, who do not see the Light of the World. The aged Simeon holds the child; Mary and Joseph, both seen from the back, kneel before him. An angel points out the Redeemer to the old prophetess Hannah. She is so inspired that she no longer has to lean on the little girl who accompanies her. On the left, Rembrandt shows the figure of a beggar, cut off by the edge of the picture — in this way the genre studies are also affecting the histories. The beggar is tottering away. Although redemption is meant for him, too, he does not perceive it. Rembrandt makes it clear again and again that the Gospel applies to the poor, but he does not for this reason present them in the foreground: poverty alone does not confer vision.

75

THE CIRCUMCISION. About 1630.
Etching 88 × 64 mm. Only one state.
Hamburg, Kunsthalle.
Bartsch 48.

THE TWELVE-YEAR-OLD JESUS IN THE TEMPLE.
Monogrammed 'RHL' and dated 1630.
Etching 109 × 78 mm. 3rd state.
Hamburg, Kunsthalle.
Bartsch 66.

THE SONG OF PRAISE OF SIMEON AND HANNAH.
Monogrammed 'RHL' and dated 1630.
Etching 104 × 79 mm. 2nd state.
Hamburg, Kunsthalle.
Bartsch 51.

REMBRANDT GAINS RECOGNITION IN AMSTERDAM

By about 1630 the two young artists, Rembrandt and Lievens, clearly felt that they had outgrown their native town; they wanted to prove themselves in the world. This desire probably has to do with the connections they had formed in the meantime. So Lievens felt impelled to go to England, and Rembrandt to Amsterdam. In 1623 he had sold A FACE *(Tronie)* to the Amsterdam patrician Joan Huydecoper, and he had already obtained his first portrait commissions from the city. Life-size portraits completed as 100 early as 1631 have been preserved (NICOLAES RUTS, Frick 77 Collection, New York, and A MAN AT A TABLE, Hermitage, 78-79 Leningrad). THE ANATOMY LESSON OF DR. TULP (The Hague) must have been commissioned in 1631 and was probably produced in the spring of 1632.

Amsterdam was the most important and richest city of the provinces which had been liberated from the Spanish yoke. It had an ideal situation at the estuary of the Amstel, in the IJssel Bay, for two arms of the river led inland. A network of canals already traversed the city. From the water, through a forest of masts, the bastions were visible which had been built around the city, with canals on their landward sides. Along these *Grachten* stood warehouses and wharves, and also, already, the opulent houses which give the city its character today. The silhouette of the city was completed by the church steeples and the watchtowers at the gates.

The real rise of Amsterdam began after the northern provinces of the Netherlands had broken away from Spain.[89] At that time the dominance of Antwerp, previously the most important trading centre, was broken by the successful blockade of its port. Many upper-class families of Antwerp, as well as artisans and traders, made their way to Amsterdam, where they found a safe home. But besides these inhabitants of the southern Netherlands, who gave the main impetus to the growth of trade, immigrants came from other European countries.

Many had left their homes for religious reasons. Jews had fled from Portugal and later from Poland and Germany; Scandinavians, Germans, Greeks, and Italians all came to Amsterdam. Within two generations the population grew from 30,000 (1585) to 115,000 (1631); in four and a half decades, therefore, it had almost quadrupled. This gave rise to an immense concentration of diverse forces which combined in common enterprises. In addition to the existing trade in the Baltic, newly discovered countries and continents were a source of trade. To establish a foothold there, merchants formed the United East India Company, and soon the Dutch had disposed of their competitors. Commod-

PORTRAIT OF A MAN AT A TABLE.
Signed: 'RHL 1631'.
Canvas 104 × 92 cm.
Leningrad, Hermitage.
Cat. 191 / Bredius 146.

Page 78-79:
DOCTOR NICOLAES TULP DEMONSTRATING THE ANATOMY OF THE ARM.
Signed: 'Rembrant ft. 1632'.
Canvas 169.5 × 216.5 cm.
The Hague, Mauritshuis.
Cat. 251 / Bredius 403.

PORTRAIT OF A YOUNG MAN SHARPENING A QUILL. About 1632.
Signed on the letter: 'RHL van Rijn'.
Canvas 101.5 × 81.5 cm.
Cassel, Gemäldegalerie.
Cat. 197 / Bredius 164.

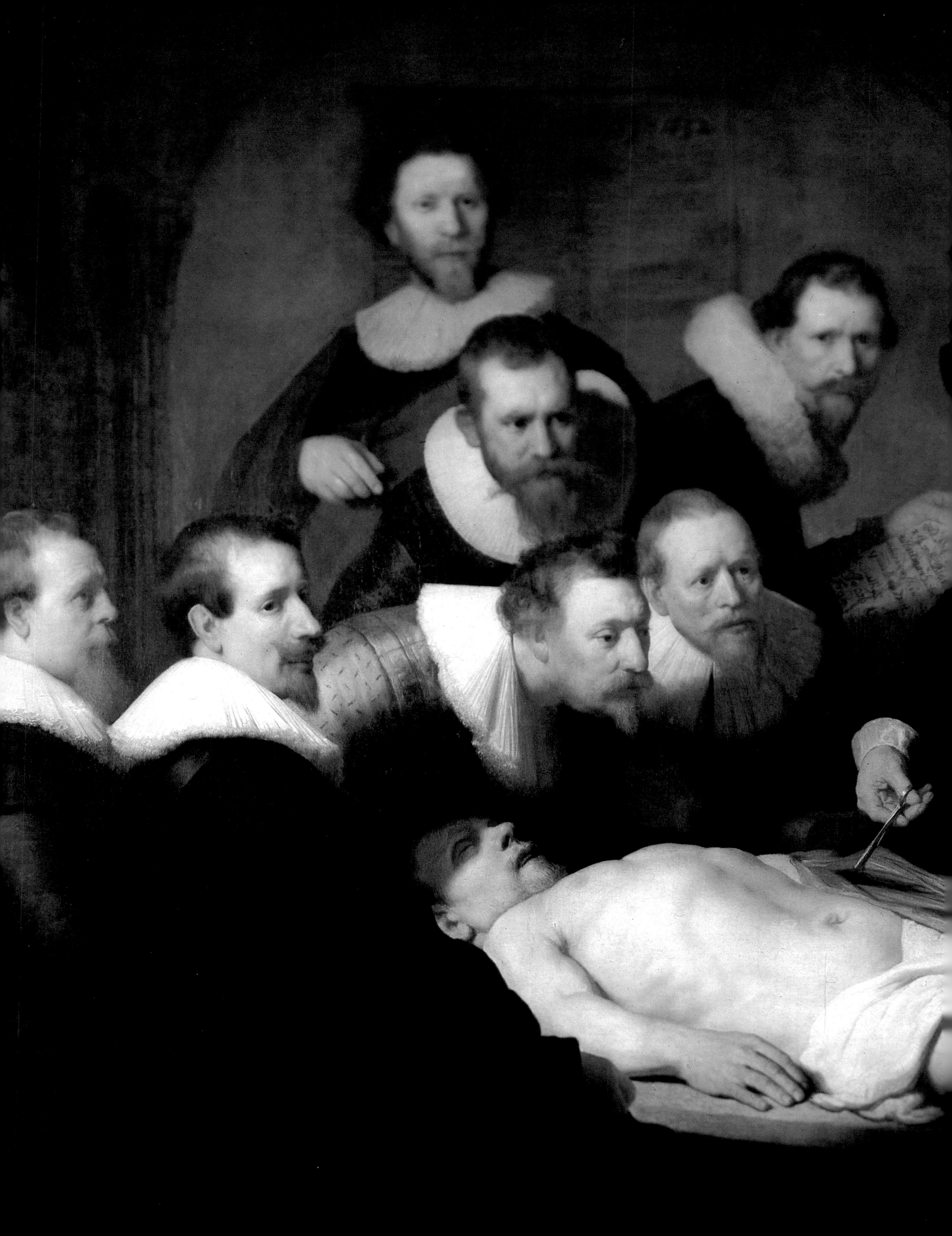

PORTRAIT OF A YOUNG WOMAN WITH PEARL-TRIMMED BERET.
Signed: 'RHL van Rijn 1632'.
Canvas 68.5 × 53.5 cm.
Zurich, private collection.
Cat. 148 / Bredius 84.

ity prices for the entire world were determined on the Amsterdam exchange. This economic expansion encouraged a blossoming of the arts in Amsterdam. Many poets and painters, including Rembrandt, came to the city. In the spring of 1631 he had probably not yet thought of moving to Amsterdam, for he bought a piece of land in Leyden; but the commissions from Amsterdam clearly became so important that he changed his mind. Hendrick Uylenburgh, an able and influential art-dealer, was probably a significant factor in this decision. This astute businessman had acquired not only a wide circle of clients but also a large number of artists interested in working with him, by making them partners in his business. Among these were Claes Moeyaert, Simon de Vlieger, Jacob de Wet, Jan Treck, and Lambert Jacobsz. Some of the partners had themselves painted by the artists who worked with Uylenburgh in order to promote the business, because a larger turnover increased their own profit. Rembrandt became a partner by contributing the large sum of 1,000 florins, which was more than the annual income of a well-paid clergyman. On the receipt he is still named as living in Leyden. It is known that Rembrandt lived with Uylenburgh in the Breestraat, so that it was presumably he who persuaded him to move to Amsterdam.

At that time portrait painting was the predominant art form in Amsterdam, which can be explained by historical factors. The self-assured bourgeoisie — merchants, clergy, and government officials — having attained prosperity, now aspired to glorification and immortality. When he arrived, Rembrandt found a well-defined art of portraiture already established. However, his colleagues had not succeeded in applying the stylistic achievements of history painting to their own field, the deficiency being particularly obvious in group portraits. The figures were generally placed side by side; only rarely were the members of the group connected by a common action. Rembrandt endeavoured to transcend this kind of portrait painting. THE ANATOMY LESSON OF DR. TULP (1632) was his first group portrait. It surpasses all of its Amsterdam predecessors, for Rembrandt makes use of insights gained from the histories. As in the painting JUDAS RETURNS THE THIRTY PIECES OF SILVER, the figures are placed in a semicircle around the main figure, on whom the attention of the onlookers is focused. Rembrandt could not, however, apply the principles of history painting entirely consistently, since this would have entailed portraying the two men on the left side in the same way he portrays the two scholars in the Judas painting, almost from behind. This contradicts the rules of portraiture; the figures on the left are therefore shown in the traditional pose, and some of the men portrayed are made to face the onlooker. This gives the painting a certain lack of unity, which was not caused by

78-79
36

Rembrandt and workshop.
PORTRAIT OF A SEATED MAN. About 1633.
Wood 90 × 68.7 cm.
Vienna, Kunsthistorisches Museum.
Cat. 198 / Bredius 163.

Rembrandt's workshop.
PORTRAIT OF A YOUNG WOMAN WITH A FAN.
Signed: 'RHL van Rijn 1632'.
Canvas 72.2 × 54.5 cm.
Stockholm, Nationalmuseum.
Cat. A55 / Bredius 85.

later additions, as has occasionally been suggested, but by the artistic conflict between the composition proper to a history painting and that of a group portrait.

Public lectures on anatomy were clearly a special event in Holland at that time; they not only fulfilled the desire for comprehensive knowledge but also recalled the transitory nature of life. The so-called anatomy theatres — like the first museums of natural history later — were stocked with illustrations and exhibits intended to make clear to the visitor that sin leads to death. In public lectures, which for reasons of hygiene usually took place in winter, only the bodies of executed criminals could be dissected; in Rembrandt's painting we know that it was that of the thief and vagrant Adriaen Adriaensz. 't Kint. It was customary for the *Praelectores Anatomiae* to commission a group portrait commemorating such an occasion, depicting themselves together with some other paying members of the guild. This was not meant to depict a specific public lecture, but rather the ideal image of such a lecture.

Dr. Nicolaes Tulp was an important anatomist who held the highly regarded post of praelector of the Amsterdam Guild of Surgeons from 1628 to 1653. As a member of the city aristocracy, he followed the usual career of a public servant, was an important member of the city council, eight times held the prestigious post of treasurer and was four times burgomaster. He was a member of the Calvinist congregation, whose interests he upheld in his political career. The well-known dictum 'I spend myself in serving' was his motto. Rembrandt particularly stresses Tulp, setting him off from the other members of the guild by his dress — for example, his hat. The spatial structure also allocates a special place to Tulp. He alone is seen before a niche; the others are in front of the large hall.

The first surgeon who did not leave the dissection to an assistant was the anatomist Andreas Vesal. As a student in Paris he had succeeded in exposing the tendons of the hand. Contemporaries praised Tulp as 'the Vesalius of Amsterdam', and the whole portrait alludes to this. Tulp is demonstrating some muscles of the arm which move the fingers, and compares his observations with the woodcut in an anatomical textbook lying open at the feet of the corpse. It is probably the one written by Adriaen van der Spiegel in 1627. In Vesalius's textbook *De humani corporis fabrica*, the author himself is shown dissecting a right arm; on the table in front of him lies a paper with the inscription 'Concerning the tendons which move the fingers'. For Vesalius, the doctor's most important instrument was his hand, and he never tired of pointing out that the word *chirurg* (surgeon) was derived from the Greek word for hand *(cheir)*. The right hand with which 'the Vesalius of Amsterdam' performs the

PORTRAIT OF A YOUNG WOMAN IN AN ARMCHAIR.
Signed: 'RHL van Rijn 1632'.
Canvas 92 × 71 cm.
Vienna, Akademie der bildenden Kunste.
Cat. 229 / Bredius 330.

Rembrandt's workshop. PORTRAIT OF A MAN. Signed: 'RHL van Rijn 1632'.
Canvas 111.8 × 88.9 cm. New York, Metropolitan Museum of Art. Cat. A81 / Bredius 167.

Rembrandt's workshop. PORTRAIT OF A WOMAN IN RICH DRESS. Signed: 'RHL van Rijn 1632'. Canvas 111.8 × 88.9 cm. New York, Metropolitan Museum of Art. Cat. A103 / Bredius 331.

Rembrandt's workshop.
PORTRAIT OF A BOY IN RICH DRESS. About 1633.
Wood 67 × 47.5 cm.
Leningrad, Hermitage.
Cat. A85 / Bredius 186.

dissection is moved by tendons exactly like those exposed in the hand of Adriaen Adriaensz. 't Kint.

In order to characterise Tulp as 'the Vesalius of Amsterdam', Rembrandt departed entirely from the normal procedure at such a dissection. Usually the abdominal cavity and the brain were opened first, and then the arms were dissected. For this purpose they were usually first separated from the torso and hung up. Rembrandt, however, depicts the whole body as untouched except for the arm. This makes it especially clear that Tulp wanted here to be seen, like Vesalius, as a surgeon of the hand and arm, so that the paper with the written explanation is no longer needed. There is some doubt whether Rembrandt painted the dissected arm from the woodcuts of anatomical textbooks or from the actual arm of 't Kint. (It is of interest, incidentally, that the 1669 inventory of his estate mentions plaster casts of four arms and legs dissected by Vesalius.)

Like THE ANATOMY LESSON, the painting THE SHIPBUILDER JAN RIJCKSEN AND HIS WIFE (Buckingham Palace, London), in its bold and consistent application of the formal principles of history painting, surpasses the tradition of portraiture. (Jan Rijcksen, as has only recently been discovered, was a partner in the East India Company and in 1620 was its most important shipbuilder.) The picture, painted in 1633, shows the couple in a scene which informs the onlooker of their social position. The shipbuilder sits at a desk, busy at his plans, and his wife has just entered his office. He interrupts his work and turns to her; this *interruption* is intended to motivate his turning towards the onlooker. The motif is cleverly generated by the action to produce the posture needed for the portrait. But it also serves to characterise the couple in another way, in stressing the professonal position of the man in contrast to the subordinate activity of his wife, who brings him a letter like a secretary.

131

The unusual conceptions of Rembrandt's paintings, the powerful narrative manner, and the picturesque chiaroscuro caused a stir among the painters and citizens of Amsterdam. By 1633, Rembrandt was already imitated by many painters and was inundated by commissions from the middle class. This factor probably strenghtened his wish to establish himself as an independent master in this city. In the year of his marriage, 1634, he joined the St. Luke's Guild and accepted students, who came in large numbers from the Netherlands, some even from Germany and one from Denmark. According to the rules of the guild, a master could teach only three students at one time. Rembrandt seems not

Rembrandt's workshop.
PORTRAIT OF A YOUNG WOMAN. Signed: 'Rembrandt ft 1633'.
Wood 63 × 48 cm.
Brunswick, Herzog Anton Ulrich-Museum.
Cat. A108 / Bredius 338.

◀ PORTRAIT OF A MAN WITH A POINTED BEARD.
Signed: 'Rembrandt f' over the signature 'RHL van Rijn' and the date (163)2.
Wood 63 × 48 cm.
Brunswick, Herzog Anton Ulrich Museum.
Cat. 192 / Bredius 159.

PORTRAIT OF A MAN RISING FROM A CHAIR. Signed: 'Rembrandt f. 1633'.
Canvas 124.5 × 99.7 cm.
Cincinnati, Taft Museum. Cat. 200 / Bredius 172.

PORTRAIT OF A YOUNG WOMAN WITH A FAN. Signed: 'Rembrandt ft. 1633'.
Canvas 125.7 × 101 cm.
New York, Metropolitan Museum of Art. Cat. 232 / Bredius 341.

MARGARETHA VAN BILDERBEECQ, WIFE OF WILLEM BURCHGRAEFF.
Signed: 'Rembrandt f. 1633'. Wood 67.5 × 55 cm.
Frankfurt, Städelsches Kunstinstitut.
Cat. 230 / Bredius 339.

to have abided by this rule, regarding his workshop as a kind of academy that could accommodate amateurs, young and old. Convinced that art could be learned through constant practice, Rembrandt devoted a great deal of time to teaching his students. Under his guidance they frequently created works which closely reflected his ideas. However, when they worked independently, most soon adapted to current taste.

Rembrandt was probably helped a good deal in establishing his livelihood by advice from Uylenburgh. A new world opened for the young man. Henceforth he lived the life of a successful artist who was not only a painter but also an art-dealer, collector, and teacher, and able to combine all

Rembrandt's workshop.
WILLEM BURCHGRAEFF (1604-1647).
Signed: 'Rembrandt f. 1633'.
Wood 67.5 × 52 cm.
Dresden, Gemäldegalerie.
Cat. A82 / Bredius 175.

Rembrandt's workshop.
A BEARDED MAN IN A WIDE-BRIMMED HAT.
Signed: 'Rembrandt f. 1633'.
Wood 69.3 × 54.8 cm.
Pasadena, Norton Simon Foundation.
Cat. A84 / Bredius 177.

Rembrandt's workshop.
PORTRAIT OF A FORTY-YEAR-OLD MAN.
Signed: 'RHL van Rijn 1632' and marked 'AET 40'.
Wood 75.6 × 52.1 cm.
New York, Metropolitan Museum of Art.
Cat. A79 / Bredius 160.

these activities. Besides an art gallery, Uylenburgh owned an academy where children from wealthy families were instructed in painting. They first learned how to copy originals. All the great artists of the time had begun their training in this way, and they commonly received the flattering comment that the copy was hardly distinguishable from the original. Since he owned a large collection of important masters, among them many Italian works, Uylenburgh benefited twice over from this arrangement. The students had to pay for their tuition, and he then sold their copies at a profit. How strong the temptation must have been to sell the work of a student as an original!

Rembrandt's workshop.
PORTRAIT OF A WOMAN.
Signed: 'Rembrandt f. 1633'.
Wood 67.9 × 50.2 cm.
New York, Metropolitan Museum of Art.
Cat. A105 / Bredius 335.

Rembrandt's workshop.
PORTRAIT OF A YOUNG WOMAN.
Signed: 'Rembrandt f. 1634'.
Wood 66.2 × 52.5 cm.
Louisville, Kentucky, J.B. Speed Art Museum.
Cat. A109 / Bredius 344.

Rembrandt's workshop.
PORTRAIT OF A FASHIONABLY-DRESSED COUPLE.
Signed: 'Rembrandt f. 1633'. Canvas 131.5 × 106.6 cm.
Boston, Isabella Stewart Gardner Museum.
Cat. A117 / Bredius 405.

BUSINESS AND TOLERANCE, POLITICS AND RELIGION, ART AND STATUS-SYMBOLS IN AMSTERDAM

The art-dealer Uylenburgh, the aristocrats Joan Huydecoper and Dr. Nicolaes Tulp, and the master shipbuilder Jan Rijcksen, along with his wife Griet Jans, all belonged to different religious denominations. Huydecoper — who had bought a painting by Rembrandt as early as 1628 — came from a family which favoured the Remonstrants, Tulp was a strict but urbane Calvinist, Jan Rijcksen and his wife were Catholics, and Uylenburgh was a member of the Mennonites, a sect derived from the Baptist movement.

The different religious denominations had in general co-existed peacefully since Amsterdam had joined the rebellion against the Spanish, and the moderate, reformist element of Remonstrants and Liberals had gained the ascendancy (with a brief interruption) in the municipal government. Thanks to the tolerant policies of the government, an intellectual, religious, and above all, economic climate was established in which minorities that were elsewhere not tolerated or were even persecuted could make an economic, cultural, and religious contribution. As a result there were in all religious denominations people able to afford to be painted by an artist who worked for the court or to buy a history painting from him. So in the course of years, the Calvinist Rembrandt painted portraits and histories for Calvinists, Catholics, Remonstrants, free-thinkers, Jews, Mennonites, and Lutherans. Most of his customers who bought paintings were from the upper classes. They were merchants, diplomats, or military men, poets, doctors, or clergymen. Many of Rembrandt's patrons and clients belonged to the civic aristocracy or were connected to it by blood or friendship. During his time in Amsterdam Rembrandt painted the portraits of four future burgomasters. Two of them had themselves painted at the beginnings of their political careers, for it was a tradition in Amsterdam that a civic aristocrat was painted with the group under him when he was appointed to a new office. Yet we also find Rembrandt's head studies and histories at an early stage in the collections of city aristocrats who later became burgomasters. The influence of these burgomasters — on cultural policy and the general artistic climate of the city — can hardly be overestimated.[90] In the whole Republic the burgomasters played a predominant role. Because Amsterdam was the richest city in the Republic and shouldered the major part of the expenditure of the seven Provinces, its voice carried much weight in the Union. The Amsterdam government consisted of the council and borough council, the court of justice, and the college of the four burgomasters. It was the burgomasters who really controlled the city's fate. Their

PORTRAIT OF AN 83-YEAR-OLD WOMAN.
Signed: 'Rembrandt f. 1634 AE(tatis) 83'.
Wood 68.7 × 53.8 cm.
London, National Gallery.
Cat. 234 / Bredius 343.

Rembrandt's workshop.
A YOUNG MAN WITH A MOUSTACHE.
Signed: 'Rembrandt f. 1634'.
Wood 70 × 52 cm.
Leningrad, Hermitage.
Cat. A86 / Bredius 196.

college was newly elected every year. The retiring burgomasters, with the lay assessors, elected three new burgomasters, and these chose the fourth from the retiring college. The burgomasters were responsible for appointing or confirming the most important civic officials, the chancellor, the commissioners of the discount house, the regents of the communal and charitable institutions, the governing boards of the guilds, the captains of the militia, and even the authorities of the Calvinist church. In this way the burgomasters could make people dependent on them and relegate trouble-makers to unimportant posts.

Joan Huydecoper, the first citizen of Amsterdam to buy a painting by Rembrandt, is a typical representative of the municipal aristocracy who, with their often unimaginable wealth, their ostentation, and their enormous influence, did much to shape the economic situation of the artists dependent on them.[91] If we consider the fortunes of his family, we realise why Rembrandt had such success in his first years in Amsterdam and why he encountered difficulties later. Originally Joan's family was simply called Bal, until it added the sobriquet Huydecoper, meaning 'leather-dealers', which later became their surname. As a tanner and trader in hides Joan's father, Jan, became very rich. As a supporter of the Orange cause, he had no opportunity, in a city then ruled by a small clique of civic aristocrats with Catholic and Spanish leanings, to help to shape its political destiny as other rich members of his class were doing. The thoughts of the rich Orange sympathisers excluded from power turned to insurrection. Many of them were captains of the militia guilds until dismissed by the municipal government on account of their liberal views. When pressure from the Orange side led to the old guild's reinstatement, the militia captains deposed the Catholic regime, deported them by ship, and chose from among themselves a new municipal council and city government. In this way Jan Huydecoper became a lay assessor and so a member of the new patriciate. The militia company led by him took the first watch after the seizure of power. In the Huydecoper family tradition this was celebrated a century later as if he had been the first to take up arms against the Spaniards. In 1580 he was made colonel of the militia. By the time of his death he had been elected lay assessor eleven times, although he never became a burgomaster. In 1578 merchants with Orangist sympathies had also been elected to the new municipal aristocracy. This broad-minded policy,

Rembrandt's workshop.
PORTRAIT OF A MAN IN A WIDE-BRIMMED HAT.
Signed: 'Rembrandt fec. 1635'.
Canvas, transferred to wood 77.5 × 64.8 cm.
Indianapolis, Earl C. Townsend Jr. Collection.
Cat. A88 / Bredius 201.

Follower of Rembrandt.
PORTRAIT OF A YOUNG WOMAN WITH FLOWERS IN HER HAIR.
Signed: 'Rembrandt f. 1634'.
Wood 71 × 53.2 cm.
Edinburgh, National Gallery of Scotland (on loan from the Duke of Sutherland).
Cat. A110 / Bredius 345.

which was intended to contrast clearly to the attitude of the Inquisition, was not entirely maintained. The Calvinists in the government ensured that the highest offices of state were reserved for Protestants. But since the new patriciate was aware that the resurgence of the Amsterdam economy could only be maintained with the cooperation of all religious denominations, it saw to it that members of other denominations could meet in secret. It was only at the beginning of the 17th century that a small, well-organised group within the aristocracy led by Gerrit Jacob Witsen and Reinier Pauw enforced the adoption of a strictly Calvinist policy. In 1619, with the help of Maurice of Orange, the municipal council was purged, even the liberal or Remonstrant militia captains being dismissed. By this measure Maurice secured the support of the simple, Calvinistically inclined population and checked the municipal aristocracy, whose self-confidence was becoming troublesome. This Calvinist predominance was not, however, long lived. As early as 1621, Gerrit Witsen and other patricians defected to the liberal faction, fearing the church might gain excessive political influence. Jan Huydecoper belonged to the liberal faction in the town hall.

Although the new municipal aristocracy had come to power by revolution, it was by no means more democratic than the preceding Catholic regime. It too kept power within its families. We can see this in the career of Jan Huydecoper's second son. Joan Huydecoper, born in 1599, grew even richer than his father and was politically more influential. In 1621 he married Elisabeth de Bischop, who came from a Remonstrant family, as was in keeping with his father's outlook. However, his wife died after only seven months of marriage. Then, in 1624, when the liberal and Remonstrant

Page 94:
Rembrandt's workshop.
JAN PELLICORNE (1597-after 1639) AND HIS SON (1628-1680).
Signed: 'Rembran(dt) ...ft'.
Canvas 155 × 122.5 cm.
London, Wallace Collection.
Cat. A118 / Bredius 406.

Page 95:
Rembrandt's workshop.
SUSANNA VAN COLLEN (1606-1660) WITH HER DAUGHTER EVA SUSANNA (born 1627). About 1634.
Signed: 'Rembrandt ft. 16 (..)'.
Canvas 155 × 122.5 cm.
London, Wallace Collection.
Cat. A119 / Bredius 407.

PORTRAIT OF A YOUNG WOMAN.
Signed: 'Rembrandt f. 1635'.
Wood 77.5 × 64.8 cm.
Cleveland, Ohio, Museum of Art.
Cat. 238 / Bredius 350.

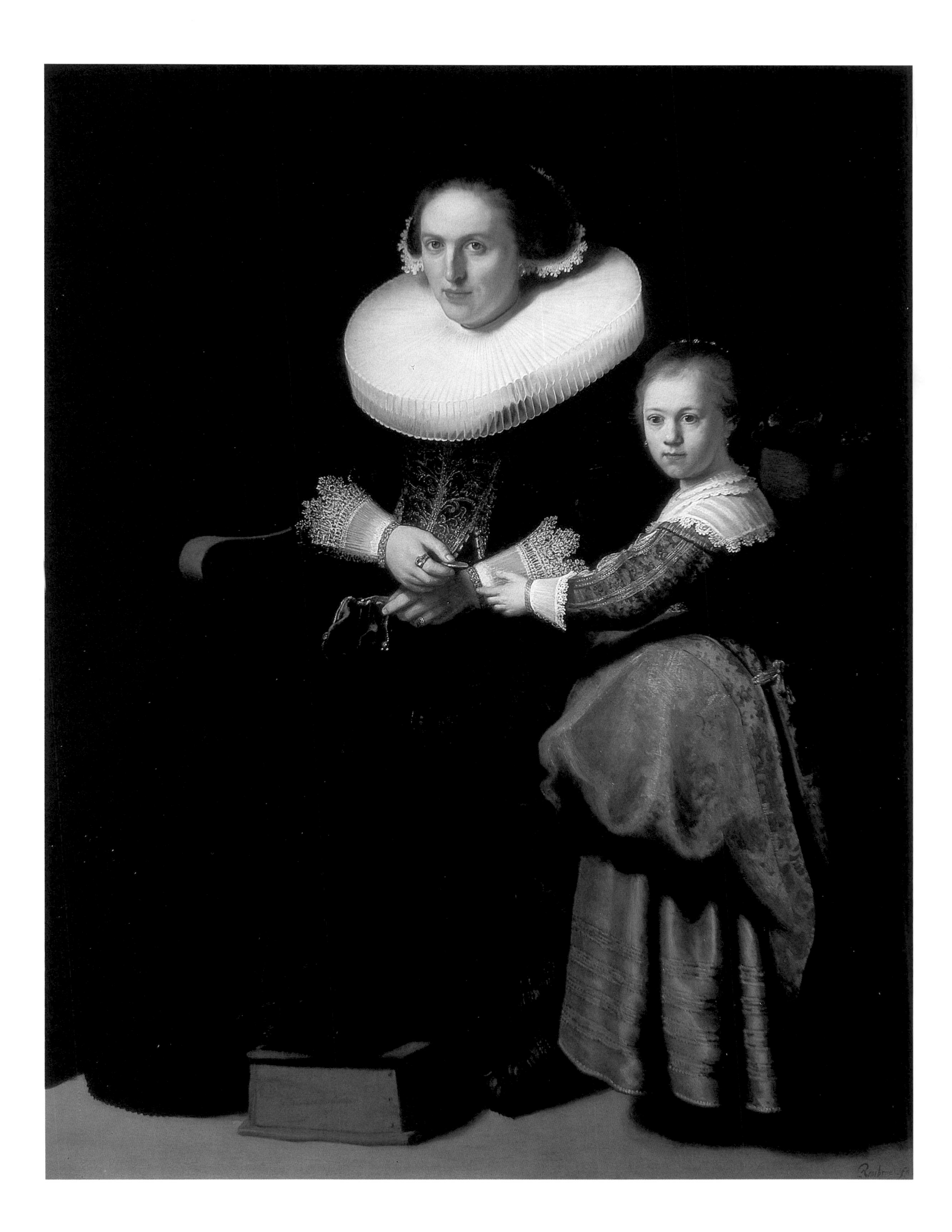

Govaert FLINCK.
MARGARETHA TULP.
Signed and dated 1655.
Canvas 138 × 103.5 cm.
Amsterdam, Bernhard Houthakker CV.

forces had gained the upper hand in Amsterdam, he married the daughter of the strictly Reformed Church merchant and banker Coymans. In keeping with the ideas then prevalent on the function of marriage, two rich families were thus united in order to act still more successfully and to pass the power they had attained to their children.

In 1620, still only 21, Joan Huydecoper was made lay assessor and thereby a member of the patriciate and the Amsterdam government. In keeping with his status, he took an interest in art, and on 15 June 1628 — as we know from the deed of sale which has been preserved — he purchased copies after Rubens and a head study by Rembrandt. He had spent his childhood and youth in Anthonisbreestraat, but these comparatively modest patrician houses no longer matched the pretensions of a merchant and politically ambitious city aristocrat. Economically, socially, and politically, he aspired to higher things. In 1634 the dream of almost all Amsterdam patricians was fulfilled for him: he was knighted by Queen Christina of Sweden. By purchasing various noble estates he was now able to call himself the Count of Tamen and Blockland, Maarseveen and Neerdijk. His new noble status had to be outwardly displayed. In 1639 he bought three houses on the Singel and had them demolished and replaced by an imposing house like a noble's palace, on the Royal Canal. The garden, protected by a gateway, was ornamented with a fountain and statues; there was also a coach-house and stables. The residence was adorned with expensive curios and works of art; the glazier and poet Jan Vos was the decorator. At Maarseveen Huydecoper erected the magnificent country seat *Goudensteyn* ('Golden Stone'). There too he had an art gallery with paintings and sculptures. Since he was guided by the taste of the international nobility determined by court life, from its beginning his collection reflected the cool classical taste of the French court and the Académie Française. Huydecoper favoured subjects taken from antiquity and had his portrait painted by artists who had adapted to the classical-courtly style, such as Govaert Flinck, Bartolomaeus van der Helst, and Janson van Keulen, and his son later had himself painted by Jan Lievens. If he had bought a work by Rembrandt in his youth, as a noble he aligned himself with international taste. So Rembrandt was unable later to sell him any more pictures. In the development of his first client, some of the difficulties that were later to beset Rembrandt were prefigured. As a patrician, Joan Huydecoper passed through the officer ranks of the militia, and on the occasion of the Peace of Münster, had himself painted with his company. The painting was intended for the Old Room at the House of Crossbowmen, where there was also a picture of the militia company of his father. A poem by Jan Vos points to the Huydecopers' importance in the liberation of Amsterdam. Just as the father with his company had been the first in the uprising against the Spaniards, his son was the first to lead his company into the Peace. High politics were understood here as a history of the influential families, and the obliging Govaert Flinck did not neglect to glorify the princely residence on the Singel in the background of the group portrait.[92] Huydecoper was a representative figure and an important presence at the municipal council. In the years between 1651 and 1660 he was burgomaster no less than six times. In this capacity he was fond of fulfilling ceremonial duties, representing Amsterdam at the courts of electors and kings, whom he regarded as equals. When in 1655 the Elector of Brandenburg sought an alliance with the City of Amsterdam on account of differences with the Swedish king, he chose the city as godfather of his youngest son. For rulers, even christenings reflected political alliances. Joan Huydecoper was assigned to represent Amsterdam at the ceremony. He was accompanied by the city secretary and later burgomaster Joan Corver and — since power was hereditary in Amsterdam — by numerous sons of burgomasters, first and foremost his own eighteen-year-old son, Joan Huydecoper Jr., who was later to become burgomaster, and then by the eldest son of Cornelis de Graeff and the son of Jan van der Poll, who was only fourteen. This ceremonial mission with its copious attendance accomplished its task with success. There was only one slight mishap: while Huydecoper was able to converse with the Electoress and Amalia von Solms the wife of Stadtholder Prince Frederick Hendrick, in Dutch, he was obliged to mumble embarrassedly when handing over the christening present, as he spoke no German.

When the delegation returned after six weeks, they spent the night at his country estate 'Goudensteyn' which was on their route; his court poet Jan Vos awaited him there. As

Rembrandt and Workshop.
PORTRAIT OF A WOMAN SEATED. About 1633.
Wood 90 × 67.5 cm.
Vienna, Kunsthistorisches Museum.
Cat. 233 / Bredius 332.

they approached Amsterdam, they were received by seventy mounted members of the patriciate and the wealthy bourgeoisie in ceremonial dress, and conducted in a triumphal procession to the newly built town hall, to the construction of which Huydecoper had been a leading contributor. From the town hall the members of the municipal council and their wives and children waved in greeting. Naturally, the knight and count Joan Huydecoper saw to it that an artist adapted to the classical taste prevalent at European courts was commissioned to decorate the building.

Through his patronage and his political position, Joan Huydecoper influenced the taste of the Amsterdam patriciate and the rich bourgeoisie. He liked to surround himself with artists who served his interests. In October 1654 he attended the banquet of the Amsterdam painters' guild, the Guild of St. Luke, which took place in the Voetboogdoelen. Vondel was also present, but not Rembrandt. Joan Huydecoper took pains to ensure that public commissions went to artists working in the courtly-classical style he approved.

The Amsterdam patriciate, of which Huydecoper was a typical representative, exerted a decisive influence on the painting of the Golden Age. The liberal group to which he belonged successfully opposed the strictly Calvinist groups who had a more distant relationship to culture and would have preferred to expel the organ from churches, prohibit the theatre, forget Antiquity, forbid dancing, and suppress luxury. Art served to heighten the fame of aristocratic families. It had a political character because it made their pretensions manifest. As Amsterdam's strength increased and its culture flowered, their claims grew; and as aristocrats they were guided by the development of the court style of painting.

The liberally inclined government promoted a climate in which art flourished. Amsterdam attracted artists, and its art market boomed. The attitude of the ruling liberals affected the whole cultural climate. The members of different religious groups aligned themselves to it. The Mennonite Uylenburgh did not just trade; he traded in art. Despite all their Puritan principles, Mennonites, like Calvinists, collected pictures. And as the Catholics, too, participated in economic and cultural life, we find many Catholics among Rembrandt's patrons, as among his colleagues and predecessors. Tolerance fostered the economic and cultural flowering that took place in Holland. A culture with pronounced national characteristics was able to develop and to leave its stamp on the culture of Europe. But the same civic aristocracy that had largely made this unfolding possible came into

Rembrandt's workshop.
PORTRAIT OF A YOUNG WOMAN.
Signed: 'Rembrandt f. 1633'.
Wood 61 × 50 cm.
New York, private collection.
Cat. A107 / Bredius 337.

Rembrandt's workshop.
PORTRAIT OF A MAN WITH A POINTED BEARD AND A WIDE-BRIMMED HAT.
Signed: 'Rembrant f. 1634'.
Wood 70 × 53 cm.
Boston, Museum of Fine Arts.
Cat. A87 / Bredius 197.

Rembrandt's workshop.
A YOUNG WOMAN WITH RICH FINERY.
Signed: 'Rembrandt f. 1634'.
Wood 69.5 × 53 cm.
Boston, Museum of Fine Arts.
Cat A111 / Bredius 346.

PHILIPS LUCASZ., COUNCILLOR OF THE DUTCH EAST INDIA COMPANY.
Signed: 'Rembrandt 1635'.
Wood 79.5 × 58.9 cm.
London, National Gallery.
Cat. 205 / Bredius 202.

conflict with the art it fostered. As it was guided by the international court style, status symbols and class taste mattered more to it than the artistic autonomy of individual painters. In Amsterdam the debate which Rembrandt had already had with the aristocrat Constantin Huygens was to be repeated. Huygens had wanted to send him and Lievens to Italy to be schooled by Antiquity and Italian Renaissance art. The very burgomaster who had been the first citizen of Amsterdam to buy a picture from him was later to measure him by the same yardstick — and place commissions elsewhere. None of the city aristocrats that Rembrandt had painted at the beginning of his career and who became burgomasters during his lifetime had themselves or their children painted subsequently by Rembrandt. They turned to artists who had adapted to the court style and who fullfilled their expectations. So Frans Banning Cocq had himself painted with his regents by Bartolomaeus van der Helst, and Margaretha Tulp, the daughter of Dr. Tulp, commissioned Govaert Flinck to paint her portrait a year after her marriage to Jan Six.

Rembrandt's workshop.
OLD WOMAN IN A WHITE CAP.
Signed: 'RHL van Rijn 1632'.
Wood 75 × 55.5 cm.
Tel Aviv, private collection.
Cat. A104 / Bredius 333.

JORIS DE CAULLERY (c. 1600-1661).
Signed: 'RHL van Rijn 1632'.
Canvas 102.8 × 84.8 cm.
San Francisco, M. H. de Young Memorial Museum.
Cat. 196 / Bredius 170.

Both Dr. Nicolaes Tulp, Rembrandt's most important client around 1630, and Rembrandt himself, belonged to the Calvinist church. Saskia, whom Rembrandt later married, was likewise of this denomination. Her uncle, Petrus Sylvius, was a minister in Amsterdam. Family relationships and friendships clearly have a bearing on the fact that most of the people whose portraits Rembrandt painted at that time were Calvinists. While they did not wield political power, they largely shaped the character of Dutch society. In the war of liberation against Catholic Spain they had proved the strongest and the most decisive religious denomination. They were able to justify the rising against an authority holding a different creed in theological terms and to take advantage of their newly won power. Since the Calvinists regarded Catholic worship as heathen, condemning even altars, crosses, devotional and memorial pictures, candles, and music, they radically purged the churches of towns liberated by the Orangists and insisted that churches be handed over to them or secularised. Although the war of liberation was waged under the banner of tolerance, they usually gained their ends; in general, town governments could allow other denominations only the freedom to hold their services in concealed churches or private houses, although the Calvinists protested against even this. If painters were thereby prevented from creating altars and church pictures, the way was open to paint portraits, landscapes, and views of towns or churches for citizens' houses, either under commission or for the free market.[93]

Although the Calvinists were an officially recognised denomination, they did not set the tone in Amsterdam society, however strident their views on many cultural and political questions of the day. Culture was determined by the liberals. The liberal climate in Amsterdam ensured that the strict Calvinists were not able to impose their ideas and had even, if they were in leading positions, to make concessions on social and cultural matters or to accustom themselves to the prevailing conditions.

Tulp belonged to the Calvinist church and to the Calvinist faction in the municipal government.[94] He was no humanist or non-religious sceptic. On the contrary, an anatomical dissection was for him a demonstration of God's omnipotence, which revealed itself even in the skeleton of an unworthy human being. He zealously asserted the interests of the Calvinist church, protesting in the reformist spirit, if unsuccessfully, against the custom of erecting statues of ancient pagan gods and goddesses at ceremonial receptions of great personages, such as Maria de Medici. Later he went

Pupil of Rembrandt.
THE TOWER OF THE WESTERKERK AT AMSTERDAM.
Pen and bistre, wash. 190 × 148 mm.
Amsterdam, Museum Fodor. Benesch A62.

Page 102:
MAERTEN SOOLMANS (1613-1641).
Signed: 'Rembrandt f. 1634'.
Canvas 209.8 × 134.8 cm.
Paris, private collection.
Cat. 202 / Bredius 199.

Page 103:
OOPJEN COPPIT, THE WIFE OF MAERTEN SOOLMANS. About 1634.
Canvas 209.4 × 134.3 cm.
Paris, private collection.
Cat. 236 / Bredius 342.

NICOLAES RUTS (1573-1638).
Signed: 'R(H)L 1631' (Only the date is clearly legible).
Wood 116.8 × 87.3 cm.
New York, The Frick Collection.
Cat. 190 / Bredius 145.

Rembrandt's workshop.
THE DIPLOMAT ANTHONIS COOPAL (1606-1672).
Signed: 'Rembrandt f 1635'. Wood 83 × 67 cm.
Greenwich, Connecticut, Neumann de Vegvar Collection. Cat. A89 / Bredius 203.

so far in the municipal council as to vote against an application by the Lutheran community to build a second church to house their growing members, justifying his action with examples from the New Testament, but again without success.

After the Synod of Dordrecht (1618-1619) the Reformed Church undertook to spread the influence of the Gospel to the whole of national life.[95] These endeavours often bore a radically puritanical stamp. Luxury was condemned; theatre, dancing, and church music rejected. In this crusade, conflicts could arise between patrician pretensions, administrative duties, and puritanical norms. Moved by such convictions, Tulp took a stand against extravagance and excess, meeting with success later, when he was a burgomaster. So a law was promulgated restricting the number of guests at a wedding and prescribing the number of courses and the nature of the food. The law even contained clauses fixing the maximum cost of the jewels the bridegroom could give the bride. This law was often infringed; the heavy fines went to the alms-house and thus served benevolent ends. Social pretensions and strict puritan morality came thoroughly into conflict in Tulp's case. He was the most successful doctor in the city, lived in one of the most select streets, and was the first doctor to afford a horse-drawn carriage in which to visit all his patients. When he had served on the city council for no less than 50 years, he invited the whole council to a festivity in his garden — an unprecedented act. Naturally the members of the council were seated in the same order of rank as that which they held in the council. At the end of the table his two sons-in-law, Jan Six and Dr. Tholinx, took their places; both, as we shall see, had their portraits done by Rembrandt in a painting and an etching. Everyone waited with furtive relish to see what Dr. Tulp would offer his guests and whether he would observe the norms he had established. Wagenaar observed later that the feast in no way differed from others in its luxury; it was appropriate to social class rather than to puritan principles. Afterwards the guests went into the house, where porcelain bowls with pipes and tobacco awaited them. When they returned to the table, it bore a dish of choice candied fruit and gingerbread. At each toast they drank to Dr. Tulp's health. Each guest received a silver medallion with Tulp's bust.

One of Rembrandt's first Amsterdam clients, Nicolaes Ruts, came from a Mennonite family but had become a member of the Reformed Church. Nicolaes Ruts was in charge of a trading house founded by his father which had connections with Moscow. Then fifty-eight, he appears life size in his portrait. The clothing with copious fur trimmings shows his wealth and may also allude to his business link with Russia, at that time an important supplier of furs. Ruts is turned towards the onlooker from a profile position, so that his body appears in a three-quarter view and his face is shown from the front. This gives the impression that the merchant is presenting the commercial letter in his left hand. Since the export business largely depended on correspondence at that time, the letter characterises the profession of the portrait's subject. For this reason it is emphasised by lighting no less than the hands and face are. The treatment of the background is also adjusted to Ruts: a kind of illuminated zone surrounds the figure, a secularised halo that is supposed to show the subject in the proper light. From 1636 at the latest, the picture hung at the commercial premises of his daughter Susanna, who exported materials and silk to Russia. Did she commission the portrait or rescue it in time from the clutches of creditors? For Ruts had had to reach a settlement with them six months before his death. In the course of the 17th century, many Mennonites went over to the Reformed Church because it promised economic benefits and the possibility of social advancement. If this was Ruts's reason, he seems to have miscalculated.

In 1634, Rembrandt completed the over-life-size portraits of the English minister Johannes Elison and his wife, Maria Bockenolle. Johannes Elison, born about 1580 in England, had studied theology at Leyden, beginning in 1589. In 1604 he was appointed preacher to the Dutch community at Norwich. Although he was offered the position of minister to the Dutch community in London in 1621, he remained true to Norwich and worked there until his death in 1639. His son Theophilus succeeded him. For a long time there was uncertainty over how this commission arose. The identity of the portrait's subjects was even doubted. The solution of the problem is very simple: two of their sons, Jacob and Johannes Jr., lived in Amsterdam. Johannes was a wealthy merchant. The parents must have visited their sons between 17 August 1633 and 26 January 1635 in Amsterdam; there is, admittedly, no documentary mention of a journey, but as their names do not appear in documents at Norwich during this period, where they otherwise occurred constantly, the assumption is very probable. On this occasion Johannes Jr. had them painted by Rembrandt; only a year later the son determined that the pictures should be bequeathed to his family in England on his death, as indeed happened. They remained in the possession of the family until 1860, keeping alive the memory of an earlier generation.

Rembrandt shows Johannes Elison at his desk; in front of him is an open book of liturgical songs; as the Reformed service differed from the Catholic Mass through 'the singing of psalms', this book was probably intended to indicate the denomination of the preacher. Further books and a rolled-up letter are also on the desk, and in the background, an extensive library is to be seen, partly concealed by a curtain. However, the portrait is not rendered in terms of action to the point where the minister is shown studying. The turning towards the onlooker and the presentation of the head *en face* are in line with tradition. In a gesture of affirmation, Elison holds his left hand to his breast. In the same year Rembrandt had shown CHRIST TEACHING with the same gesture, and a year earlier the preacher JOHANNES UYTTENBOGAERT. The attitude of Maria Bockenolle matches that of her husband.

Rembrandt's next major portrait commission after THE ANATOMY LESSON OF DR. TULP came from MAERTEN SOOLMANS and his wife OOPJEN COPPIT. They ordered life-size full-length figure portraits; each painting is almost as large as the group portrait. As the price of portraits was governed by their size, these must have been very costly. The wealthy couple could afford them; the husband was a grandson of the rich sugar manufacturer Jan Soolmans, who had emigrated as a Protestant from Antwerp to Amsterdam about the end of the 16th century. As chance would have it, the client and Rembrandt had visited the same notary in Leyden on the same day, one

THE REFORMED-CHURCH MINISTER JOHANNES ELISON (c. 1581-1639). Signed: 'Rembrandt ft. 1634'. Canvas 174.1 × 124.5 cm. Boston, Museum of Fine Arts. Cat. 204 / Bredius 200.

after the other; whether they met in so doing is not known. Maerten Soolmans had studied from 1623 to 1633 in Leyden, but does not seem to have taken any examinations. The couple present themselves in elegant dress. The husband's dark suit is delicately striped, her dark dress soberly relieved with light dots. Ornamental accessories such as lace collars, cuffs, belts, and shoe buckles are in both cases executed in the most expensive manner. Such luxurious shoulder-width lace collars have been met up to now in Rembrandt's earlier works only in the portraits of AMALIA VON SOLMS and MAURITS HUYGENS. The artist devotes much attention to the sumptuous fashionable accoutrements which display wealth and

135
134

MARIA BOCKENOLLE,
WIFE OF JOHANNES ELISON.
Signed: 'Rembrandt f. 1634'.
Canvas 175.1 × 124.1 cm.
Boston, Museum of Fine Arts.
Cat. 235 / Bredius 347.

underline the link between the couple, rendering them carefully and with especial brilliance, in the manner of Amsterdam *Feinmalerei* (very detailed painting) of that time. The directions of the movements of the two figures arrested in portrait poses also stress their belonging together. The tiled floor, the pedestal, and the curtain are interrelated, yet Rembrandt has not presented a unified space with a central perspective. Puritan severity and the claims of social position were not always easy to reconcile in liberal Amsterdam. Portraits such as Rembrandt's of the Soolmanses make it clear that considerations of social status often took precedence over the strict observance of religious principles.

Rembrandt probably met Saskia van Uylenburgh through the art-dealer Hendrick Uylenburgh. She was Uylenburgh's cousin and had come to live and work at a relative's house in Amsterdam at about the age of ten. Her mother had died when the girl was about six. Saskia, like Rembrandt, was a late child, the youngest of nine children. Her father was the Leeuwarden delegate to the States of Friesland, and as a member of the deputy states, one of the Frisian envoys at The Hague. For Rembrandt, who was of bourgeois origin on his father's side and of noble blood on his mother's, Saskia's lineage may, consciously or unconsciously, have played a part in his wish to marry her. It would only be in keeping with the natural development of a boy if his mother's image was more deeply impressed on him than his father's, and all the evidence we have suggests that this was so. Saskia and Rembrandt met in 1633, as can be inferred from a number of portraits of her that he painted in that year. As an orphan, Saskia had a guardian, the Reformed Church minister Jan Cornelisz. Sylvius. He was married to Aaltje van Uylenburgh, a first cousin of Saskia's. In 1634 he was already 70, but still served in the Groote Kerk, where he had worked for more than 28 years. In 1633 or 1634, Rembrandt etched a 110 portrait of him. One may assume that Rembrandt wanted thereby to win over Saskia's guardian or thank him for his consent to the marriage. Sylvius was a highly esteemed clergyman; eight years after his death an etching was 110 commissioned showing him in the pulpit. Such a picture was not intended only for art collectors, but for people who honoured and wished to remember him.

On 10 June 1634, Rembrandt and Saskia presented their banns to the Commission of Marriages. Saskia was accompanied by Sylvius. The document is worded as follows: 'On 10th June 1634...Rembrandt van Rijn, of Leyden, 26 years old, living in the Breestraat, (declaring that) his mother will assent to this marriage, appeared with Saskia V(an)Uylenburgh from Leeuwarden, 21 years old, resident in St. Anne's parish...'[96] Rembrandt's mother signed the agreement assumed in this document on 14 July, four days later, at the office of a notary in Leyden, thanking the Marriage Commissioner in an appendix for having presupposed her assent in accepting the banns; her agreement should be accepted as if she had been personally present.[97] The wedding took place on 2 July in the Reformed Church of St. Anne, which belonged to the parish of Het Bildt in Friesland, where Saskia's brother-in-law, Gerrit van Loos, was secretary.[98]

109 Rembrandt made an enchanting portrait sketch of Saskia which he inscribed as follows: 'This is my wife when she was

SASKIA. Dated 1633.
Silver stylus on white-primed parchment. 185 × 107 mm.
Berlin-Dahlem, Staatliche Museen Preussischer Kulturbesitz, Kupferstichkabinett. Benesch 427.

SASKIA AS FLORA.
Signed: 'Rem (br)a(.) 1635'.
Canvas 123.5 × 97.5 cm.
London, National Gallery.
Cat. 105 / Bredius 103.

JAN CORNELISZ. SYLVIUS.
Signed: 'Rembrandt ' and dated 1646.
Etching 278 × 188 mm. 2nd state.
Hamburg, Kunsthalle.
Bartsch 280.

21 years old on the third day of our marriage, June 8, 1633'. Through the choice of materials normally used for documents, this portrait of Saskia, in silverpoint on parchment, has an almost documentary character. Rembrandt undoubtedly made a slip in his inscription: either he gave the wrong date for the wedding or he mistook Saskia's age, for she was only 21 at the time of the wedding in July 1634; in 1633 she was still 20.

In 1634, 1635, and 1641, Rembrandt painted SASKIA AS FLORA, the Roman goddess of flowers and therefore of youth, of the enjoyment of life, and of expectant mothers.[99] She is symbolized by flowers. During her festival, women in ancient Rome adorned themselves with flowers. The goddess was depicted as a blooming virgin decked in flowers; these statues were known in Holland through engravings, and the Dutch were fond of presenting Flora as a live picture on festal occasions such as processions in honour of a king. Rembrandt was therefore making use of familiar associations when he presented Saskia as Flora in the London painting of 1635, her head adorned with flowers and holding a garland in her left hand, while her right hand rests on a staff wreathed in flowers. For him Flora may have been above all an allegory of the hopes of motherhood, for Saskia was expecting a child that was born at the end of the year. Bearing in mind the trite analogies which Rembrandt's contemporaries established between themselves and figures from the past, the possibility of such an allusion seems by no means farfetched.[100] In later years Saskia also served as model for DELILAH; in the Dresden painting REMBRANDT AND SASKIA IN THE SCENE OF THE PRODIGAL SON IN THE BROTHEL, he gave the harlot on the lap of the Prodigal Son the features of his young wife.[101] Before he met Saskia, Rembrandt had painted hardly any portraits of women. The first female portraits are decidedly stiff, sometimes boring; it was only through the free studies of Saskia's face that he learned to convey the charm and grace of feminine features. How far he identified his wife with the roles in which he painted her will probably never be quite clear; this can be seen in the case of the Dresden portrait of Rembrandt and Saskia, painted as a testimony to their overflowing happiness, which is all the more surprising since the connection of the picture with portrayals of the Prodigal Son in the brothel was pointed out as early as 1925. Rembrandt himself produced a series of drawings on this subject, which show remarkable similarities to the painting. In both, the Prodigal Son is dressed as a

115, 108, 116
108
160
117
114

JAN CORNELISZ. SYLVIUS. 1633 or 1634.
Etching 166 × 141 mm. 2nd state.
Hamburg, Kunsthalle.
Bartsch 266.

SASKIA SMILING WITH A PLUMED HAT.
Signed: 'Rembrandt ft. 1633'.
Wood 52.5 × 44.5 cm.
Dresden, Gemäldegalerie.
Cat. 181 / Bredius 97.

THREE FEMALE HEADS. About 1634.
Etching 126 × 104 mm. 2nd state.
Bartsch 367.

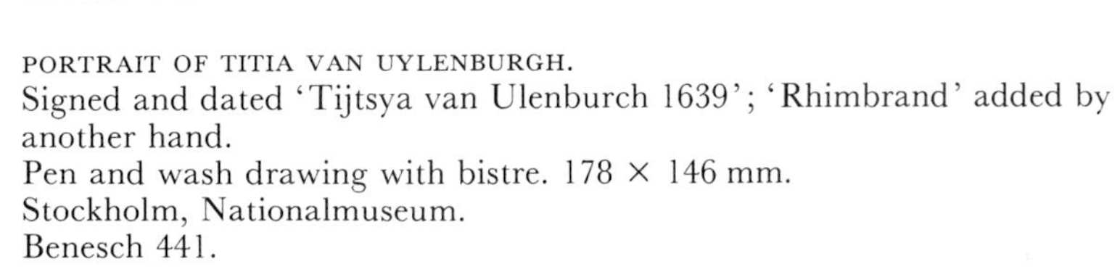

PORTRAIT OF TITIA VAN UYLENBURGH.
Signed and dated 'Tijtsya van Ulenburch 1639'; 'Rhimbrandt' added by another hand.
Pen and wash drawing with bistre. 178 × 146 mm.
Stockholm, Nationalmuseum.
Benesch 441.

SASKIA. About 1633/34. ▶
Wood 99.5 × 78.8 cm.
Cassel, Gemäldegalerie.
Cat. 182 / Bredius 101.

SASKIA WITH A VEIL.
Signed: 'Rembrandt ft. 1633'.
Wood 65 × 48 cm.
Amsterdam, Rijksmuseum.
Cat. 180 / Bredius 94.

THE PRODIGAL SON SQUANDERING HIS INHERITANCE.
Pen and bistre, wash, 177 × 210 mm.
Basle, Robert von Hirsch Collection.
Benesch 529.

Copy from Rembrandt.
THE PRODIGAL SON SQUANDERING HIS INHERITANCE.
Pen and bistre. 185 × 222 mm.
Orléans, Museum.
Benesch 528a.

SASKIA. About 1634.
Wood 60.5 × 49 cm.
Washington DC, National Gallery of Art (Widener Collection).
Cat. 183 / Bredius 96.

nobleman in officer's uniform with a plumed hat and sword, and the harlot sits on his lap while he raises his glass. The table is richly laden, and on the wall the drinks have been marked on a slate. As these pictures are all in horizontal format and the objects on the left edge of the Dresden painting seem oddly truncated, I asked the museum in 1966 whether the picture might have been cut and whether X-ray photographs existed. Both questions were answered in the negative, but a later investigation by Anneliese Mayer-Meintschel confirmed my supposition. The X-ray does not show the usual tensioning marks along the left edge, so that the picture must be a fragment. There was a further surprise, for the X-ray showed an overpainted nude woman playing the mandolin. In the original version, therefore, the painting was a history piece in horizontal format showing the Prodigal Son in the brothel. It was then cut — by Rembrandt? — and concentrated around the main figures. Perhaps Rembrandt had difficulty in finishing the picture and restricted it to the main figures in the course of composition.

To present oneself in the role of the Prodigal Son, who squanders his inheritance on wayward paths and sinks into abject poverty, but then, returning home repentant, is joyfully received by a good father, was by no means an unusual idea for painters at that time. Karel van Mander mentions that Dürer had depicted himself in the engraving THE PRODIGAL SON AS A SWINEHERD. The Utrecht artist Jan Bijlert portrayed himself in a brothel scene. As the Prodigal Son in a number of Utrecht works clearly takes on the characteristics of a self-portrait by turning his eyes to the

SASKIA AS FLORA.
Signed: 'Rembrandt f. 1634'.
Canvas 125 × 101 cm.
Leningrad, Hermitage.
Cat. 104 / Bredius 102.

SASKIA AS FLORA.
Signed: 'Rembrandt f. 1641'.
Wood 98.5 × 82.5 cm.
Dresden, Gemäldegalerie.
Cat. 107 / Bredius 108.

onlooker, it was natural to present oneself in this role. There are several self-portraits by Rembrandt in the form of anti-heroes. As he acquired more and more wealth, he represented himself as a beggar, and later as one of the soldiers who raised Christ's cross. At a time of abundance he was mindful of the transience of riches, as a Christian, of guilt, in marriage, of human lust. Love was often described in a negative sense in contemporary poetical works. Rembrandt therefore did not stand outside the theology of his time, which interpreted biblical stories in terms of the present.

72
133

Saskia, her guardian Sylvius, and her uncle Uylenburgh undoubtedly facilitated Rembrandt's access to clerical and patrician circles thanks to their family connections. Rembrandt therefore particularly cultivated his contacts with Saskia's relatives. The baptismal documents are of interest in this respect, for these richer relatives were witnesses at the baptisms of all of his four children, never his own much poorer brothers and sisters. Rumbertus and Titus were named after Saskia's ancestors. Only the two daughters, born in 1638 and 1640 — the first died soon after birth — were given the name Cornelia after Rembrandt's mother. Did Rembrandt think of himself as someone so special that he neglected his own family? It is noteworthy that in all the documents dealing with his parents' legacy, he is distinguished from his brothers and sisters by the honorary title of 'Mr.' ('Sr.').

Hendrick TER BRUGGHEN.
THE PRODIGAL SON IN THE BROTHEL.
Monogrammed and dated 1624.
Canvas 103 × 86 cm.
Krefeld, Kaiser Wilhelm Museum.

REMBRANDT AND SASKIA IN THE SCENE OF THE PRODIGAL SON AT THE BROTHEL. About 1636. ▶
Signed: 'Rembrandt f.'.
Canvas 161 × 131 cm.
Dresden, Gemäldegalerie.
Cat. 54 / Bredius 30.

THE AMSTERDAM MENNONITES AND REMBRANDT

On Rembrandt's attitude to the various Protestant denominations we have only a single contemporary comment. The Florentine Baldinucci writes that Rembrandt was a Mennonite, citing Rembrandt's Danish pupil Keil as his authority. The Mennonites, he asserted, embraced a false religion. They deviated even from the Calvinist doctrine, for they were only baptised at thirty. Their clergy had not studied and were just ordinary people, even though respected, honest, and just. For the rest, they lived *a lor capriccio* — as they saw fit. Baldinucci declared that he did not know whether Rembrandt later adhered to this false creed.[102]

This inaccurate statement has led many critics astray. It has misled important art historians such as Carl Neumann, Julius Held, and Jakob Rosenberg into forgetting the church documents which prove him to have been a member of the Calvinist Church and the other documentary evidence about Rembrandt, and into explaining his choice of subjects as arising from the Mennonite spirit.[103] In this they entirely overlook the fact that to the Catholic Italian with his Classicist taste, much as for Houbraken, Rembrandt's capricious art was a breach of the rules. Baldinucci liked to give his judgement a sociological foundation: in religious matters as well, he saw Rembrandt as consorting with bizarre folk who did not live according to court rules but *a lor capriccio*, ordinary but respected, honest and just. Just as he had a false religion, Rembrandt had the wrong style. Baldinucci's sources show how he arrived at these comments. He reports on Uylenburgh's academy–again basing himself on information from Rembrandt's pupil Keil. Rembrandt's art-dealer was a Mennonite. But as Baldinucci does not want to say anything adverse about Uylenburgh, he suppresses this information with reference to him and transfers it to Rembrandt. Have we here a case of art criticism founded on religious psychology?

The Mennonites originated in the Anabaptist movement which was formed in Zürich in 1523-1525. When, in December 1523, Zwingli, while trying to introduce the Protestant Holy Communion, gave way to opposition from the authorities, many of his most loyal followers saw this as a betrayal; from their circle the Anabaptist movement was formed. They insisted on unconditional obedience to the Gospel, the question of the correct form of baptism being only one among many. But the conflict was sparked by the issue of adult baptism. From their inception the Anabaptists were persecuted, not only by the Catholics. Most of the martyrs of the Reformation period were Anabaptists. The Imperial Laws of 1528 had supplied the basis for this. The peaceful Anabaptist

THE AMSTERDAM MERCHANT MARTEN LOOTEN (1585-1649).
Monogrammed: 'RHL' and dated 1632.
Wood 91 × 74 cm.
Los Angeles, County Museum of Art.
Cat. 195 / Bredius 166.

THE MENNONITE PREACHER CORNELIS CLAESZ. ANSLO AND HIS WIFE AALTJE GERRITSDR. SCHOUTEN, *detail*.
(see p. 121).

movement was distorted by Melchior Hofmann, who wanted to bring about the Kingdom of God by force of arms. In Münster he instituted a reign of terror that ended in the catastrophes of Münster and Amsterdam. In Amsterdam, Anabaptists had stormed the town hall. They were all executed. In Rembrandt's time, pictures by Dirck Barendz. showing the Anabaptist rising and the executions still ornamented the town hall. Between 1536 and 1576, 51 Anabaptists were executed, mostly by burning. Nevertheless, Menno Simons and his companions succeeded in giving the survivors new heart. In Groningen and Emden, on the Lower Rhine, in Holstein and Prussia, he worked as Elder, as the Anabaptists called their bishop. In his writings he opposed the militant Anabaptists of Münster and elsewhere. He thus became an influential teacher and leader of the peaceful and long-suffering Anabaptists, who called themselves Mennonites after him. When the Netherlands became Calvinist in about 1578, the persecution of the Anabaptists ended. The Anabaptists wanted to purify the community uncompromisingly; their model was the early Christian community. They admitted only those who professed their religion and were baptised as adults. To act well and do good were the demands placed upon believers. After the persecutions the Anabaptists turned away from the world, refusing war service and public offices. But gradually they gave up the principle of isolation, engaged in trade, and took part in social and cultural life, but were outwardly distinguished by very simple dress and hairstyle.

Through his Mennonite art-dealer, Uylenburgh, Rembrandt came into contact not only with the Mennonite community but with other groups opposed to the Calvinist Church.[104] He cultivated these connections although himself a Calvinist.

Hendrick Uylenburgh came from a Frisian Mennonite family which had left Holland and fled to Cracow on account of their faith. He later lived for a few years in Danzig. His brother Rombout was court painter, and his father furniture-maker, to the King of Poland. Not later than 1628 he returned to Holland. There the descendants and friends of these families had returned to power and after 1578 had transferred offices from Catholics to Protestants and adopted liberal policies. Uylenburgh clearly had good friends and patrons among them. He rented a house in the Breestraat and was soon able to fill the gap left by the deaths of Pieter Isaacsz., and Lastman's friend Cornelis van der Voort. To conduct his art trade Uylenburgh had to borrow money. He did so primarily from people with Mennonite beliefs. Four of Uylenburgh's investors were relations of powerful regents. To finance his business Uylenburgh had to walk a tightrope; he appears to have repeatedly infringed the rules observed by strict Mennonites. In April 1639 he assigned all his pictures to two fellow-believers against a credit of 1,600 florins. In January 1640, he declared before a notary that he had mortgaged 'his whole shop of paintings and art' to eighteen other creditors. From 1647 to 1650, Uylenburgh rented a house on the Dam but was unable to pay the rent, and was two years in arrears when he left. The burgomasters remitted 60 per cent of the debt and gave him a new commission into the bargain: he was to varnish the paintings owned by the city. It is clear from Uylenburgh's vicissitudes how difficult it was for Mennonites to remain true to their principles in an economically flourishing city. Commerce demanded its tribute. When his existence was at stake, Uylenburgh, too, does not appear to have weighed every word.

Rembrandt painted several portraits of Mennonites. In 1632 he produced the portrait of the merchant MAERTEN LOOTEN. 119 Looten came from a Reformed family. His parents had fled from the Spanish and with many thousands of refugees had given Rembrandt's native town a new impulse. About 1615 he had gone to Amsterdam as a merchant and lived there, beginning in 1625, on the Keizersgracht near the Prinsenstraat. Although wealthy, he had himself painted in simple, sober black clothing. Rembrandt puts a letter into the merchant's hand, dated 17th January and bearing his monogram; the writing is illegible.

The rich and esteemed lay preacher CORNELIS CLAESZ. ANSLO had a portrait of himself and his wife, AALTJE GERRITSDR. SCHOUTEN, 121, 118 painted by Rembrandt. As the Mennonite community was among Uylenburgh's creditors, it is likely that he arranged the commission. Rembrandt stresses Anslo's importance both as preacher and cloth merchant. As was customary in the Netherlands, there is a heavy cloth on the table, but on it a second, especially fine material is piled; on this lie a Bible, another book, and some manuscripts, as if Rembrandt wanted to show that the cloth and carpet trade was the basis of Anslo's activity as a preacher. In his group portraits Rembrandt always avoids a slack juxtaposition of figures. He wanted to show people in a situation typical of their lives, often using elements or compositional structures developed for other genres, such as history painting. In the double portrait of the Anslos, the preacher is shown in his study, finding words of comfort in the Holy Scriptures for a woman seeking advice, who is his wife. She looks up to him, and the view from below places the onlooker in the position of someone listening to a sermon from the pulpit. The model for the composition is the theme of JESUS IN THE HOUSE OF MARY AND MARTHA. Mary listens spellbound to Jesus while Martha prepares the meal. In this way Rembrandt elucidates Anslo's rank as a preacher, as he also does in the etching dated 1641 123 on which Jos van den Vondel wrote the verses: 'Rembrandt, paint the preacher's voice, / the outward man we can forgo. / In him the ears alone rejoice. / To see him we must hear Anslo'. It is inappropriate to read a criticism by Vondel into these lines, as some have done; and to surmise that the poem induced Rembrandt to include the woman in the painting in order to render the listening visible is certainly mistaken, for in a preliminary study dated 1640, 122 Anslo is presented in such a way that a complementary listener is needed. Cornelis Claesz. Anslo performed his preaching duties very conscientiously and also practised what he enjoined on others. When his son went bankrupt in 1642, he redeemed debts amounting to 60,000 florins, although not legally obliged to do so. This was many times the sum later owed by Rembrandt, at present values, several million florins. This episode not only throws light on Anslo's morality but also on his wealth and the economic emancipation of the Mennonites. And it shows us why Anslo had himself painted wearing a fur coat; not because it was winter, as an archivist has argued, but because the expensive garment expresses his wealth.

THE MENNONITE PREACHER CORNELIS CLAESZ. ANSLO (1592-1646) AND HIS WIFE AALTJE GERRITSDR. SCHOUTEN (1598-1657).
Signed: 'Rembrandt f. 1641'.
Canvas 176 × 210 cm.
Berlin-Dahlem, Staatliche Museen Preussischer Kulturbesitz, Gemäldegalerie.
Cat. 253 / Bredius 409.

Other portraits of Mennonites have been transmitted only through documents.[105] In the inventory of the cloth trader Jan Pietersz. Bruyningh we find a double portrait of him with his wife and a portrait of Pieter Jansz. Moutmaker ('mede van Rembrandt'), his father-in-law. As the cloth-trader's wife had died in 1640 and her father probably before 1635, it is probable that both pictures are from Rembrandt's early Amsterdam period, in the 1630s. These inventories are also revealing in other ways. They show how tolerant the Mennonites were in their choice of artists. Almost always, pictures by Catholics, Calvinists, and Remonstrants are listed beside those by Mennonite painters. They owned pictures of saints, a HERMIT or a ST. LAWRENCE ROASTED ON A SPIT.[106] Subjects from mythology are also to be found, although the Mennonites, like the Reformed Church, rejected the classical tradition. It even emerges that no specifically Mennonite subjects for pictures can be derived from the inventories. Finally, they prove one other thing. The Mennonites had long since attached themselves to the

PORTRAIT OF CORNELIS CLAESZ. ANSLO.
Signed: 'Rembrandt f. 1640'.
Red chalk, red wash, heightened with white oil paint, corrected with body white. 157 × 143 mm.
London, British Museum.
Benesch 758.

cultural trends of the time. Hendrick Uylenburgh's wife had been presented by Rembrandt as an Oriental (biblical) figure.[107] Jan Pietersz. Bruyningh had even had himself painted by S. Koninck 'in the ancient manner': in short, the role portrait had also been accepted by the Mennonites.[108]

Between 1642 and 1657, Rembrandt does not seem to have produced any portraits of Mennonites. This was probably due not only to Rembrandt's mode of life after 1642, which by no means conformed to Mennonite standards, but also to the deteriorating economic situation. Finally, taste too was changing, and the Mennonites had enough recognised painters in their own circles, who competed strongly with Rembrandt in other quarters as well, and secured far more commissions, in particular Jacob Adriansz. Backer (1608-1651) and Govert Flinck (1615-1660). It was only at the end of the 1650s that he again produced portraits of members of the Mennonite community, but these were of somewhat peripheral figures, CATHARINA HOOGHSAET (1657) and LIEVEN WILLEMSZ. VAN COPPENOL.

281

PORTRAIT OF CORNELIS CLAESZ. ANSLO.
Signed and dated 1641.
Etching 186 × 157 mm. 2nd state.
Hamburg, Kunsthalle.
Bartsch 271.

THE PREACHER JOHANNES UYTTENBOGAERT (1557-1644).
Signed: 'Rembrandt f. 1633' and 'AET 76'.
Canvas 132 × 102 cm.
England, private collection.
Cat. 201 / Bredius 173.

In 1633 Rembrandt produced a portrait of the seventy-six-year-old preacher JOHANNES UYTTENBOGAERT. In 1610, with his treatise *Remonstrantism*, Uyttenbogaert had unleashed a violent dispute within the protestant Church and prepared the ground for a schism by his sect, whose members were called 'Remonstrants' after this text.[109]

124

The argument began at Leyden University as a theological debate between two professors, Jacob Arminius (a friend of Uyttenbogaert) and the strict Calvinist Frans Gomarus. The conflict rapidly spread to the wider population, combining with political and social issues and developing into a crisis of the young Republic.

In this situation Arminius's adherents handed a copy of *Remonstrantism* to the States of Holland and Western Friesland in order to secure recognition of their opinions. The treatise demanded a revison of Calvinist doctrine, according to which God had preordained man both to good and to evil. Against this, Uyttenbogaert argued that Christ had won atonement for all men, although it was only to be granted to believers. The faithful could expect divine mercy. The possibility that a believer might fall from grace was not excluded. The Remonstrants became, in a sense, the moderate, liberal wing of the Reformation, which asserted the predominance of the state in church matters. They were stamped by the Humanism of Erasmus. They were especially strongly represented in the municipal aristocracy. Among their number was the illustrious councillor of the States of Holland, Oldenbarneveldt, as well as Hugo Grotius. The strict Calvinists were outraged by Uyttenbogaert's views. In 1611 the treatise *Counter-Remonstrance* appeared. State intervention in the dispute was unavoidable, particularly as Oldenbarneveldt had gravely provoked the Calvinists by deploying troops.

Political factors decided the outcome. Maurice of Orange wished to secure the support of the predominantly Calvinist population and free himself from the troublesome policies of the town aristocracy, many of whom were Remonstrants. At the Dordrecht Synod, held from 1618 to 1619, Arminianism was repudiated. Two hundred ministers were dismissed. Despite his distinguished services, the seventy-two-year-old leader of the Republican party at the States, Oldenbarneveldt, ended on the scaffold. Hugo Grotius was condemned to life imprisonment, but successfully escaped detention. Municipal governments, and even militia captains, were vetted for correct beliefs. In 1618, with Prince Maurice's help, the Amsterdam city council was purged of Remonstrants, who were replaced by Calvinists. But by 1622 the

JOHANNES UYTTENBOGAERT (1557-1644).
Signed: 'Rembrandt f.' and dated 1635.
Etching 225 × 184 mm. 5th state.
Hamburg, Kunsthalle.
Bartsch 279.

DIRCK JANSZ. PESSER (1587-1651).
Signed: 'Rembrandt ft. 1634 AET 47'.
Wood 67 × 52 cm.
Los Angeles, County Museum of Art.
Cat. 203 / Bredius 194.

liberal patricians had already regained power since many Calvinists turned to them for political reasons.

When his portrait was painted, Johannes Uyttenbogaert was engaged in writing a church history, which began with the events of 400 AD and was to extend to the present. In this work he sought to defend the creed of the Arminians. Following the death of his friend Arminius, whom he had met while a student at Basle, he was the head of the Arminian sect. While an army chaplain under Prince Maurice and as court chaplain at The Hague, he had argued for greater state influence in church administration. He was now subjected to the historical irony of being himself proscribed through state intervention in the church. As court chaplain he had been responsible for the education of Prince Maurice's two children. He became a close friend of the son, Hendrick (later Rembrandt's client), so that when Hendrick came to power, he tolerated the Arminians and allowed Uyttenbogaert to return to The Hague.

Despite many requests, Uyttenbogaert seldom had his portrait painted. We know from the theologian's diary that Rembrandt painted him on 13 April 1633[110]. We must imagine that on that day Rembrandt put in the outlines and painted the head and hands; he added the clothes and background in his studio, using a dummy. He had received the commission for this picture from Abraham Anthonisz., a prominent Remonstrant. He lived on the corner of the Warmoesgracht and the Herengracht and had displayed Oldenbarneveldt's portrait in his cellar. The life-size portrait shows the cleric from knee height. Rembrandt chose a broad vertical format with a well-lit background, giving an impression of spaciousness around the preacher. The heavy fur-trimmed mantle has room to spread wide, conveying figuratively the substance of this personage.

In the background we see a broad black slouch hat on a table to the right and, above all, a folio upright against the wall, with clearly visible writing. The significance of this writing is stressed by a corner of wall rising exactly behind it. The portrait conveys an impression of calm and concentration. The left hand rests slightly open on the breast. This gesture makes it clear that he truly stands for what he has

HAESJE JACOBSDR. VAN CLEYBURG (1583-1641).
Signed: 'Rembrandt f. 1636'.
Wood 68.6 × 53.4 cm.
Amsterdam, Rijksmuseum.
Cat. 239 / Bredius 354.

taught and fought for throughout his life. A few years later, he said repeatedly on his deathbed that he had performed his duties with a clear and upright conscience in the sight of God, and that he had never wished for anything other than to further divine truth, peace, and concord among Christians, and an honest Christian life in godliness for the happiness of all.

The right hand holds the costly gloves, a sign of social rank. However, owing to its relative unimportance, this hand is not clearly visible in its full size. The face, surrounded by a loosely folded ruff, expresses serenity. It is marked by age; the eyes, wide open, almost as in meditation, seem to hold a deep and earnest knowledge and the wisdom of age.

Rembrandt's portrait, of which numerous copies were made, found such favour, owing to the preacher's popularity, that there was a demand for an etched portrait reproduced in large numbers. Rembrandt was commissioned two years later to produce an etching. It shows the preacher at his desk, which is covered with folios. Other volumes stand on a shelf in the background; the abundance of books indicates the churchman's erudition. In the painted portrait, by contrast, the emphasis is rather on the dignity of the personality. In the third version of the etching, Rembrandt made the originally rectangular plate octagonal, adding a poem on Uyttenbogaert by Hugo Grotius below the picture, as well as his signature and the date, 1635.

A year earlier, in 1634, Rembrandt had painted an influential Rotterdam Remonstrant, the brewer Dirck Jansz. Pesser and his wife, Haesje Jacobsdr. van Cleyburg. He belonged to a large Remonstrant family. His sister-in-law was married to Simon Episcopus (de Bischop), who in 1610 took over Arminius's university chair. As Rembrandt had painted Uyttenbogaert the previous year, it seems likely that the later commission resulted from the earlier one.

Altogether, Rembrandt painted relatively few Remonstrants. If in a later biography he is turned into a Remonstrant, it will be in disregard not only of all the entries in church registers, but of this fact as well.

The Dutchmen of Catholic beliefs whose portraits Rembrandt painted include JAN RIJCKSEN and GRIET JANS.[111] As has already been mentioned, Jan Rijcksen was one of the most important shipbuilders of the East India Company and a partner in it. In Amsterdam, Catholics like Jan Rijcksen were able to attain important economic positions as the patriciate ruled very tolerantly in the interests of general prosperity and their own. The Catholics were excluded only from high political office, both because of the War of Liberation against Catholic Spain (1568-1648) and through fear of intervention by the Pope. They gathered to celebrate mass in private houses, since public worship was forbidden to them.[112]

From outside, these hidden churches *(schuilkerken)* were unrecognisable; inside (for example, in spacious attics) large church halls were equipped with every artistic and liturgical ornament. So in Amsterdam there was The Church of the Good Lord in the Attic; one of the Catholic Pre–Rembrandtists, Claes Moeyaert, later furnished it with altar paintings. A Venetian envoy reported in 1620 that the authorities turned a blind eye, so that one could hear twelve to fourteen masses each day in private houses in Amsterdam alone.[113] Of course, the Reformed clergy complained continually about the Catholic services, 'the sacrilegious worship of idols and superstitious ceremonies', but these protests were brushed aside by the government in Amsterdam.[114] (In the country there were occasional clashes; on their country estates, city patricians like Frans Banning Cocq had to be much less accommodating towards their Catholic subjects.) Catholics also took part in the social life of the city. They were permitted to serve in the militia guilds and appointed to the governing bodies of social, economic, and cultural institutions.

130 THE MERCHANT ALBERT CUYPER and his wife, NEELTGEN CORNELISDR. PRONCK, were also Catholics. Like many Catholic merchants he moved to Amsterdam in the second decade of the century. He registered there in 1614 and traded with the Baltic area and Moscow. Through his marriage with Neeltgen Pronck, who came from the demoted Catholic patriciate, he was admitted to management of his father-in-law's gunpowder factory. The couple had themselves painted by students working with Rembrandt at his studio.

The portrait of the pallid-looking woman makes clear the difficulty the painters in Rembrandt's workshop experienced in rendering the faces of young women and girls. While Rembrandt's student places strong accents on the head of the grey-haired Cuypers, setting the left half in deep shadow and

THE DEATH OF THE VIRGIN.
Signed: 'Rembrandt f' and dated 1639.
Etching 409 × 315 mm. 1st state.
Bartsch 99.

THE POET JAN HERMANSZ. KRUL (1601-1646).
Signed: 'Rembrandt f 1633'.
Canvas 128.5 × 100.5 cm.
Cassel, Gemäldegalerie.
Cat. 199 / Bredius 171.

Rembrandt's workshop.
CORNELIA PRONCK, WIFE OF AELBERT CUYPER (1600/01-1667).
Signed: 'Rembrandt ft 1633' and 'AET 33'.
Wood 60 × 47 cm.
Paris, Louvre.
Cat. A106 / Bredius 336.

leaving a broad zone of shade on the collar, Neeltgen Pronck's face is in bright light. Rembrandt's student clearly takes pains to convey the typical traits of the young woman, the smooth skin, the softer contour, the lighter complexion, her beauty, yet he does not entirely succeed. Rembrandt's own earlier portraits of young wives are also distinctly weaker than those of their husbands.

When Rembrandt created the portrait of THE POET JAN HERMANSZ. KRUL, a Catholic, in 1633, Krul was at the height of his success. A group of mainly Catholic lawyers and doctors supported his project of founding a new musical theatre. The revenue was to go to The House of Old Men and Women, whose governors included numerous descendants of the old deposed Catholic patriciate. In May 1634 the theatre was opened amid much publicity, but scarcely a year later the curtain fell for the last time. This plunged Krul into grave financial difficulties, from which he was not to recover. So in his life he experienced the transience of wealth and the world which he had described in many of his poems. But the painting gives no premonition of this failure. In the three-quarter-length portrait Rembrandt shows the prosperous poet in bourgeois dress. He does not even omit the costly gloves appropriate to his status. Krul stands in a dark interior, the plan of which, as we can see from the sill, is circular. This is clearly intended to evoke the theatres of antiquity. Krul is thus presented as a poet who can invoke antiquity. The light falls on his face and right hand. Krul meets the onlooker with a firm gaze. 128

Biographers of the poet have suspected, no doubt rightly, that the portrait was intended to enhance Krul's fame and so promote his plans for the theatre.

No further portraits of Catholics are known at present. But as many of the later portraits are unidentified, it is probable that members of all denominations, including Catholics, are among them.

The tolerant climate had a many-sided influence on Amsterdam life. Despite their divergent political views, the individual religious groups did not isolate themselves from each other. In bodies such as the militia, on the governing boards of the guilds, the theatre, and the social institutions, Calvinists came together with Remonstrants, Lutherans with Mennonites, Catholics with agnostics.

In a picture of a Haarlem debating chamber we find a description of this situation:

> Here, one speaks for Calvin, another for Arminius. Yet another pleads for Luther, and Menno's side too is taken.

Rembrandt's workshop.
AELBERT CUYPER (1585-1637).
Signed: 'Rembrandt ft. 1632. AE 47'.
Wood 61 × 45 cm.
Paris, Louvre.
Cat. A80 / Bredius 165.

JAN RIJCKSEN (1560/61-1637) AND GRIET JANS (1560-after 1653).
Signed: 'Rembrandt f. 1633'.
Canvas 114.3 × 168.9 cm.
London, Buckingham Palace, Collection of Her Majesty The Queen.
Cat. 252 / Bredius 408.

And another praises Socinus — the freethinker extols Libertinus. Even the old Jewish doctrine is here reinstated. Some condemn the office of preacher, as gossiping wives are apt to do. Mohammed praises the Koran — the zealot cleaves to the Sophists. But the Council of Trent banished all these arguments.[115]

It was natural for Catholic communities to award commissions for their secret churches to their own painters. This indeed happened frequently later. But earlier, tolerance went so far that Calvinists and Remonstrants were also invited to create altar pieces for Catholic churches or private chapels, just as Calvinist painters produced works for Lutheran churches or, conversely, Catholic artists for Reformed churches.[116] This tolerance among all the political and religious groups is of great significance in the context of art history, for it was the precondition for the work of many artists. Rembrandt, too, did not become a representative of a particular group in Amsterdam, but worked for members of all the denominations and parties.

Rembrandt f. cum pryvl. 1633. Amstelodami Hendrickus Vlenburgensis Excudebat.

REMBRANDT'S COMMISSIONS FROM PRINCE FREDERICK HENDRICK

Rembrandt had not been long at Amsterdam when — probably in 1632 — he was commissioned through Constantin Huygens to paint three portraits at The Hague. He painted Huygens's brother Maurits and his friend Jacob de Gheyn Jr, and also the wife of Stadholder Prince Frederick Hendrick, Amalia von Solms. In 1632 Maurits Huygens took over from his father the honourable office of Secretary to the Dutch State Council, which he held until his early death. He was a close friend of the painter Jacob de Gheyn Jr, who was canon at the Church of Mary at Utrecht, a kind of sinecure. The two portraits were conceived as pendants, and Jacob de Gheyn subsequently bequeathed his portraits to Maurits Huygens. On the back is the following inscription in Latin: 'Jacob Gheyn the Younger (bequeathes) his portrait to Huygens as his last duty on his deathbed'.[117] De Gheyn had a high regard for Rembrandt's art, for he owned his painting PETER AND PAUL IN DISCUSSION (Melbourne), produced in 1628, and his OLD MAN SLEEPING BY A FIRE (Turin), which he bequeathed to the tax-collector Jan Uyttenbogaert.[118] A year after it was painted, Constantin Huygens wrote this couplet on the portrait of de Gheyn: 'This is Rembrandt's hand and the face of de Gheyn. Marvel, reader, for this both is and is not de Gheyn'.[119] The epigram makes clear that every portrait is only an image of its subject, and not the subject himself. He who would know the person should look at him and not the portrait. This view is in line with neo-platonic ideas and is to be found in numerous descriptions of pictures in the 17th century.[120]

The portrait of Amalia von Solms was probably intended to be a pendant to that of Prince Frederick Hendrick painted by Gerard van Honthorst the previous year, for it has a similar decorative painted false frame. In its conception, too, Rembrandt followed Honthorst, giving the portrait a stiffness matching court etiquette, but quite untypical of his own style. It is dated 1632. In the palace inventory of the same year it is entered as 'A likeness of Her Excellency in profile, painted by Rembrandt...'.[121] Curiously, it was not at that time hung in the same room as the Prince's portrait. Amalia von Solms was the daughter of Count Albrecht von Solms-Braunfels and had lived at The Hague as a maid of honour before the prince married her in 1625, the year of his election as stadholder.

For almost two decades Prince Frederick Hendrick was one of Rembrandt's best clients.[122] We shall therefore say something more about him. When Stadholder Prince Maurice died in 1625 without legitimate offspring, Prince Frederick Hendrick, the youngest son of William of Orange, who

THE RAISING OF THE CROSS. About 1633.
Canvas 96.2 × 72.2 cm.
Munich, Alte Pinakothek.
Cat. 46 / Bredius 548.

THE DESCENT FROM THE CROSS.
Etching 530 × 410 mm. 3rd state.
Signed and dated: 'Rembrandt f. cum pryvl: 1633'.
Bartsch 81 (pl. 2).

Gerard VAN HONTHORST.
PORTRAIT OF FREDERICK HENDRICK.
Signed and dated 1631.
Canvas 77 × 61 cm.
The Hague, Huis Ten Bosch.

had been murdered at the instigation of the Spanish, was elected to this office by the States General. Most of the provinces which had declared themselves sovereign states after the rising against the Spaniards agreed retrospectively to the decision and elected him stadholder to their regions also. When the northern provinces had seceded from Spanish rule, which had been represented in the Netherlands by the stadholder, the office had lost its meaning. Nevertheless, there was reluctance to abolish the office. It was redefined. The prince became the supreme commander of the army, elected by the representatives of the provinces at the States General, and had a say in appointments to the municipal councils. On his election Frederick Hendrick found himself in a difficult political situation, for the Spanish general Spinola was a dangerous opponent of the Republic. However, he dealt brilliantly with the difficulties, and also avoided conflict with the regents of the cities, who saw their power threatened by the increasing authority of the stadholder. While Maurice's special interest had been in military matters and the construction of fortifications, Prince Frederick Hendrick competed with the French court in the extension to his palace, Honselaarsdijk, and its park. He had received a French education. His mother was a daughter of the murdered Huguenot leader Coligny, and he had often visited the court of his godfather, the French king Henri IV. He had the palace decorated by well-known artists and chose no lesser an artist than Honthorst as court painter. He also assembled a large collection of paintings, in which he was probably advised by Huygens, for he acquired masterpieces of Netherlandish painting.

We may suppose that it was Huygens who drew Rembrandt to his attention, and the prince commissioned a series depicting THE PASSION OF CHRIST. The first order probably comprised five paintings: THE RAISING OF THE CROSS, THE DESCENT FROM THE CROSS, THE ENTOMBMENT, THE RESURRECTION, and THE ASCENSION. Later THE ADORATION OF THE SHEPHERDS, and THE CIRCUMCISION were added. This commission is especially interesting because seven letters by Rembrandt to the go-between, Constantin Huygens, have been preserved and give us at least fragmentary information on the genesis of the pictures and on Rembrandt's artistic intentions.[123] Unfortunately, Huygens's replies have been lost.

133
138, 136, 137
247, 138

Characteristically, Rembrandt conducted his correspondence in Dutch, while educated people of his time mostly wrote in Latin. As more than a decade had passed since he had attended Latin school, he clearly could no longer express himself in that language. His handwriting, compared to that

MAURITS HUYGENS, SECRETARY TO THE DUTCH COUNCIL OF STATE.
Signed: 'RHL van Rijn 1632'.
Wood 31.2 × 24.6 cm.
Hamburg, Kunsthalle.
Cat. 193 / Bredius 161.

AMALIA VON SOLMS (1602-1675).
Signed: 'RHL van Rijn 1632'.
Canvas 68.5 × 55.5 cm.
Paris, Musée Jacquemart-André.
Cat. 228 / Bredius 99.

of his mother, for example, is extremely flowing and individual. But the letters make it plain that he is no *homme de lettres*:

> At the beginning of the 17th century a broadly uniform style of writing emerged among the upper classes, who had a distinct awareness of their culture, language and status. Rembrandt was remote from these tendencies, in which he felt no need to engage. Often, and not only in the case of proper names or words of foreign derivation, he writes casually, in harmony with the north-western Netherlands accent with which he spoke. In this respect, too, he did not belong to the world of contemporary education, of literary men and scholars. This must have become plain once again to Huygens, the exponent of modernity, despite all the admiration Rembrandt aroused in him at times, as he read the letters. Polite formulae at the beginning and end of letters were a normal part of letter-writing in society at that time, even in friendly or familiar letters. They are a social convention, not the expression of personal or socially determined behaviour. Words of foreign derivation, which Rembrandt used, were also conventional. Yet the style of these letters is not governed by formal polish, but by an expressive intention largely guided by the spoken word and its emphases. Where emotions, affects, come into play a sentence can break off abruptly, succinct memos can replace well-formed sentences, and anger at the matter being discussed can lead to clumsy accumulations of words.

Thus does Anne-Marie Hübner, a lecturer in the Dutch language, characterize Rembrandt's style.[124] Rembrandt's letters are usually very direct. He comes straight to the point, states what he wants, and candidly offers Huygens his own works as gifts in exchange for help.

Before the victory of Calvinism, the sequence of subjects in this commission had been a normal feature of altar programmes. In the wake of Calvinist iconoclasm they were to be found, in the northern Netherlands, only in graphics or in domestic altars and cabinet pictures, if we disregard the ornamentation of Catholic and Lutheran churches. Rembrandt therefore had an opportunity to compete with Flemish art, which still depicted these scenes in altar paintings. Where it was not already prescribed by the client, Rembrandt chose a vertical format with rounded top, as is frequent in altar pictures. The commission aroused him to match himself against the greatest Flemish masters, Rubens, van Dyck, and Jordaens, whom Huygens favoured in his purchases for the stadholder.

133 In the first two paintings produced, THE RAISING OF THE

THE PAINTER JACOB DE GHEYN III.
Signed: 'RHL van Rijn 1632'.
Wood 29.9 × 24.9 cm.
London, Dulwich Picture Gallery.
Cat. 194 / Bredius 162.

THE ENTOMBMENT OF CHRIST. About 1636-39.
Canvas 92.5 × 68.9 cm.
Munich, Alte Pinakothek.
Cat. 57 / Bredius 560.

138 CROSS and THE DESCENT FROM THE CROSS, he was influenced by compositions by Rubens which he probably knew through engravings. Yet the structures are considerably revised. In 139 Rubens's DESCENT FROM THE CROSS, the body of Christ is parallel to the picture axis and is framed by all the helpers. Rembrandt has broken them up into different groups, which stand mourning around the cross or help in taking down the body. The cross is set aslant. Rubens wanted to characterise the women and disciples below the cross as faithful bearers of Christ. In contrast to Rubens, Rembrandt shows the deep sympathy and toil of the friends as they lower the lifeless, sunken body from the high cross. On the right, in keeping with the story, he shows Nicodemus. On the left, Mary has collapsed in her grief and is supported by two women. In the biblical text this episode is not mentioned. It came into being as a legend in the Middle Ages, when Mary's part in redemption was established on the basis of her compassion during Jesus' life and at the foot of the cross. The portrayal of such legendary episodes had been forbidden by the Council of Trent,[125] but the Protestant Rembrandt consciously took up this Catholic motif in order to include the element of compassion. Like Mary, the onlooker was to be overcome by pain. Accordingly, at about the same time, Rembrandt wrote below a drawing of Mary at the foot of the cross, that the words of Jesus to John were 'a treasure of modesty that we should keep in our hearts, to comfort the compassionate soul'.[126] How much he understood this event in terms of contemporary hymns, in which the faithful describe themselves as mourners and sinners below the cross, can be seen from the fact that he depicts himself as one of the helpers at the foot of the cross.

Rembrandt is concerned to portray the personal experience of encountering the crucified Christ; all narrative elements, such as the drawing of lots for Christ's cloak, would only have distracted from this. On the other hand, he emphasized all the motifs that recall Christ's suffering: on the beams of the cross the bloody traces of the nailing, the crowning with thorns and the piercing of Christ's side are to be seen. By means of chiaroscuro he concentrates his depiction on the cross and the body of Christ, on the faces and hands of the mourners. The departing Jews and the city are lost in darkness. Although he took over much from the engraving after Rubens, Rembrandt did not regard its use as intellectual theft. For him his work, which made the event of salvation vividly present, was a creative act in its own right. For this reason he reproduced his painting in an etching 132 which had the unusually large format of the engravings from Rubens, and had it protected by a copyright which forbade reproduction by engraving. Such privileged reproductions were customary in Rubens's circle, with which Rembrandt is clearly competing here. The etching shows an earlier stage of the painting, which Rembrandt subsequently altered because, as so often, he was not satisfied with the solution he had found. In the engraving we find, instead of Mary's fainting, a group of mourners holding out a linen cloth. The original intention was clearly to show the shroud as well as the actual descent from the cross in order to point forward to the burial. In the final version Rembrandt dispensed with this contextual allusion in order to depict the mother's grief more poignantly.

In the painting THE RAISING OF THE CROSS, he had shown 133 himself as one of the soldiers setting up the cross, in keeping with contemporary theology. In a similar spirit Paul Gerhard composed the following verses at the same time: 'What of these cruel torments is the cause? / Alas, Lord Jesus, it is by my guilt / Your blood is spilt'.[127] Neither painting is dated. Rembrandt must have delivered them in 1633 or 1634. In a letter of 1636 he asks Huygens to tell the stadholder that he is eagerly at work on the completion of the three Passion pictures which belong together with THE RAISING OF THE CROSS and THE DESCENT.[128] THE ASCENSION is complete, he writes, and the two other pictures (THE RESURRECTION and THE BURIAL) are more than half finished. He asks whether the Prince would like to have THE ASCENSION at that stage or all three pictures together later. To secure Huygens's favour he announces that he will send him some of his latest works (he probably meant etchings) to express his thanks. It was obviously known at The Hague how difficult Rembrandt found it to consider a painting as finished and how strong was his inclination to paint over his works and make major alterations. He was therefore asked to

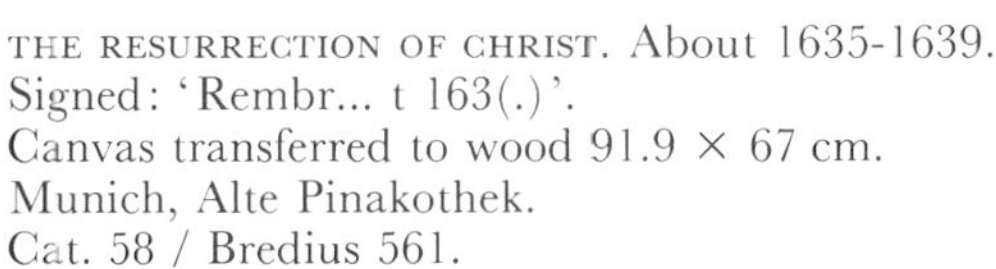

THE RESURRECTION OF CHRIST. About 1635-1639.
Signed: 'Rembr... t 163(.)'.
Canvas transferred to wood 91.9 × 67 cm.
Munich, Alte Pinakothek.
Cat. 58 / Bredius 561.

THE ASCENSION OF CHRIST.
Signed: 'Rembrandt f. 1636'.
Canvas 92.7 × 68.3 cm.
Munich, Alte Pinakothek.
Cat. 53 / Bredius 557.

137 deliver THE ASCENSION at once.[129] In the accompanying letter Rembrandt agreed with Huygens that it would be sensible for him to go to The Hague soon to see how THE ASCENSION fitted in with the other pictures.[130] He asks for 1,200 florins for this relatively small picture, but leaves the final decison on the price to the Prince. This price says much about Rembrandt's self-confidence, for he had acquired the large painting HERO AND LEANDER, by Rubens, at an auction for about a third of this amount. The court thought the demand too high and paid 600 florins. THE ASCENSION OF CHRIST, too, as X-ray pictures show, has been overpainted several times. From his formal model, Titian's painting THE ASSUMPTION OF MARY, he had taken the figure of God the Father awaiting Christ, who is borne up on a cloud, with open arms.[131] But then Rembrandt seems to have had doubts whether this might infringe the Calvinist prohibition against making images of God, and overpainted the figure with a radiant wreath, at the centre of which he showed a dove as a symbol of the Holy Spirit.

In the faces and gestures of the disciples, reverence and terror find manifold expression. The conception of THE ASCENSION goes back to 1634, when Rembrandt created the etching THE ANNUNCIATION TO THE SHEPHERDS. 165 Contrary to the biblical text, he has presented the Ascension as almost a night scene. Only the mountain peak, the palm and the cloud concealing Christ from the eyes of the disciples, are visible. He therefore adds as a precaution, in the accompanying text, that the picture should be hung in bright light. Anyone who now expects a speedy completion of the next, half-finished pictures does not know Rembrandt. The Hague was far away, and his duties as teacher, portraitist, and etcher occupied the foreground for him. He would probably have deferred delivery of the two pictures still longer had he not bought in 1639 a house in the Breestraat, in the vicinity of 144 the house earlier occupied by Uylenburgh. As it was an expensive area, the high-bourgeois residence cost 13,000 florins; 1,200 fl. were due on moving in. Although Rembrandt had claimed in a libel action the previous year that he had not squandered Saskia's inheritance — later estimated at 40,700 fl. — he lacked cash. He therefore finally resolved to finish the two paintings, and wrote to Huygens on 12 January asking for his mediation.[132]

However, he clearly has not a very clear conscience, for he emphasizes in an apologetic way that the work has only

THE DESCENT FROM THE CROSS. About 1633.
Signed: 'CRHmbrant' (faked signature).
Wood 89.4 × 65.2 cm.
Munich, Alte Pinakothek.
Cat. 47 / Bredius 550.

dragged on so long because he has 'observed the greatest and most natural movement' in the pictures. This observation takes up the theme of earlier conversations with Huygens. The latter had been impressed by Rembrandt's indefatigable industry, and had felt it to be Rembrandt's essential achievement to have succeeded in conveying the inner mood of persons through their movements. Huygens also admired how, in small paintings, he attained effects in a concentrated form that one could look for in vain in the colossal pictures of others. X-ray pictures and copies of an earlier version of the painting show us how intensively Rembrandt actually did concern himself with the story of the Resurrection and how deeply he studied the many different solutions in painting tradition.[133] In the course of this he must have been struck by the fact that the Resurrection, really an unimaginable event, is not described at all by Matthew. So, in the first version, he follows a very uncommon pattern, used only in graphic art, in which Christ is not actually represented, his Resurrection being merely announced by an angel shining like lightning. This first version, a genuine innovation in painting, was later amended by Rembrandt, who finally depicted the resurrected Christ. But even the second version is exceptionally bold. It is based on portrayals of the raising of Lazarus: as the dead Lazarus only gradually returned to life, Christ too will only awaken slowly from the sleep of death. Rembrandt therefore sought to present Christ in the act of Resurrection by the most natural movements. 137

Some critics see in THE ENTOMBMENT OF CHRIST the first signs of a change of style, since it seems harmonious in comparison to THE RESURRECTION.[134] This is a fundamental misunderstanding. The outward gestures have to match the inner movement. Rembrandt was guided by what was natural, that is, what the onlooker felt to be natural on the basis of art tradition and custom. At a burial or funeral the mourners express their grief in a quiet, patient manner. Lastman, too, had depicted the Resurrection turbulently and the Burial through calm gestures. 136

Rembrandt was probably not quite sure whether Huygens would advocate the acceptance of pictures so long delayed, for he promised him in appreciation of his trouble a painting which was to be as large as 240 x 300 cm. He does not mention the title, but he probably means THE BLINDING OF SAMSON, which has roughly these dimensions.[135] The offer was excessively generous, but Rembrandt needed money to pay the first instalment on his house, not to mention the next one in the autumn and the third the following spring. In the course of the subsequent transaction Rembrandt shows a hectic style of conducting business. Huygens asks him first of 160

Copy after a hidden picture by Rembrandt.
THE CIRCUMCISION OF CHRIST. 17th century.
Canvas 98 × 73 cm.
Brunswick, Herzog Anton Ulrich Museum.
Cat. K3.

Peter Paul RUBENS.
THE DESCENT FROM THE CROSS. 1611/1612.
Wood 420 × 310 cm.
Antwerp, Onze-Lieve-Vrouwekathedraal.

all to deliver the two pictures. Rembrandt sends them at once and writes on the accompanying invoice that they are of such high quality that each has a value of not less than 1,000 florins, but that he will be content with the valuation of the Prince.[136] When Rembrandt has not received any payment by 27 January, he writes a further letter,[137] saying that he has in the meantime talked with the tax-collector Jan Uyttenbogaert, who visited him when he was in the act of packing the two paintings. Uyttenbogaert, who esteemed Rembrandt's work very highly, wanted to see the pieces commissioned by the Prince. He offered to have the bill paid by his Amsterdam office, provided the Prince agreed. Rembrandt informed Huygens of this in his letter and sent him the painting THE BLINDING OF SAMSON. In his reply Huygens advised him not to expect the sum he had requested in payment. Rembrandt answered that he would be content to receive 600 fl. for each picture as previously, together with the cost of framing and packing.[138] But the payment should be made as quickly as possible. How desperate he was is shown by the last letter that has been preserved, which he sent a few days later.[139] He reports that Uyttenbogaert has informed him that the treasurer, van Vollbergen, is at that moment receiving large sums in taxes and could therefore hand over the money for the pictures. This reminder was unnecessary, for in the meantime Huygens had on his side instructed van Vollbergen to pay the sum. Rembrandt now felt obliged to Uyttenbogaert and etched a portrait of him.[140] The artist's nervous antics had therefore brought him little reward: he had to prepare the etching of Uyttenbogaert and had made Huygens a present of one of his largest works. The gift did not produce the effect that Rembrandt had hoped for. He had clearly wanted to commend himself to Huygens as a history painter in the style of Rubens and Jordaens, for THE BLINDING OF SAMSON surpasses them in the realism of its cruel action and in its narrative consistency. However, he misjudged Huygens's taste, for while the latter appreciated cruel pictures, he preferred to see them in the houses of friends rather than in his own.

Prince Frederick Hendrick later commissioned two more paintings to complement the Passion series, an ADORATION OF THE SHEPHERDS and a CIRCUMCISION OF CHRIST.[141] Rembrandt completed and delivered them in 1646. For each picture he at last received the sum which in his opinion they were worth, 1,200 florins. But it was his last commission from the Dutch court. After Frederick Hendrick's death in 1647, the only artists in demand at The Hague were those who had adapted to the French classical taste that had come into fashion since 1640.

JAN UYTTENBOGAERT (1606-1689).
Signed: 'Rembrandt f.' and dated 1639.
Etching 250 × 205 mm. 2nd state.
Hamburg, Kunsthalle.
Bartsch 281.

ECCE HOMO.
Signed and dated 1636.
Etching 549 × 447 mm. 3rd state.
Berlin-Dahlem, Staatliche Museen Preussischer Kulturbesitz, Kupferstichkabinett.
Bartsch 77.

The Breestraat, usually called the Jodenbreestraat, where 144 Rembrandt lived from 1632 to 1636 and again from 1639 to 1658, was on the edge of what later became the Jewish quarter.[142] This has given rise to frequent flights of fancy among critics. Ever since Eduard Kolloff wrote in somewhat belittling terms of Rembrandt's preoccupation with Jewry (Jüdelei) in his paintings,[143] critics have pictured the artist discovering the world of the Old Testament in the picturesque Jewish quarter. This view, now almost a legend, has coloured much of the literature on Rembrandt. Even the great master of iconographic research Erwin Panofsky fell victim to it:

> The foreign became identified with the patriarchal, southern vivacity and brilliance with the biblical, and men believed that by observing the contemporary Jews they could lay hands on the past. Their black-haired, dark-eyed, brown-skinned appearance, unfamiliar to northern eyes, their rich, foreign jewelery, their gesticulating manner of speech, doubly conspicuous among the phlegmatic Dutch—all this drew attention irresistibly to them. And if the rich and educated members of Amsterdam's Jewish community seemed to represent the patriarchs, high priests, and scribes, then the pale beggars in rags, whose faces and gestures aroused sympathy, were seen as the brothers of Lazarus and of all the poor and oppressed. So artists were particularly drawn to the Jews.[144]

The area around the Breestraat was seen as a picturesque quarter stamped with the image of the Jews. Involuntarily, this notion became linked to images of a different, colourful, Oriental world. Art historians believed that Rembrandt withdrew in solitude to study the life of the Old Testament at its source. They thought they could see something of the colourfulness of this world in his biblical scenes. The truth is, however, that this world was quite different from the one they imagined, so that Rembrandt's reasons for moving there must be reconsidered. As the name indicates, the Breestraat, the 'Broad Street', was lined with tall upper-class homes where successful artists had settled next to Amsterdam merchants such as Hendrick Uylenburgh. Well-to-do Flemish emigrants followed later, and only then the rich and aristocratic elements among the Spanish and Portuguese Jews,[145] among them Rembrandt's Jewish neighbours whose names are mentioned in an account of the auction of his home.

It is important to call to mind the unhappy history of the Iberian Jews who had found a new home in Amsterdam and who gratefully called it their 'New Jerusalem'. Their ances-

THE JEWISH DOCTOR EPHRAIM BUENO (1599-1665). About 1647.
Wood 19 × 15 cm.
Amsterdam, Rijksmuseum.
Cat. 210 / Bredius 252.

tors, who had immigrated to the Iberian peninsula in the early Middle Ages, became the élite among European Jews. They not only upheld the cabbalistic and rabbinic tradition, but also transmitted the heritage of Greek and Arab scholarship. They quickly became assimilated, some abandoning their faith and obtaining high posts in the Catholic church or in the military and legal professions. Some married into the highest nobility and even held positions at court. But after the highly educated and religiously tolerant Moors lost their last stronghold in Spain in 1492, the Jews were forced to leave. In 1531, the Vatican established the Inquisition to deal with the Marranos, or 'pigs', as those Jews who had been converted to Christianity were disparagingly called. This was the beginning of a time of great suffering for them. Many of those who had accomplished most, who had become rich or entered the ranks of the nobility, left the Iberian peninsula to seek refuge in other Mediterranean countries and reverted to the faith of their fathers. The separation of the northern Netherlands from Spain encouraged a considerable number to settle there. Many lost their wealth in their flight, but their education and business abilities opened new possibilities to them, particularly in Amsterdam. The Amsterdam government had really only one fear: that they might be clandestine Catholics. After the Catholic élite, who had been Spain's allies, had been deprived of power, many being forced to leave the city, a new group of people who might secretly support Spain was not wanted. However, investigations proved these suspicions groundless. No concealed pictures of Catholic saints were found, only Hebrew writings. As the financial world of Amsterdam hoped to gain from the arrival of these immigrants with international business connections, the Jewish community was not forced to live apart. Disregarding some minor regulations which were not strictly enforced, they were allowed to develop freely. As a consequence, Jews became important bankers and merchants, and the Jewish community developed a rich intellectual and social life of its own, founded its own hospitals and orphanages and built three synagogues. The Jewish immigrants did not differ from the Dutch in their dress. Contemporary prints depicting Jewish citizens or whole families cannot be distinguished by a layman from portraits of Dutch burghers. The Jews' most conspicuous peculiarity was that they spoke Spanish or Portuguese, and so were called 'Spaniards' by the common people.

This applies also to Rembrandt's neighbours, the Belmontes, Pintos, and Rodrigos. Josef Belmonte's family was related to the Spanish nobility and had been Catholic until the emigration. In Holland they rebuilt their life, and contemporary prints soon show the house of 'Baron Belmonte', as he was called. The Pinto family had connections in all parts of the world and transacted business on a large scale. Rembrandt's Jewish neighbours, therefore, did not help him to obtain a historical picture of biblical times; rather, they showed him that in their outward appearance the descendants of Old Testament Jews were just as modern as the Dutch. They were not a living image of biblical people; but because some of them knew Hebrew, they could give him direct access to the sources of the Old Testament.

Rembrandt's purchase of a house in the Breestraat did not reveal an inclination to live in picturesque surroundings, but a desire to be among rich upper-class merchants. In this connection, we recall that in one document he actually referred to himself as a 'merchant', so that the purchase of a house in this wealthy quarter expresses a wish to establish himself as a painter beside these wealthy businessmen. There may have been sentimental reasons as well, for he had met Saskia in the Breestraat.

Rembrandt's picture of the Old Testament Jews was at first influenced less by their descendants than by what he had learned about them while studying with Lastman.[146] He had served his apprenticeship in Amsterdam at a time when notions about the world of the Bible were very vague. To be sure, interest in biblical archeology was awakening in the more free-thinking theologians, but ethnographic studies were rare. Ethnology and comparative religion were in their infancy. Artists therefore depicted the people of Abraham and the story of Jesus in a world akin to that of rural Italy, which bore little resemblance to the actual historical setting. One of the reasons, of course, was lack of information. Who among artists had ever seen the Arabian desert or the flora and fauna of Canaan? Which of them knew Abraham and his family lived as nomads? Only educated artists such as Rembrandt knew that in Oriental countries such as Turkey there existed age-old customs that had been unchanged since the time of the Old Testament. It was for this reason that such artists depicted scenes of Turkish life when they wanted to add historical local colour to their biblical stories. There was, however, a very definite attitude at this time to the presentation of a biblical history painting. History was understood, not as a distant event, but rather as a moral guide or cautionary example for one's own actions. People were supposed to see biblical history as an analogy of their own lives and identify with characters in sacred and even secular history, which also supplied examples. Artists did not dissociate themselves from this distant world by depicting its strangeness, but tried to make it appear as close to their own times as possible. They were apt to use knowledge of antiquity acquired on their own travels, for none wanted to follow the reconstructions of engravers and scholars slavishly.

No-one was willing to relinquish his artistic freedom. Although complete plans of the city of Jerusalem had been published by this time, each painter created his own Jerusalem and his own temple, using traditionally accepted motifs. In these pictures, an oasis was never a real Oriental oasis: one looks in vain for palms. Rather, the model was the Dutch well and the Dutch water-trough. To these artists, a too accurate reconstruction of the ancient world would have led to estrangement from the history in question. What was supposed to be movingly immediate would have become over-exotic if it had been historically authentic.

This attitude also influenced the view of the Bible and its people, the Jews. Concern with the reality of biblical times gave rise to a certain interest in how the people of Israel looked and lived and how they dressed. Nevertheless, this interest was quite limited. Because the artists and public identified themselves with the people of the Bible on account of the moral and spiritual implications of the histories, Dutch models were chosen to portray the Jews of the Old and New Testaments.

Only when the figure in question was to be distanced from the onlooker, did the archeological interest in manners and customs show itself. It is revealing that Jesus' enemies, the High Priests and Pharisees, were the first to be given a Semitic appearance.

At first, Rembrandt's relationship to Judaism was coloured by this attitude. When painting exemplary figures from the Bible, he chose Dutch models and dressed them in 25 Oriental garments. We may suppose that his own mother 11 served as the model for various biblical figures. Rembrandt gave Jews Semitic features only when characterising Pharisees and Scribes as persecutors of Jesus or as the rabble-rousers who caused his death, as in his large early etching 140 ECCE HOMO, produced in 1636.[147] Distortion of their faces had been present in art as early as the Middle Ages; in making use of these models, Rembrandt intensified such characteristics. One of the High Priests has seized the staff of judgement from Pilate. Rembrandt uses this idea, his own invention, to indicate the High Priest's responsibility for the death of Jesus. Pilate raises his hand defensively to indicate that he is against the death sentence.

Not later than the year in which he produced such a distorted picture of Jesus' enemies, Rembrandt made the acquaintance of a Jewish scholar, the influential and erudite Rabbi Menasseh ben Israel, with whom he soon formed a friendship that lasted more than two decades and led him to a deeper understanding of Judaism and the Jews. Menasseh's father, too, had emigrated from Portugal after having been tortured three times by the Inquisition. He fled from Lisbon to Madeira, from there to the Huguenot stronghold of La Rochelle, and finally to Protestant Amsterdam, where he died in 1622, a broken man.

Menasseh ben Israel, his son, soon became well known. At eighteen he had written a Hebrew grammar, which was distributed in manuscript form because there was no Jewish publisher or printer in Amsterdam. He became a teacher in the Jewish community, instructing the newly arrived Marranos in the faith of their fathers. Although poor, Menasseh managed, through his own energy and with the help of friends, to establish the first Jewish printing press in Holland. For his first publication, in 1627, he had to have the Hebrew letters specially made. By the end of his life he had published eleven of his own works and more than sixty by other authors. He soon acquired a reputation and influence among philologists and theologians because, more than anyone else, he knew the Hebrew writings in the original, as well as the extensive commentaries with their long tradition. Menasseh supported them in their efforts to go back to the sources and to study the history of religion, by giving them access to rabbinic and cabbalistic commentaries and teaching them Hebrew. He had contact with professors at the Atheneum (which later developed into the University of Amsterdam), with Gerhard Johannes Vossius and Casparus Barlaeus; he was friendly with the Remonstrant Simon Bischop and corresponded with scholars and theologians throughout Europe, among them Hugo Grotius and Jakob Böhme. Although he knew ten languages, he did not have a sure command of Latin; some of his works were therefore translated by friends from Portuguese into Latin, the language of scholarship. He also published many works in

YOUNG JEW. About 1648.
Wood 25.1 × 21.5 cm.
Berlin-Dahlem, Staatliche Museen Preussischer Kulturbesitz, Gemäldegalerie.
Cat. 140 / Bredius 250.

Rembrandt's house in the Jodenbreestraat, 1606.

Portuguese because the Iberian Jews had been brought up in that language.

When Rembrandt etched a portrait of this Jewish scholar 146 in 1636, the peculiarities of the Jewish physiognomy may have been made clear to him, but he did not portray Menasseh with what were considered typical Semitic features. His friendship with Menasseh was important to Rembrandt because he could consult him on the interpretation of difficult texts. Although it is certain that Rembrandt did not study Hebrew with Menasseh, he did obtain the Hebrew texts for his paintings from him, although he was not generally convinced by Menasseh's apocalyptic reading of the Bible. This involved a complicated interpretation of figures and letters through which the scriptures were seen as a collection of hidden predictions and connections. The apocalyptic passages which were most significant for Menasseh were not important to Rembrandt, although he sought Menassah's advice when confronted — whether through commissions or from choice — with a difficult subject in this field. So Rembrandt must have turned to Menasseh when, at the end of the 1630s, he was concerned with a story from the 161 apocalyptic book of Daniel. This story, typical of Rembrandt's choice of subjects, tells how King Belshazzar, during a bacchanalian feast during which vessels stolen from the temple were being desecrated, suddenly saw a hand writing on the wall the words '*mene mene tekel upharsin*'.

Rembrandt is sure to have asked Menasseh how it came about that Daniel could read the writing while Belshazzar could not. The cabbala had a simple explanation:[148] the inscription was not written horizontally from right to left, as is customary in Hebrew, but vertically, beginning from the upper right:

S	U	T	M	M
		e	e	e
I	PH	K	N	N
	a	e	e	e
N	R	L		

Such hidden meanings were common in the cabbala. In 1639, shortly after the painting was produced, Menasseh published this interpretation in his book *De terminu vitae*. He was, then, an adviser who could explain mysterious passages not only to humanist scholars but to the artist, who, influenced by Lastman, developed a great interest in antiquity. It was probably through him that Rembrandt also met the Jewish doctor Ephraim Bonus, likewise a member of the Portuguese Jewish community, who supported Menasseh's publishing house and published religious works there himself. Rembrandt depicted him as a rich, respected citizen of 141, 146 Amsterdam.

Rembrandt discovered the 'Jewishness' of the Spanish Jews only in their facial characteristics. It was only at the beginning of the 1650s that he produced studies of Jews. He 143 became interested in their physiognomic peculiarities because not only the high priests but all Jews, even Jesus Christ, had looked like this. In the 1650s a young Jew frequently served as his studio model, and Rembrandt and his students used his face in their paintings of Christ.[149] This reflects the change in Rembrandt's attitude towards the Jewish people: this people, who were distinguished because Jesus Christ came from their midst, had not ceased to be brothers of the Christians by remaining true to the faith of their fathers.

When Rembrandt went bankrupt in 1656, these works were listed in his inventory under the title PAINTINGS OF CHRIST FROM LIFE. Some later paintings also stress Semitic characteristics in the followers of Jesus, so that Rembrandt no longer used these characteristics negatively as in his 140 earlier etching ECCE HOMO.[150] Criticism of the Scribes and Pharisees is directed mainly at the ceremonial, the literal interpretation of the law, and the pomp of the temple service. The High Priests, resplendent in costly ceremonial robes, are blind to the poor Son of God, who is at one with the simple people. Undoubtedly Rembrandt was also aware that the conflict between a powerful church, fond of ostentation, and the true followers of Jesus, with their concern for simple people, also emerges in Christian society. The biographer Arnold Houbraken later told how Rembrandt answered the accusation that he mixed with simple people and did not uphold his social position by saying: '*When I relax, I look for freedom, not honour*'.[151] This attitude is consistent with Rembrandt's interpretation of biblical history, although he did not learn to apply it to himself until later in life.

In the mid-1650s, Menasseh ben Israel asked his neigh- 147 bour in the Breestraat for four illustrations for his book *Piedra Gloriosa*, which was particularly close to his heart because of its Messianic implications.[152] For it was generally believed that the Messiah would come as soon as Jews had settled everywhere, even at the ends of the earth. Since the traveller Aaron Levi de Montezinos had returned to Amsterdam in 1644, claiming to have met the ten lost tribes of Israel in the interior of South America, there had been considerable unrest in the Jewish community. Menasseh was only too receptive to this hope-inspiring report. If Jews really were living in the heart of South America, there was only one country from which they had been expelled completely since 1290, and which Menasseh considered the 'end of the earth', for this was how Jewish scholars translated the word *Angleterre* (England). In 1653 the active and influential Menasseh wrote a tract entitled *The Hopes of Israel* which he dedicated to the English Parliament, and he resolved to go in person to ask Cromwell to allow Jews to return to England. As the journey was postponed because of the first sea war between England and Holland (1652-1654), he published the book *Piedra Gloriosa* in 1655, reinforcing the Messianic hopes of his people. Then he and his son left on their journey.

He returned from his mission two years later, gravely ill and completely impoverished. He brought with him the body of his son, who had died in England, and his own death followed a few weeks after his son's burial. As the Jews did not yet have their own cemetery in Amsterdam, Menasseh was buried in the famous Jewish cemetery near Ouderkerk on the Amstel, immortalised in a painting by Ruysdael.

147 Rembrandt's illustrations for *Piedra Gloriosa* deal with four biblical stories, which Menasseh explained in Messianic terms. A stone of great importance to Israel is mentioned in three Old Testament stories. Menasseh believed that these were not three different stones, but one and the same stone, which was a symbol of the coming Messiah. He believed that the stone which loosed itself and struck the clay feet of the statue representing the four empires and destroyed it was identical with the stone on which the patriarch Jacob (later Israel) slept when he saw in a dream the angels of God climbing up and down a ladder reaching to heaven (Genesis 28: 11) and with the stone that David had used to kill Israel's enemy, Goliath (1 Samuel 17: 49). The subject of the fourth etching was the vision of Daniel, in which four animals arose from the sea. According to Menasseh, these symbolised the four empires, which were to be followed by Israel as the fifth, as soon as the Messiah came. In Menasseh's interpretation, therefore, the four stories dealt with the coming of the Messiah, who will destroy the four empires and establish the new Jerusalem.

When Rembrandt created his small etchings, he started as usual from the graphic tradition, in this case mainly the Protestant Bible illustrations. This, however, brought him into conflict with Menasseh's allegorical explanation of the texts. For while Rembrandt was interested in an artistic interpretation of the stories, Menasseh wanted a literal rendering of his reading. This led to numerous corrections of the etchings THE STATUE and JACOB'S DREAM. In the first state of the etching of the statue, the stone strikes the clay legs, not the feet, as described by Menasseh. This has been changed by the third state. In the fifth, the four names of the empires have been added to the statue for clarity, which was in keeping with tradition but not with Rembrandt's narrative style. In the first state of JACOB'S DREAM, the ladder reached only to the ground where Jacob is lying; in the later state this is corrected, as Menasseh believed the centre of the ladder to be the symbol of Jerusalem, and that according to his interpretation Jacob should sleep there. For this reason Rembrandt extended the ladder to the lower edge of the print, which artistically is not a happy solution, for Jacob now floats above the ground.

Rembrandt's frequent deference to Menasseh in spite of his own artistic conceptions is proof of his great tolerance as well as of his respect for his friend. He was usually reluctant to make changes. But Menasseh, too, who as a Jew was bound by the Second Commandment forbidding representations of God, generously overlooked the fact that Rembrandt, following early Protestant Bible illustrations, had portrayed God the Father. It is not known whether it was his liberal attitude that made him so tolerant or the pressure of preparations for his impending journey to England.

In the second edition of *Piedra Gloriosa*, which appeared after Menasseh's death, the original etchings were replaced by restrikes containing substantial changes.[153] The figure of God the Father, which Menasseh had tolerated, was now symbolised by a circle of light, in keeping with the Second Commandment.

After his bankruptcy, not later than 1658, Rembrandt was forced to leave his house in the Jodenbreestraat and his rich Jewish neighbours. As we have seen, these Jews certainly had not given him a colourful picture of the world of the Old Testament, but they had made him aware that the descendants of Israel were human beings like all other people.

EPHRAIM BONUS. 1647.
Etching 241 × 177 mm. 2nd state.
Hamburg, Kunsthalle.
Bartsch 278.

MENASSEH BEN ISRAEL. 1636.
Etching 149 × 103 mm. 2nd state.
Hamburg, Kunsthalle.
Bartsch 269.

Four illustrations (etchings) for the book *Piedra gloriosa o de la estatua de Nebuchadnesar* by Samuel Menasseh ben Israel. 1655.
a) THE STATUE. 96 × 76 mm. 2nd state.
b) JACOB'S DREAM. 106 × 69 mm. 3rd state.
c) DAVID AND GOLIATH. 106 × 74 mm. 2nd state.
d) DANIEL'S VISION OF THE FOUR BEASTS. 97 × 76 mm. 3rd state.
Berlin-Dahlem, Staatliche Museen Preussischer Kulturbesitz, Kupferstichkabinett.
Bartsch 36.

THE BIBLICAL HISTORIES OF THE FIRST AMSTERDAM PERIOD

Since Rembrandt's training with Pieter Lastman, which in 1631 was seven years behind him, the artistic scene in Amsterdam had changed fundamentally. Pieter Lastman was in ill health and no longer productive. Of his successors, only Claes Moyaert was still fully active, but had remained at Lastman's level and shown little originality in his development. So Rembrandt's history paintings met with hardly any competition, and he was soon to surpass even his teacher, who up to then had exerted the major influence on the young painter. After only two years, many Amsterdam artists were imitating Rembrandt's style, above all, his chiaroscuro. It was he who restored Amsterdam history painting to a European level, after it had sunk to insignificance at the end of the 1620s.

As before, Rembrandt continues to paint history pieces, mostly on wood and in small formats, having been encouraged by a commission to paint a Passion series in this format for the stadholder. But he also has a burning wish to paint monumental histories with life-size figures.

The Dutch painters observed, not without a certain envy, how their colleagues in Flanders and Italy were painting scenes from the life of Jesus for the gigantic altars of the Counter-Reformation and presenting the doctrine of the Catholic church in pictorial terms. These compositions were disseminated in engravings. Rembrandt referred to them in his Passion series, for example, thus giving monumentality to his small-format pictures. As the Calvinist church strictly rejected altar-pieces, this area of work was largely closed to the northern-Netherlandish artists.[154] Only occasionally did one or other of them paint gallery pictures for Catholic or Lutheran churches in Holland or outside it, and an altar picture or side-pieces for the organ in a Calvinist church[155].

Rembrandt could therefore only hope to receive commissions comparable to those of his Flemish or Italian colleagues, at least in the field of cabinet painting or decoration. He was acquainted with their works through the art trade and major collections. As early as 1635 he acquired a large-format history painting by Rubens showing a mythological scene.[156] If, alongside the small histories, Rembrandt created some Old Testament histories with life-size figures after the mid-1630s, he must have hoped that such works would one day also be saleable in the northern Netherlands. The stadholder, who held his office for life, wanted to established a hereditary monarchy; he affected the style of the great courts, following above all the French model, erecting castles with magnificent gardens and assembling a

Pieter LASTMAN.
ABRAHAM'S SACRIFICE. About 1612.
Grisaille. Monogrammed.
Wood 40 × 32 cm.
Amsterdam, Rembrandthuis (on loan from Dienst Verspreide Rijkscollecties).

THE ANGEL STOPPING ABRAHAM FROM SACRIFICING ISAAC TO GOD. Signed: 'Rembrandt f. 1635'.
Canvas 193 × 132.5 cm.
Leningrad, Hermitage.
Cat. 9 / Bredius 498.

DANIEL AND KING CYRUS BEFORE THE IDOL OF BEL.
Signed: 'Rembrandt 1633'.
Wood 22.5 × 28.7 cm.
England, private collection.
Cat. 7 / Bredius 491.

THE DESCENT FROM THE CROSS.
Signed: 'Rembrandt f. 1634'.
Canvas 158 × 117 cm.
Leningrad, Hermitage.
Cat. 48 / Bredius 551.

considerable art collection. Rembrandt clearly hoped, through his connections to the court, to offer life-size history paintings to the international high nobility. He also counted on the aspirations of the rising, newly rich Dutch city patriciate and of the great merchants. These hopes were not unfounded, for despite all their initial restraint, the Amsterdam patricians, descendants of the insurgents of 1578, were beginning to be ashamed of their modest style of living. They built ostentatious palaces in the city, acquired the estates of the earlier Catholic nobility and took over their fine-sounding titles, and were now barons or even knights. For the state-rooms of their town palaces and estates, some of them had life-size portraits and histories painted. At first, Rembrandt was primarily occupied with portraits in Amsterdam, but at the same time he was already working on the conception of the biblical and mythological history paintings which were completed in 1632 and 1633. In 1633 the religious history painting once again takes an important place beside the numerous portraits in Rembrandt's work. In the Passion series he clearly evinces the urge to come to grips with the works of the Flemish and Italian Baroque. But by the manipulation of light he cancels the heavy, physical quality of the powerful bodies caught in violent movement and turns the turbulent epic into a contemplated scene. The paintings he created alongside the Passion group differ from this commission in their choice of subjects. Again and again he depicts conversations, scenes of recognition or mistaken identity, and the meeting of the elevated with the lowly. Even if the great Passion series is disregarded, the New Testament histories preponderate in the 1630s. Above all, the story of the childhood and the passion and resurrection of Christ is chosen as his theme. In dealing with the Old Testament, his emphasis is on the stories of the patriarchs, the hero Samson, and the apocryphal books of Daniel and Tobias. Apart from histories with one or only a few figures, he creates numerous crowd scenes, developing forms of composition which open up the whole picture space as a stage. In Leyden, Rembrandt had already attempted, like his teacher Lastman, to represent topics in painting that had previously been treated only in graphic art. The models used by Lastman and Rembrandt were produced by the great 16th-century interpreters of the Bible, above all Maerten de Vos and Maerten van Heemskerck. Stylistically, these works are often very antiquated, yet Rembrandt, like Lastman, succeeds in translating motifs from them into his own style. If Lastman had, in general, presented his scene in several distinct layers on a flat stage, Rembrandt often arranges the figures in a semicircle around the main event, the onlooker thereby becoming a spectator of the scene. As compared to his predecessors, Rembrandt clarifies the scene by stressing the main figure through composition and brushwork and introduces chiaroscuro in order to emphasize main figures and make secondary ones recede into semi-darkness. The figures just arriving or leaving remind us of impending or completed actions.[157]

133, 136, 137, 138

The small picture DANIEL AND KING CYRUS BEFORE THE IDOL OF BEL, produced in 1633, shows a story only rarely treated in art, which must have appealed to Rembrandt because it shows the dangerous conflict between one of the mighty, who has been betrayed and deluded by his priests, and a boy sent by God. The Jewish prophet Daniel lived at the court of the

ESTHER BEFORE THE MEETING WITH AHASUERUS or BATHSHEBA AT HER TOILET. About 1633.
Signed: 'Rembrandt f. 16(.)'.
Wood 110.5 × 94.3 cm.
Ottawa, National Gallery of Canada.
Cat. 8 / Bredius 494.

SUSANNA AT HER BATH.
Signed: 'Rembrandt f. 1636 f'.
Wood 47.2 × 38.6 cm.
The Hague, Mauritshuis.
Cat. 14 / Bredius 505.

CHRIST SHOWING HIS WOUND TO THE UNBELIEVING THOMAS.
Signed: 'Rembrandt f. 1634'.
Wood 50 × 51 cm.
Moscow, Pushkin Museum.
Cat. 49 / Bredius 552.

Persian king Cyrus. When the king called him to account for not worshipping Bel, Daniel defended himself: 'I do not serve idols made by human hands, but the living God'.[158] Daniel questioned whether the idol consumed the offerings left for him. The angry king had his priests summoned and announced: 'If you can prove that the idol eats the food, Daniel shall die; otherwise, you die'[159]. The king placed food in the temple, but Daniel cunningly spread ashes everywhere. Then the doors were sealed with the king's ring. The priests entered the temple, as always, by a secret door and ate the offerings with their wives and children. When the king went into the temple the next morning, he believed the idol had been proved to be alive. But Daniel pointed out the footprints to him. The king grew angry, had the idol destroyed by Daniel and the priests executed.

Fully illuminated, the king is shown in his splendid purple mantle in a raised position at the centre of the picture. He points with his sceptre to the empty dishes on the table. But Daniel, standing as a courtier on a lower step, knows better: bowing reverentially, he holds his left hand to his breast in protestation, emphasising his prudent words with his right. His figure is largely in the shade, only the hands and profile being illuminated. The altar table is decorated with a glowing red cloth embroidered in gold. Above it rises the dark image of Bel. To the right of the table we see a cover which — as we know from Heemskerck's series — conceals the secret entrance. In the background stand the priests with their crosiers. They are wide eyed, as if anticipating the end. The flickering light heightens the dramatic quality of the scene.

A year later, in 1634, Rembrandt again painted a revelation scene, THE RISEN CHRIST SHOWING HIS WOUND TO THE APOSTLE THOMAS. After the Resurrection, Christ had shown himself to the disciples. Thomas, however, had not been present and had said he would only believe if he could put his hand into the nail-marks and the wound in his side. A week later the disciples were together again, and this time Thomas was there. Christ again appeared to them and said to Thomas: 'Hold out your finger and see my hands, and hold out your hand and put it into my side, and be not unbelieving, but believe'.[160] This moment is portrayed. Most of the disciples are crowded in awe around Christ, who forms the light-filled centre of the group. He takes the cloth from his breast and turns to Thomas, who stands close to Him. The loosely open right hand points to the wound in his side. Thomas, caught in a strong physical movement, moves a step down as if he wishes to abase himself before Christ. His attitude expresses utmost astonishment, almost terror, at his disbelief, now turning into belief. He has not yet put his finger into the wound; his raised hands still show disbelief; but his wide-open eyes, gazing at the wound in Christ's side, already show acceptance and wonderment. The halo around Christ's head burns like flames. Most of the light falls on Thomas, his form seeming especially colourful and plastic. The figures of the other disciples reflect varying degrees of surprise. Those on the left turn to their Lord with utmost attention. Some crowd around him; some fall to their knees or worship with clasped hands. Some push close to him, as if they cannot grasp the miracle of the resurrection even at this second meeting. A woman opens her mouth in amazement. One, however — who is not reported in the Bible — does not perceive Christ. He has turned his back in his sleep, a foil to the deeply moved Peter, whose agitation is particularly vivid in contrast to this unconcerned, sleeping figure.

In his composition Rembrandt deliberately disregards the modern solutions to this scene that had been found by Rubens and Caravaggio, for example.[161] They had detached the main group of Christ and Thomas from the throng of disciples, concentrating the scene on a few figures. Rembrandt, by contrast, wishes to depict varying reactions of amazement and realisation in the many disciples and witnesses and to encompass a crowd scene in a dark interior at night.

155

In the first of the large biblical histories, CHRIST IN THE STORM ON THE LAKE OF GALILEE, Rembrandt also shows a conflict between the seeing and the blinded, here the imperilled and frightened disciples, who are still fighting the waves or pleading with the calm Christ, not noticing that he is already threatening the sea and that his words are already having their effect. Rembrandt impressively paints the unleashed power of the sea. The boat has become a plaything of the waves, which are washing over the sides. With their last strength the despairing disciples are trying to reef the sails. These are already tearing under the violence of the wind. A rope has broken, and the wind plays with it. One of the disciples vomits. Peter pleads with Christ. But he has already calmed the storm. Through the rent clouds, radiance falls on a sea that is already smooth behind the ship. So Rembrandt stresses the transition from peril to peace in the depiction of the sea as of the figures. While the disciples have succumbed to frenetic activity, Christ remains calm.

CHRIST IN THE STORM ON THE LAKE OF GALILEE.
Signed: 'Rembrandt f. 1633'. Canvas 160 × 127 cm.
Boston, Isabella Stewart Gardner Museum. Cat. 45 / Bredius 547.

ST JOHN THE BAPTIST PREACHING. About 1635/36.
Canvas mounted on wood. Enlarged from 38 × 52 cm to 62 × 80 cm.
Berlin-Dahlem, Staatliche Museen Preussischer Kulturbesitz, Gemäldegalerie.
Cat. 52 / Bredius 555.

T.P.C. HAAG. Copy from Lastman.
THE SERMON OF JOHN THE BAPTIST.
Pen and wash drawing.
London, J.H.J. Mellaert Coll. (1921).

In the composition Rembrandt's starting point is an engraving by Maerten de Vos. Even in his early Leyden paintings, in compositions modelled on Lastman, and later in miniature painting, Rembrandt had depicted the power of the word. Now he expresses it in a Baroque language of forms; the movements are violent, agitated, rough. He succeeds in representing reactions both calm and violent, quiet and shrill, hesitant and decisive. In this narrative, sequentiality plays a decisive part. In Rembrandt the two protagonists seldom speak simultaneously; usually one reacts to the words of the other: action and reaction are shown.[162] They are temporally linked. The echo follows the call.

THE HOLY FAMILY. About 1635.
Signed: 'Rembrandt f. 163(.)'.
Canvas 183.5 × 123 cm.
Munich, Alte Pinakothek.
Cat. 51 / Bredius 544.

SAMSON THREATENING HIS FATHER-IN-LAW.
Signed: 'Rembrandt fc 163(5)'.
Canvas 158.5 × 130.5 cm.
Berlin-Dahlem, Staatliche Museen Preussischer Kulturbesitz, Gemäldegalerie. Cat. 10 / Bredius 499.

SAMSON POSING THE RIDDLE TO THE WEDDING GUESTS.
Signed: 'Rembrandt f. 1638'.
Canvas 126.5 × 175.5 cm.
Dresden, Gemäldegalerie.
Cat. 17 / Bredius 507.

162 In the grisaille painting ECCE HOMO, Rembrandt shows a crowd seething with fanaticism, calling for Christ's death in a stadium atmosphere. One of the high priests turns round, as if he were conducting the crowd's protest. Pilate rises from his judgement seat. He finds no guilt and dismisses the high priests. One of them has picked up Pilate's rod of judgement. In this way Rembrandt conveys that while Pilate is unwilling to have Jesus executed, the high priests are determined, and have themselves adopted the language of the law: 'We have a law, and according to this law he must die...'.[163]

157 In ST JOHN THE BAPTIST PREACHING, Rembrandt depicts how people of different races and classes listen to the preaching of Christ's forerunner, moved or indifferent, distracted or dismissive. The composition is based on a lost 157 painting by Pieter Lastman, of which only a copy has survived, and the Gospel accounts are supplemented by important details. Bathed in bright light, John stands in an eloquent posture on a rise in the ground, surrounded by the crowd which has rushed to hear him. At the Baptist's feet, Rembrandt has portrayed himself and his mother among the listeners. According to the rules of art at his time, he places

Cornelis MASSYS.
SAMSON SPEAKING WITH HIS FATHER-IN-LAW.
Engraving 80 × 103 mm.
Hollstein XI, 10.

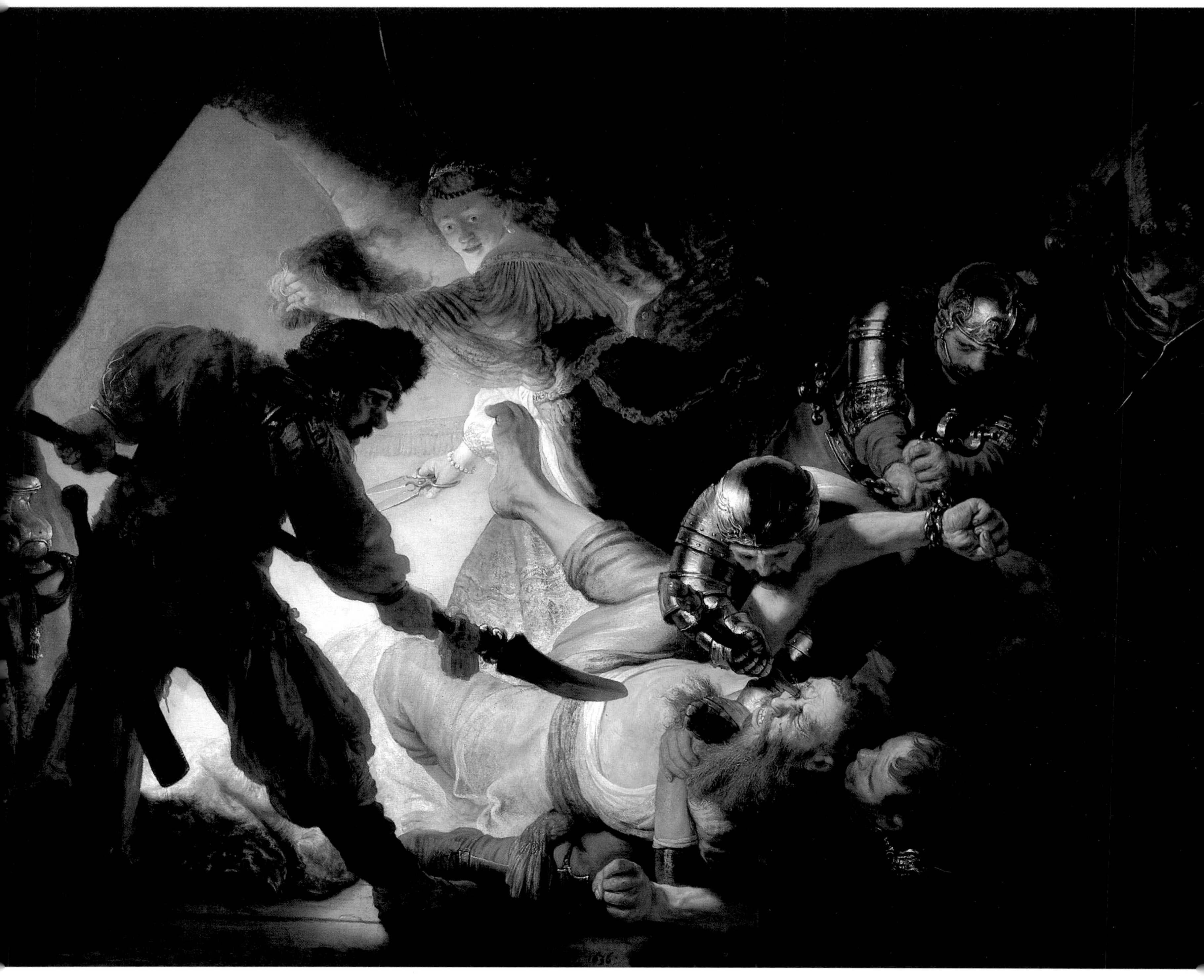

THE BLINDING OF SAMSON.
Signed: 'Rembrandt f. 1636'.
Canvas 205 × 272 cm.
Frankfurt, Städelsches Kunstinstitut.

Cat. 12 / Bredius 501.

people who are listening to the sermon close to John. At the edge, by contrast, he shows mothers with their children, who are quite unable to understand a sermon or are performing natural functions. In the crowd at the Baptist's feet, we discover two fighting children who are arousing the adults' displeasure. At the edges stand spectators who have come from far countries, with little understanding of the Old Testament religion, but so moved by John's preaching that they wish to be baptised.

162 As in ECCE HOMO, Rembrandt shows a group of people who are ill disposed towards the divine message: the high priests. This group, whom Rembrandt places at the centre of the picture, low down below a shadowy column supporting the bust of a Roman emperor, have turned away to confer[164]. For in his sermon John violently attacks the specious piety of the Sadducees and Pharisees: 'Ye brood of vipers, who has taught that ye shall not escape the wrath to come? Behold, and do righteous deeds of penitence.'.[165] To this group Rembrandt adds a motif which by tradition was only associated with scenes of extreme lasciviousness and violence: to make clear the bestial aspect of a rape scene, for example, Raphael included mating dogs. Rembrandt cites this motif 'probably' from an engraving by Agostino Veneziano (dei Musi) after Raphael's painting of the rape of Lucretia.[166] Rembrandt's pupil Samuel van Hoogstraten, who made an admiring note on the way the varying attention

THE FEAST OF BELSHAZZAR. About 1635.
Signed: 'Rembrandt fecit 163(.)'.
Canvas 167.6 × 209.2 cm.
London, National Gallery.
Cat. 11 / Bredius 497.

THE LAST SUPPER (after Leonardo da Vinci).
Signed: 'Rembrandt f. 1635'.
Pen and bistre wash, white body colour. 128 × 385 mm.
Berlin-Dahlem, Staatliche Museen Preussischer Kulturbesitz, Kupferstichkabinett. Benesch 445.

CHRIST BEFORE PILATE AND THE PEOPLE.
Signed: 'Rembrandt f. 1634'.
Paper on canvas 54.5 × 44.5 cm.
London, National Gallery.
Cat. 50 / Bredius 546.

JOSEPH RELATING HIS DREAMS. About 1637/38.
Signed: 'Rembrandt 163(.)'.
Paper on wood 51 × 39 cm.
Amsterdam, Rijksmuseum.
Cat. 16 / Bredius 504.

CHRIST TEACHING HIS DISCIPLES.
Signed: 'Rembrandt f: 1634'.
Black and red chalk, pen and bistre, wash in various tones, heightened in gouache. 355 × 476 mm.
Haarlem, Teylers Museum.
Benesch 89.

of the spectators is depicted in ST JOHN PREACHING, found this motif quite unsuitable — natural, but unseemly in this biblical history. One might conclude, he argued, that the dog-like Diogenes was preaching, rather than John. (Diogenes is supposed to have taught that people could couple in public like dogs; hence his followers were called cynics — canines.) The classicist Hoogstraten criticises Rembrandt's imagery: 'Such images make the master's simple-mindedness obvious; they are the more ridiculous in that they are the result of thoughtlessness'.[167]

In 1635 and 1636 Rembrandt raises the biblical history to monumental power. Three life-size Samson pictures are produced. In the Berlin painting SAMSON THREATENING HIS FATHER-IN-LAW, he depicts Samson's angry reaction when his Philistine father-in-law will not admit him to his house to see his wife, because he has given her in the meantime to another man, whereupon Samson says: 'I have a just cause against the Philistines. I shall bring ruin upon you'.[168] Rembrandt convincingly makes visual the cause and content of the exchange. The onlooker sees Samson standing before the locked door. He cannot enter the house. The father-in-law looks fearfully from a casement and speaks to the wronged hero. Samson, a powerful, imposing figure, raises his clenched fist at him; he bears a sword, Moorish servants

158, 159, 160
158

TOBIAS HEALING HIS FATHER'S BLINDNESS.
Signed: 'Rembrandt f. 1636'.
Wood 47.2 × 38.8 cm.
Stuttgart, Staatsgalerie.
Cat. 13 / Bredius 502.

CHRIST APPEARING TO MARY MAGDALEN.
Signed: 'Rembrandt f. 1638'.
Wood 61 × 49.5 cm.
London, Buckingham Palace, Collection of Her Majesty The Queen.
Cat. 56 / Bredius 559.

hold his train, by which his rank as a hero of Israel is shown. The flickering play of light that runs from Samson's sword over his angry face and clenched fist to the face of the frightened father-in-law indicates the course of the story: Samson's revenge will strike the old man. Already the shadow of his fist has fallen on his house.

If we look at Rembrandt's model, an engraving by Cornelis Massys, we can only admire Rembrandt's great ability to translate stories into pictures. Massys has presented the motifs of the story: the sisters, the gift of a goat, and the locked door. But the conflict between the two, the hero's status — none of this is conveyed by Massys's engraving.

Rembrandt paints the reactions of people not only to the spoken but to the written word. The mysterious writing on the wall in THE FEAST OF BELSHAZZAR causes a violent change of mood. The King starts up and turns towards the apparition, knocking over his goblet. Likewise a woman on the right shrinks back and spills her wine. Rembrandt took the complex foreshortening of this figure from Veronese's famous painting THE ABDUCTION OF EUROPA (which was at that time in the collection of a governor of Amsterdam).[169] Two other revellers look up fearfully. On the left Rembrandt places a woman as a dark repoussoir-figure who has not yet seen the

161

THE ENTOMBMENT. About 1639.
Wood 32.2 × 40.5 cm.
Glasgow, University, Hunterian Museum.
Cat. 59 / Bredius 554.

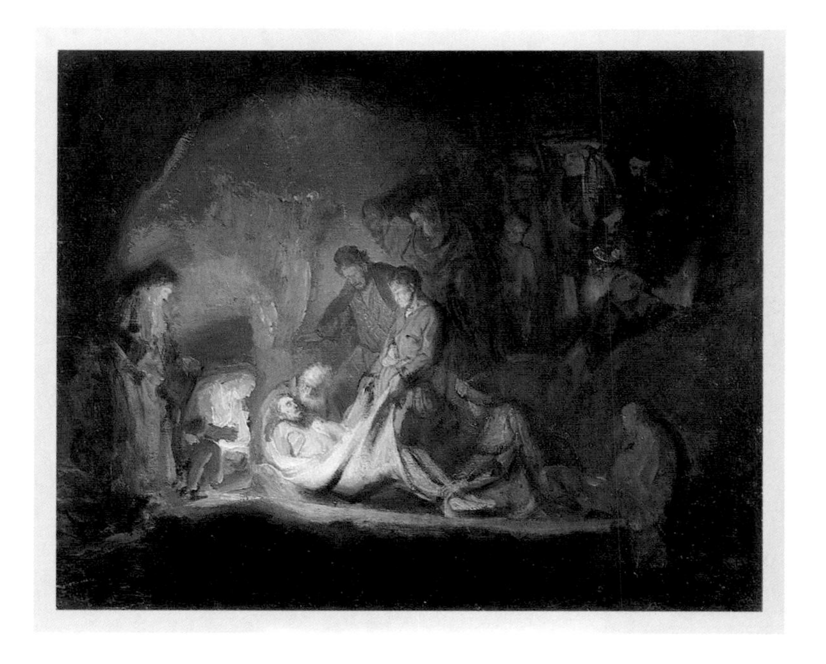

THE ANGEL LEAVING TOBIAS AND HIS FAMILY.
Signed: 'Rembrandt f. 1637'.
Wood 68 × 52 cm.
Paris, Louvre.
Cat. 15 / Bredius 503.

THE PARABLE OF THE LABOURERS.
Signed: 'Rembrandt f. 1637'.
Wood 31 × 42 cm.
Leningrad, Hermitage.
Cat. 55 / Bredius 558.

apparition and is looking up at the members of the court. The musicians in the background are still absorbed in their playing. Here the culminating point is shown, when the mood changes. The individual figures are assigned different ways of behaving: some are reacting to the writing, others are just noticing it, others still revelling.

In the painting THE ANGEL STOPPING ABRAHAM FROM SACRIFICING ISAAC TO GOD, too, the moment is depicted in which everything is changed by a word of God: Abraham, at God's command, was on the point of sacrificing his own son. Then the angel of the Lord called on him from heaven, saying: 'Abraham, Abraham! Lay not your hand on your son and do him no harm. For now I know that you fear God and did not spare your own son for my sake'.[170] To convey these words and their effect visually, artists before Rembrandt, Lastman among them, had turned them into an action: the angel stays Abraham's hand. Rembrandt takes up this motif and develops it further: as Abraham is about to perform the sacrifice, the heavens have opened. The angel has come down. In an attitude which expressively conveys both his flight and his coming to rest, he hovers above Abraham, holding his wrist with his right hand and restraining him from his action with his left. His sudden grasp has knocked the knife from Abraham's hand. The richly ornamented curved dagger is shown falling, still pointing like an arrow at the boy's throat, but destined not to strike it but to fall to the ground. The boy, undressed except for a loin cloth, lies on the ground with legs sharply bent and arms twisted behind his back, which is pressed against the pyre on which he is to be burnt after the sacrifice. Abraham's left hand completely covers his face and at the same time presses the head down, so that the throat arches forward to the knife. This gesture of the father's gives an impression of both cruelty, in its determination, and of protectiveness, as if he wanted to spare the boy the sight of the knife at the moment of death. The onlooker's gaze first meets the body of the boy, for his skin glows brightly in the light from above. The sight of the exposed body with the head forced down has a shocking effect.

148

149

In the verisimilitude of the depiction Rembrandt converges with Caravaggio. In the latter's painting, Abraham presses Isaac so brutally on to the sacrificial stone that he cries out in pain and fear[171]. Rembrandt's work, however, despite its cruelty, still has human traits: Abraham's hair — as described in a Jewish legend — has turned grey in the course of his terrible act; his eyes are staring in horror. He is still so marked by God's inhuman demand that the joy at his deliverance does not yet show in his face.

Rembrandt bases himself on a work by Lastman in which the latter had clearly been heavily influenced by two famous paintings by Caravaggio that he must have seen in 1603 in Italy: ST MATTHEW WITH THE ANGEL and THE SACRIFICE OF ISAAC.[172] Although Rembrandt probably knew only Lastman's work, he comes closer to Caravaggio's realism than does his teacher. In the background Rembrandt places a mountain landscape and thus shows the long distance that Abraham and Isaac have had to walk together to the place of sacrifice. The delicately painted landscape is reminiscent of the work of Hercules Seghers.

149

THE ANNUNCIATION TO THE SHEPHERDS.
Signed: 'Rembrandt f.' and dated 1634.
Etching 261 × 218 mm. 3rd state.
Hamburg, Kunsthalle.
Bartsch 44.

Few paintings by Rembrandt have been so ill used in the course of centuries as the DEPARTURE OF THE SHUNAMMITE WIFE. This powerful painting, that Rembrandt produced while he was working on the so-called NIGHT WATCH, was in the 18th century turned into a 'genuine' Rembrandt. To make it look more Rembrandt-like, an unknown artist painted the sky black and added more dark sky on an additional panel. Now the owner had a 'nocturnal' Rembrandt. The legend of Rembrandt's chiaroscuro, that had pronounced Rembrandt a painter of night moods, had claimed its sacrificial victim.

But our picture was to be maltreated a second time: for more than two hundred years it has been almost continuously misinterpreted.[173] For it depicts an episode from the Old Testament so rarely illustrated that even the auctioneers of the 18th century did not know which story it alluded to and called it simply THE DISMISSAL OF HAGAR. So it has since been called. Although a number of critics noticed that it did not coincide with the story of Hagar, the interpretation was not doubted. Firstly, the title was old — what did it matter if in the 18th century Rembrandt's biblical histories had sometimes been given extremely odd titles in the auction catalogues, since the tradition had been broken off? Of more moment was the fact that in the 19th century Rembrandt had been elevated to a genius who observed no rules. For the art historians of the French Revolution he was the republican artist with whom, unlike his Catholic, royalist rival Rubens, all democrats who repudiated the old norms could identify. At a time when religious and national differences were intensifying, he later became the embodiment of the Protestant Dutch bourgeoisie, while Rubens represented Catholic Belgian national feeling. In Bismarck's struggle with Catholicism, the thesis that Rembrandt exactly followed the Bible was given a denominational twist: while Rubens had adhered to art tradition and dogma, the Protestant Rembrandt had respected the text alone. Here, then, was the Luther of painting (as he had already been called during the French Revolution), who rose up against Emperor and Pope.

The critics were naturally aware that Hagar had gone into the desert on foot when she was sent away by Abraham. This is how the story had always been represented. But with a genius like Rembrandt such difficulties could be disregarded, for he was bound by no traditions.

Cornelis Hofstede de Groot accordingly found the following explanation:

THE DISMISSAL OF HAGAR..., for example, must have been

THE DEPARTURE OF THE SHUNAMMITE WIFE.
Signed: 'Rembrandt f. 1640'.
Wood 39 × 53.2 cm.
London, Victoria and Albert Museum.
Cat. 18/Bredius 508.

HANS COLLAERT after Maerten de Vos.
Six engravings, 212 × 290 mm each.

THE PROPHET ENTERING THE HOUSE OF THE SHUNAMITE WIFE. HE CALLS THE SHUNAMITE WIFE. Hollstein IV, 5-8 (1).

THE SHUNAMITE WIFE GIVES BIRTH TO A SON. THE SON IS SENT TO HIS FATHER. Hollstein IV, 5-8 (2).

THE SON FALLS ILL IN THE FIELDS. HE DIES IN HIS MOTHER'S ARMS. Hollstein IV, 5-8 (3).

THE DEPARTURE OF THE SHUNAMITE WIFE TO VISIT THE PROPHET ELISHA. THE ARRIVAL. Hollstein IV, 5-8 (4).

THE PROPHET DISPATCHING HIS SERVANT GEHASI. Hollstein IV, 5-8 (5).

THE PROPHET ELISHA AROUSES THE BOY. Hollstein IV, 5-8 (6).

originally intended as a Flight to Egypt. For it is striking that Hagar is riding off on a donkey, and the praeternatural light surrounding her also seems quite inappropriate to a slave sent away at God's command. With the flight, however, both the animal and the divine radiance emanating from the Christ child are explained by tradition. When Rembrandt decided to change the subject of the picture, he left these two subsidiary [sic!] issues alone.[174]

Carl Neumann noticed, to be sure, that 'on the left grazing animals and shepherds, and on the right a person washing at a trough' were to be seen, concluding percipiently: '...it is not, therefore, night.'[175] But it did not occur even to him to doubt the interpretation of the picture's subject.

A few years later Werner Weisbach, in his great book on Rembrandt, gave an explanation that was unintentionally replete with the clichés of Rembrandt's classicist adversaries:

> The painting shows...how Abraham accompanies the woman, who has already embarked on her journey, through the gateway of his house. On an ass led by the trimly-dressed Ishmael, Hagar departs not like a maidservant expelled into the desert, but in rich attire — like a fairytale princess, like Mary in the 'Visitation'.... The invention of the scene...bears witness to the originality and fertility of Rembrandt's imagination which, starting from literary tradition, elaborates the episode from a particular aspect into a romantic fairytale.[176]

The author of the next monograph on Rembrandt, Richard Hamann, reaches the following heights in his description:

> Hagar's departure...is one of the images in which it is not deep human understanding but the traversing of wide spaces that is artistically important. The whole scene is as if a princess were leaving on her travels, accompanied a small part of the way by her husband, and as if beyond the garden wall the people were waiting to break into hurrahs when the resplendent personages came into view from the depths.[177]

It occurred to none of the authors to question the identity of the subject of this picture in which content and form seem in such disagreement. For them the painting was a proof of Rembrandt's 'fairytale imagination' and 'independence of the pictorial tradition'.

THE DISMISSAL OF HAGAR.
Signed: 'Rembrandt f.' and dated 1637.
Etching 126 × 96 mm. Only one state.
Berlin-Dahlem, Staatliche Museen Preussischer Kulturbesitz, Kupferstichkabinett.
Bartsch 30.

169 The iconography of the Baroque — in which we situate Rembrandt's work — had been decisively shaped by painting and graphic art, and above all by book illustration, since the late 15th century. In this Rembrandt is no exception.[178]

At the beginning of the 16th century the iconography of biblical histories, both in the choice of subjects and in the manner of representation, was still largely determined by the medieval typological and symbolic interpretation. According to the typological interpretation, the events of the New Testament are prefigured in those of the Old, so that the Old Testament is not seen historically. Only the connecting meaning is important to theology. So, in the medieval view, the story of 'Joseph Lowered into the Well', like the scene of 'Jonas Thrown into the Sea', refers to the burial of Jesus.

The beginnings of the overthrow of this typology are to be found in lay piety and among theologians influenced by rabbinical exegesis.[179] In the history Bibles, the stories were handed down orally in their literal sense.[180] Finally, the translation of the Bible into the vernacular allowed the stories to be read in context by those who could not read Latin. This must have led to a new understanding of the biblical heritage.

This new understanding of the historical context also showed itself in the development of Bible illustration. More and more often the Bible or individual books are illustrated as a whole, or the stories of particular heroes, such as Abraham, Lot, or Noah, are made the subject of a series of pictures. The illustrations representing in detail the Old Testament, above all, were also collected as picture Bibles, or picture Bibles were compiled from the whole range of previous illustrations. It is these series of illustrations which exerted a still underestimated influence on the iconography of the Renaissance, of Mannerism, and of the Baroque.

Artists collected such books and drew inspiration from the often weak or mediocre illustrations, even taking from them most of the motifs needed to clarify the subject. It is known that Rubens drew as a boy from Tobias Stimmer's *New Artistic Figures from Biblical Histories...* (1576), and that even later, when he painted his DISMISSAL OF HAGAR (1618, Leningrad), he referred back to this picture Bible.[181] In the guilds of St Luke and the painters' corporations the members were given graphic material to work from.[182] The Netherlandish art theorists required that the borrowings should be translated into the artist's own style.[183] Poussin summarised the teaching about invention as follows: innovation in painting did not consist in the choice of a subject that had not been painted before, but in a good and novel composition and expressive form, through which an old, traditional theme was renewed.[184] The poets of antiquity had already taught this. The conservative Horace, for example, advised against the choice of new themes, though he did not forbid it; he recommended dramatists to keep to subjects which tradition had made generally known.[185] The theorists among the artists held the same view. Poussin makes us aware by his dictum that this question was obviously discussed in artists' circles and that the problem was not quite uncontroversial. Indeed, Poussin himself sometimes deviated from this rule,

J. A. BACKER.
UNKNOWN SCENE, identified here as THE ANGEL APPEARING TO CORNELIUS, THE CENTURION OF CAESAREA, WHEN HE PRAYED AND FASTED. About 1640.
Canvas 100 × 115 cm.
Milwaukee, Collection of Dr. A. and Mrs. Bader.

Philip GALLE after Johannes Stradanus.
THE VISION OF CORNELIUS. Engraving.
Hollstein VIII, 306-340, III.

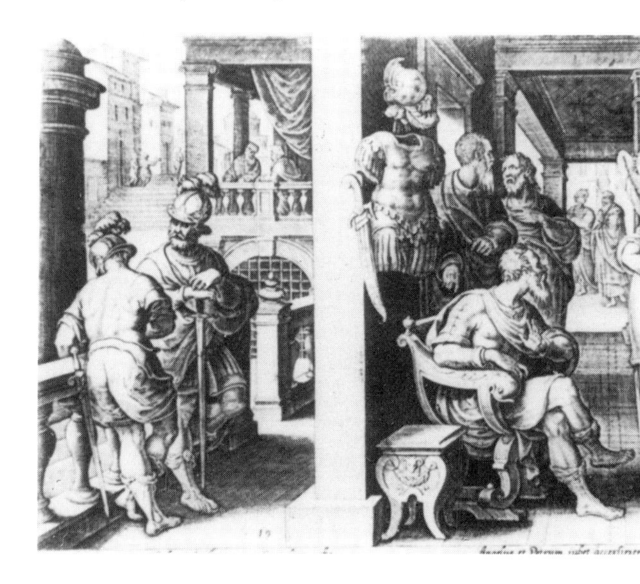

Pieter LASTMAN.
ELISHA AND THE SHUNAMMITE WIFE. About 1616 (?).
Canvas 74 × 125 cm.
Moscow, Pushkin Museum.

Jan VICTORS.
THE SHUNAMMITE WIFE EMBRACING HER REVIVED SON.
Signed: 'Johanes Victors f.'
Canvas.
Milwaukee, Collection of Dr. and Mrs. L. Parker.

Claes Cornelisz. MOEYAERT.
ELISHA AND THE SHUNAMMITE WIFE.
Monogrammed 'CLM'. Before 1624.
Wood 33.5 × 43.5 cm.
Moscow, Pushkin Museum, Depot.

painting subjects that had previously only appeared in graphic art. The old dictum derived from antiquity conflicted with the great encyclopaedic interest of his century.[186]

Let us return to Rembrandt's painting THE DEPARTURE OF THE SHUNAMMITE WIFE, so long misinterpreted. His starting-point was a series of engravings by Hans Collaert after drawings by Maerten de Vos, which copiously illustrated the story of the Shunammite wife (2 Kings 4: 8-37). It concerns a woman from Shunem who was unhappy at being childless; she offered her hospitality to the prophet Elisha, who foretold in gratitude that she would bear a child (Plate 1). The Shunammite woman indeed bore a son (Plate 2). One day the child, now grown to boyhood, accompanied his father to the fields, where he was afflicted with a severe headache, was taken back to his mother, and died in her arms; she laid him on his bed (Plate 3). She asked her husband, whom she did not tell of his son's death, for a boy and an ass so that she could journey to the Prophet Elisha on Mount Carmel (Plate 4). The prophet saw her from far off and sent his servant to ask if she was well. When she reached the prophet, she fell to the ground and clasped his feet (Plate 5). The servant wanted to thrust her away, but the prophet listened to her lament. He sent his servant with his staff to the Shunammite's house, but the servant was unable to help (background). Then the prophet went himself. He lay down on the child, breathing on it and waking it to new life (Plate 6).

167
166

Pieter Lastman was the first to draw inspiration from this series. In two paintings he represented the scene in which the Shunammite wife comes to the prophet and begs for his help.[187] Artists from Lastman's circle took up the same theme.[188] As far as we know now, Jacob Pynas was the first to show this story from Elisha's viewpoint. Pynas paints the prophet in the foreground, sending his servant away with his staff to the Shunammite woman, who has arrived on the mountain with her boy.[189] Claes Moyaert, in his painting, stays closer to his model, Lastman: the Shunammite kneels before the prophet, the servant tries to hold her back but is restrained by Elisha. As in the model by Maerten de Vos, the boy who has accompanied the Shunammite wife leans on an ass.

169
170

Astonishing: a subject that for centuries had led a shadowy existence, had been disregarded in art, arouses such interest in Amsterdam because Pieter Lastman had taken the engravings by Maerten de Vos as the model for his paintings.

167

Rembrandt too was stimulated to concern himself with the story. He did not choose the moment of arrival which had fascinated Lastman, but the scene of misunderstanding and departure. The two parents have lost their only child, but the husband does not yet know. The wife has seen her son die and, seeing a last source of hope, leaves to visit the Prophet Elisha so that he may help. This was a theme that engaged Rembrandt. Perhaps it affected him personally, for Saskia and he had lost three children shortly after birth.

In this Baroque phase of Rembrandt, when he was concerned with staggering his persons within the picture space, it can be taken for granted that he did not dispose them in the monotonously parallel way used by Maerten de Vos. But in the next plate de Vos offered a composition that attracted him more. The ass was seen almost frontally, its head bent to the right. This strongly foreshortened structure better suited his style, so he borrowed the composition from this plate in reverse.

Later, Rembrandt's pupils were affected by his and Lastman's enthusiasm for this story. Gerbrandt van den Eeckhout painted the arrival of the Shunammite wife at Elisha's dwelling in two paintings; like Rembrandt he shows the Shunammite's servant as a boy.[190] Up to a few decades ago his picture, too, was thought to be of the expulsion of Hagar, because this boyish servant was taken to be Ishmael. An anonymous pupil of Rembrandt's (Horst?) painted the scene in which Elisha bends over the dead boy and calls him 170 back to life.[191] Finally, Jan Victors treated the scene in which the prophet hands the resuscitated boy back to the Shunammite. Almost all these pictures were for a long time misinterpreted.

What I have demonstrated here in the case of a single series could be shown to apply to other series by Maerten de Vos and Maerten van Heemskerk. All had a major influence. Lastman and his circle used them as models again and again, and Rembrandt followed them. Lastman was a Catholic,[192] as were most of his pupils. This reminds us how senseless is the old dogma that Rubens took tradition as his starting point, whereas Rembrandt worked from the text alone, thus being the first to represent many themes. It was not the Calvinist Bible reader who discovered the themes, but artists inspired by the Reformation and Humanism, who in their graphic series opened up the Bible both chronologically and thematically. From these the Baroque artists merely made a selection typical of themselves.

Poussin had warned against working on subjects that lacked a long tradition. But Rembrandt was encouraged by Lastman, who has been called 'the Poussin of the Netherlands', to address himself also to arcane themes. His genius resides in the fact that he was able not only to recast 171 convincingly a traditional theme in a great creation in its own right, but to produce masterpieces from very weak compositions, and so was independent of the artistic quality of his models. This is a central and hitherto unrecognised feature of Rembrandt's art.

NATHAN ADMONISHING DAVID. About 1654-1655.
Reed pen and bistre wash. 146 × 173 mm.
Berlin-Dahlem, Staatliche Museen Preussischer Kulturbesitz, Kupferstichkabinett.
Benesch 947.

ELI INFORMED OF THE DEATH OF HIS SONS. About 1656.
Pen and bistre wash. 184 × 248 mm.
London, Victoria and Albert Museum.
Benesch 1011.

Why did Rembrandt paint so few stories from classical antiquity? This question has always exercised critics. But until now no convincing answer has been given.[193] Gary Schwartz argues that Rembrandt consciously remained aloof from classical themes since he had not finished his course at the Latin school.[194] A glance at the work of other Amsterdam history painters would have apprised Schwartz of his error. Pieter Lastman and his successors also painted few stories from antiquity, and Rembrandt followed their choice of subjects. For while in the 17th century the Bible was known to a broad public through numerous illustration series, many books from classical antiquity had yet to become more widely known through translation and illustration. Up to now there has been no comprehensive study of how the works of classical authors were handed on, edited, translated, and illustrated in the Middle Ages and the Renaissance, and how, through their texts and illustrations, they influenced iconography and the subject matter of art in the Middle Ages, the Renaissance, Mannerism, and the Baroque. But just because the rules of the history of their reception, which can certainly be established, are not yet known, uncertainty still reigns concerning not only the evaluation of Rembrandt's choice of subjects, but also the naming, description, and interpretation of many works of art with mythological themes. So, as many as three of his few paintings on these themes have been ambiguously or wrongly interpreted. They include the early uninterpreted HISTORY PAINTING (35), the picture variously interpreted as SOPHONISBA RECEIVING THE POISONED CUP or as ARTEMISIA (183), and finally the DANAË-painting (180). In attempting to establish a basis for interpreting the paintings, I shall sketch the history of the reception of classical authors is the Middle Ages and the modern period.

The reception of the historical and mythological works of classical authors in the Middle Ages was very varied. This is bound up with the initially critical attitude of Christian doctrine to antiquity. The early Church was not interested in handing down works regarded as pagan — on the contrary, it often obstructed the process; this was responsible for the loss of many ancient literary works. In the Middle Ages there was a more relaxed relationship to ancient culture and its books, which were often seen as useful exemplary tales; the typological manner of interpretation was often applied. The Italian Humanists take the credit for having edited the works of classical authors for printing and thus for making them known to a broader educated public. In the course of the 16th century the books were translated into many languages

THE ABDUCTION OF EUROPA.
Signed: 'RHL van Rijn 1632'.
Wood 60 × 77.5 cm.
New York, private collection (on loan in the Metropolitan Museum of Art).
Cat. 95 / Bredius 464.

◀ BELLONA.
Signed: 'Rembrandt f. 1633 Be(ll)on(a)'.
Canvas 127 × 97.5 cm.
New York, Metropolitan Museum of Art.
Cat. 103 / Bredius 467.

Hendrik GOLTZIUS.
THE ABDUCTION OF EUROPA.
Engraving.

and illustrated by woodcuts, which the publishers often re-issued in picture volumes with explanatory texts. In general, artists only knew those works which had been translated into their native tongues, for few of them had mastered Latin or Greek. How few authors an artist needed to know emerges from a contemporary textbook. The art theorist and painter Gerard de Lairesse, in his treatise *Grondlegginge der Tekenkunst* (1701), enumerates the works an artist should know in order to practise his profession through a conversation between the pupil (Probus) and the teacher (Iudicio): 'Herodotus, Tacitus, Livy, Justin, Flavius Josephus, Plutarch, and especially, Holy Scripture'.[195] The selection made by Lairesse is determined by his theory of art. He therefore ranks Ovid's *Metamorphoses* as low fables and does not mention them, although scenes from them are the classical subject matter most often treated in the 16th, 17th, and 18th centuries. 'Knowledge of his (Ovid's) work was never extinguished, making its appearance in the early Middle Ages and reaching a high point in the 11th century'. (Walter Kraus).[196] In *Ovide moralisé* the *Metamorphoses* were given a Christian interpretation and divested of their scandalous character. Ovid was first introduced to Netherlandish artists in the Dutch language through the translation by Joanes Florianus (1552). The Haarlem art theoretician, painter, and poet Karel van Mander considered the *Metamorphoses* so important that he devoted a large part of his *Schilderboeck* (1604) to them and offered artists a *Uitlegginghe op de Metamorphoses* ('Interpretation of the Metamorphoses'). He interpreted the *Metamorphoses* for the reader, as *Ovide moralisé* had done earlier. In these fables, he said, general truths and teachings were concealed. He distinguishes three kinds of interpretation: historical, natural-historical, and moral, the last being given the greatest importance.

More than half of all the ancient histories represented by Baroque artists show scenes from Greek and Roman mythology that are to be found in Ovid. Compared to these, stories from Greek or Roman history were of far less significance. This was true for Rembrandt too: they make up less than a third of his surviving works on antique themes. This is clearly bound up with the fact that most of the historical works were edited only at a late stage and made known to a broader public through translations and collections of illustrations even later. This can be illustrated by Livy's monumental work *Ab urbe condita*.[197] Livy's description of the history of Rome from its foundation to the death of Drusus was regarded in the Imperial period as the most authoritative account of the history of the Roman Republic. Only 35 of the 142 books are extant today. Livy's work was rediscovered during the Italian Renaissance. In 1469 it was republished in Rome for the first time. In 1541 a Dutch translation

THE ABDUCTION OF GANYMEDE. About 1635.
Pen and wash drawing with bistre. 183 × 160 mm.
Dresden, Staatliche Kunstsammlungen, Kupferstichkabinett. Benesch 92.

THE ABDUCTION OF GANYMEDE.
Signed: 'Rembrandt ft. 1635'.
Canvas 177 × 130 cm.
Dresden, Gemäldegalerie.
Cat. 98 / Bredius 471.

THE NAUGHTY CHILD. About 1635.
Inscription added later.
Pen and wash drawing with bistre, heightened with white body colour, some black chalk. 206 × 143 mm.
Berlin-Dahlem, Staatliche Museen Preussischer Kulturbesitz, Kupferstichkabinett. Benesch 401.

THE ABDUCTION OF PROSERPINE. About 1632.
Wood 84.5 × 79.5 cm.
Berlin-Dahlem, Staatliche Museen Preussischer Kulturbesitz, Gemäldegalerie.
Cat. 96 / Bredius 463.

appeared: *Roemsche historie, nu eerstmael in Nederlantscher Spraken ghedruckt. Antwerp 1541.* ('Roman Histories, Now Printed for the First Time in Dutch. Antwerp, 1541'). Of the German translations I shall mention the one published by Feierabend in 1571 in Frankfurt. In place of the lost books, summaries of the individual books compiled in antiquity were printed.

Unlike Livy's work, the *Facta et dicta memorabilia* by Valerius Maximus was much appreciated in the Middle Ages.[198] The work offers a collection of examples of model behaviour from the spheres of religion, political institutions, virtue, and the other areas of life. 'Valerius Maximus's *Exempla* have significance as an historical source..., as a symptom of the practice of history in the early Imperial period, and finally in mediating an anecdotally structured image of Antiquity to the Middle Ages and the early Renaissance' (Peter L. Schmidt).[199] In 1476 a Latin edition appeared, to be followed by a flood of further editions. In 1560 Feierabend published a German edition in Frankfurt, and in 1614 a Dutch one appeared in Rotterdam.

Rembrandt owned 15 books, including an old Dutch Bible (probably influenced by Luther's version), a complete High German edition of Flavius Josephus, probably a High German edition of Fronsberger's *War Book*, and eleven other books.[200] The titles of most of these other books are unknown. Ovid's *Metamorphoses* tin the version by van Mander, a German or Dutch translation of Livy's Roman history with illustrations by Jost Amman after Johann Bocksperger the Younger, and a translation of Valerius Maximus were probably among them. But even if Rembrandt did not own one of these works, there is much evidence of books being borrowed. We can therefore assume that he was able to read the stories. However, it was not only the texts but the illustrations that were decisive for artists. In them Rembrandt could see how the stories had been treated by artists before him. This influenced him decisively, for in the case of many subjects the pictorial tradition had become detached from the texts during the Middle Ages. Motifs were added which are not included in the texts, and Rembrandt often adopted such motifs. Further, it is of fundamental importance that the educated artists in particular sometimes invented motifs that were adopted by later artists and also applied to other themes. Therefore we must know the language of Renaissance and Baroque art, the court style, and the semiotics of the time to be in a position to interpret such works adequately.

The early Leyden period, up to the move to Amsterdam, is dominated by the Bible, head studies, and genre works. Only once is there a HISTORY, not yet interpreted, and a mythological scene with ANDROMEDA. In etchings Rembrandt portrayed DIANA and a SLEEPING ANTIOPE who is visited by Jupiter in the form of a satyr.[201] It was only in Amsterdam that Rembrandt dealt more frequently with classical themes. The stimulus clearly came from the Dutch court, for in 1632 he produced THE ABDUCTION OF PROSERPINE for it. In the painting he followed closely an etching by Sautman after Rubens's ABDUCTION OF PROSERPINE, which was based in its turn on a relief on an ancient sarcophagus.[202]

35 43 176

Rembrandt takes up this depiction and dramatises it. It matched his desire to portray reactions to unexpected events in a vivid way. Ovid describes how Proserpine, the daughter

MINERVA. About 1632.
Said to be monogrammed.
Wood 60.5 × 49 cm.
Berlin-Dahlem, Staatliche Museen Preussischer Kulturbesitz, Gemäldegalerie.
Cat. 102 / Bredius 466.

of Ceres, was gathering violets and lilies with her companions on the grassy bank of Lake Pergus when she was surprised by Pluto and abducted to the Underworld. 'In fear the goddess called to her mother.... The seam of her garment was rent, she scattered the flowers.... (Pluto) drives on the horses with mighty shakes of the iron-dark reins on the necks and manes of the coursers. Through bottomless lakes he hastens on...',[203] taking Proserpine to his shadowy underworld. Ceres sought her daughter throughout the world until a nymph revealed her fate. The mother implored Zeus to help, so that Proserpine might be allowed to spend at least two-thirds of the year in the upper world. Zeus complied with this request. The meaning of the myth is not difficult to guess: the perennial drama of the death and rebirth of the vegetable world.

Rembrandt has dramatised Rubens's composition, subordinating the figures, which in Rubens are parallel to the picture plane, to the diagonal movements of horses and chariot. Pluto appears suddenly and drags Proserpine onto his chariot, while the horses charge forward. The movement runs from the left background to the right foreground, so the picture is divided into a light side with Pluto and Proserpine on the chariot, and a dark side into which the horses are already vanishing. From the bright world of humans the vehicle careers into the dark forest and lake of the underworld. With all her strength Proserpine resists Pluto, who has grasped her by the shoulders and knees; she tries to push away his shoulder and scratch his cheek. Her two playmates hold fast to her train which is stretched full length. The chariot and the foreground are distinctly painted. A large herb-like plant and some flowers are visible on a brightly lit slope. The chariot is a splendidly ornamented gold-coloured vehicle with a lion's head showing bared teeth on the front. Proserpine's resistance makes Pluto turn his head so that he is seen in profile. But as he has a firm grasp on the woman and the horses are galloping forward, it is clear that he has already won. The two playmates have already fallen so far back that only their heads and outstretched arms are visible, so the outcome of this dramatic scene is beyond doubt at the moment of highest tension: Proserpine will vanish with Pluto into the dark of the Underworld.

173 In the painting THE ABDUCTION OF EUROPA, produced in 1632, Rembrandt likewise shows a scene in which Europa and her companions see the danger only when it is too late. Jupiter has approached the Tyrian princess Europa in the shape of a white bull as she is playing with her maidens on the beach. The royal maiden dares to sit on the back of the bull. 'Then the god steps softly from the shore, setting treacherous hooves in the waves.... She looks fearfully back to the desolate strand, her right hand grasping a horn and her left hand braced on his back; her garment is swelled by the breath of the wind'.[204] The girls on the shore realise the danger. One raises her arms over her head and utters a cry; another beside her wrings her hands in despair. An intuition of what is happening fills all the participants. A girl standing near the carriage turns towards the scene, and even the coachman has sprung up. In the staggered arrangement of figures, the rendering of local colour, and the invention of accessories that fit the story, such as the fine coach and four with its immense sunshade, Rembrandt follows suggestions in similar paintings by Pieter Lastman. However, he is far removed from Lastman in his painting of details, the realistic treatment of the figures, and the use of chiaroscuro, as in the presentation of a continuous space stretching deep into the background.

Van Mander gives the story of Europa a moralising interpretation. He quotes a classical source in which the abducted princess is compared to the human soul, which is led away from the divine by the cares of this world. On a less profound level, he says that the bull could also be interpreted as a ship taking the beauty of the East to the western continent, to which Europa then gives her name. Perhaps the harbour in the background of this picture is to be understood not only as the harbour of the royal city, but also as an allusion to this second layer of meaning.

If in these two paintings Rembrandt has avoided showing 179 the figures naked, the scene of THE GODDESS DIANA BATHING, [in the presence of] ACTAEON, WHO IS BEING TRANSFORMED INTO A STAG, AND THE DISCOVERY OF THE PREGNANCY OF CALLISTO gives him the opportunity to present nude female bodies. Rembrandt interprets the two stories in an entirely new way: he combines two scenes which do not belong together and are even taken from different books of the *Metamorphoses*. By simultaneously presenting two turbulent events, he can establish a tension between two sets of movements, and so achieve the 'greatest amount of...movement', the meaning of which here includes a multiplicity of outward movements.[205]

The hunter Actaeon is turned by Diana into a stag when he surprises her and her companions while they are bathing; his own dogs then tear him apart. Callisto is turned into a bear when the maidenly nymphs discover that she is with child. In the foreground of his picture Rembrandt shows the nymphs innocently bathing around Diana, sporting in the water. Turning to the left, Diana sees Actaeon, whom she splashes with water so that he begins to turn into a stag, antlers sprouting from his head. On the right, the nymphs on the bank are shown discovering Callisto's pregnancy. One of them holds Callisto by the shoulders as she lies on her back; another exposes her rounded body by pushing up her garment and feeling her belly with her hand. Rembrandt shows the gloating reaction of the girls, who see what is happening and rush from the water. Through the behaviour of Actaeon's dogs — two of them are romping together — he makes clear how the stories will end: the victims will be defeated.

Although the figures are divided into three groups — Actaeon with his pack, Diana bathing, and Callisto with the nymphs — they are bound together by gestures and glances. Diana and the two nymphs with her look towards Actaeon; the others are trying to reach the group around Callisto; and one of the girls with Callisto shades her eyes with her hand as she looks towards Actaeon. Much space is given to the landscape. Although the figures are small, the glowing flesh tint of their bodies gives them prominence. Blue and light green are the predominant colours, the bright skin of the women shimmering in contrast.

Though in his early history pictures on mythological subjects Rembrandt preferred scenes with many figures in a landscape, organising the composition through chiaroscuro, this changes about 1633. He is then no longer concerned to achieve a unity of landscape and figures. He again uses Caravaggio's style, interpreting him in a Venetian sense. The cabinet pictures with small figures, usually painted on wood, give way to life-size canvases with few figures or only one. Apart from historical figures (BELLONA, SASKIA AS FLORA), he paints a life-size half-length figure picture (ARTEMISIA) and two life-size full-length figure pictures (GANYMEDE, DANAË). 172, 108, 115, 116 174 180

172 Bellona, the goddess of war, played a major part in the political allegories of the war-torn 17th century (for example, in royal processions and political pamphlets). Rembrandt shows Bellona in front of an old fortification with arches, in bright, clear illumination. She holds a steel-grey shield, the front of which is formed into a powerful relief: the Gorgon's head with snake hair protrudes frighteningly. Her right hand rests confidently on her sword. Shining silver armour with gold ornamentation protects her shoulders, breasts and body; below the armour a shimmering purple and gold hip-length cloak with gold-embroidered seams appears, in its turn covering a green dress. The head is covered by a silver helmet with a gold vizor and a resplendent green plume. Abundant brown curls fall on Bellona's shoulders. The light comes from the left, so one side of Bellona's full face is

THE GODDESS DIANA BATHING, WITH SCENES FROM THE STORIES OF ACTAEON AND CALLISTO.
Signed: 'Rembrandt fe. 1635'.
Canvas 73.5 × 93.5 cm.
Schloss Anholt, (Lower Rhine), Collection of the Prince of Salm-Salm.
Cat. 99 / Bredius 472.

brightly illuminated while the other is in semi-darkness. It is this play of bright light on the fine armour and the face of the war goddess that gives this picture its special enchantment. At the same time, the portrayal is informed by the dignity and self-confidence emanating from Bellona's whole posture.

The Baroque ideal of beauty which Rembrandt follows in his BELLONA had been rejected by the Classicists, although the Flemish and Dutch artists and sculptors had taken pleasure in developing it. He here invokes the style and models of the Roman Baroque.

174 In Rembrandt's ABDUCTION OF GANYMEDE the Classicists and most art historians after them claimed to see a parody of antiquity. In this they misunderstood the picture entirely. To be sure, Rembrandt gives his own interpretation of the subject and opens new levels of interpretation with his concealed symbolism, but the picture certainly does not represent an attack on antiquity.

Sir Kenneth Clark, the famous English cultural historian, has interpreted the painting as a Protestant protest against pagan sexual customs,[206] the depiction of the boy being understood as deliberately anti-classical. A glance at Dürer's well-known drawing of a weeping angel or at Michaelangelo's depiction of the young Christ would have corrected this misapprehension. The Ganymede myth was allegorised at an early stage: 185

> The myth of Ganymede, the most beautiful of mortals, whom the gods abducted to heaven so that he should live for ever there, was already interpreted allegorically in antiquity... For Xenophon it is proof that spiritual rather

DANAË.
Signed: 'Rembrandt f. 16(36)'.
Canvas 185 × 203 cm.
Leningrad, Hermitage.
Cat. 100 / Bredius 474.

than physical qualities could win the gods' love. On Roman tombs we find it as a symbol of the elevation of the human soul above earthly things.... On the Enamel Cross of Engelberg (12th century) Ganymede is represented as an allegory of the air. In the *Ovide moralisé*, Ganymede is seen as prefiguring the favourite disciple John who was taken up into Heaven, and the eagle as symbolising Christ.

In the neo-platonic interpretation Ganymede is 'the human spirit; the companions left behind are the lower qualities of the soul; the eagle is divine love. God loves the soul and bears it aloft, parted from its base earthy qualities, to Heaven' (Herbert von Einem).[207] The allegorical interpretation explains the acceptance of the theme into the picture programme of a church dignitary and justifies the boy's assent to his abduction, expressed in many pictures. In Karel van Mander's interpretation of the *Metamorphoses*, Ganymede stands for the pure human soul which is carried up to God. Purity of soul was associated with young children; since antiquity, the Ganymede myth had implied the taking away of a child from its parents. In antiquity and later in the Renaissance, the myth was therefore used to symbolise the loss of a child. Rembrandt's pupil Nicolaes Maes produced a number of Ganymede pictures showing children painted in a portrait manner being carried to Heaven by an eagle. The works are clearly intended as mementos of children who have died young. In these pictures the children sit on the eagle's back and look at the onlooker.[208]

In Rembrandt's work this symbolic meaning, if such was his intention, is embodied in an action. In a preliminary 175 drawing, Ganymede's parents are seen lifting their hands in horror, as if they wanted to hold on to the child. The father's attitude has been interpreted in various ways: he is said to be trying to hit the bird with his crossbow, or he has plucked out some tail-feathers which he now holds in his hand.[209] In the painting Rembrandt has concentrated the scene on Ganymede and the eagle. His presentation contains a new interpretation which does not go back simply to the text. The entirely natural, elemental reaction of the abducted boy is made the subject: his terror, his helpless resistance, and his revulsion. The boy does not yet recognise the god or divine messenger in the eagle, as in the preceding and later tradition. He pushes against the bird, and the twig in his hand shows that he has tried to hold fast to a cherry tree. None of this is in the original story, and this representation was only possible because artists had begun to ask about the natural reactions of the child and to introduce such questions into the story, as is shown by the inscriptions on 16th-century German woodcuts. Into the realistic presentation Rembrandt, following a suggestion from Karel van Mander, has incorporated a symbolic meaning. Since Ganymede, as a cupbearer, holds a goblet or urn, he was identified with the demon at the sources of the Nile, and even given a place among the stars by astrologers as Aquarius.[210] Therefore Rembrandt depicts Ganymede urinating. Van Mander pointed out the linguistic origin which the humanists assumed to underlie such an interpretation, and added: 'Ganymede, (is) winter, in Greek *hyein*, which means rain. Thus Ganymede is transformed into the heavenly sign of the Watercarrier, who makes water, if not nectar, flow in plenty for us'. This motif was not at all indecent to the Baroque age, as is shown by the MANNIKEN PISSING FOUNTAIN, by Jérome Duquesnoy the Elder, in Brussels; Rembrandt clearly owned a reproduction of this famous figure.[211] Interpretations of it had included one which related it symbolically to the Christ child, in which the outflowing water was described as the urine of the little Jesus. It is characteristic of Rembrandt that he embodies his symbolic interpretation in the natural reaction of the abducted boy.[212]

180 In a similar way, in the famous DANAË painting he presented the symbolic meaning only in a concealed form. Danaë was the daughter of the Argive Acrisius and Aganippe. Her father locked her in a bronze tower or vault, to prevent her from having contact with any man. However, Zeus visited her in the form of a golden rain, and she gave birth to Perseus, who later turned King Polydectes to stone with the Medusa's head.

Even in antiquity artists were fond of the myth of Danaë. Zeus appearing to Danaë as a golden rain was very often portrayed. Rembrandt does not show the golden rain itself, but renders it through a warm light falling on Danaë. (In deciding to make the appearance of the god visible through light, Rembrandt follows a conception that can be observed, for example, in Lastman's GOD'S APPEARANCE TO ABRAHAM.

Franz MENTON after Frans Floris I.
DANAË.
Signed.
Engraving 213 × 267 mm.
Hollstein XIII, 35.

This painting exerted a great influence, for example, on Moeyaert, Potter and Saftleven).[213] In Titian's DANAË in 22 Naples, the cloud from which the rain falls has become 'a flickering vision of flames, inaugurating a development that was to lead to the complete elimination of the actual cloud...'.[214] In the pictures from the 16th and 17th centuries with which Panofsky illustrates this development, the golden rain was still shown, but in the Renaissance and Mannerism there was already a type of treatment that replaced it by a 181 beam of light. Rembrandt decided in favour of this type, following the general trend towards symbolising divine apparitions, yet creating something new and original. The special feature of Rembrandt's treatment emerges from Fechner's account:

> It is not a rain of gold coins but a warm light that flows over Danaë's naked body, giving it a delicate golden gleam. It falls on the high forehead, glows on the rosy fingertips, and pours over the whole form. And the whole figure seems permeated by the golden, shimmering light which, emphasising the main subject, surrounds the reclining woman with a warm radiance, lighting up the gold of the wood-carvings and penetrating the half-light of the room.... The red carpets, the greenish-brown curtains, and the golden glow scattered across the picture provide the dominant colour tone, harmonising wonderfully with the nuances of the body.[215]

In his treatment Rembrandt indicates the golden rain indirectly; the picture is entirely attuned to the golden glow. It thus becomes clear that he did not intend to symbolise venal love by the myth of Danaë. A further iconographic detail confirms this: Danaë's sumptuously carved bed shows a chained Eros, Anteros, above her head. Love always has two poles, the lover and the beloved, and in mythology Eros is therefore paired with Anteros, the god of requited love. From this conflict between two kinds of love, Platonic philosophy asserts the victory of the true, divine — because

Peter Paul RUBENS.
ARTEMISIA.
Wood 97 × 105 cm.
Potsdam-Sanssouci, Bildergalerie.

rational — love over earthly, sensual love. The requital of love, Anteros, is reinterpreted as pure, non-sensual love on which this ethical-philosophical principle confers the absolution of chastity. The angel with pain-distorted face and bound hands at the head of the bed is also to be understood in these terms. Danaë preserves her chastity. She will not soil divine love with sensual lust, for the hands of the latter are bound, since Anteros protects her.[216] Kieser has pointed out that a bird-like creature is shown on the left side of the bed.[217] It resembles a parrot. The parrot is a symbol of Mary's Immaculate Conception, since, according to Conrad of Würzburg, its green coat of feathers is not wetted by rain. (In the Middle Ages, Danaë's conception could be interpreted analogously as prefiguring the Virgin Birth). Rembrandt uses the parrot and Anteros motifs to make clear Danaë's divine love. In the final version of the painting, he stressed the varying degrees of the perception of the divine. The maid, to be sure, opens the curtain and gives free passage to the light, but she does not look towards the divine, does not recognise it. Danaë, by contrast, lifts her head and gazes at the approaching god. So of this picture, too, Rembrandt has made a recognition scene. But as it was this level of meaning that concerned him, he has cancelled all the materialisation of love that is present in the myth by a symbolic imagery appropriate to his time.

Although Rembrandt has depicted the theme of Danaë in a manner typical of an erudite Baroque artist in its references to tradition, the painting continually inflames the imaginations of critics and laymen who prefer to see Rembrandt as a genius independent of his time and tradition, who created at his own whim. It was recently reinterpreted as 'Aegina visited by Zeus in the shape of a blazing fire',[218] without adequate justification and although this theme is not represented in earlier printed graphics or picked up from them by Baroque art.

The fact, which has received insufficient attention up to now, that in his treatment of ancient themes Rembrandt always took earlier depictions as his starting-point, is the main reason why the subject of the painting mentioned at the outset, Artemisia or Sophonisba, has not yet been securely identified. (A further reason may be the poor reproductions that have often been used.) 183

Interestingly, Rembrandt's painting shares the fate of doubtful interpretation with a picture by Rubens depicting the same scene. Early on (1632/33), this was in the possession of the stadholder, and we are including it in our study because it may have inspired Rembrandt to produce his own version. 182

The story and death of Sophonisba are recounted by Livy (Book 30, Ch. 5). During the war between Rome and the Numidians, the patriotic queen of the Numidians had succeeded in keeping her long-estranged husband, Syhax, on the Carthaginian side; yet the Romans were victorious and the couple imprisoned — Syhax by the Romans and Sophonisba by the Romans' ally Massinissa. Asked to protect her from the Romans, Massinissa gave way to Sophonisba and married her. However, the Romans soon demanded that she be handed over, for Syhax had excused his disloyalty to them by pleading Sophonisba's influence, so that Rome now feared for Massinissa's loyalty. Massinissa, however, did not release Sophonisba, but sent her a goblet of poison and a message: she had asked him either to kill her or to protect her from the Romans. As he could no longer do the latter, he sent her the draught. Unafraid, she took the poison and died.

The story of Artemisia (Valerius Maximus 4, 4 Ext. 1), too, tells of a heroic woman in a high position. She had been the wife of her brother, Mausolus of Mylasa, and on his death had succeeded him to the throne. She erected a monumental tomb to him, the Mausoleum, which in the ancient world was counted among the wonders of the world. Yet Artemisia wished to be herself a living tomb for her beloved spouse and sent for his ashes, which she mixed in a drink and consumed. Shortly after magnificent obsequies for Mausolus she died of sorrow.

The previous research on the two paintings shows that there are numerous arguments for seeing the vessel as containing either poison or the drink of ashes. No sure interpretation can be arrived at by relating the pictures back to the text alone. On the other hand, a clear answer is obtained if we examine the pictorial tradition relating to the two themes. Both were repeatedly treated in the printed graphics of the 16th century.[219]

The iconography of the death of Sophonisba was established by the Nuremberg-born minor master Georg Pencz in an engraving: Sophonisba sits in an interior on a bench, drinking the poison from a goblet. The armed messenger still has his hat, which he has removed in humble greeting, in his left hand. With his right he gives emphasis to his words. He is pictured distinctly smaller than the Queen; though standing, he hardly looks down on her. In this way the artist stresses the difference in rank and in addition clearly emphasises the chief protagonist. 184

ARTEMISIA RECEIVING THE ASHES OF HER HUSBAND MIXED WITH WINE.
Signed: 'Rembrandt f. 1634'.
Canvas 142 × 153 cm.
Madrid, Prado.
Cat. 97 / Bredius 468.

Dutch and German editions of Livy from the last third of the 16th century are often illustrated by a woodcut by Jost Amman, after Johan Bocksberger the Younger, which shows the scene in a palace.[220] Several messengers have appeared, holding goblets in pairs, and Sophonisba, accompanied by three ladies-in-waiting, drinks the poison.

The iconography of Artemisia, too, evolved from an engraving by Georg Pencz. 184 He shows the Queen sitting in a palatial building on a bench. In her right hand she holds a goblet. A female servant standing before her in a bowed position carefully pours her husband's ashes into it from a sack. Armour and weapons in the foreground remind us of Mausolus, while in the background a cremation (and the Mausoleum?) is indicated.

Both the ashes and the container in which they are preserved are clearly shown and related to the dead king. Maerten van Heemskerk, in his etchings of the Seven Wonders of the World, showed the Mausoleum as an immense pyramid, in front of which Artemisia holds the ashes of her husband in a wine cup.[221] In Baroque painting, motifs from both graphic works could be combined.[222]

Constituent motifs can be identified for the iconography of

Georg PENCZ.
SOPHONISBE. About 1539.
Engraving 187 × 124 mm. Only one state.

Georg PENCZ.
ARTEMISIA.
Engraving 192 × 134 mm. Only one state.

both Sophonisba and Artemisia: the Sophonisba scene includes the messenger with the goblet of poison, and the Artemisia scene includes, in addition to the goblet, the ash container, the contents of which are often being poured into the cup.

On this basis the common theme of Rubens's and Rembrandt's paintings can be determined with certainty; in both cases the subject is Artemisia.

182 The queen is characterised by Rubens as a widow by means of a black veil and presses her left hand with her handkerchief against her breast in lamentation. With grief-stricken eyes she gazes towards heaven. In her outstretched right hand she holds the cup, into which a young servant is pouring the ashes. He appears to have taken them by means of a small dish from the mighty urn which is placed in the foreground. Young chambermaids behind Artemisia and aged counsellors in Oriental head-dresses clearly situate the scene in an ancient court.

Rubens interpreted the original engraving very freely, adding the detail of the widow's veil, extending the court appartenances, and replacing the sack by an urn more appropriate to the solemn theme. But he, too, adopted the moment chosen by Georg Pencz. This work makes us aware once again of the rules governing the translation of a theme into Baroque pictorial language. By means of gestures, glances, movements, and particular motifs the text is converted into imagery which in its turn is stamped by the nature of the theme and the context in which it originates. Thus Rubens's presentation of the royal subject painted for a prince is determined in large measure by court etiquette and certain fixed rhetorical formulae.

By comparison, formulae are less prominent in Rembrandt's painting. He can manipulate the Baroque pictorial 183 language more freely and so heighten the picture's emotive content by adding further motifs. At first sight his treatment of Artemisia is less simple to interpret than Rubens's.

The queen sits magnificently robed on her throne. Her hair falls to her shoulders. With her left hand resting for support on the table, she points with her right to her stomach. A girl situated far lower in the picture area walks up to her with the goblet. In the dim background an aged servant can be seen holding a sack. This sack, which owing to the darkness of the background can only be seen in the original painting, is the key to the unambiguous identification of the theme. It contains the ashes of Mausolus. The banal pouring of the ashes is not shown, having happened already. Rembrandt has depicted the solemn moment in which the young girl brings the composed queen the ashes of her husband. For this reason the chambermaid holds the goblet in a cloth (as Simeon holds the Christ child with hands covered by a cloth in mediaeval pictures); she holds something holy, numinous, the transient remains of a mighty personage, a king. The queen points to her body, which will now be the living tomb of the dead king. The old servant is a mute witness of this exemplary action, the narrative context of which he provides and which he characterises by his oriental dress as an event in the ancient world.

Carl Neumann observed in 1922:

> There is a life-size seated female figure...who is offered something to drink in a vessel made of a nautilus shell. This picture is now called 'Sophonisba with the Poisoned Cup'. Earlier she was called Cleopatra or Artemisia; nothing in her expression helps us to identify such an emotive moment; she is a mannequin for a magnificent costume.[223]

Werner Weisbach objected in 1926: 'Anyone who takes exception to the calm, almost apathetic bearing of the woman at a moment of such agitation should be reminded that this is a costume portrait and not a history as such'.[224] In this way Rembrandt's intention is entirely mistaken, the Baroque artist's language ignored, the quiet tones of the picture disregarded — perhaps partly because the authors knew the picture only through indifferent reproductions.

The woman's calm bearing is explained by the solemn, almost sacred situation and the dignity of the action. Artemisia becomes herself the living tomb of her husband and does so in freedom and royal dignity. Her rich attire does not indicate a costume piece but is inherent in the theme: Artemisia is a queen. Even artists before Rembrandt emphasised this, which does not mean that great care and artistic subtlety have not been expended in rendering the precious materials.

Albrecht DÜRER.
BUST OF A WEEPING CHERUB. About 1521.
Led-tin stylus on blue-primed paper, heightened in white. 214 × 199 mm.
Berlin-Dahlem, Staatliche Museen Preussischer Kulturbesitz, Kupferstichkabinett.

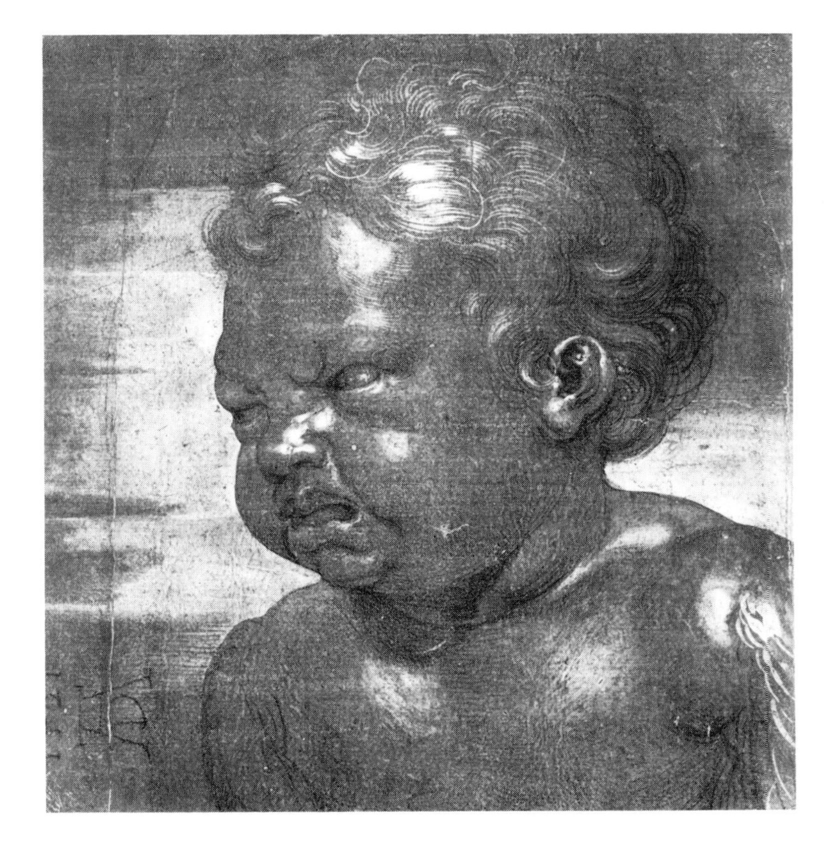

In Leyden Rembrandt had primarily painted less-than-life-size studies of heads. In Amsterdam, for the heads as well as for the histories, he chooses a larger format, depicting most historical figures life size. The choice of subjects also changes. In the Leyden period he had done studies of his mother, his father, and Leyden models which were incorporated in his histories as the prophetess Hannah, Jeremiah, and other prophets and as disciples, apostles, and onlookers. Now he paints Turkish or Oriental potentates, heroes or scholars. (186, 192, 194, 195) As in the histories, he clearly wants to give more attention to the study of the great biblical heroes (as in the histories of Abraham and Samson). The usually life-size heads of Old Testament of Oriental princes and scholars are frequently impossible to name, being usually referred to in contemporary sources only by general titles; unless they hold specific iconographic motifs in their hands, we can interpret them in many different ways. However, Rembrandt or his client may have had particular historical figures in mind. Only if we recognise the model used by Rembrandt can we identify a figure. For example, in the painting in Chatsworth not correctly interpreted until now, he portrays the Old Testament hero DAN, (193) following an engraving by H. Goltzius. Dan was one of the early fathers of Israel, whose symbol was a snake and who was a judge in Israel. Rembrandt shows the snake coiled round a staff on a table in the background.

As compared to the Leyden period, when Rembrandt overpainted many of the heads he had produced for study purposes or to be incorporated in histories, in the 1630s the studies of heads and historical figures lose this subordinate function, becoming a class of subjects in their own right. They are no longer produced in preparation for the large histories. Rather, it can be said that in the studies of heads, too, it is now the great heroes which concern him. There are few women among the heads he painted in the 1630s and 1640s. If Rembrandt painted heroines, they were often modelled on Saskia, while heroes were often based on his own self-portraits. In this way the histories were brought temporally close to the onlooker, while they also preserved Saskia's and Rembrandt's own images for posterity.

For Rembrandt's contemporaries, the head studies and historical figures were laden with historical and exotic interest. The Oriental figures were representatives of a strange, distant world that most of them would never have the opportunity to visit, of which travellers, explorers, merchants, and artists brought back novel, remarkable, and bizarre reports. In this remote world, people still lived as they had in biblical times. Motifs from that world could be used in depicting the world of the Old and New Testaments, and portrayals of Eastern princes could serve as models for biblical heroes.

AN OLD MAN.
Signed: 'Rembrandt 1633'.
Wood 9.5 × 6.5 cm.
Queenstown (Maryland), Arthur A. Houghton Jr Collection.
Cat. 134 / Bredius 183.

ORIENTAL NOBLEMAN.
Signed: 'RHL van Rijn 1632'.
Canvas 152.7 × 111.1 cm.
New York, Metropolitan Museum of Art.
Cat. 132 / Bredius 169.

AN OFFICER WITH A GOLD CHAIN. About 1631.
Monogrammed: 'RHL'.
Canvas 83.1 × 75.7 cm.
Chicago, Art Institute.
Cat. 131 / Bredius 81.

AN OLD MAN WITH A TALL FUR CAP.
Signed: 'RHL 1630'.
Wood 22.2 × 17.7 cm.
Innsbruck, Museum Ferdinandeum.
Cat. 129 / Bredius 76.

Rembrandt circle (Jan Lievens?).
OLD MAN. About 1631.
Wood 73.3 × 59.7 cm.
Boston, Museum of Fine Arts.
Cat. A33 / Bredius 73.

Isaac JOUDERVILLE.
YOUNG MAN WITH A GOLD CHAIN.
Faked signature: 'RHL van Rijn 1632'.
Wood 57.8 × 43.8 cm.
Cleveland, Museum of Art.
Cat. A37 / Bredius 156.

Rembrandt's workshop.
YOUNG WOMAN IN A ROBE WITH EMBROIDERED BORDER.
Signed: 'RHL van Rijn 1632'.
Wood 55 × 48 cm.
Milan, Brera Gallery.
Cat. A35 / Bredius 87.

THE STANDARD-BEARER.
Signed: 'Rembrandt f. 1636'.
Canvas 125 × 105 cm.
Paris, private collection.
Cat. 138 / Bredius 433.

Page 191, above:
OLD MAN IN A CAP. About 1630.
Wood 46.9 × 38.8 cm.
The Hague, Mauritshuis.
Cat. 130 / Bredius 77.

Rembrandt's workshop.
AN OFFICER. About 1631.
Faked signature: 'Rembrandt f.', covering the remains of the genuine monogram 'RHL'.
Wood 65 × 51 cm.
Malibu, The J. Paul Getty Museum.
Cat. A34 / Bredius 79.

Page 191, below:
Jan LIEVENS.
REMBRANDT'S MOTHER AS AN HISTORICAL FIGURE. About 1630.
Wood 61 × 47.4 cm.
Windsor Castle, Royal Collection.
Cat. A54 / Bredius 70.

Pupil of Rembrandt (Govaert Flinck?).
REMBRANDT'S MOTHER AS THE PROPHETESS HANNAH.
Signed: 'Rembrandt f. 1639'.
Wood 79.5 × 61.7 cm.
Vienna, Kunsthistorisches Museum.
Cat. A15 / Bredius 71.

Pupil of Rembrandt.
AN OLD MAN IN HISTORICAL COSTUME.
Signed: 'Rembrandt f. 1643'.
Wood 73.7 × 50.7 cm. England, Woburn Abbey.
Cat. A39 / Bredius 185.

Pupil of Rembrandt.
AN OLD MAN WITH BEARD AND GOLD CHAIN.
Signed: 'RHL van Rijn 1632'.
Wood 59.3 × 49.3 cm. Cassel, Gemäldegalerie.
Cat. A36 / Bredius 152.

Rembrandt
f.

A MAN IN ORIENTAL COSTUME. Signed: 'Rembrandt f. 1633'. Wood 85.8 × 63.8 cm. Munich, Alte Pinakothek. Cat. 133 / Bredius 178.

DAN (one of the twelve sons of Jacob). Signed: 'Rembrandt f. 1635'. Wood 101 × 79 cm. Chatsworth, Devonshire Coll. Cat. 77 / Bredius 179.

P. 194:
A MAN IN ORIENTAL COSTUME.
Signed: 'Rembrandt f. 1635'.
Wood 72 × 54.5 cm.
Amsterdam, Rijksmuseum.
Cat. 136 / Bredius 206.

P. 195:
Rembrandt's workshop.
AN ORIENTAL HERO. About 1635.
Signed: 'Rembrandt ft.'.
Canvas 98 × 74 cm.
Washington DC, National Gallery of Art.
Cat. A38 / Bredius 180.

BIBLICAL FIGURE AT A STUDY DESK.
Signed: 'Rembrandt f. 1634'.
Canvas 145 × 135 cm.
Prague, National Gallery.
Cat. 135 / Bredius 432.

A MAN IN HISTORICAL COSTUME.
Signed: 'Rembrandt f. 1636'.
Wood 97 × 66 cm.
Washington DC, National Gallery of Art.
Cat. 137 / Bredius 211.

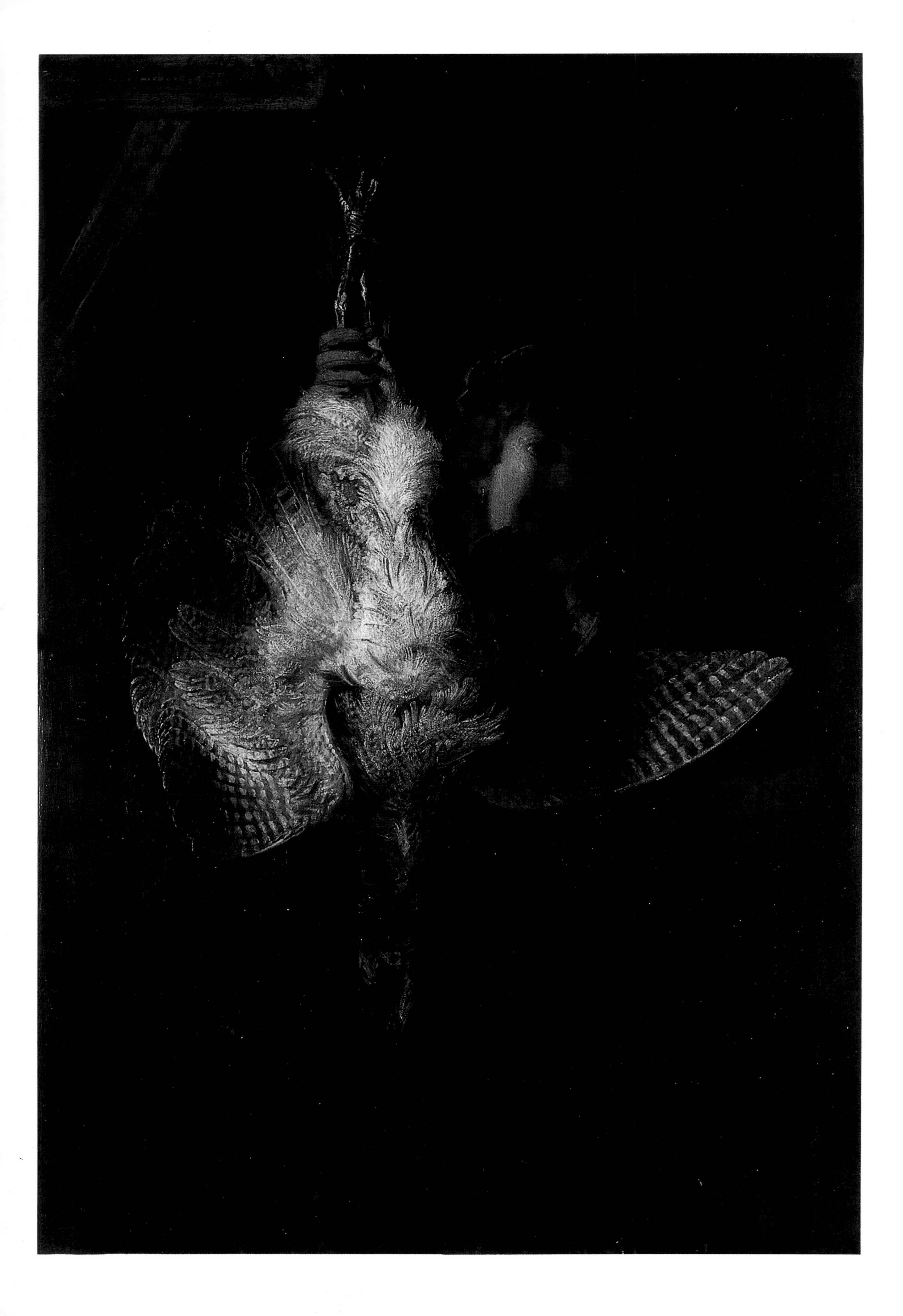

69 What had been prefigured in Rembrandt's self-portrait of 1631 becomes the predominant feature in his first Amsterdam 200 SELF-PORTRAIT, that of 1632: Rembrandt presents himself as a bourgeois personage, with collar and coat and even a hat.[225] He is clearly guided here by the Amsterdam portrait style, in which the oval format for portraits was in fashion. The upper body, with steeply sloping shoulders, is turned slightly to one side, but the face is seen frontally. The clothing, which expresses solidity rather than modishness, imparts to Rembrandt a certain gravity. Accordingly, he no longer emphasises his youthful traits, but those that show the adult. Below the brightly illuminated right eye, the first wrinkles show themselves. Colour and the play of light are concentrated on the face. Bright light falls from the left, illuminating the lobe of the ear, the cheek, and the chin as well as the nose. The flesh colour gleams; on the cheekbone a delicate reflection has formed. The left half of the face, except for a part of the cheek, is in shadow. This graceful interplay sets the head off vividly against the drab, rather flat clothing and the monochrome greyish-brown background. The overall impression is governed by the calm but insistent gaze that 200, 201 rests on the onlooker. The self-portraits produced in 1633 and 1634 are far more animated. Rembrandt presents himself as if he is years older; a deep furrow in his forehead gives him a thoughtful appearance; below the eyes deep wrinkles have appeared; the face has grown fuller. These pictures, too, have been heightened into role portraits; emphasising his rank, he presents himself wearing a golden chain and a slashed beret.[226]

In 1634, the year of his marriage to the daughter of a 199 patrician family, Saskia van Uylenburgh, he paints himself in the SELF-PORTRAIT IN A SATIN CAP AND A COAT WITH A FUR COLLAR as a rich, elegant artist, who clearly takes pleasure in his social success. The composition is far more complex and animated than in either the self-portrait of 1632 or portraits done by others at the same time, because Rembrandt emphasises the asymmetry of the figure's vibrantly drawn outline. Through the structure he creates movements in two opposed directions: the shoulders are aligned diagonally towards the front of the picture, giving its space an appearance of depth, while the head is seen frontally, cutting across this movement. The hair is covered by a beret-like cap which, compressed to the left, gives the figure a somewhat jaunty air. Again the light falls from the left. It illuminates Rembrandt's right shoulder, gleaming on the fur of the collar and the finely woven cloth and making the right cheek the most brightly lit area. The right eye is shaded by the cap;

SELF-PORTRAIT.
Signed: 'Rembrandt f. 1634'.
Wood 58.3 × 47.5 cm.
Berlin-Dahlem, Staatliche Museen Preussischer Kulturbesitz, Gemäldegalerie.
Cat. 164 / Bredius 21.

SELF-PORTRAIT WITH A DEAD BITTERN.
Signed: 'Rembrandt fc. 1639'.
Wood 121 × 89 cm.
Dresden, Gemäldegalerie.
Cat. 167 / Bredius 31.

SELF-PORTRAIT.
Signed: 'RHL van Rijn 1632'.
Wood 63.5 × 47 cm.
Glasgow, Art Gallery and Museum (on loan from the Burrell Collection).
Cat. 161 / Bredius 17.

SELF-PORTRAIT.
Signed: 'Rembrandt f. 1633'.
Wood 60 × 47 cm.
Paris, Louvre.
Cat. 162 / Bredius 18.

SELF-PORTRAIT.
Signed: 'Rembrandt f. 1633'.
Wood 70 × 53 cm.
Paris, Louvre.
Cat. 163 / Bredius 19.

yet, like the shaded left eye, it is not painted altogether dark, giving intensity to the gaze. The light also touches the background. A bright area exactly behind the head glows with reflected light. There are no sharp contours or pronounced colour contrasts in the composition. Colours and tone values are finely attuned to each other. Rembrandt shows himself here to be a painter able to place colour and values at the service of portrait painting.

In the High Baroque phase of his work he makes the heads of some of his heroes, for example, Samson's, resemble his own from a distance. His history painting benefits from the studies of facial expression that he made of himself and, above all, of Saskia. But his portrait painting is also reflected in his history painting. In the famous painting THE PRODIGAL SON IN THE BROTHEL, Rembrandt presents himself as the Prodigal Son, Saskia as a harlot. The portrait-like qualities of the picture, which originally had a horizontal format, are made clearer by the reduced size, the overpainting, and the concentration on two people. The 'first-person formula' of the painting, which was also common in Baroque poetry, gives the story actuality. It is a Prodigal Son painted from life, a Prodigal Son of today.[227]

158
117

The SELF-PORTRAIT WITH A DEAD BITTERN (1639), also a role portrait, is one of the most complex conceptions of Rembrandt's Baroque period. The main theme is the bittern, which, however, is not rendered in a still-life manner (like

198

Pupil of Rembrandt.
REMBRANDT ('SELF-PORTRAIT').
Signed: 'Rembrandt f. 1634'.
Wood 80.5 × 66 cm.
Cassel, Gemäldegalerie.
Cat. A66 / Bredius 22.

Rembrandt's workshop.
REMBRANDT ('SELF-PORTRAIT'). About 1633/34.
Wood 56 × 47 cm.
Berlin-Dahlem, Staatliche Museen Preussischer Kulturbesitz, Gemäldegalerie.
Cat. A65 / Bredius 23.

Imitator of Rembrandt.
REMBRANDT ('SELF-PORTRAIT'). About 1643.
Signed: 'Rembrandt f. 164(.)'.
Wood 67.5 × 57.5 cm.
Windsor Castle, Royal Collection.
Cat. A69 / Bredius 37.

SELF-PORTRAIT (?). About 1636/37.
Wood 62.9 × 46.8 cm.
The Hague, Mauritshuis.
Cat. 165 / Bredius 24.

SELF-PORTRAIT. ▶
Signed: 'Rembrandt f. 1640', inscribed by another hand: 'conterfeycel'.
Canvas 102 × 80 cm.
London, National Gallery.
Cat. 168 / Bredius 34.

Pupil of Rembrandt.
REMBRANDT ('SELF-PORTRAIT'). About 1640.
Signed: 'Rembrandt '.
Wood 64 × 49 cm.
London, Wallace Collection.
Cat. A68 / Bredius 27.

Govaert FLINCK.
REMBRANDT ('SELF-PORTRAIT'). About 1640.
Signed: 'Rembrandt '(by a later hand).
Wood 57.5 × 44 cm.
São Paulo, Museum of Art.
Cat. A67 / Bredius 26. ▼

SELF-PORTRAIT. About 1638.
Signed: 'Rembrandt f. 163(.)'.
Wood 63.2 × 50.1 cm.
Pasadena, Norton. Simon Museum of Art (The Norton Simon Foundation).
Cat. 166 / Bredius 32.

SELF-PORTRAIT, LEANING ON HIS ARM.
Signed: 'Rembrandt f.' and dated 1639.
Etching 207 × 164 mm. 2nd state.
Hamburg, Kunsthalle. Bartsch 21.

RAPHAEL.
PORTRAIT OF BALDASSARE CASTIGLIONE. 1514/15.
Canvas 82 × 67 cm.
Paris, Louvre.

PORTRAIT OF BALDASSARE CASTIGLIONE (after Raphael). Dated 1639.
Pen with bistre and white paint. 163 × 207 mm.
Vienna, Graphische Sammlung Albertina.
Benesch 451.

206 the birds in the CHILD WITH DEAD PEACOCKS, for example), but is incorporated into an action. Rembrandt has painted himself life size in a three-quarter-length portrait as an aristocratic huntsman hanging a shot bittern by its feet on a hook. The wings fill almost the full width of the picture, and the rich, variegated structure, the diversity of the feathers, and the down on the body are displayed in their full beauty. The light falls from the left on to the bittern's body. 'What a symphony of colours is kindled by this light! What polyphony unfolds in this cool grey, warm smoke-brown and brownish-gold white, fiery reddish accents at the neck and head' (Otto Benesch).[228] However, Rembrandt does not fully illuminate the bird: only a few rays fall on the head and neck, and the right wing remains in darkness except for its tip. The bittern with its spreading feathers fills the foreground parallel to the picture plane. Rembrandt himself remains largely in shadow in the middle ground. Only a narrow strip of his face, the corner of his right eye, and the edge of his cap are touched by light, as is his gloved right hand that holds up the rare bird. Over the bittern Rembrandt's gaze from the semi-darkness is directed straight at the onlooker.

The content of the picture has many layers. The dead bittern with the hook reminds us of the transience of all earthly things, and of the beauty of nature which art approaches. But like the Amsterdam kitchen still life, the presentation of the bird killed during a hunt has a moralising aspect, calling to mind the nullity of the things with which we occupy ourselves. An erotic meaning is also often assigned to pictures of hunters who have killed birds. The dead creature is naturally also a hunting trophy, and the depiction of a bird as uncommon as the bittern satisfies our delight in curiosities.

203 The SELF-PORTRAIT of 1640, one of his finest, also shows Rembrandt in a role. He presents himself as an aristocrat, as 204 Raphael had painted Count Castiglione. When Lucas van Uffelen's extraordinary collection of paintings was auctioned on 9 April 1639, it included Raphael's portrait of Baldassare 204 Castiglione. Rembrandt made a sketch of the picture and annotated it: 'Count Batasor de Kastijlijone by Raphael, sold for 3,500 guilders; the entire proceeds to van Nuffelen amounted to 59,456 fl. — 1639'.[229] At the auction Alphonso Lopez, arms dealer to the king of France, financier and diamond trader, who supervised the building of warships for Louis XIII in Amsterdam, outbid the painter Joachim von Sandrart. Lopez's collection also included the so-called PORTRAIT OF ARIOSTO by Titian, which Rembrandt must have seen there.[230] Both these works of the Italian Renaissance inspired the self-portrait. The aristocratic pose was also suggested by Titian's so-called PORTRAIT OF ARIOSTO, who likewise turns towards the onlooker and rests his elbow self-confidently on a balustrade, so that his garment bulges to form a base. In Rembrandt's picture there is, in addition, a cloak with voluminous folds hung over the right arm, on which he leans.

SELF-PORTRAIT WITH SASKIA.
Etching 104 × 96 mm. 1st state.
Paris, Bibliothèque Nationale.
Bartsch 19.

Still life and genre scenes, which became increasingly popular in Dutch art in the 17th century, are very uncommon in Rembrandt's painting.

206 The still life A CHILD WITH TWO DEAD PEACOCKS derives from the Amsterdam Mannerist kitchen still life, in which a rich array of fruit and animals on one hand glorifies the majesty of the Creator and on the other, through an interpretative biblical or genre scene, warns against the seductive dangers of wealth. (In modern art history the first aspect — the celebration of the Creator through the beauty of Creation, which was central to the natural theology of the Golden Age — is usually overlooked.)

Rembrandt does not overload his picture with animals and fruit: he concentrates on a few motifs, two peacocks and (as the interpretative scene) a child looking on. Rembrandt did not choose peacocks for his still life without reason, for these birds were regarded as especially beautiful in the Baroque period. Their glorious plumage revealed the majesty of God, who, contrary to human notions, had in his goodness bestowed such a gift on so stupid a creature.

But the peacocks are not only symbols of the beauty of Creation. H. H. Frey, in 1595, presented a spiritual and moral interpretation of the qualities of animals, their attributes symbolising those of human beings. Peacocks are regarded as vain and spiteful, like monkeys.

Rembrandt depicts two examples of this bird that has been laden with so much significance in the long history of its interpretation. One hangs by its feet from a window shutter, the feathers of its wings spread out while those of its fine tail project towards the onlooker. A second lies on the table, with 198 its blood draining from it. As in the SELF-PORTRAIT WITH A BITTERN, the glorious plumage of the majestic bird calls to mind the beauty of Nature, behind which the omnipotence of the Creator is visible. At the same time, the dead creatures remind us of transience, which is symbolised not only by their death and the flowing blood, but by the peacocks' typical characteristics and the human vanity they represent, as well as the nullity of all extravagant wealth.

Not without reason does Rembrandt depict, as the contemplator of this kitchen still life, a child whose meditative mood is meant to reflect and guide that of the onlooker.

Among Rembrandt's paintings — leaving aside the con- 30, 31 troversial early works — genre scenes play a less important 207 part. In the case of A SCHOLAR IN A ROOM WITH A WINDING STAIR, I am not even sure that this really is a genre scene. It might equally well be an Old Testament history or an allegory of the seasons. Seymour Slive has shown that Rembrandt's use of perspective in the interior is based on an engraving by Vredeman de Vries in a book on perspective. Rembrandt took the spatial and linear structure of the stair from his model and embellished it with masterful chiaroscuro values in his complex rendering of space. The old man is illuminated by natural daylight, the young woman in the foreground by artificial light at the open fireplace. The old woman climbing the stair is shown in dim semi-darkness. Rembrandt used variations of this complex spatial structure in two history scenes: the etching ST JEROME IN HIS STUDY and the painting TOBIAS HEALING HIS BLIND FATHER. 163

A SCHOLAR IN A ROOM WITH A WINDING STAIR.
Signed: 'RHL van Rijn 163(2)'.
Wood 28 × 34 cm.
Paris, Louvre.
Cat. 120 / Bredius 431.

A CHILD WITH TWO DEAD PEACOCKS. About 1636/37.
Signed: 'Rembrandt '.
Canvas 145 × 135.5 cm.
Amsterdam, Rijksmuseum.
Cat. 121 / Bredius 456.

Rembrandt: f: 1639

REMBRANDT AGAIN ACCEPTS PORTRAIT COMMISSIONS

From 1631 to 1634 Rembrandt received a flood of portrait commissions. He painted almost 40 portraits in this period, and his students participated in the execution of some of these. After that his success abated. In the following years he produced few portraits, mostly pendants to others painted earlier. How is this to be explained? Baldinucci writes in 1686:

> He would have been able to secure commissions for a large number of portraits, thanks to the good reputation he owed to his use of colour, which certainly outstripped his skill in drawing. But as soon as it became generally known that anyone who wanted their portrait done by him would have to sit for two or three months, few were found willing.[231]

According to Baldinucci, Rembrandt worked too slowly and frightened off possible clients. I do not agree that this was the real reason. It conflicts with Uyttenbogaert's diary entry to the effect that Rembrandt had painted his portrait in one day. It is more likely that Rembrandt almost stopped accepting portrait commissions because he wished to devote himself again to history painting, etching, and instructing his pupils. In the first Amsterdam phase, his earnings had been good, and his wife, Saskia van Uylenburgh, had brought a fortune of some 40,700 guilders into the marriage, three times as much as the fashionable house in the Antonisbreestraat was to cost. So he was no longer obliged to paint portraits, which were ranked lower than history paintings by art theoreticians and were regarded merely as a source of income. In commercial terms Rembrandt did not make very adroit use of his wife's 'dowry of millions'. When he bought the expensive house on the Antonisbreestraat in 1639, he could not afford the down payment; he had finally to complete the two pictures for the stadholder, which had stood half finished in his workshop for three years, and again accept portrait commissions. But after raising Amsterdam portrait painting for three years to a new level, he now had to contend with competition in style and price from his own pupils and from new portrait painters.

After all that we have learned up to now about Rembrandt and his clients and about the function of portraits as status symbols, it does not surprise us that the clients came from the same circles as previously: the city patricians, rich merchants, and Rembrandt's own circle.

208 Andries de Graeff (1611-1678), who was immortalised by Rembrandt in a full-length portrait in 1639, came from a very successful patrician family.[232] He was twelve years younger than his brother Cornelis. In 1633 the latter

PORTRAIT OF A MAN HOLDING A GLOVE. About 1641.
Signed: 'Rembra... f. 164.'.
Wood 81 × 67 cm.
New York, Metropolitan Museum of Art.
Cat. 209 / Bredius 221.

ANDRIES DE GRAEFF (1611-1679).
Signed: 'Rembrandt fc. 1639'.
Canvas 200 × 124.2 cm.
Cassel, Gemäldegalerie.
Cat. 206 / Bredius 216.

ALETTA ADRIAENSDR.
Signed: 'Rembrandt 1639' (?). Wood 64.7 × 55.3 cm.
Rotterdam, Boymans-van Beuningen Museum (Willem van der Vorm Foundation).
Cat. 240 / Bredius 355.

MARIA TRIP, DAUGHTER OF ALETTA ADRIAENSDR. (1629-1683).
Signed: 'Rembrandt f. 1639'.
Wood 107 × 82 cm.
Amsterdam, Rijksmuseum (on loan from the Van Weede Foundation).
Cat. 241 / Bredius 356.

THE FRAME-MAKER HERMAN DOOMER (1595-1650).
Signed: 'Rembrandt f. 1640'.
Wood 75.2 × 55.2 cm.
New York, Metropolitan Museum of Art.
Cat. 207 / Bredius 217.

took as his first wife the burgomaster's daughter Geertruyd Overlander, the second daughter of the enormously rich Mr. Volckert Overlander, thereby becoming the brother-in-law of Dr. Frans Banning Cocq. On his father's death he inherited his noble title, took his place in the municipal council, and became a captain of the militia. His company, like that of Cocq, belonged to the Cloveniers; if Cocq had himself and his company painted by Rembrandt, Graeff engaged Jacob Adriaensz. Backer. When a brother-in-law of Cornelis de Graeff, Dr. Jan Bicker, was elected burgomaster in 1653, the government of Amsterdam was again in the hands of a few closely related families. After the early death of Frans Banning Cocq in 1655, Andries de Graeff became burgomaster, supporting the rule of his brother Cornelis ans later becoming his successor.

218
224

Andries de Graeff had himself portrayed as a rich patrician's son. Then twenty-eight, he had received a good education, obtaining a licentiate at the University of Poitiers in 1634. In 1646, seven years after Rembrandt had painted his picture, he became a lay assessor and thereby a member of the municipal council. In the same year, he married a burgomaster's daughter, Elisabeth Bicker van Swieten. Rembrandt paints the young de Graeff already dressed as a member of the municipal council, so certain was his career. He placed the young patrician at his full height before a fireplace; with his right elbow resting on the mantlepiece, he leans slightly back. The wide cloak folds decoratively over a projection in the wall and opens expansively. Except for his collar, Andries de Graeff is dressed entirely in black. So the broad, full face and long hair are enclosed and given special emphasis by the broad white collar and the broad-brimmed black hat. The left arm hangs loosely, the hand gloved. The right glove lies on the floor. The legs, in silk breeches with frills at the calves, are in a loose stepping position, so that the posture conveys calm and movement at once. Beyond a curved step, an adjoining room with a tiled floor is to be seen on the right; a side wall frames a heavy, iron-studded door. The glimpse of this room stresses the rich furnishings of patrician houses and also their military aspect. Cornelis de Graeff had himself painted in a similar milieu.

In 1639 Rembrandt painted two ladies from the richest Amsterdam society: ALETTA ADRIAENSDR. and her beautiful daughter MARIA TRIP. The Trips came from Zaltbommel. They came to Amsterdam via Dordrecht. Elias Trip (1570-1636), Aletta Adriaensdr.'s husband and Maria's father, had begun as a metal trader. Arms production and arms trading were added later. By marrying into the de Geer family, he and his brother gained part-ownership of Swedish copper mines, and the Trip brothers' firm grew into a world-wide concern. Despite their wealth they did not have a share of power in Amsterdam. The clan of the de Graeffs and the de Bickers still held all the strings in their hands. Only when Gillis Valckenier succeeded in depriving Andries de Graeff of power, in 1672, were the Trips admitted through him to the city aristocracy.

210
211

Although the Trips were not recognised by the city aristocracy, they kept up relations with the stadholder's court. This probably influenced the commissioning of the two portraits which Rembrandt produced in 1639. In 1638 the banished queen, Maria de' Medici, arch-enemy of Richelieu, paid a surprise visit to the northern Netherlands. On 14 August she was officially received at Den Bosch. Four days later the municipal council heard from The Hague that she wished to see Amsterdam. To the newly rich patricians of Amsterdam, the reception of a queen, even a deposed one, was a welcome opportunity. Although they had only two weeks' notice, they prepared a magnificent reception. The queen was welcomed by the entire militia, bearing arms. She was honoured with triumphal arches and tableaux vivants. As the preparations had been made in some haste and the performances were not comprehensible to everyone, Barläus, in a work published in Latin, French, and Dutch, recorded the events and documented them with illustrations after paintings by Gerard Honthorst and Thomas Keyzer, and after drawings by Jan Maertsen de Jonge, Claes Moeyaert and others.[233] During her stay in Amsterdam Maria de' Medici had her portrait painted by the court painter at The Hague, Gerard Honthorst, and presented the picture to the Amsterdam burgomasters. Maria de' Medici, who spent the night at the Prinzenhof, was accompanied by Amalia von Solms, who for her part spent the night at the house of Aletta Adriaensdr. It seems to have been Amalia von Solms who brought Rembrandt to Aletta Adriaensdr.'s notice; as we recall, he had painted her portrait in 1632. So Rembrandt was commissioned to produce a half-length-figure portrait.

210 The portrait of ALETTA ADRIAENSDR. radiates dignity. One hand rests on the edge of a painted table covered by a red cloth, only a narrow strip of it being visible. The shape of the body is concealed by a heavy black garment. About the neck is a shoulder-width double ruff; the hair is covered by a simple black bonnet. It is a costume which reduces all signs of personality to the face. The upright posture of the head matches the subject's clear, steadfast gaze. A barely perceptible smile plays at the corners of the mouth.

While the portrait of the widowed mother has a certain astringent severity, the life-size three-quarter-length portrait 211 of her twenty-year-old daughter has great charm and delicacy. Here Rembrandt displays the full pyrotechnics of his technique, showing himself a master of fine-detail painting (*Feinmalerei*), and brilliantly rendering the sumptuous dress, the precious gems, the expensive lacework, the soft skin, and the fine hair in their substantiality. Maria Trip stands in front of a broad arch, resting her hand on the back of an armchair. The view of the interior is lost in darkness. On the left, the grotesque caryatid of a fireplace is half visible; behind Maria Trip there is a heavy wall-hanging. The three-quarter-length figure, in contrast to these shaded areas, is brightly illuminated. Everything combines to emphasise the status of the portrait's subject. She wears a glistening, richly ornamented black satin robe. The high waist is emphasised by an embroidered belt, from which a similarly embroidered sash hangs over the skirt. On her shoulders lies a threefold white collar hemmed with white lace, which half covers an embroidered shirt-front of finest cambric. It is wonderful how Rembrandt has here captured both materiality and transparency: where the lace lies directly on the satin, there is a gleaming dark undertone, but where several layers of lace are superimposed or where skin colour is visible through the lace, the white is brighter. The locket chain and the pearl necklace shine through the lace where it covers them. Broad double-layered white cuffs adorn the sleeves; they have the same lace edges as the collar. At the seams the sleeves reveal the bright lining material. There are four strings of pearls around each wrist, and the necklace has especially large pearls. The ear-rings with large, drop-shaped pearls match the heavy brooch, which is similarly decorated with hanging drop-shaped pearls. All these details appear clear and plastic in the bright light. The face, the reddish-blond ringlets of hair, the throat, and the hands all give the same clear, bright impression. Maria Trip seems to smile a little, yet her expression speaks at the same time of the dignity and aloofness of her high social status. The dress of Maria de' Medici, the queen mother, had been similarly rich and elegant.

Rich and elegant, likewise, is the couple that Rembrandt painted in 1641 and whose name was discovered only two decades ago through the very meritorious research of an outstanding archivist, I. van Eeghen, who has uncovered the secrets of numerous portraits.[234] In the light of what we know of the social status of those whose portraits Rembrandt painted, it is not surprising that in this richly dressed woman we have before us a burgomaster's daughter, married to a successful exporter: Agatha Bas. Her father, Dr. Dirck Jacobsz. Bas, had been burgomaster on a number of occasions since 1610, and her grandfather and great-grandfather had also filled this office. Dr. Dirck Jacobsz. Bas was especially esteemed by his contemporaries for his tolerance towards those of different denominations. He was active in the diplomatic service, including that of the States General. We are not surprised to learn that, like many Amsterdam city aristocrats, he was knighted (in 1616 by King Gustav Adolf of Sweden).

BAARTJEN MARTENS, WIFE OF HERMAN DOOMER (1596-1678).
Signed: 'Re(.)brant'.
Wood 76 × 56 cm.
Leningrad, Hermitage.
Cat. 242 / Bredius 357.

His daughter was married on 27 April 1638 to Nicolaes van Bambeeck. By the standards of the day she was at 27 no longer a young bride, but bore this with dignity, giving her age correctly in the marriage banns. Nicolaes van Bambeeck, fifteen years her senior, made himself a few years younger. He came from a rich merchant family that did not belong to the city aristocracy. His business, primarily in Spanish wool, must have been very profitable. The parental house was in the Anthonisbreestraat. It is this that probably brought Bambeeck into contact with Hendrick van Uylenburgh, to whom in 1640 he advanced money for his art dealing. Uylenburgh still owed him money in 1655.[235] It is likely that

Uylenburgh was the middle-man in this portrait commission, if Rembrandt did not himself know Bambeeck.

214 In the portrait of NICOLAES VAN BAMBEECK he heightens the complex composition of Titian's painting of ARIOSTO, which served as his model, using motifs taken from paintings by Frans Hals. Bambeeck rests his left hand on the painted frame of the picture. In his right hand he holds gloves which cut across this painted frame.

These trompe-l'oeil effects are also used by Rembrandt in 215 the portrait of AGATHA BAS. She holds a spread fan which likewise cuts across the painted picture frame. She leans with her left hand against the painted side of the frame, her thumb overlapping it.

By cutting across space in this way, the figures are no longer confined to the picture plane; we have the impression that they are present before us, standing in a darker interior.

The trompe-l'oeil effect was undoubtedly suggested to Rembrandt by paintings by Frans Hals. The prestigious 214, 215 presentation of the figures in the two portraits of married 212, 213 couples produced shortly before also shows Hals's influence.[236] They can be compared, for example, to the double portraits of ANDRIES VAN DER HOORN and his wife, MARIA OLYCAN PIETERSDR. But from these suggestions Rembrandt produces something quite new. Through the painted picture frames we are given the impression that the subjects are looking from an open door or window, behind which a 215 room is lost in darkness. AGATHA BAS is fully illuminated. The expensive robe with insertions at bodice and waist and the threefold lace-trimmed collar, the hand with the fan that overlaps the frame, lace-trimmed cuffs — all of these are both exquisite and plastic. In the bright illumination her skin seems very delicate. The brightly lit face is turned towards the visitor; the thin curls gleam reddish blond. Grace is allied to the dignity of a married woman. In contrast, BAMBEECK, who is shown in three-quarter profile, is placed in 214 shadow, so that the shadow emphasises the manly tonality of the flesh colour beside the light feminine tones.

In the portraits of the couple HERMAN DOOMER and 212 BAERTJEN MAERTENS, Rembrandt also made use of composi- 213 tions which had been developed by Frans Hals in the 1630s. Even the way in which Rembrandt paints the wife's slight smile is influenced by the great Haarlem portraitist.

Herman Doomer was a craftsman. He produced ebony frames and had obtained a patent on frames made of whalebone. Perhaps Doomer also made picture frames for Rembrandt; his son Lambert was apprenticed to the artist. Doomer, like many citizens of Amsterdam, was of German origin; in 1618 he married Baertjen Maertens, a simple girl who could not even write her own name. After her husband's death, Baertjen Maertens made various wills in which the portraits by Rembrandt are mentioned. Her son Lambert was to inherit them and make copies for all his brothers and sisters; the originals were always to go to the eldest son.

If we compare these impressive portraits of an artisan couple with those of the patricians and wealthy merchants from 1639 and 1641, we are struck by a great difference both in the dress of the persons and in Rembrandt's style. How much more modest is the clothing: the artisan couple does not play coquettishly with gloves serving as status symbols;

Page 214:
NICOLAAS VAN BAMBEECK (1596-1661).
Signed: 'Rembrandt f. 1641'. Additional inscription: 'Ae(tatis) 44'.
Canvas 105.5 × 84 cm.
Brussels, Musées Royaux des Beaux-Arts.
Cat. 208 / Bredius 218.

Page 215:
AGATHA BAS (1611-1658), WIFE OF NICOLAAS VAN BAMBEECK.
Signed: 'Rembrandt f. 1641' and 'AET 29'.
Canvas 105.2 × 83.9 cm.
London, Buckingham Palace, Collection of Her Majesty the Queen.
Cat. 243 / Bredius 360.

we look in vain for a fan. In place of a many-layered lace collar, we find an old-fashioned Spanish ruff. Rembrandt's style, as in the double portrait of CORNELIS ANSLO AND HIS WIFE, is much freer; he indicates the materials more summarily, using abbreviations in the rendering of the husband's collar, for example, whereas in the portraits of the noble and rich he had adhered to an almost draughtsmanlike manner of painting reminiscent of Mierefeldt, exactly reproducing each detail.

121

In the four years from 1639 to 1642, Rembrandt received fewer portrait commissions than in 1631-34. Had he become too expensive? Was he being undercut by painters like Nicolaes Eliasz., Jacob Adriaensz. Backer, Bartholomeus van der Helst, Joachim von Sandrart, and his own pupil Govert Flinck? At all events, the competition had grown stiffer, for apart from the painters just mentioned, who like Rembrandt were commissioned to paint group portraits for the new Doelensaal, there were other young portrait painters who had been attracted to Amsterdam. Some had even been trained by Rembrandt.

But there was something else. Rembrandt obviously felt impelled to create new, unknown solutions on the basis of great masterpieces. In the so-called NIGHT WATCH, on which he had been working since about 1639/40, he was investing far more time than was economically justified. So he could no longer accept commissions for full-length portraits, although he earned considerably more from them, in relation to his time, than from the group portraits.

For the first time, too, criticism of Rembrandt's chiaroscuro seems to have been voiced. At any rate, Joachim von Sandrart was already painting his group portraits in the classical style especially prized by the patricians.[237] He later censored Rembrandt's style in his famous *Academia* (1675) on grounds of deficient draughtsmanship.[238] It is noteworthy that at this time we hear for the first time of a conflict between Rembrandt and a client: Andries de Graeff — for unknown reasons — refused to pay. The intervention of Hendrick Uylenburgh was needed to resolve the disagreement.[239] At all events, at the beginning of the 1640s there seems to have been a debate on style in portraiture, for in 1644, Rembrandt drew a satire on art critics: a connoisseur with donkey's ears (as complacent and obtuse as Midas, who grew ass's ears as punishment) criticises, before a group of spectators, a portrait lying at their feet. The artist, in the right foreground, excretes (on the criticism).[240] He is not ready to bow to the style of the time.

225

At about the time Rembrandt moved to the Jodenbreestraat, he must have received the commission for the so-called NIGHT 218 WATCH, his most famous painting, and one surrounded by legends.[241] Three widely held views on this picture are pure inventions. Firstly, the title NIGHT WATCH does not describe the actual contents. Secondly, it is not true that Rembrandt portrayed his subjects performing a scene from a well-known contemporary play. Thirdly, it is not correct that the unusual composition of this group portrait brought Rembrandt into disrepute as a portraitist.

The inaccuracy of the name NIGHT WATCH is clear from the fact that in the 17th and 18th centuries the painting was referred to as THE COMPANY OF FRANS BANNING COCQ, the name NIGHT WATCH only emerging about the end of the 18th century, when the numerous layers of varnish had darkened, giving the impression of a night scene.

78-79 The painting, like THE ANATOMY LESSON OF DR. TULP, is a group portrait of a guild. The people portrayed are Captain Cocq, Lieutenant Willem van Ruytenburgh, and members of the militia. They belonged to the 'Cloveniers' or marksmen. Seventeenth-century Amsterdam had three guilds of marksmen, dating back to the Middle Ages.[242] The oldest and most honourable of them was the Guild of Crossbowmen, which had received its name from that medieval weapon. As the city expanded, two further guilds were formed, which chose the longbow and crossbow as their respective weapons. In 1520 a guild for firearms, the Cloveniers' Guild, was formed and received all the rights and honours of the oldest guild, which was disbanded. While in the course of time the two other guilds also took up firearms, they kept as their emblems the weapons after which they had been named, the longbow and the crossbow. The duties of the guilds were various. In times of emergency they had to defend the city against the enemy, carry out night watches, and parade on festive occasions. Each guild met regularly on its shooting range, and these training sessions were always connected with meetings in the guildhouses, or 'target houses', (*doelen*), as they were called. So the guilds were social unions and often represented political groupings of citizens. In 1580, the Citizens' Militia was formed and absorbed these three old guilds. The city was divided into districts and the citizens of each were formed into a company whose officers came from the leading families.

The guildhouse of the Cloveniers was the Swijg Utrecht Tower, which stood on the strategically important road to Utrecht and had an adjacent shooting range. In the 1630s they built a new guard-house nearby in the recently opened

Unknown artist.
COAT-OF-ARMS OF THE COUNCIL OF WAR OF THE CITY OF AMSTERDAM (with the original weapons of the three guilds of guardsmen and the coat-of-arms of the city of Amsterdam). About 1650.
Water-colour from the family album of Frans Banning Cocq.
Amsterdam, Rijksmuseum (on loan).

CAPTAIN FRANS BANNING COCQ GIVES HIS LIEUTENANT THE ORDER FOR THE MILITIA COMPANY TO MARCH (so-called NIGHT WATCH)
Signed: 'Rembrandt f. 1642'.
Canvas 363 × 437 cm.
Amsterdam, Rijksmuseum.
Cat. 254 / Bredius 410.

J. Th. DE BRY after J. Amman.
A SECTION MARCHING. Detail.
Engraving 46 × 285 mm.
Hollstein IV, 27.

Doelenstraat. In proud remembrance of the history of the old guild, the doorway was decorated with its weapons and emblems, including crossed muskets and claws. As the guildhouses were often leased to excellent innkeepers and also had large banqueting halls, they were used for receptions. In 1638, Maria de' Medici and her entourage were entertained there after having been escorted into the city by the militia guilds.

Seven group portraits were commissioned between 1638 and 1645 to decorate the banqueting hall of the Cloveniers' Guild, most of them going to the Rembrandt circle. (Flinck received two, Backer one, and Rembrandt one.) The German Joachim von Sandrart, the old-fashioned Pickenoy, and the young and ambitious Bartholomeus van der Helst also participated in the decoration. 224, 225 224 225, 222 220-221

Like THE ANATOMY LESSON OF DR. TULP, this commission presented Rembrandt with a serious problem. How was he to incorporate the older levels of meaning in the portrait and at the same time avoid the frequently very dry manner used by his predecessors? His solution, similar in principle to that used in THE ANATOMY LESSON OF DR. TULP, showed the company of citizens in a typical situation which connected the various people portrayed. The spoken word has a part to play. On the order of Captain Frans Banning Cocq, 78-79

Bartholomeus VAN DER HELST.
THE MILITIA COMPANY OF CAPTAIN ROELOF BICKER AND LIEUTENANT JAN MICHIELSZ. BLAEUW.
Signed and dated 163(9).
Canvas 235 × 750 cm.
Amsterdam, Rijksmuseum.

Lieutenant Willem van Ruytenburgh gives the order to march. The central, commanding figure of the Captain thus gathers the group behind him. If this scene is compared with THE ANATOMY LESSON OF DR. TULP, it is clear that Rembrandt has here chosen a different moment, for he has caught the action at its inception, not during its progress. The order to march has just been passed to the lieutenant. Some members of the company have heard the order and have begun to form ranks, but the formation is not yet complete.

The idea of achieving order underlies the whole picture and its composition. The two officers are moving towards the centre of the picture, and the rhomboid arrangement of many spears and muskets gives an idea of the principle of order in military exercises, as shown in textbooks and illustrations of the time. The tension between *what has already occurred* and *what has not yet occurred* provides the particular charm of this composition.

Rembrandt has included the emblems of the ancient Guild of Cloveniers in the action at this moment of departure and falling into line. These emblems were the claw and the musket, for the word *clovere* for musket was mistakenly understood in the 17th century as coming from the word *claw*. Rembrandt includes the musket in his painting, not as an added motif divorced from the action, but rather as an integral part of it: it is not merely represented, but actually used. Three marksmen preparing themselves for the march are seen in the foreground of the painting, carrying out a training exercise with their muskets. One is loading his musket, one is shooting, and a third is blowing the powder away.[243] Rembrandt also represented the claw, the old emblem of the guild, at the second centre of the composition.[244] He had noticed that old military prints depicted not only powder boys but also female camp followers, who clearly belonged to the company. They usually carried a chicken or some other fowl in their belts, as they were obviously responsible for the bodily well-being of the soldiers. These women were often as small as children in 16th century paintings because of their relative unimportance.[245] So it occurred to Rembrandt to use little girls as allegorical personifications of the guild. One is carrying in her belt a chicken whose claws are visible and fully lit, but whose head is covered. She also carries the valuable guild drinking horn and a peacock pie, which can be explained only through her allegorical function, for they suggest the banquet celebrating the guild's solidarity.[246] This meal in the *doelen* had a central function within the brotherhood. In 16th-century paintings of such banquets the marksmen are pictured displaying their valuable drinking vessels and pointing to the meal. The

223
222
220

Schets van de Schilderije op de groote Sael van de Cleveniers Doelen, daerinne de Jonge Heer van Purmerlandt, als Capiteyn, geeft last aen Synen Lieutenant, de Heer van Vlaerdingen, om syn Compaignie Burgers te doen marcheren.

Nicolaesz ELIASZ. (called PICKENOY).
THE COMPANY OF CAPTAIN JAN CLAESZ. VLOOSWIJCK AND LIEUTENANT GERRIT HUDDE.
Canvas 340 × 527 cm.
Amsterdam, Rijksmuseum.

banquet was of particular importance in the history of the guilds, for among the privileges they received at their foundation in exchange for their services was a grant of wine from the city on certain days and permission to hold a large banquet. And, after all, THE NIGHT WATCH was commissioned to hang in the hall where the guild's banquets were held.

So in this composition full of movement and gestures, in which every detail was very carefully planned, Rembrandt succeeded not only in emphasizing symbolic embodiments of the guild, but in portraying the most important military members of the company in the central position. To the left and right of the commanders are two clear aisles which give depth to the room. The two little girls have stepped into the aisle on the left. Behind them is the standard bearer, the soldier of highest rank after the officers. He appears as a three-quarters-length figure who is just on the point of raising the flag which bears the coat of arms of Amsterdam. The Dutch word for 'flag' and 'company' are identical. In keeping with their rank, the two sergeants are also shown as almost complete figures. On the left side, Rembrandt has made Sergeant Reimer Engelen stand out from the group by having him seated on the wall of a little canal, and the group opens in front of the second sergeant, Rombout Kemp. Within one company the soldiers fought with various weapons; some were musketeers and others carried pikes or lances. By suggesting further figures, Rembrandt creates the illusion of a complete company. He even shows a drummer who was employed during parades because the drum-roll was a necessary part of the departure. Some soldiers are dressed in a uniform dating from the time of the revolt against the Spaniards. The composition and the manner in which the painting is built up bear witness to an excellent knowledge of the history, tradition, and importance of the guild, to which there are many allusions. An attempted reading of the painting without this detailed knowledge is bound to lead to the most ludicrous interpretations. For example, one scholar came to the conclusion that Rembrandt had depicted the company performing a famous contemporary theatrical piece, because in that particular play the hero wore gloves, as did Frans Banning Cocq. It is almost superfluous to point out that in older depictions of musketeers the captains, who were members of the city aristocracy, wore gloves as a sign of their rank.[247]

Within the history of such portraits of guardsmen, Rembrandt's work represents the most logical solution to the

J. Th. DE BRY after J. Amman.
A SECTION MARCHING.
Engraving 46 × 285 mm.
Hollstein IV, 27.

Two pages from the family album of Frans Banning Cocq, with a copy of the NIGHT WATCH. Water-colour, about 1650.
Amsterdam, Rijksmuseum.

Unknown sculptor.
GABLE STONE FROM THE SWIJG-UTRECHT TOWER. About 1560.
Stone, 28 × 56 × 12 cm.
Amsterdam, Amsterdams Historisch Museum.

DRINKING-HORN OF THE AMSTERDAM CLOVENIERS'GUILD.
Buffalo-horn and silver. Stamp: Amsterdam, C (1547); master's sign: shield with trade-mark.
Height: 37.5 cm.
Amsterdam, Rijksmuseum.

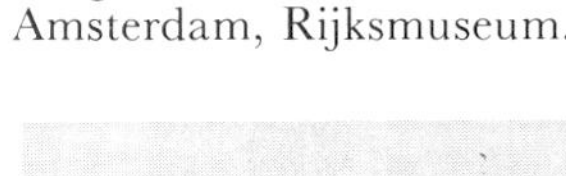

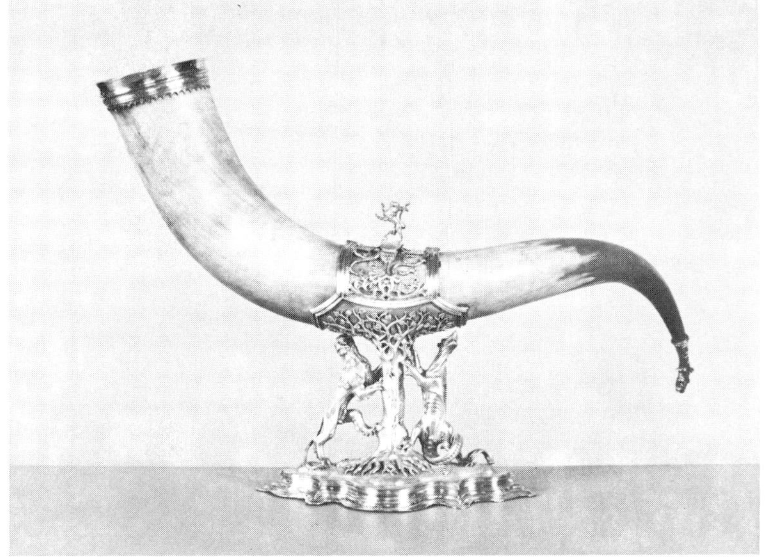

Jacob Adriaensz. BACKER.
THE COMPANY OF CAPTAIN CORNELIS DE GRAEFF AND LIEUTENANT HENDRICK LAUWRENZ. Dated 1642.
Canvas 367 × 511 cm.
Amsterdam, Rijksmuseum.

Govaert FLINCK
THE COMPANY OF CAPTAIN ALBERT BAS AND LIEUTENANT LUCAS CONIJN. Signed and dated 1645.
Canvas 347 × 244 cm.
Amsterdam, Rijksmuseum.

problems posed. It appears, however, that he was not very well paid for this painting. Contemporary sources speak of 1,600 florins, which was about the price of two history paintings.[248] One of his students wrote later, in 1678, about this painting:

> It is not sufficient for a portrait painter to arrange his figures in rows, side by side, as is all too often seen here in Holland in the militia guild halls. The true masters manage to subject their works to one unifying idea. In his piece in the Hall of Guardsmen in Amsterdam, Rembrandt has succeeded in this very well, too well in the opinion of many, for in this large painting he is more concerned with his total concept than with the individual portraits for which he was commissioned. And yet, in my opinion, this picture, however open to criticism, will survive all similar works, because it is so picturesque in its conception, so complex in its composition, and so powerful in its effect that, in the opinion of many, all other group portraits of guardsmen look like playing cards. Even so, I should have preferred him to have introduced somewhat more light into the picture.[249]

After this monumental painting Rembrandt did not receive any major commissions for a long time. This was not because of dissatisfaction with the so-called NIGHT WATCH, but was probably connected with the crises which overtook him in 1642.

Gerrit LUNDENS after Rembrandt.
COPY OF THE SO-CALLED 'NIGHT WATCH'.
Wood 66.5 × 85.5 cm.
London, National Gallery (on loan to Amsterdam, Rijksmuseum).

Govaert FLINCK.
FOUR WARDENS OF THE CLOVENIER'S GUILDHOUSE WITH THEIR HOST. Signed and dated 1642.
Canvas 203 × 278 cm.
Amsterdam, Rijksmuseum.

Joachim VON SANDRART.
THE MILITIA COMPANY OF CAPTAIN CORNELIS BICKER AND LIEUTENANT FREDERICK VAN BANCHEM. About 1638.
Canvas 343 × 258 cm.
Amsterdam, Rijksmuseum.

THE CONCORD OF THE STATE. About 1642.
Signed: 'Rembrandt f. 164(.)'.
Wood 74.6 × 101 cm.
Rotterdam, Boymans-van Beuningen Museum.
Cat. 116 / Bredius 476.

Rembrandt was well informed on the Dutch constitution and the politics of his city. This is shown by his painting THE 227 CONCORD OF THE STATE. He clearly produced it as preparation for a political etching, which was to be provided with explanatory texts at the top and bottom edges of the picture. The commission came to nothing. Rembrandt therefore still owned this picture in 1656. It is mentioned in his inventory. The most convincing account of the details of the picture has been given by Wolfgang Schöne, whose interpretation is reproduced in shortened form below:

> The left complex represents in concentrated form the constitution of the United Free Netherlands and its historical origin. The column stands for their autonomous state power; the parchment volume with four seals which is leaning against it is certainly the document of the Utrecht Union. Into the great throne of the Spanish king, who has lost his seat, the throne of the Netherlands' own sovereignty has been inserted. In the Act of Secession the supreme power in the provinces of the Utrecht Union, denied to the Spanish king, is described by three concepts: princely highness, jurisdiction, and sovereignty over the lands. In Rembrandt's CONCORD OF THE STATE, the slim volume with two seals in the right pan of the scales of justice must signify the declaration of independence; the slender crown on the seat of the throne, the princely highness of the Orange stadholder; the inner seat of the throne with its cushions, sovereignty. The fact that the scales are tilting to the right indicates that independence, 'libertas', weighs more than money and goods. Finally, the four treasure chests arranged around the throne express the idea that the wealth of the land, the 'divitiae', are under the protection and in the service of its sovereignty and constitution. On the carpet lies the Leo Belgicus (the Belgian Lion), a bundle of arrows under its paw. It is chained to the seat of the inner throne and, on the right, to the rock below the coat of arms of Amsterdam; on the left it is chained to the constitution and sovereignty of the United Free Republics and to Justitia, and on the right, to Amsterdam as the leading town in the province of Holland and to the device 'Soli Deo Gloria'. Its anger, which finds expression in the twisting round of its head to roar, while its tail thrashes and its claws tear the ground, is directed [according to Schöne] at the difficult political circumstances of the time. It is probably to these that one of the arrows, which has detached itself from the harmonious bundle and lies aslant, is pointing. This motif is so unusual that it must signify something specific. Above the winged rock the tree of Orange, as mighty as it is old and already strikingly denuded of leaves, rises into the thundery sky. To the left of the tree of Orange, a fortress manned by soldiers firing cannons and muskets. Before the fortress, a horseman in a statuesque pose, not the gallop but a most dignified equestrian gait, the Courbette or Levade. By this horseman Rembrandt undoubtedly meant Prince Frederick Hendrick. The fortress is behind him, the roaring lion below him, the tree of Orange above him. The fortifications extend behind the tree to the edge of the picture at the right. They are also visible in the left background, where a battle is in progress. It is the fortress of Holland and at the same time the pictorial representation of Starters's verses of 1622: '*Ons Eendracht is ons Macht, ons Eendracht sijn ons wallen*' ('Our concord is our might; our concord is our rampart').

It is particularly striking that many horsemen in the background are following Prince Frederick Hendrick into battle, while others are returning to the fortress. In the foreground two riders are mounting their horses. But precisely a knight on a grey horse, whose long saddle-cloth bears the coat of arms of Amsterdam, does not join in these preparations for battle but rides in the opposite direction. He is followed by numerous other horsemen. In these divergent actions of the horsemen (joining and leaving the battle) the political conflict that smouldered in the early 1640s seems to be expressed. Holland, and above all Amsterdam, had in 1640/41 grown weary of Frederick Hendrick's conquests in the border regions, since they had to contribute large sums for them that they would have preferred to spend on the enlargement of their fleet. The states of Holland began to withdraw their troops. The Dutch cities, therefore, were in clear opposition to the stadholder on this point.

> What is entirely new, however, is the way he combines the creation of allegorical emblems with the depiction of action, how he makes the allegorical signs and objects participants in the action while, conversely, the human and animal figures involved in the action become actors of the allegory (Schöne).[250]

This widely disseminated political graphic, working with a known vocabulary, needs verbal inscriptions to accompany its allusions to concrete political situations. As the texts originally intended for the upper and lower margins of Rembrandt's painting have not been passed down to us, only a lucky document find will be able to determine whether the identification suggested here correctly deciphers the political situation to which the scene refers.

LANDSCAPE WITH THE GOOD SAMARITAN.
Signed: 'Rembrandt f. 1638'.
Wood 46.5 × 66 cm.
Cracow, Czartoryski Museum.
Cat. 258 / Bredius 442.

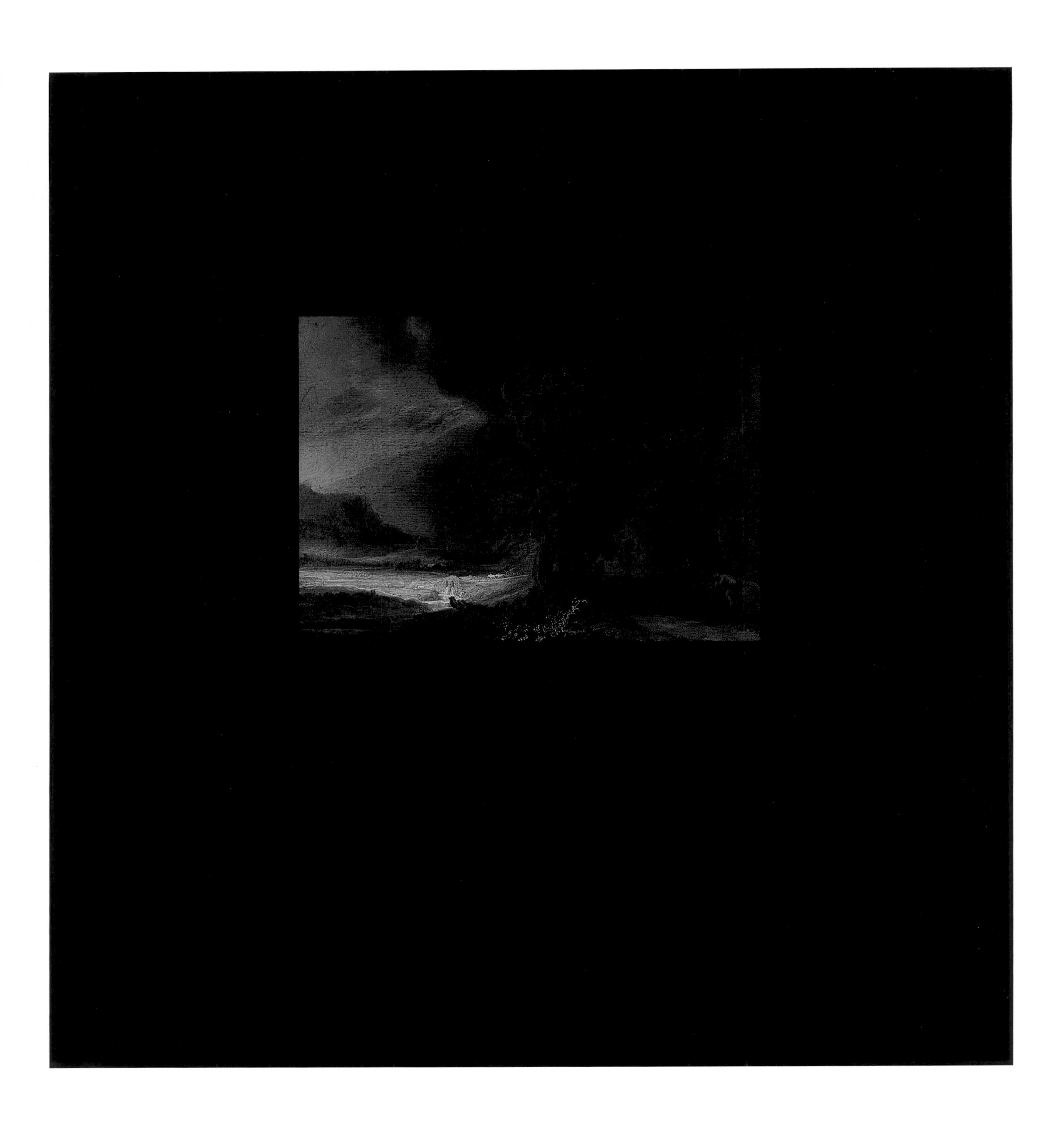

Landscapes make up only a small proportion of Rembrandt's paintings, less than a twentieth of his total output. He began relatively late to produce pure landscape pictures. This was probably because, like most history painters and art theoreticians, he ranked landscapes lower than histories. Unlike his drawings and etchings, which alongside fantastic landscapes show topographically exact reproductions of his surroundings in the manner of his Haarlem models, the landscapes of the paintings are usually invented rather than copied from nature. Just as Rembrandt based his histories on engravings and models, he followed earlier artists in his landscapes as well. As early as 1600, Dutch artists had accepted the proposition disseminated by the Italian Mannerists, and widely adopted in practice, that while Nature should be studied it should never be slavishly copied. It was the artist's duty to improve a landscape in the light of the idea he had formed of it. So Rembrandt is best understood in his paintings as a Baroque interpreter of a Mannerist concept of landscape. But whereas for Mannerism landscape offered a 'world stage' for historical or mythological scenes and was built up strictly in a three-colour perspective in distinct, overlapping planes, Rembrandt treats landscape in his paintings as a unity animated by atmosphere.

His conception of landscape painting was influenced above all by Hercules Seghers. From his inventory of 1656 we know that he owned eight of the latter's rare paintings. Seghers did not paint the typical Dutch landscape, but mountain ranges in a sunlit south, giving them a dramatic effect by illumination, waterfalls, and cliffs. In the earliest dated landscape painting from Rembrandt's workshop, the 230 LANDSCAPE WITH THE BAPTISM OF THE CHAMBERLAIN in Hannover, a rocky landscape blocks the view on the right, while on the left the river in which the baptism has taken place recedes into the distance. The river cascades over waterfalls and is accompanied by rugged groups of trees. In the background a town is visible. The landscape is further dramatised by the use of light and shadow. The foreground and the rocky part are in darkness, but glistening light falls on the group with the chamberlain in the centre and on the waterfall, emphasising the blue of the water and the yellow of the rock in contrast to the blueish-grey tones of the mountain.

228 About 1638 Rembrandt painted the LANDSCAPE WITH THE GOOD SAMARITAN, which is full of dramatic movement. A mighty group of trees painted in reddish-brown tones divides the picture into two halves. To the left, the eye passes over a plain bounded by a ridge on the left and lit by bright sunlight

A COTTAGE AMONGST TREES. Drawing 172 × 271 mm. New York, Metropolitan Museum of Art.

at the centre, since the clouds above it have parted. On the right, by contrast, dark clouds loom. That side of the picture is plunged in darkness. A sunken road is painted in dark brown tones, though it is dimly lit in the foreground and background. Here past and present merge. At the left edge he shows hunters shooting birds. By adding the Good Samaritan leading the wounded man through the defile, he characterises such roads as dangerous, menacing. Govert Flinck, in his Boston painting LANDSCAPE WITH AN OBELISK, 230 took this composition of Rembrandt's as his model. About 1638, Rembrandt painted his STORMY LANDSCAPE. Here he 231 shows a wide view with an agitated sky. From the foreground a broad plain stretches into the distance, bounded on the horizon by a chain of hills rising slowly towards the right. On the left, a high plateau rises towards the background. This is bathed in a livid light, while the slopes falling steeply to the plain are in semi-darkness or darkness.

This concern to dramatise landscape explains Rembrandt's fondness for thunderstorms in his landscapes. They enable him to intensify contrasts between parts shadowed by dark clouds and others where the sun breaks through. This brings movement and tension to the picture and makes the landscape a mirror of the struggles of life. The landscapes are embellished with ruins, viaducts, old churches, castles, and obelisks, which give a heightened exotic character reminiscent of the South and the world of antiquity. The fissured, gnarled trees are to be understood as signs of age and transience. Here, as in many other landscape depictions by contemporaries such as Jacob van Ruysdael, the Baroque idea of the transitoriness of all things emerges. In his life man

passes through storms, but the sun constantly breaks through. At the end of his life's path, golden sunlight falls on the man of faith.

230 In the LANDSCAPE WITH A CASTLE (about 1640), in contrast to the landscape pictures discussed so far, architecture plays a major part. Behind a flat lake flanked to the right by trees, the castle mount juts commandingly, surrounded by mighty walls, bridges, and buildings and painted in brownish-red tones. The landscape lies in darkness. But the low sun's rays strike the right side of the castle, which stands in bright clear light.

Within this group of landscapes the painting LANDSCAPE WITH A STONE BRIDGE is closest to the drawings made directly from nature. In a broad format Rembrandt shows a flat river 230

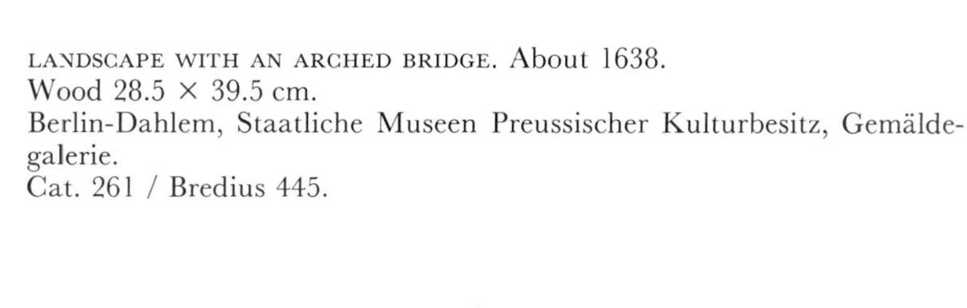

LANDSCAPE WITH AN ARCHED BRIDGE. About 1638.
Wood 28.5 × 39.5 cm.
Berlin-Dahlem, Staatliche Museen Preussischer Kulturbesitz, Gemäldegalerie.
Cat. 261 / Bredius 445.

LANDSCAPE WITH A STONE BRIDGE. About 1638.
Wood 29.5 × 42.5 cm.
Amsterdam, Rijksmuseum.
Cat. 260 / Bredius 440.

STORMY LANDSCAPE. About 1638.
Wood 52 × 72 cm.
Brunswick, Herzog Anton Ulrich Museum.
Cat. 259 / Bredius 441.

LANDSCAPE WITH A CASTLE. About 1640.
Wood 44.5 × 70 cm.
Paris, Louvre.
Cat. 262 / Bredius 450.

WINTER LANDSCAPE.
Signed: 'Rembrandt f. 1646'.
Wood 16.7 × 22.4 cm.
Cassel, Gemäldegalerie.
Cat. 264 / Bredius 452.

RIVER LANDSCAPE WITH RUINS. About 1650.
Wood 67 × 87.5 cm.
Cassel, Gemäldegalerie.
Cat. 265 / Bredius 454.

landscape with an arched bridge. Dark clouds shadow the landscape, but above the horizon the sky is lit momentarily by a strong low sun that has broken through. Unique among 231 Rembrandt's landscape paintings is the Kassel WINTER LANDSCAPE dated 1646. In this small sketch (of only twice postcard size) Rembrandt seems to have captured an impression just received.

Rembrandt's workshop.
LANDSCAPE WITH THE BAPTISM OF THE CHAMBERLAIN.
Signed: 'Rembrandt ft. 1636'.
Canvas 85.5 × 108 cm.
Hanover, Niedersächsische Landesgalerie (on loan).
Cat. A120 / Bredius 439.

Govaert FLINCK.
LANDSCAPE WITH AN OBELISK. About 1638.
Wood 55 × 71 cm.
Boston, Isabella Stewart Gardner Museum.
Cat. A121 / Bredius 443.

LANDSCAPE WITH A MOATED CASTLE. About 1641.
Wood 45.1 × 63.8 cm.
London, Wallace Collection.
Cat. 263 / Bredius 451.

THE MARRIED COUPLE AND DEATH. About 1639.
Etching 108 × 78 mm. Only one state.
Hamburg, Kunsthalle.
Bartsch 109.

In the late 1630s, Rembrandt and Saskia lost a near relative each year; their son Rumbertus in 1636, one of Saskia's sisters in 1637, their daughter Cornelia in 1638, Rembrandt's mother and their second daughter in 1640, and Saskia's sister Titia and brother-in-law Gerrit van Loo in 1641.[251] It was as if Death were stretching out his hourglass towards the young family. Rembrandt must have felt it so, for in 1639 he etched a young couple meeting Death, an unusual subject in his work.

232

The news of her sister's death must have affected Saskia very deeply, for she was particularly close to Titia who, we may suppose, had given her the warmth and security she needed after their mother's death. When Saskia gave birth to a son two months after her sister's death, he was named Titus in memory of the beloved sister who had died so young, and Titia's husband was chosen as one of the godparents.

Saskia's health seems to have suffered as a result of the quick succession of births. Three months after the birth of the second daughter, Cornelia, she was again pregnant, and after Titus's birth she remained sickly. Rembrandt, who had not usually included his private life in his art and had shown little of his home surroundings in his works, now drew Saskia while he sat in her sickroom. In one drawing she lies in bed, and Titus, already crawling, is playing on the bed-cover.[252]

Saskia did not recover from this birth, and on the morning of 5 June 1642, she called a notary and made her will. In it she named her son Titus, and any subsequent children, should she recover, as sole heirs. Her husband was to have the use of her capital until he married again or until his death, in return for which he was to provide suitable education for Titus. Here, as is often the case, a well-meant clause turned out to be a pitfall. Rembrandt was named as Titus's guardian, so excluding the Board of Orphans, which was neither to act as guardian to Titus nor to administer his estate. So the inventory of Titus's inheritance, which would otherwise have been necessary, was not drawn up. Had this been done, Titus's possessions would not have been auctioned during Rembrandt's later bankrupty.

Saskia died on 14 June, one week after the signing of this will, and was buried in the Oude Kerk. Geertghe Dircx, a young widow from Friesland who had been married to a trumpeter, was brought into the house to care for Titus, then 9 months old. But although Titus and the household were now provided for, Rembrandt suffered a grave crisis through the loss of his wife. As the earliest portraits show, Saskia's grace had inspired him; her illness and death affected the artist deeply, paralyzing his creative powers. The small etching of Saskia, wan and stricken by illness, shows how much Rembrandt suffered with her.

Rembrandt's workshop.
SASKIA. (posthumous portrait).
Signed: 'Rembrandt f. 1643'.
Mahogany 75.2 × 60 cm.
Berlin-Dahlem, Staatliche Museen Preussischer Kulturbesitz, Gemäldegalerie.
Cat. A74 / Bredius 109.

REMBRANDT'S CRISIS AND THE ART OF THE 1640S

Up to the year of Saskia's death Rembrandt had been enormously productive, but from 1642 on his creative activity suddenly declined. As compared to previous periods, he produced only a few paintings and hardly any etchings. Many biographies and older studies have attempted to explain this by saying that the original composition of the so-called NIGHT WATCH had cost him the goodwill of potential clients, and that many of those portrayed had felt themselves slighted. This is not a convincing explanation. The audacious composition of THE MILITIA COMPANY OF CAPTAIN FRANS BANNING COCQ (the painting's correct title) did not receive unanimous praise, but it was nevertheless copied and imitated because many admired the boldness of its conception. If Rembrandt had indeed been rejected as a portraitist because of this work, it might explain why he subsequently painted so few portraits, but not why he produced hardly any histories. And why were there not more etchings? His graphic art was in demand throughout Europe in the 1640s; it was collected and often copied in engravings. It was used as models for altar paintings in Protestant and Catholic churches.[253] Large etchings like the ECCE HOMO were sold for sums which other masters received only for paintings. The cause of the decline in Rembrandt's productivity is not to be sought, therefore, in a rejection of his art. Various other factors contributed.

218

140

As a young widower Rembrandt identified himself to an extraordinary degree with his new role as father, which he was now able to play fully for the first time, as all of Saskia's earlier children had died very young. He had already longed for children in the 1630s, and the many drawings of children from this period not only prove that Rembrandt was trying to grasp the entire reality of human life; they also mirror his hopes and expectations. Now he had a son, and after Saskia's death he alone bore the responsibility for the child; he had to replace Saskia.

This is reflected in a drawing with an unusual iconographic subject: a man is shown feeding his year-old son.[254] This subject, probably somewhat odd at that time, shows how Saskia's death had abolished the normal distribution of roles. Probably we see here the origin of the identification which developed between Titus and Rembrandt, for the portrayal of his son was to engage him more and more intensely as the boy became a real companion with whom he could communicate. Titus met his father's expectations completely, accepting the role allocated to him. But he did not develop artistically under his dominating father. Rembrandt, for his part, took the task of fatherhood seriously, living so much for

JAN SIX.
Signed: 'Rembrandt f.' and dated 1647.
Etching 243 × 194 mm. 3rd state.
Hamburg, Kunsthalle.
Bartsch 285.

CHRIST AND THE WOMAN TAKEN IN ADULTERY.
Signed: 'Rembrandt f. 1644'.
Wood 83.8 × 65.4 cm.
London, National Gallery.
Cat. 63 / Bredius 566.

THE WINDMILL.
Signed: 'Rembrandt f.' and dated 1641.
Etching 144 × 207 mm. Only one state.
Hamburg, Kunsthalle.
Bartsch 233.

THE BRIDGE OF JAN SIX.
Signed: 'Rembrandt f.' and dated 1645.
Etching 131 × 225 mm. 3rd state.
Hamburg, Kunsthalle.
Bartsch 208.

LANDSCAPE WITH HUT AND GREAT TREE.
Signed: 'Rembrandt f.' and dated 1641.
Etching 126 × 320 mm. Only one state.
Hamburg, Kunsthalle.
Bartsch 226.

the present that his own creative activity receded.

However, it was not only the family situation that led Rembrandt into a crisis in which he called into question what was traditionally acceptable. In his development as a painter he had reached the summit of Baroque art with histories such as THE BLINDING OF SAMSON or THE TRIUMPH OF MORDECAI. 160, 256 His works surpassed even those of Rubens in their narrative logic, their portrayal of emotion through movement, and their realistic conception. Which direction was he to follow now?

About 1640, when he posed this question, Dutch art was coming slowly but steadily under the influence of Classicist tendencies. Artists who had been profoundly influenced by Caravaggio returned to a lighter manner. Colours became brighter, and more attention was paid to draughtsmanship, perspective, and decorum. Classical compositions were taken as models, countless etchings being made after compositions by Raphael, which were elevated to the standard for all art. Also pre-eminent were sequences of engravings after works from antiquity.

Rembrandt had begun at an early stage to take his stand against this classical tendency, represented in Amsterdam by the German painter Joachim von Sandrart. In the 1630s, Rembrandt had heightened the compositions of Italian Renaissance artists in the Baroque manner by dramatising movement and action. But he was now captivated by the stillness and serenity which had previously seemed a fault in these Renaissance paintings. Calm, spacious works replace his earlier intricate, towering compositions; but he did not allow himself to be forced into a radical change of style. Although he vied with the artists of the Renaissance — since 1633 he had self-confidently signed only his first name, as they had done — the rules of their art did not become the sole criteria for him. The contrast between light and dark and the understanding of the psychological content of a scene meant more to him, since both were closely allied to his conception of a history. His self-portrait of 1639 therefore 203 included compositional elements from Raphael's CASTIGLIONE 204 and Titian's ARIOSTO, yet his manner remained picturesque. So his works in the 1640s contain progressive as well as regressive elements. He turns to nature, no longer painting his landscapes after models by Hercules Seghers and Hans Bol, and seeing the specific qualities of the flat landscape of his native Holland in a new light. If at the end 236, 237 of the 1630s his first landscape paintings had been heroic, with castles and obelisks, mountains and waterfalls, he is now concerned with distant prospects and the play of the wind with the clouds. The few works that he created at this time are of great mastery; among them is the etching THE THREE TREES, 237 which shows a landscape after a thunderstorm. What became significant to him was the individual beauty of his own country and its historic buildings, the witnesses of a venerable history.[255]

Even more clearly than his search for a new view of landscape and the world around him, the regressive features of his histories reflect that he was living through a period of crisis at this time. He went back to his own compositions of the Leyden period, when he was as yet little influenced by Rubens's dramatic structures. This is particularly apparent in the painting THE ADULTERESS (1644), 234 similar in composition to his PRESENTATION IN THE TEMPLE of 1631. 46 As the form became calmer, cooler tones assumed a greater importance, harmonising with the few warm tones more successfully than in his early work. A glowing red is used, contrasting with the darker tones. Yet despite this regression, a development is also visible. The composition is more complex and more carefully planned. The history is portrayed on two levels, or stages. The onlooker seems to climb the high steps of the temple and become part of the group around Jesus and the adulteress. Christ appears here with his disciples as a poor rabbi in simple clothes, confronting the sumptuously robed priests, a contrast which for Rembrandt is not simply external. He is consciously stressing the difference between the love of God, which touches all mankind regardless of rank and knows renunciation and forgiveness, and the religion which seeks its fulfilment in absolute obedience to the law and stylises itself in the splendour of worship. This external service, which enthralls but does not liberate, is shown on the upper stage, where the high priest sits enthroned before a splendid altar above a humble throng. Rembrandt has described the emotions of the Pharisees in this scene in a note on a drawing: 'They were so anxious to make Jesus contradict himself that they could hardly wait for his answer'.[256] He shows them as attentive listeners anxiously awaiting Jesus's reply, whereas in other scenes the Pharisees are characterised as disputatious opponents.

235 The PORTRAIT OF JAN SIX (1647) is one of the masterpieces 237 of these years, and is on the same level as the THREE TREES 254 and THE HUNDRED GUILDER PRINT, completed about 1649/50, which is probably his most famous etching.

Rembrandt must have met the author Jan Six in the mid-forties. He was much younger than Rembrandt. His father, who belonged to a rich Huguenot family, owned a silk factory in Amsterdam. Six was a great lover of the arts, collecting paintings and drawings by Dutch and Italian artists as well as sculptures, marble reliefs, and other objets d'art. Probably it was this passion which brought the patrician's son into contact with the older artist, whose collection had already become famous. A close acquaintance, perhaps even a friendship, developed from this meeting. Rembrandt composed the title page for one of Six's dramatic works and made two drawings for his *Liber Amicorum.* In his turn, Six left the silk-manufacturing business in 1652 and began the usual career of a public official, which culminated in his becoming burgomaster in 1691. When Rembrandt got into financial difficulties in 1653, Six at first lent him money, but then their ways parted.

When Six was twenty-nine, he sat for a portrait in the medium for which Rembrandt, now forty-one, had become famous throughout Europe: etching. The composition and conception are extremely bold. Six is leaning on a window-sill, reading a manuscript. Only a small part of the room is visible, but through the subtle play of light and shadow we have the impression of a large, elegant room. The genre-like motifs caught by the light coming through the window prove on closer inspection to be clues to the social position and private interests of the sitter. He is probably not wearing the sword and sash, the attributes of nobility, because Rembrandt is here characterising him as a poet, but they are visible on the chest. Books are piled on the chair in the foreground, showing Six as an author and scholar. The altar picture on the wall characterises him as a collector of old, valuable art. This etching became a model for many later artists, and it is said that another of Rembrandt's clients asked to be portrayed in a similar manner to Jan Six.[257]

THE THREE TREES. 1643.
Etching 211 × 280 mm. Only one state.
Hamburg, Kunsthalle.
Bartsch 212.

THE SKIFF UNDER THE TREES.
Signed: 'Rembrandt' and dated 1645.
Etching 129 × 133 mm. 2nd state.
Hamburg, Kunsthalle.
Bartsch 231.

Rembrandt's workshop (?).
PORTRAIT OF A WOMAN IN AN ARMCHAIR (ANNA WIJMER? 1584-1654).
Signed: 'Rembrandt f. 1641'.
Djati wood 96 × 80 cm.
Amsterdam, Six Foundation. Cat. A112 / Bredius 358.

AN OLD MAN IN FANCIFUL COSTUME HOLDING A STICK.
Signed: '... f 1645'.
Canvas 128 × 112 cm.
Lisbon, Museu Calouste Gulbenkian.
Cat. 139 / Bredius 239.

Rembrandt's workshop.
AN OLD MAN IN A FANCIFUL COSTUME.
Signed: 'Rembrandt f. 1651'.
Canvas 78.5 × 67.5 cm.
Chatsworth, England, Devonshire Collection.
Cat. A46 / Bredius 266.

Rembrandt circle.
AN OLD MAN IN A FUR-LINED COAT.
Signed: 'Rembrandt f. 1645'.
Canvas 110 × 82 cm.
Berlin-Dahlem, Staatliche Museen Preussischer Kulturbesitz, Gemäldegalerie.
Cat. A42 / Bredius 236.

Rembrandt circle.
A MAN IN AN ARMCHAIR.
Signed: 'Rembrandt f. 1637'.
Canvas 133 × 104 cm.
Mertoun, Berwickshire, Duke of Sutherland's Collection.
Cat. A90 / Bredius 214.

Rembrandt's workshop.
PORTRAIT OF A WOMAN SITTING IN AN ARMCHAIR. (AALTJE VAN UYLENBURGH, the widow of J.C. Sylvius?).
Signed: 'Rembrandt f. 1644'. Canvas 124.5 × 100 cm.
Toronto, Art Gallery of Ontario. Cat. A113 / Bredius 369.

Pupil of Rembrandt.
AN OLD WOMAN WITH A BOOK.
Signed: 'Rembrandt f. 164(7)'. Canvas 109 × 91.5 cm.
Washington DC, National Gallery of Art.
Cat. A58 / Bredius 362.

Rembrandt's workshop.
HENDRICK MARTENSZ. SORGH (c. 1611-1670).
Signed: 'Rembrandt f. 164(7)'. Wood 74 × 67 cm.
England, private collection. Cat. A92 / Bredius 251.

Rembrandt's workshop.
ARIAENTJE HOLLAER, WIFE OF THE PAINTER HENDRICK MARTENSZ. SORGH.
Signed: 'Rembrandt 1647' (?). Wood 74 × 67 cm.
England, private collection. Cat. A114 / Bredius 370.

THE HOLY FAMILY (WITH PAINTED FRAME AND CURTAIN). Detail.
(See page 243).

THE BIBLICAL HISTORIES OF THE 1640S: THE HIDDEN SYMBOLISM OF NEW TESTAMENT DEPICTIONS

The first works of the 1640s still belong to Rembrandt's Baroque phase. If they are compared with the works produced five years earlier, however, both the style and the choice of subjects have grown strikingly quieter. The figures are caught in calm movements on a single picture level; they seldom break through several levels with violent movements and do not form complex, superimposed groupings. In place of violent events, we now usually find tranquil scenes. In the course of the decade the format also changes. Though, in Leyden and in his first decade in Amsterdam, Rembrandt had preferred the vertical format because it allowed him to pile the composition upwards, after the mid-1640s the horizontal format plays a greater role, as it had for Pieter Lastman. The narration is again more expansive, and landscape or spatial elements are lovingly sketched, contributing to the atmosphere.

Local colour once again takes on greater importance — here too Rembrandt could not escape the general artistic trends of his time — but retains its function as the bearer of light.

In the 1630s Rembrandt had studied Pieter Lastman's pictures primarily with regard to the grouping of crowds and the gestures of people in special situations. A decade later, he is interested in how the figures are integrated into the landscape or space and how the architectonic or landscape milieu reinforces the history. This shift can be clearly demonstrated by the two paintings on the Susanna theme. If in the picture in The Hague (1637) Rembrandt had isolated Susanna from the scenic context and reduced the milieu, in the Berlin picture completed in 1647 he depicts it in detail and also shows the two elders. Almost all the Old Testament histories were inspired directly or indirectly by Lastman's works. In the New Testament, however, he is interested, with few exceptions, in the life of the Holy Family and the rejection or acceptance accorded to the child Jesus.

The following observation is most noteworthy: like the early Dutch masters, Rembrandt includes symbolic motifs in his New Testament histories. Apparently natural movements, everyday objects, plants, and animals often have a deeper meaning and draw attention to the significance of the history in relation to the passion and salvation of Christ. Rembrandt uses in his paintings of New Testament subjects the same symbolic language he had already used in his histories depicting ancient subjects in the 1630s.[258]

244 In his painting THE VISITATION, dated 1640, Rembrandt took issue with Rubens's magnificent version on the side panel of the altar of St Christopher in Antwerp Cathedral; its

THE HOLY FAMILY (WITH PAINTED FRAME AND CURTAIN). Signed: 'Rembrandt ft. 1646'. Wood 46.5 × 68.8 cm. Cassel, Gemäldegalerie. Cat. 66 / Bredius 572.

Hugo VAN DER GOES.
ADORATION OF THE SHEPHERDS. About 1480. Detail. Oak 97 × 245 cm. Berlin-Dahlem, Gemäldegalerie.

THE MEETING OF MARY AND ELIZABETH (THE VISITATION).
Signed: 'Rembrandt ... 1640'.
Wood 56.5 × 47.9 cm.
Detroit, Institute of Arts.
Cat. 60 / Bredius 562.

centre panel depicting the Descent from the Cross had already acted as the inspiration for his Passion series. As in the painting tradition, he made the meeting between Mary and Elizabeth take place in front of the house to make the arrival clearer.[259] In 1640, Rembrandt had a strong interest in architecture. He did not paint the palace of Zacharias, as Rubens had, in classical terms, but with the heavy, rounded, pasty forms of lingering late Mannerism. Elements clearly taken from Gothic architecture are fused with motifs from late antiquity and the Baroque to form a strange, imposing portal.

Elizabeth who, although of advanced years, is pregnant with John, has descended the steps to greet the pregnant Mary, who has climbed the steps to the portal. The bent old woman, her stick in her right hand, puts her arms around the younger woman, who stands upright and so seems taller. These age-induced postures have symbolic meanings. Mary as the Mother of God stands above Elizabeth, who will bear the forerunner of the Messiah. A servant takes off Mary's green cloak, which is still enveloping her like a canopy. Most of the light falls on Mary. Supported by a boy, old Zacharias comes down the steps. He is visible in almost his full stature, one side being slightly hidden. Joseph is only half visible, in keeping with his lesser importance in Christ's life. He has not climbed the stairs, but has stayed with the ass, which is tied to its halter — a reference to the flight to Egypt.

Rembrandt took the composition of the figures, in reverse, from an engraving after Maerten van Heemskerck showing young Tobias greeted by his aged parents. Through the language of gesture Rembrandt has rendered in pictorial terms an essential aspect of the story he portrays. Only through God's grace can Zacharias (who like the blind Tobias must be supported by a young servant while descending the stairs) and the aged Elizabeth become parents of the prophet John. The meeting with Mary, who is expecting the Saviour, lends wings to Elizabeth's steps, so that, forgetting her age and stick, she stretches out her arms towards Mary and speaks of the child, who will come as the Redeemer.

The picture is spendidly embellished. In the background a rich urban landscape extends over a chain of hills. The details — for example, the family of peacocks in the left foreground and the vines growing up the side wall of the portal are both carefully painted and harmonised with the picture as a whole. Rubens's painting contains similar details, which give a deeper meaning to the depiction.

Peacocks had been introduced into Israel at the time of Solomon; they were regarded as royal creatures and make the onlooker aware that the story took place in elevated circles in the ancient world. Joseph was a descendant of David. But in Rubens and Rembrandt the peacock probably had an additional meaning. It could have been a symbol of virtue, which shines like the peacock's magnificent tail. In a 17th-century book of emblems, the peahen with her chicks symbolises the royal house's abundance of children, which brings what power and wealth cannot bestow.[260] Elizabeth points to the Annunciation, when the angel says that God shall give Jesus the throne of his father, David: 'And he shall reign over the House of Jacob forever; and of his kingdom shall be no end'. And Mary answers Elizabeth's greeting: 'Behold, from henceforth all generations shall call me blessed. For he that is mighty hath done to me great things'.[261] On the wall beside the portal vines grow. Through the symbolism of this motif Rembrandt makes the onlooker aware that Christ brought about the redemption of men through his suffering, which is represented in Holy Communion.[262] As in the DANAË, the symbolic motifs are embodied in a realistic depiction, so that they have not been recognised previously.

180

Rembrandt's HOLY FAMILY (1640) in the Louvre was believed in the 18th century to be a portrayal of the carpenter's family in the manner of a genre scene.[263] Even leading Rembrandt experts have misunderstood this picture, interpreting its theme as the quiet happiness of the Holy Family in a dark, homely corner of existence. This interpretation in genre terms fails to do justice to Rembrandt's intention, for he heightens the depictions of the Holy Family into quiet recognition scenes.

246

In a room in which the furnishings are shown in detail Mary sits suckling the child Jesus. Next to her sits her old mother, Anna. She has just been reading the Bible, and some words on the Saviour have caused her to experience an illumination. She has taken off her spectacles and is now removing the cloth from the child's head to see it better. Sunlight streams through the open window. It falls exactly on the child Jesus. His naked skin shines in the light, as does Mary's breast, from which the child is drinking. Anna's hand pulling the cloth from the child's head is also illuminated.

Joseph is working at his carpentry in a recess by the window. He is so engrossed in his work that he does not perceive what Anna has seen, and turns his back to the two women. He is a peripheral figure, who has little to do with the story of salvation. On the right, there is a view into an adjoining room where an alcove is visible. In the foreground the composition is rounded off by a large fireplace with imposing columns.

245 In the Leningrad painting of 1645 Rembrandt developed the recognition motif further. The Holy Family is again shown in the carpenter's workshop, but only segments of the room are shown. In the foreground the child slumbers in a wicker cradle. Mary, who has just come across words about the Saviour in the Bible, is making certain of her insight: she carefully lifts a cloth from the arched roof of the cradle and can see the child properly, giving us, too, a clear view of the sleeping child. The sky opens above her and heavenly light descends, illuminating her and the scripture. Putti float down from the opened Heaven. One of them flies down in a peaceful attitude with arms outstretched over Mary and the Christ child. The arms of the putto seem to be outstreched in a gesture of protection and of blessing, but the posture also recalls that of the crucified Christ. So this idyllic picture calls to mind the Passion. Mary recognises that the Saviour, the Light of the World, must die on the cross.[264] As was his practice, Rembrandt has depicted the working areas, Mary's place at the fire and Joseph's workbench, in detail, but in such shadow that they do not take on undue importance. What a contrast exists beween the meagre earthly fire and the heavenly light that breaks into the carpenter's dwelling with the angels. Behind Mary, Joseph is visible. He is half in shadow.[265] He is bending to fashion a yoke with a mighty axe, seemingly merely a realistic motif, but really another allusion to a biblical prophecy, for two Old Testament passages foretell that the Saviour will break the yoke of Israel's burden.[266] The better-known passage is in Isaiah (9: 1-6), and this is the one that Rembrandt probably had in mind:

> The people that walked in darkness have seen a great light: they that dwell in the land of the shadow of death, upon them hath the light shined.... For thou hast broken the yoke of his burden, and the staff of his shoulder, the rod of his oppressor, as in the day of Midian.... For unto us a child is born, unto us a son is given: and the government shall be upon his shoulder: and his name shall be called Wonderful, Counsellor, The Mighty God, The Everlasting Father, the Prince of Peace. Of the increase of his government and peace there shall be no end, upon the throne of David, and upon his kingdom, to order it, and to establish it with judgement and with justice from henceforth for ever and ever.

Joseph, who lives in semi-darkness and has not yet recognised the Saviour, is bent under the burden; perhaps we are also to interpret the fragments of wood in the foreground as a broken staff.

246 If with this knowledge we look back at the Louvre picture, it is noteworthy that Joseph is shown fashioning a yoke. The same hidden symbolism is also present there.

In the second Epistle to the Corinthians, St Paul uses the metaphor that the Old Testament is hidden by a veil unless

THE HOLY FAMILY WITH THE ANGELS.
Signed: 'Rembrandt f. 1645'. Canvas 117 × 91 cm.
Leningrad, Hermitage. Cat. 65 / Bredius 570.

it is related to Jesus.[267] Anna and Mary interpret the Old Testament in relation to Jesus and so draw the veil aside. The motif of the veil over the child and the idea that the meaning of Jesus is only revealed by pushing back that veil reappear in a profound variation in the Kassel painting of 243 1646. Around the picture Rembrandt painted a costly carved frame. The right third of the picture is covered by a painted red curtain that is swung slightly to the right as if it has just been drawn aside. (Obviously Rembrandt was prompted to choose this motif by an example provided by one of the early Dutch painters. In the Berlin ADORATION OF THE SHEPHERDS, 252 by Hugo van der Goes, the curtain is being drawn aside by 243 prophets.)[268] We as onlookers are thus given a view into the room of the Holy Family. Only because the curtain opens for us do we discover the secret of this night scene that appears in a sacral light. For the Holy Family is not illuminated by the small fire, but by the light that falls into the room from high on the left. It seems as if the picture itself were hanging in a dark room and were only made visible by a strong light falling on it, which is reflected by the frame, the rod and the curtain. Past the drawn curtain there is a view into a large room. Mary is sitting on a chair, behind her stands the child's cradle. She has taken the child on her lap to soothe it. The little Jesus stands with unsteady legs upright on her lap; she presses him to her and bends towards him. In the background a large grating or lattice window bounds the space to the outside. To the right of the lattice a segment of landscape appears somewhat abruptly. If we look at the

THE REST ON THE FLIGHT INTO EGYPT.
Signed: 'Rembrandt f. 1647'.
Wood 34 × 48 cm.
Dublin, National Gallery of Ireland.
Cat. 68 / Bredius 576.

arched wooden ceiling, it is intact on the side where Mary 242 and the child are, but in total disrepair on the side of Joseph and the curtain. Outside, Joseph is hacking the branches from a tree trunk from which he is probably again to fashion a yoke. The bright room is oriented towards Mary and the child, while Joseph outside the door is so occupied with his work that he does not perceive the child. As he who does not recognise Christ he is consigned to an unredeemed, dilapidated world given over to decay. It is the world of the *Vetus Testamentum Velatum* — the Old Testament behind a veil.[269]

Rembrandt had used a comparable division of the space of a painting into two sections in 1644, two years before the Kassel picture, to make clear the difference between Old Testament worship and the New Testament message of redemption. In this painting THE WOMAN TAKEN IN ADULTERY 234 is brought into the hall of the temple to Jesus so that he can condemn her. Jesus challenges those who are without sin to stone her, and so secures her freedom. He too forgives her, and for this reason Rembrandt has shown her in a white garment. Opposite this New Testament service, an Old Testament service is shown on a higher podium. On a mighty throne resplendent with gold sits the high priest. The priests worshipping there and the people ascending to them do not perceive, in their blindness, Christ's disputation with the Pharisees on guilt and forgiveness.

The two paintings produced in 1646 for the stadholder as part of the Passion series, THE ADORATION OF THE SHEPHERDS 247 and THE CIRCUMCISION OF CHRIST, were also conceived by 138 Rembrandt as scenes of recognition and dazzlement. In the pitiful stable the shepherds and even the children visit the child Jesus and worship him as the light of the world. In the temple glittering with gold and sumptuous furnishings, the priests are so preoccupied with their ceremony that their eyes are unseeing and they perform the circumcision obliviously. Nor does the throng of elegantly dressed young women recognise in Mary the mother of Jesus.

In the London ADORATION OF THE SHEPHERDS, the Munich 250 composition has been laterally reversed by a gifted pupil of Rembrandt.

In 1647, Rembrandt produced the painting THE REST ON 246 THE FLIGHT INTO EGYPT. It was suggested by Elsheimer's Munich picture, which until 1628 was in the possession of the Utrecht artist Hendrik Goudt and was disseminated by him in an engraving. The Holy Family is advancing into the dark night of their journey. The landscape is faintly lit by the stars and moonlight along a river in which the sky is

THE ADORATION OF THE SHEPHERDS. ▶
Signed indistinctly and dated 1646.
Canvas 97 × 71.3 cm.
Munich, Alte Pinakothek.
Cat. 67 / Bredius 574.

THE HOLY FAMILY.
Signed: 'Rembrandt f. 1640'.
Wood 41 × 34 cm.
Paris, Louvre.
Cat. 61 / Bredius 563.

reflected. In the middle ground, under tall trees, a group of shepherds is visible, camped with their animals around a fire. In the engraving by Goudt the inscription runs: 'Into the darkness flees the light of the world, and the Creator of the orb hides as an exile — a wonderful thing — among the Pharaonic tyrants'.[270] Even in comparison with the nocturnal lights, the child, the light of the world, is hardly to be seen, but is concealed from the world.

Rembrandt has adapted Elsheimer's composition in a revealing way. Mary and Joseph are warming themselves at the fire; some shepherds have drawn near with their flocks; one has knelt to tend the fire. This attitude seems almost like a gesture of worship and adoration of the Holy Family.

The picture is dominated by the nocturnal landscape which is lightened around the fire of the resting people and in the strip of sky above. The landscape seems spacious and dim, as if to indicate the long and laborious terrain that the Holy Family must cross on their flight to Egypt. If the figures seem small in relation to the whole picture, the group is nevertheless given weight by being reflected in the river.

As the exact depiction of the stable and the evocation of the inhospitable river landscape serve to make clear to the onlooker the hardships the Holy Family had to contend with, and to show that they nevertheless encountered charitable people in their wretchedness, the architecture of THE APPEARANCE OF JESUS TO THE DISCIPLES AT EMMAUS (1648), now in the Louvre, serves to make us aware that the story has a significance and influence extending to the present. Rembrandt shows Christ with the two disciples at the moment when he breaks the bread and is recognised by them as the risen Christ. Before him lies the loaf from which he breaks a piece. He lifts up his eyes in thanksgiving. A halo with strong, irregular beams radiates from his head. The figure sitting on the left, seen from the back, starts back and clasps his hands in supplication, and the disciple on the right has also shrunk back somewhat as if afraid, one arm on the back of his chair, his right hand on the table. The servant in the background is bringing in a meal on a dish; he does not recognise Christ, so he takes no part in the miracle.

248

'A miraculous work that must be numbered among the masterpieces of this master', Fromentin called this picture.[271] The treatment of the light, in particular, makes the judgement comprehensible. The sunlight falls obliquely through a high unseen window and lights the white tablecloth. The cloth glows, reflecting the light on the figure of

ABRAHAM SERVING THE ANGELS.
Signed: 'Rembrandt f. 1645'.
Wood 16 × 21 cm.
Aurora Trust.
Cat. 21 / Bredius 515.

CHRIST AT EMMAUS.
Signed: 'Rembrandt f. 1648'.
Wood 68 × 65 cm.
Paris, Louvre.
Cat. 69 / Bredius 578.

Rembrandt's workshop.
CHRIST AT EMMAUS.
Signed: 'Rembrandt f. 1648'.
Canvas 89.5 × 111.5 cm.
Copenhagen, Statens Museum for Kunst.
Cat. A8 / Bredius 579.

Christ. The sacral nimbus about Christ's head is also enlarged and intensified.[272]

In the picture as a whole, the table seems almost like an altar. For the scene takes place in a high room built of stone and reminiscent of a church, the more so since Christ is seated before a wide, very high niche that encloses him like a chancel. So the picture also recalls Communion in a church, as celebrated by Christians in memory of the Risen Christ.

In the 1640s Rembrandt painted few Old Testament histories. He usually shows scenes of recognition or shock, and there are two pictures of departures. In most of the Old Testament pictures the impulse came from Lastman, either the scene being entirely regrouped (DAVID AND JONATHAN), or an earlier moment in the story being painted (THE DEPARTURE OF THE SHUNAMMITE WIFE), or, finally, the composition 251 being varied (SUSANNA SURPRISED BY THE ELDERS and ABRA- 248 HAM SERVING THE ANGELS).

249 In the Berlin picture ANNA ACCUSED BY TOBIAS OF STEALING THE KID (1645), the old, blind Tobias sits in the middle of a spacious but shabby room, raising his right arm as he accuses Anna of theft — wrongfully, as we know, since she has earned the goat honestly by spinning. Anna stands obliquely behind her husband, pulling the somewhat refractory goat behind her. She looks at her husband, but he does not turn towards her. In this story he is blind twice over. The light falls into the room from the left through an open window, illuminating in detail the utensils of the meagre household, the dilapidated wall, and the two old people who spend their declining years in this twilit world. A small fire burns at Tobias's feet, giving them warmth and shedding its feeble light on them. To the right and towards a partly open garret, the large room is lost in darkness.

248 In the small painting ABRAHAM SERVING THE ANGELS, Rembrandt started from a composition by his teacher, but raised it to the level of a revelation scene.[273] The Bible story tells how Abraham and Sarah waited in vain for the child promised by God. Then the Lord appeared to Abraham. Abraham invites him to a meal under the tree before his house and affords him hospitality. God confirms his promise. The text speaks alternately of the Lord and of the three men. Rembrandt represents the messengers — as often happened in the pictorial tradition — as angels, identifying one with the Lord and emphasising him through illumination. He shows the moment at which this angel foretells the birth of Isaac. Under a mighty tree in front of Abraham's house, the three angels have taken their place, reclining on the ground. The angel sitting under the tree and emphasised by it holds his wings spread wide, with his foot stretched out on a pedestal. His appearance determines the whole picture. His robe shines brightly and is the source of light in this picture confined to brownish, earthen tones.

The angel raises his hand and speaks to Abraham. The latter, who has half fallen to his knees, holds cutlery for the

JOSEPH'S DREAM IN THE STABLE AT BETHLEHEM.
Signed: 'Rembrandt f. 1645'.
Wood 20 × 27 cm.
Berlin-Dahlem, Staatliche Museen Preussischer Kulturbesitz, Gemäldegalerie. Cat. 64 / Bredius 569.

ANNA ACCUSED BY TOBIAS OF STEALING THE KID.
Signed: 'Rembrandt f. 1645'.
Mahogany 20 × 27 cm.
Berlin-Dahlem, Staatliche Museen Preussischer Kulturbesitz, Gemäldegalerie. Cat. 20 / Bredius 514.

Rembrandt's workshop.
JUPITER AND MERCURY VISITING PHILEMON AND BAUCIS.
Signed: 'Rembrandt f. 1658'.
Wood 54.5 × 68.5 cm.
Washington, National Gallery of Art.
Cat. A26 / Bredius 481.

Rembrandt's workshop.
THE ADORATION OF THE SHEPHERDS.
Signed: 'Rembrandt f. 1646'.
Canvas 65.5 × 55 cm.
London, National Gallery.
Cat. A7 / Bredius 575.

table and looks rigid and dazzled. On the left sit the other two angels, one seen from the back and one in profile. Both are struck by the radiance from the first angel, which they reflect back from the parts of their bodies turned toward him. Abraham, however, is only slightly illuminated, so the picture is as if divided in two. On the left is the world of the angels with the landscape behind them, from which they have come and to which they will return; on the right is the world of Abraham, with the façade of his house and an open door, in which Sarah stands listening.

The unification of the colour tones of the picture, with an accentuation of some tones, is to be found also in the Berlin SUSANNA. In 1647, Rembrandt revised this picture, probably 251 first painted in the 1630s, as Hans Kauffmann has recognised. While his analysis has been contested, the theory is confirmed by several drawings of both the original and the 251 final versions that have been preserved and by X-ray photographs. In keeping with the development of his style in the 1640s, Rembrandt has softened or eliminated all motifs involving violent movements. He depicts Susanna, the faithful wife of the rich Joiakim of Babylon, who has laid her garment on a balustrade and descends the curved stone steps into the water. One of the two lewd judges reaches for her robe, bends over her and warns her to be silent. The other is just walking through the gate into her garden. As if entreating help, Susanna — bending forward — turns towards the onlooker and defensively covers her breast.

On the left, Rembrandt has painted a lake, on the bank of which the heavy fortifications of an ancient palace or fortress built on a slope are seen. He has placed this left half of the picture in shadow, so that it acts as a dark foil against which the maidenly figure of Susanna stands out. While the old man grabs her garment, he does not touch her. Threatened as Susanna is, she also seems as if detached by the strong accentuation of her bright form.

Jan Kelch aptly writes:

> The final version offers a composition of two distinct halves, the left half receding into a shadowy 'emptiness' against the schematic outlines of the palace architecture, while the right half, with a rocky arch covered in foliage jutting into the foreground, is entirely reserved for the compact narrative episode, throwing the most intense concentration of light on Susanna's body and on the red of her sumptuous dress. It is the soft, atmospheric chiaroscuro that indivisibly unites the unlike halves, making them appear as parts of one and the same world saturated with mood and light.[274]

In the painting SARAH AWAITING TOBIAS, Rembrandt also 253 used a work by Lastman as his starting-point, the WEDDING NIGHT OF TOBIAS AND SARAH.[275] Raguel's daughter was 252 possessed by an evil spirit which killed seven men to whom she had been married, each on his wedding night. When Tobias married Sarah, he overpowered this spirit with the help of the angel. He put part of the liver and heart of a fish on the coals. Then the angel took the spirit prisoner and

Rembrandt and an imitator.
THE LAMENTATION OVER THE DEAD CHRIST. About 1635-1642.
Paper on canvas, mounted on wood. 31.9 × 26.7 cm.
London, National Gallery.
Cat. 62 / Bredius 565.

SUSANNA AT THE BATH SURPRISED BY THE TWO ELDERS.
Signed: 'Rembrandt f. 1647'. Wood 76.6 × 92.7 cm.
Berlin-Dahlem, Staatliche Museen Preussischer Kulturbesitz, Gemäldegalerie. Cat. 22 / Bredius 516.

Pieter LASTMAN.
SUSANNA AND THE ELDERS.
Signed: 'Lastman fecit 1614'. Wood 43 × 59 cm.
Berlin-Dahlem, Staatliche Museen Preussischer Kulturbesitz, Gemäldegalerie.

SUSANNA AND THE ELDERS.
Signed, about 1637.
Red-chalk drawing, 235 × 364 mm.
Berlin-Dahlem, Staatliche Museen Preussischer Kulturbesitz, Kupferstichkabinett. Benesch 448.

Pieter LASTMAN.
THE WEDDING NIGHT OF TOBIT AND SARAH.
Signed and dated 1611. Wood 42 × 57 cm.
Boston, Museum of Fine Arts.

THE PARTING OF DAVID AND JONATHAN.
Signed: 'Rembrandt f. 1642'. Wood 73 × 61 cm.
Leningrad, Hermitage.
Cat. 19 / Bredius 511.

banished him far off to the dessert. It is this decisive moment that Lastman shows. Sarah looks on in fascination from the marriage bed as Tobias burns the liver and the angel overpowers the evil spirit. Probably the curtain of the marriage bed, thrown ceremoniously back, provoked Rembrandt to use this motif more effectively in a recognition scene: Sarah draws back the curtain and, rising up, sees the cause of her terrible destiny and its conquest. Her emotions and gestures reflect the redemption she is witnessing. Here too, therefore, Rembrandt has used the pictorial form of detachment to heighten the emotive content of the history.[276]

Hugo VAN DER GOES.
THE ADORATION OF THE SHEPHERDS. About 1480.
Oak 97 × 245 cm.
Berlin-Dahlem, Staatliche Museen Preussischer Kulturbesitz, Gemäldegalerie.

SARAH AWAITING TOBIAS. About 1649/50.
Signed: 'Rembra (...) f. 164(.)'.
Canvas 81.1 × 67.8 cm.
Edinburgh, National Gallery of Scotland.
Cat. 23 / Bredius 110.

THE HUNDRED GUILDER PRINT: AND THE SUGGESTION OF HOW THE STORY HANGS TOGETHER

Rembrandt's most famous etching is the so-called HUNDRED 254 GUILDER PRINT (B. 74).[277] This name, dating back to the 17th century, refers to the remarkably high price, equivalent to the monthly salary of a university professor, which the work fetched at the time. Even in Rembrandt's lifetime, the public clearly appreciated the beauty and the special composition of this etching and valued it accordingly. In this print, with its many figures and its narrative breadth, Rembrandt summarised a whole chapter of the Bible in an entirely new way, combining its parts in a new unity of time and space. His object was to sum up the special nature of Jesus's activity, his miracle-working, his teaching, and his call for followers. In this sense, the etching is a kind of characterisation of Jesus. People of the most varied origins and ages — each caught in his unique individuality — crowd around Jesus. Their gestures and faces communicate a knowledge of Jesus's special powers, and for this very reason a group sets out to prove the contrary, seeking trick questions with which to expose Jesus. Belief and unbelief are both represented. Jesus stands above them all.[278]

Even in the choice of his etching plate Rembrandt seems to have realised the peculiar nature of his composition. For, compared to the compact proportions of his other etchings, he opts here for an unusually wide format. The extended breadth is emphasised by the wedge-shaped structure of figures running from left to right and stretching as far as the gateway. The gaze is led through this opening, with its illuminated inner wall, and further and further to the right into the roofed space beyond. Areas of strong shadow in the right half of the picture emphasise the breadth. The accustomed direction of the gaze from left to right thus finds a correlative. But at the same time a counter-current from the right edge of the picture is generated by the turning and the varied movements of the figures, leading back to the figure of Jesus, who is not at the exact centre of the picture. Coming through the gateway, the figures move outwards into the picture. In this way the compositional form just described is constantly broken and intersected. No matter how much the different figures attract notice, the dominant form is Jesus. Displaced slightly to the left of centre, he stands tall and bright amid the forms crowding round him, stretching out his hands in calm gestures. The centre of the picture is occupied by the chest-high stump of a pilaster, which emphasises Jesus's upright posture. The attitude of Jesus expresses serenity. The picture space is not deep, being closed at the back by masonry that is only vaguely structured and reveals no architectonic coherence. Instead, the division

THE BEHEADING OF JOHN THE BAPTIST.
Signed: 'Rembrandt f.' and dated 1640.
Etching 129 × 105 mm.
Hamburg, Kunsthalle.
Bartsch 92.

THE HUNDRED GUILDER PRINT. About 1649.
Etching 283 × 395 mm. 1st state.
Berlin-Dahlem, Staatliche Museen Preussischer Kulturbesitz, Kupferstichkabinett.
Bartsch 74.

THE TRIUMPH OF MORDECAI. About 1640.
Etching 176 × 216 mm.
Hamburg, Kunsthalle.
Bartsch 40.

Jan VAN DE VELDE.
THE GOOD SAMARITAN.
Etching 258 × 208 mm. 1st state.
The 4th state is signed and dated.

into light and shaded parts is governed by the structure of the group of figures. So a strong shadowy shape rising behind Christ marks out — immensely enlarged — a dark patch on the back wall that no longer has any similarity to a human shadow but resembles a kind of canopy, like those spread above the thrones of rulers. Jesus's halo shines in extremely fine rays against this dark background. The overall composition, therefore, is simple and easily grasped. But in terms of iconography and narrative, the picture is executed with particular artistry. Each figure has its special significance. The thematic structure determines the arrangement of the figures.

Following an essay by Jordan, the view has become accepted among critics that Rembrandt has here represented various scenes from the 19th chapter of the Gospel of St Matthew.[279] The central act that is just being performed is the blessing of the children. This scene was recognised in the artist's lifetime, as is known from a poem written by Rembrandt's friend Waterloos on a print, which refers to this scene.[280] A woman is setting foot on the steps leading up to Jesus; she carries a small child in her arms. Jesus stretches out his open right hand towards her, raising his left hand in a sign of blessing. While stretching out his right hand to welcome the woman, at the same time — in keeping with the biblical text — he restrains a disciple who is trying to prevent her from approaching. In the text this disciple is not mentioned by name. However, Rembrandt characterises him unmistakably by his half bald head, snub nose, and beard as Peter. He thereby incorporates into the picture the conversation between the fisherman and Jesus on the succession of Christ.[281] This was possibly suggested by Merian's *Icones biblicae* or by his model.[282] This interpenetration of scenes recorded successively in the Bible is also found in the group around Jesus and in the group on the left. A small boy, still below the steps but running towards them, pulls his mother by the apron, pointing excitedly to Jesus. The urgency of the entreating gestures of small children is impressively captured. It is clear that the impetus comes from the child. The woman with the child on her arm and the small child urging his mother are moving in a kind of aisle that leads obliquely from the bottom left corner into the picture and up to Jesus and is flanked by the spectators.

Seen from the back at the left edge of the picture is an imposing male figure who, while looking at the spectators on the left, is turned towards Jesus. The three figures seen from behind — the man, the child, and the woman with the child on her arm — lead the onlooker's gaze along the empty aisle to Jesus. The children are probably intended as an allusion to the words referring to those who follow Christ: 'And everyone that hath forsaken...father, or mother...for my name's sake...shall inherit everlasting life' (Matthew 19, 29).[283] Gathered around a broad stone pedestal as around a table is the group of Pharisees, apparently engrossed in argument and counter-argument to decide which artful question would best lure Jesus into a wrong answer. Some members of this group therefore look away from Jesus to the speaker — as always in a large gathering, there are figures everywhere whose attention is distracted from the main personage. Although their interest is diverted, this group is marked by attentive listeners. They too are affected by

THE GOOD SAMARITAN.
Etching 247 × 203 mm. (The 5th state is signed and dated: 'Rembrandt . inventor . et . Fecit. 1633').

THE ENTOMBMENT. About 1645.
Signed: 'Rembrandt'.
Etching 131 × 108 mm. Only one state.
Hamburg, Kunsthalle.
Bartsch 84.

Jesus's influence.[284] A figure not screened by others stands out within this group: a richly dressed young man with curly hair, sitting on the ground and turned pensively towards Jesus. His cheek rests in his palm, the classical gesture of reverie. The 19th chapter of Matthew tells of this man; he is the rich youth who engages Jesus in discussion and is told that he must give away his entire wealth if he is to have treasure in heaven. Jesus sums up the rich man's resistance to this idea by telling his disciples: 'It is easier for a camel to go through the eye of a needle, than for a rich man to enter into the kingdom of God'.[285] Schrey remarked on this in his interpretation of the etching:

> With humorous effect Rembrandt includes in his picture the camel mentioned symbolically to the rich young man, pointedly placing it under the high arch of the gateway to demonstrate the enormity of the utterance.[286]

Here too Rembrandt was stimulated by earlier graphic art: Joos Bruyn has pointed to an engraving after Heemskerk which shows the camel confronted by the eye of a needle.[287]

From the right, figures crowd towards Jesus, hoping for him to perform miracles and heal the sick. The light coming through the gateway gives the impression that the space beyond it leads further. The arrangement of the people coming through the gate makes it appear as if they are only the tip of a procession that fills the imaginary space far behind the gate. This impression is aroused by the multiplicity of the individuals. An old man is supported by a woman; a woman is brought in on a barrow; the faces are marked by exhaustion and distress. At Jesus's feet lies a woman totally prostrate on a straw bed; the onlooker looks straight into her sorrowful face with its closed eyes. A woman seen half from the back kneels before Jesus, holding her clasped hands towards him in entreaty. Right at the front of this procession of wretchedness a woman has stretched out her arms so far that her shadow falls on Jesus's garment, as if to indicate literally that Jesus is *touched* by all this suffering.[288]

There had earlier been graphic works making the contents of whole chapters of the Bible visible in one print.[289] However, there is an essential difference between these and Rembrandt's summary of the 19th chapter of Matthew. The Bible illustrations of the 16th and early 17th centuries showed the successive events in separate sequences, each with its own sphere of action, which were juxtaposed. Often, to show the correct sequence, the scenes were numbered, which, of course, made the artificiality of the arrangement obvious. Rembrandt made the successive images coexist and interpenetrate, for all the figures are placed within the same sphere of action and the same time, as was stated above. The calm, impressive figure of Christ which dominates the whole picture is a further unifying feature — even if there are interactions and distractions within the group.

Inspired by pictorial tradition, by series, simultaneous depictions and by the iconography of scenes both preceding and following a story, Rembrandt adds motifs which remind one of the entire story but which do not actually belong to the scenes or which are not part of the pictorial tradition. As we know, Rembrandt was moved by an etching of Jan van de Velde to add an eye-catching motif which does not accord with the text. THE GOOD SAMARITAN pays the innkeeper for the

256
257

wounded man when they arrive, whereas in the biblical parable, he pays when he leaves the following day. During 258 the ENTOMBMENT which took place on the evening of Good Friday, Rembrandt shows people on the mountain still 259 watching the crucifiction. In the etching ABRAHAM TALKING TO ISAAC, Rembrandt shows the story as Josephus tells it: Abraham explains to Isaac who is to be sacrificed, so that Isaac knows. In the biblical report, Abraham avoids replying to Isaac's question about the sacrifice. In many works we see the various places where the heroes of the stories have been. 259 In the BAPTISM OF THE CHAMBERLAIN we still see the empty seat in the carriage where the chamberlain had been sitting. We see the African boy who is holding the clothes which the chamberlain had taken off for the baptism. In the etching 256 THE TRIUMPH OF MORDECAI, B40, Esther and Ahasuerus are 255 watching the triumph of Mordecai. In the BEHEADING OF JOHN THE BAPTIST Rembrandt shows Herod and Herodias in the background, even though the presence of the royal couple is excluded by the text. Rembrandt, however, depicts them in the spirit of a higher truth: he clarifies the entire story, how it happened, and the human background and its relationship to fate.

THE ANGEL LEAVING THE FAMILY OF TOBIAS.
Signed: 'Rembrandt f.' and dated 1641.
Etching 104 × 153 mm. 1st state.
Bartsch 43.

THE BAPTISM OF THE CHAMBERLAIN.
Signed: 'Rembrandt f.' and dated 1641.
Etching (178/182) × (214/212) mm. 2nd state.
Berlin-Dahlem, Staatliche Museen Preussischer Kulturbesitz, Kupferstichkabinett.
Bartsch 98.

ABRAHAM TALKING TO ISAAC.
Signed: 'Rembrandt' and dated 1645.
Etching 160 × 131 mm. Only one state.
Hamburg, Kunsthalle.
Bartsch 34.

Geertghe Dircx came to Rembrandt's house as a nurse for Titus.[290] The recently widowed Rembrandt painted and 262 drew her, gave her Saskia's jewelry, and made her his mistress. She felt so close to Titus that when she fell very ill in 1648, she made him the chief heir in her will. Later, however, arguments arose between Rembrandt and Geertghe. It is not known whether the cause of these was the housemaid, Hendrickje Stoffels, who at twenty-two was considerably younger and who had come to the house before the summer of 1649. Rembrandt tried to reach a peaceful settlement with Geertghe, offering to pay her 150 guilders at once, and then an annual allowance of 160 guilders. But this agreement was not legalized at once. Geertghe moved out, had to pawn Rembrandt's gifts in order to live, and denounced her former master in court for marital quarrels and defamation of character. She demanded that he marry her or pay her a pension. Rembrandt did not appear before the court, but he finally consulted a lawyer. In a contract he stressed the social differences between himself and Geertghe, styling himself 'the famous painter', whereas Geertghe is referred to as a penniless nursemaid. But this did not satisfy him. Because of her fondness for Titus, Geertghe had named him as her chief beneficiary, but Rembrandt demanded her property. Everything she had, she had received in his house, so that the annual payments should be made to her only on the condition that she would not change her will or pawn her property. When Geertghe was shown this contract, she clearly felt trapped and became uncertain. She did not want to sign it, objecting that with such an annual payment she would not even be able to have a nurse if she became ill. So Rembrandt was not spared a third summons. He submitted the draft of his contract. The judges concurred, but raised the annual payments to 200 guilders.

Unfortunately, the matter had a sad sequel. When Geertghe broke the contract by pawning a valuable ring, Rembrandt's suppressed hatred erupted and he collected material to incriminate her. Neighbours bore witness that she had behaved badly. She was taken to the House of Correction in Gouda, Rembrandt paying for the transportation in advance. In 1651 he did his best to have her kept in prison for another 11 years, but in 1655 her friends secured her release despite his objections. The matter did not end there. When he got into financial difficulties in 1656, and was himself threatened with the debtors' gaol, Rembrandt remembered the 160 guilders he had paid for her transportation. Although he still owed money to Geertghe, he tried every possible means of recovering these 160 guilders. Her

STUDY OF A WOMAN IN ZEELAND COSTUME, SEEN FROM BEHIND. About 1636.
Pen and wash drawing with bistre. 220 × 150 mm.
Haarlem, Teylers Museum.
Benesch 315.

A YOUNG GIRL AT A WINDOW.
Signed: 'Rembrandt f 1651'.
Canvas 78 × 63.6 cm.
Stockholm, National Museum.
Cat. 150 / Bredius 377.

GEERTHGE DIRCX (?). About 1643.
Pen and wash drawing with bistre. 130 × 78 mm.
London, British Museum.
Benesch 314.

brother, a ship's carpenter, had guaranteed the sum, and although Rembrandt owed a sum a hundred times as large and was dependent upon the good will of his creditors and the courts, he had this brother thrown into a debtors' prison when he could not pay. Geertghe probably died shortly after her release, for her name appeared for the last time on the list of Rembrandt's creditors in 1656.

This rather unedifying story shows how self-righteous and implacable the artist could be who time and again had depicted mercy and forgiveness in his works. Yet we must temper our judgement by admitting that we have too little documentary evidence on the character and failings of Geertghe to decide with certainty whether Rembrandt may not merely have been following the legal views of his day.

A YOUNG GIRL LEANING ON A WINDOW-SILL. ▶
Signed: 'Rembrandt ft. 1645'.
Canvas 81.6 × 66 cm.
London, Dulwich Picture Gallery.
Cat. 149 / Bredius 368.

Rembrandt's workshop.
A YOUNG WOMAN AT A DOOR.
Signed: 'Rembrandt f. 1645'.
Canvas 102 × 84 cm.
Chicago, Art Institute.
Cat. A57 / Bredius 367.

Follower of Rembrandt.
A GIRL HOLDING A BROOM.
Signed: 'Rembrandt f. 1651'.
Canvas 107 × 91 cm.
Washington DC., National Gallery of Art.
Cat. A59 / Bredius 378.

After Rembrandt had separated from Geertghe Dircx, Hendrickje Stoffelsdr. Jaeger became his housekeeper and mistress. She was 22 when Rembrandt separated from Geertghe, who must have been nearly 40. But it was not just her youth which attracted this man of 43. Whereas he had seldom painted Geertghe, who had lived in his house for seven years, he painted Hendrickje, as he had earlier painted Saskia, over and over again, as Flora and Bathsheba, Juno and Lucretia.

273, 289, 356, 348

Hendrickje, like Geertghe, was of simple origin, the daughter of a sergeant. From the little that is known of her, she seems to have been a loyal companion to Rembrandt, for the neighbours later referred to her as his wife. Their relationship could not be legalised because Saskia's will stated that if Rembrandt remarried, half her estate was to be paid to her relatives. According to a later valuation, that would have been 20,350 guilders, which after the unproductive 1640s he would have been hard pressed to pay. His financial position was so bad by 1649 that he stopped payments on his house and could not even pay the interest and taxes. Yet he took upon himself the difficulties which were bound to be caused by his living with Hendrickje at a time of strong church discipline and double-standard morality.

When Hendrickje was expecting a child in 1654, she was called before the church courts. She did not appear until the fourth summons and admitted 'that she had whored with Rembrandt, the painter', for which she was 'punished, exhorted to penance, and excluded from the Lord's Table'. A few months later, in October, she gave birth to a daughter, who was called Cornelia after Rembrandt's mother and was baptised in the Oude Kerk. This must have reawakened old memories in Rembrandt, for Saskia's two daughters, who had died so young, had been baptised with the same name. Rembrandt admitted that the child was his and appeared as the father in the church register.

Anyone who believes Rembrandt's work to be merely a reflection of his life or who naively interprets art as a mirror of economic conditions will find no corroboration for his views in the works of the years that followed. It is true that Rembrandt now painted the people within his circle, Hendrickje, Titus, his friends, art-dealers, and even the auctioneers of his estate, but his artistic development was not influenced by financial need. He neither followed fashionable taste in order to sell nor does his style mirror his critical situation in these years. On the contrary, the compositions of precisely this period radiate calm and serenity.

264, 266, 267, 268, 270, 271, 276

A GIRL SLEEPING. About 1655-1656.
Pen and bistre wash. 245 × 203 mm.
London, British Museum.
Benesch 1103.

HENDRICKJE BATHING IN A RIVER.
Signed: 'Rembrandt f. 1654'.
Wood 61.8 × 47 cm.
London, National Gallery.
Cat. 122 / Bredius 437.

HENDRICKJE STOFFELS. About 1652.
Canvas 74 × 61 cm.
Paris, Louvre.
Cat. 187 / Bredius 111.

HENDRICKJE STOFFELS AT THE OPEN DOOR. About 1656/57.
Canvas 88.5 × 67 cm.
Berlin-Dahlem, Staatliche Museen Preussischer Kulturbesitz,
Gemäldegalerie. Cat. 188 / Bredius 116.

TITUS AT HIS WRITING-DESK. Signed: 'Rembrandt f. 1655'. Canvas 77 × 63 cm. Rotterdam, Boymans-van Beuningen Museum. Cat. 184 / Bredius 120.

The impending loss of his collection led to an even more intense involvement with the works of the great Renaissance artists. He copied the most valuable and the rarest graphic works of European artists as well as Indian miniatures and statues from antiquity. Yet he did this not only to retain images of the treasures he was about to lose, for he often used the motifs and pictorial solutions of these works in his later compositions.

The single figure predominates in the paintings he produced at this time, and only towards the middle 1650s did he complete a number of compositions with several figures. He therefore developed his new pictorial technique first in life-size portraits and single figures, influenced by the late styles of Titian and Frans Hals. Areas of colour were applied with broad brush-strokes or with a palette knife, and the drying colour was modelled with the brush or finger. These compositions have a predominance of horizontal and vertical lines, whereas diagonal lines had been used in the 1630s. The compositions are now aligned with the plane of the picture, so that figures seen in profile or frontally become more and more important.

Rembrandt also developed his etching technique in the 1650s. In his early work he had principally used the engraver's tool, but since the 1630s he had made increasing use of dry point, and in the 1650s he often did so without chemical treatment of the plate. He preferred this technique in his later works also. In using it, he achieved gradations from the strongest to the most delicate lines with utmost assurance. The ridges of the incised lines intentionally produce a patchy effect resulting in a deep tonal unity.

Between 1650 and 1653, half of his landscape etchings 275 were produced, based on numerous drawings. In contrast to his practice when drawing from nature, in these etchings he 275 superimposes block-like motifs such as groups of trees and towers on the flat landscapes which he actually observed, in order to unify the composition. His technique with dry point, now at the apex of perfection, creates impressions of light and colour of an almost unbelievable delicacy that no earlier artist had achieved.

Naturally this artist, who was so well educated in art history, could not be unaware of his own importance, particularly as his fame had spread even to Sicily, where he

School of Rembrandt (?).
TITUS VAN RIJN. About 1660.
Canvas 72 × 56 cm.
Paris, Louvre.
Cat. A75 / Bredius 126.

Rembrandt circle.
BOY IN FANCY DRESS (so-called TITUS). About 1660.
Canvas 64.8 × 55.9 cm.
Pasadena, The Norton Simon Museum of Art.
Cat. A99 / Bredius 119.

TITUS READING. About 1658.
Canvas 70.5 × 64 cm.
Vienna, Kunsthistorisches Museum.
Cat. 185 / Bredius 122.

TITUS. About 1658.
Monogrammed: 'R'.
Canvas 67.3 × 55.2 cm.
London, Wallace Collection.
Cat. 186 / Bredius 123.

TITIAN.
FLORA. About 1515-1516.
Canvas 79 × 63 cm.
Florence, Uffizi.

had received commissions. This explains why, during the 1650s, Rembrandt occupied himself with the masterpieces of his illustrious predecessors and even tried to outdo them. His large-scale etchings ECCE HOMO and THE THREE CROSSES were intended to surpass the masterful etchings of Lucas van Leyden, which he had acquired at enormous cost. 274, 278

Attempts have been made to interpret his later works by suggesting that the ageing artist was striving only for universal truth and elevated spirituality, no longer for concrete history. The truth is the exact opposite[291]. His intense preoccupation with the works of his predecessors and contemporaries meant that during this period he was particularly concerned with tradition, borrowing subjects from it and correcting its solutions. His virtuosity in the technique of etching enabled him even with dry point to represent night scenes and even natural catastrophes, which no previous artists had been able to do.

In his large etching THE THREE CROSSES, Rembrandt dramatized and interpreted the scene on Calvary. To symbolise the world-shaking event of Christ's death, the evangelists relate that a darkness came, and that after the death of Jesus, the earth shook, the rocks split, and the graves opened. 278

Rembrandt's workshop.
A YOUNG WOMAN (so-called HENDRICKJE). About 1655.
Canvas 65.5 × 54 cm.
Los Angeles, County Museum of Art (on loan from Mrs Lucille Ellis Simson).
Cat. A76 / Bredius 112.

Rembrandt's workshop.
THE PROPHETESS HANNAH IN THE TEMPLE. In the background: THE SONG OF PRAISE OF SIMEON.
Signed: 'Rembrandt f. 16(50)'.
Mahogany 42.9 × 34.8 cm.
Edinburgh, National Gallery of Scotland. Cat. A9 / Bredius 577.

HENDRICKJE AS FLORA. About 1657.
Canvas 100 × 91.8 cm.
New York, Metropolitan Museum of Art.
Cat. 111 / Bredius 114.

ECCE HOMO. Etching 383 × 455 mm. 1st state.
From the 6th state on dated 1655.
Berlin-Dahlem, Kupferstichkabinett. Bartsch 76.

THE RUINS OF THE OLD TOWN HALL AFTER THE FIRE OF 7 JULY 1652.
Pen and wash drawing in bistre, and red chalk. 145 × 197 mm.
Dated 1652.
Amsterdam, Rembrandthuis. Benesch 1278.
Inscription by Rembrandt in translation:
' be seen here the Town Hall of Amsterdam after it had burned down. 9 July 1652. Rembrandt van rijn.'

VIEW OVER THE IJ FROM DIEMERDIJK. About 1650/51.
Pen and wash drawing with bistre, some body white. On toned paper.
76 × 244 mm.
Chatsworth, Devonshire Collection.
Benesch 1239.

LANDSCAPE WITH TREES, FARMHOUSES AND TOWER. About 1652.
Etching 124 × 320 mm. 3rd state.
Hamburg, Kunsthalle. Bartsch 223.

LANDSCAPE WITH FRINGE OF FOREST.
Signed: 'Rembrandt f.' and dated 1652.
Etching 124 × 212 mm. 2nd state.
Hamburg, Kunsthalle.
Bartsch 222.

LANDSCAPE WITH OBELISK. About 1650.
Etching 83 × 162 mm. 1st state. Bartsch 227.

A COTTAGE AMONGST TREES NEAR A RIVER. About 1650.
Pen and wash drawing with bistre and some body white.
133 × 204 mm.
Chatsworth, Devonshire Collection. Benesch 1232.

A ROAD NEAR A RIVER WITH BOATS. About 1650/51.
Pen and wash drawing with bistre. 127 × 200 mm.
Chatsworth, Devonshire Collection.
Benesch 1252.

JAN SIX (1618-1700). 1654.
Canvas 112 × 102 cm.
Amsterdam, Six Foundation.
Cat. 214 / Bredius 276.

NICOLAES BRUYNINGH (c. 1629-1680).
Signed: 'Rembrandt f. 1652'.
Canvas 107.5 × 91.5 cm.
Cassel, Gemäldegalerie.
Cat. 212 / Bredius 268.

THE THREE CROSSES. 1653.
Etching 385 × 450 mm. 1st state.
Berlin-Dahlem, Staatliche Museen Preussischer Kulturbesitz, Kupferstichkabinett.
Bartsch 78.

THE RISEN CHRIST APPEARING TO MARY MAGDALEN.
Signed: 'Rembrandt 165(1)'.
Canvas 65 × 79 cm.
Brunswick, Herzog Anton Ulrich Museum.
Cat. 70 / Bredius 583.

> Now when the centurion and they that were with him watching Jesus saw the earthquake and those things that were done, they feared greatly, saying, Truly this was the Son of God. And many women were there beholding afar off, which followed Jesus from Galilee. (Matthew 27: 54 ff.).

In his etching, Rembrandt dispenses with all narrative details such as the soldiers casting lots for Christ's robe. Instead, he concentrates on the three crosses and the reactions of the onlookers to the death of Christ and the natural phenomena. He depicts actual darkness and destruction and shows people truly shattered by the death of Jesus and the happenings of nature. The centurion has gone down on his knees; a man is led away in shock; women have fallen to the ground. Some hide their faces in their hands in grief. This concentration on the actions of those present, on the portrayal of despair, grief, and fear through movements, shows us how true to himself Rembrandt has remained even in his late works. If in THE RESURRECTION (137) he used dramatically agitated figures, some of whom were taken from Baroque works, here he borrows the subtle gestures from works of the Renaissance and antiquity. For example, the group on the left, where a man who has been overcome by the event is being led away, is based on an etching by Lucas van Leyden; Rembrandt used the solution which van Leyden had found to show the shock of the apostle Paul after his conversion. The conversion of the centurion in Rembrandt's etching is borrowed from a composition by Raphael. Beams of light break from the sky, accentuating the sacred character of the picture through their geometric structure. They fall on Christ and the good thief while the bad thief remains in darkness.

(247) Rembrandt's etching ECCO HOMO, produced two years later, entirely with dry point, is influenced by Lucas van Leyden.[292] Again he concentrates the action on Pilate, who is showing Christ to the people, and on the excited throng. Yet how much more clearly are the main groups distinguished and the secondary figures mentioned in the text accentuated. The city hall is unmistakably characterized by the symbolic figures as the seat of justice. Pilate asks the people: 'Whom will ye that I release unto you? Barabbas, or Jesus which is called Christ?'[293] Rembrandt depicts in detail the reaction of the throng, young and old men, women, and children. Some loudly demand the death of Jesus; others look on more

Rembrandt's workshop.
DAVID PLAYING THE HARP BEFORE SAUL. About 1655.
Canvas 130 × 164.3 cm.
The Hague, Mauritshuis.
Cat. A3 / Bredius 526.

Pupil of Rembrandt.
JOSEPH ACCUSED BY POTIPHAR'S WIFE.
Signed: 'Rembrandt f. 165(.)'.
Canvas 106 × 98 cm.
Washington, National Gallery.
Cat. A2 / Bredius 523.

FLORIS SOOP (1604-1657).
Signed: 'Rembrandt f. 1654'. Canvas 140.3 × 114.9 cm.
New York, Metropolitan Museum of Art.
Cat. 213 / Bredius 275.

CATRINA HOOGHSAET (1607-1685).
Signed: 'Rembrandt f. 1657' and on two shields in the top left corner:
'CATRINA HOOGH/SAET/ OUT 50/Jaer'.
Canvas 123.5 × 95 cm. England, private collection. Cat. 244 / Bredius 391.

THE AMSTERDAM DOCTOR ARNOUT THOLINX (1607-1679).
Signed: 'Rembrandt f. 1656'. Canvas 76 × 63 cm.
Paris, Musée Jacquemart-André.
Cat. 216 / Bredius 281.

indifferently. In the window on the left we see Pilate's wife, who has sent a messenger to her husband to tell him of her dream and to warn him. The boy on the far left at the altar is holding a bowl and so points to Pilate's washing of his own hands. Whereas in Lucas van Leyden's etching the main group with Christ is obscured by a strong foreshortening of the composition, Rembrandt emphasises it by a conscious disregard for perspective. Pilate and Christ in the centre are as large as the people in the foreground, so that they come closer to the onlooker and are emphasised. Rembrandt depicts the scene from below, the action appearing to the spectator from the viewpoint of the people who are demanding Christ's execution.

The study of tradition led Rembrandt to an old theme of graphic art, the history of the youth of Jesus, which he depicted in a loose series of etchings.[294] The etchings, created in 1653 and 1654, are all about the same size. The connection with tradition is particularly close in this group of subjects, and yet in several instances he has departed from the customary treatment, which does not correspond to the text. This is most striking in the etching THE CIRCUMCISION OF CHRIST.[295] 285 Since the 4th century, iconographic tradition had shown the scene as taking place in the Temple, even though the gospel of St. Luke tells that the circumcision of Jesus took place on the eighth day after his birth, in the stable. For this reason, writings of the Counter-Reformation condemned the erroneous depiction of the scene in the Temple.[296] However, only one artist before Rembrandt, Anton Wierix, had placed the scene in the stable, in keeping with the biblical text. Perhaps Rembrandt knew this etching and, having been made aware of the problem, informed himself on the correct interpretation of Luke's text. Moreover, the portrayal of this scene requires an exact knowledge of the ritual procedure. Rembrandt interprets the event through lighting. Mary, Joseph, and a woman who is watching with interest appear in the full light which falls from heaven onto the stable. By contrast, the priests, their helpers, and witnesses who are engaged in the ritual or are following it with understanding are left in darkness, since they do not know that it is the Son of God on whom they are inflicting this pain. Thus, in his histories, Rembrandt does not depart in any way from what was actually given in the texts. On the contrary, precisely in his late works he often uses a rare motif, or even one which has never been used before, if it clarifies the meaning of the text. However, if a solution has already been found by earlier artists which explains a person's behaviour more correctly or more convincingly than one which is true to the text, in his late works he sometimes prefers the more human interpretation. For example, his early painting THE SACRIFICE OF ISAAC 148 shows an Abraham who has bound his son like a beast for

A COURTESAN AT HER MIRROR.
Signed: 'Rembrandt f. 165(4)'.
Wood 39.5 × 32.5 cm.
Leningrad, Hermitage.
Cat. 151 / Bredius 387.

PORTRAIT OF A MAN IN A FUR-LINED COAT. About 1654.
Signed: 'Rembrandt f.' with an illegable date.
Canvas 115 × 88.3 cm.
Boston, Museum of Fine Arts (on loan from Fuller Foundation).
Cat. 215 / Bredius 278.

PORTRAIT OF A FAIR-HAIRED MAN (CLEMENT DE JONGHE?).
Signed: 'Rembrandt f.'.
Canvas 94 × 75 cm.
Buscot Park, Berkshire, Faringdon Collection.
Cat. 211 / Bredius 265.

slaughter, while the later representation evinces compassion; Isaac kneels before his father, who embraces him with emotion.

In a certain sense, what has been said about the histories applies also to the portraits. The late painting THE ANATOMY LESSON OF DR. JOAN DEYMAN, produced in 1656, shows the actual proceedings more faithfully than the earlier group portrait, THE ANATOMY LESSON OF DR. TULP. The opened abdomen and the exposed brain of the corpse are visible. This was the order in which an autopsy was usually begun, because those parts of the body which decomposed quickly had to be removed. Dr. Deyman had succeeded Dr. Tulp in 1653 and had himself painted with other members of the guild during an anatomy lesson in 1656. The painting hung originally in the Anatomical Theatre and was largely destroyed in a fire in 1723. Luckily, the museum in Amsterdam owns a sketch of the composition, which Rembrandt made when designing the heavy ornamental frame, and he also indicated where it would best be hung in the room.[297] This drawing allows us to make a reconstruction of the entire conception. The composition is symmetrical and shows the body in the central axis, strongly foreshortened. Dr. Deyman is standing behind it, dissecting the brain. In the left foreground, the university lecturer, Gysbrecht Calkoen, holds the top of the skull. The other people pictured are behind the barrier that surrounds the circular stage of the Anatomical Theatre, and they are so arranged that the two groups appear to be equally balanced. What is special in this work is its unusual conception. We look first at the feet of the body, then at the abdomen, and finally at Dr. Deyman, who is seen from below. The formal composition is inspired by the famous LAMENTATION FOR CHRIST by Mantegna, as is the inverted perspective which reduces the size of the feet of the man who has been executed, while clearly enlarging the abdomen and the brain, the parts important for the study of anatomy. Rembrandt made a careful study of the dissection of the brain, and for his depiction of it he used a famous woodcut from a medical textbook known to us.[298]

285
78-79
284

THE ANATOMY LESSON OF DOCTOR JOAN DEYMAN. About 1656.
Pen and bistre. 110 × 133 mm.
Amsterdam, Rijksprentenkabinet.
Benesch 1175.

THE ANATOMY LESSON OF DOCTOR JOAN DEYMAN (1620-1666).
Signed: 'Rembrandt f. 1656'.
Canvas 100 × 134 cm, originally 275 × 200 cm.
Amsterdam, Rijksmuseum.
Cat. 255 / Bredius 414.

THE CIRCUMCISION IN THE STABLE. About 1654.
Etching 95 × 144 mm. 1st state.
Hamburg, Kunsthalle.
Bartsch 47.

לאתרצח
לאתנאף
לאתגנב

In his late work Rembrandt again used a form of composition that had fascinated him in his early Amsterdam period: he created half-length figure pictures in the manner of Caravaggio, endowing the form with new life. In so doing he made use of the Venetian colourist style, the late Titian being a particular model.[299] The language of gesture and facial expression was exploited more sensitively and quietly, less dramatically, than in the 1640s. Because he diverged from the stylistic mainstream of his time in this reversion to earlier techniques, he had to contend with attacks from the art trade and from clients. These must have been difficult to withstand. For two decades his stylistic development had determined that of an older and a younger generation in the northern Netherlands. After he had produced self-portraits which had given a new interpretation to the artist's role, many young artists painted self-portraits as Rembrandt had done. Since he had plumbed the possibilities of chiaroscuro in the history, in the night scene, in fine-detail painting (*Feinmalerei*), and in portraits, hundreds of painters had followed him, not only in Amsterdam and Leyden but in other Dutch cities as well. His graphics had been influential throughout Europe. But after 1640 there was a break.[300] Many artists turned back to classicist art. The works of Raphael, above all, became the normative models. Over and over again, the great Italian's loggia frescoes were copied in engravings, even by artists who had worked previously in the style of Caravaggio. The works of the great German and Dutch engravers of the Renaissance and Mannerism, the enchanting works of the Venetian colourists, and the Italian and Dutch Caravaggisti were thought old-fashioned. Rembrandt was not able to escape this trend entirely and occupied himself again with the works of the Italian Renaissance, seeing them with new eyes and learning to appreciate their temperate gestures, which he had dramatised in his Baroque phase.

This did not prevent him from continuing to admire and study the works of the great colourists and Caravaggisti and the great engravers of the Renaissance and Mannerism or from developing his own characteristic style further in adapting them, in renewing old forms, and in transforming new ones.

But because the masterpieces he admired were no longer rated highly, he saw his own influence, his market value, his stock sink in the course of years. New comets flared in the artistic firmament of Amsterdam and set the trend. Among them were some of his pupils, who all too quickly turned with the wind.[301]

In this situation Rembrandt remained true to himself. Throughout Europe there were also, beside the admirers of the bland court style, sensitive collectors who admired Rembrandt's continuing development. They included the Venetian nobleman Ruffo, already mentioned. With his commission for half-length figure pictures, such as the ARISTOTLE of 1653, he stimulated Rembrandt to concern himself again with life-size histories. So in the 1650s he painted a number of unusual masterpieces. 360

A year after the ARISTOTLE, Rembrandt produced one of his most beautiful works, the Louvre BATHSHEBA of 1654. Through a comparison with an earlier painting on the same theme, made by a student in 1643, which is now in New York, Hans Jantzen grasps the essence of this painting, which shows a figure detached from her historical context: 289 288

> While the earlier picture has the character of a 'biblical history', with a copious depiction of the situation that makes the figures look like accessories, in the later painting in the Louvre the merely narrative element is suppressed as far as possible, and the purely human content of the event is condensed into something wonderfully profound. The life-size naked figure of the beautiful woman now dominates the picture. The upper body of the old woman in the corner of the picture at Bathsheba's feet and merging into the background colour is hardly noticed.... A poised calm and a rich transparency flood from the closed square of the painting, intensified by the warm splendour of the progression of red and brocade golds rising from the brown ground tone. Transparency in the spatial values created by unfolding planes, the relief-like disposition of the body that follows the movement of the picture plane, tranquillity in the secure, organic construction of the figure. Never has Rembrandt portrayed 'sitting' with such decisive clarity as here. Moreover, all the formal movements of the figure are closed on themselves. The head is aligned to the planes of the whole figure, is seen in profile and slightly inclined. There is nothing which leads outside this closed form. And this matches the underlying conception. The Louvre Bathsheba seems detached from the present, quietly harbouring her thoughts. Her fingers mechanically hold the king's momentous letter.... This

MOSES SMASHING THE TABLETS OF THE LAW.
Signed: 'Rembrandt f. 1659'.
Canvas 168.5 × 136.5 cm.
Berlin-Dahlem, Staatliche Museen Preussischer Kulturbesitz, Gemäldegalerie.
Cat. 27 / Bredius 527.

Pupil of Rembrandt.
BATHSHEBA AT HER TOILET SEEN BY KING DAVID.
Signed: 'Rembrandt ft 1643'.
Wood 57.2 × 76.2 cm.
New York, Metropolitan Museum of Art.
Cat. A1 / Bredius 513.

Rembrandt's workshop.
CHRIST AND THE WOMAN OF SAMARIA.
Signed: 'Rembrandt f. 1655'.
Wood 48 × 40.5 cm.
Berlin-Dahlem, Staatliche Museen Preussischer Kulturbesitz, Gemäldegalerie.
Cat. A10 / Bredius 588.

mood of complete self-absorption only became accessible to Rembrandt in the fifties.... Yet now in the Bathsheba painting the mood is deepened spiritually. What Rembrandt had failed to achieve in his youth, to show the spiritual form of such a figure, is accomplished here. This form encompasses a human fate ensnared in guilt.... In it the gathering and denouement of the whole Bathsheba tragedy is condensed.[302]

Of particular importance in characterising the figure's detachment, it seems to me, is the observation that the history is by no means abolished, but that its special dimension — the tragic content of human entanglement — is heightened as compared with the merely narrative motifs.

It is of interest to know that Henrik Bramsen discovered in 1950 the formal model for this Bathsheba, an engraving by Perrier from his *Icones et segmenta illustrium e marmore tabularum quae Romae adhuc extant* (Rome, 1645), which provides the group of a bathing woman with a servant.[303] So one may suppose that here, as in THE PRODIGAL SON IN THE BROTHEL, 117 Rembrandt may have been stimulated by the formal model to detach Bathsheba from her historical context.

In the year of Rembrandt's financial collapse, 1656, he produced one of his masterpieces, JACOB BLESSING THE CHILDREN OF JOSEPH, 290 which communicates a sense of deep tranquillity.

Critics have long been struck by how far Rembrandt's depiction departs from the biblical text; but they have never given a convincing explanation. Yet the reason must be obvious to anyone who is familiar with Rembrandt's narrative style as a whole. According to the biblical text, Joseph brought his two sons, Manasseh and Ephraim, to the dying Jacob, wishing his elder son, Manasseh, to receive the blessing of the first-born and Ephraim only a general blessing. He therefore placed Manasseh at Jacob's right hand and Ephraim at his left. Jacob, however, opposed Joseph's intention by *crossing* his hands and giving Ephraim the first-born's blessing. To Joseph's protest he replied prophetically that Ephraim would be the progenitor of a greater people than Manasseh.

In earlier art this story of Ephraim and Manasseh was interpreted in terms of the relationship between Christianity and Judaism. The story was seen as implying that it was not the first-born people, the Jews, who received the true blessing, but the younger people, the Christians.

Various typical representations of the story were developed in the painting tradition. In the most common, the crossing of the arms was heavily accentuated. But there were also works which dispensed with this motif and depicted a simple blessing or tried to show more clearly in pictorial terms which of the two had received the first-born's blessing.

All these attempts must have left Rembrandt dissatisfied. In many works showing Jacob with crossed hands he looks decidedly vigorous. Rembrandt, by contrast, stresses the frailty of the dying man and makes Joseph support the right hand that gives the blessing. In this way Jacob's extreme age and the significance of the last act before his death are poignantly conveyed. But the theme of dying is combined in an impressive way with the old symbolic treatment of the

BATHSHEBA WITH KING DAVID'S LETTER.
Signed: 'Rembrandt f. 1654'.
Canvas 142 × 142 cm.
Paris, Louvre.
Cat. 24 / Bredius 521.

blessing. Jacob blesses the blond Ephraim who, as the archetype of the Christians, receives the first-born's blessing, according to the early Christian interpretation. The devoutly clasped hands, symbolising Ephraim's Christianity, also allude to this typological meaning. Joseph's supporting hand crosses Jacob's arm and touches Manasseh's head. But Jacob's left hand, too, raised almost invisibly — only three fingers are seen — touches the dark-haired son's head. Only through Joseph's mediation, and almost incidentally, does Manasseh receive a share of Jacob's blessing. Meanwhile, Ephraim has his eyes devoutly closed while Manasseh looks unsuspectingly towards the onlooker. The real meaning of the history and of its early Christian interpretation is here expressed by Rembrandt far more profoundly, and more convincingly in pictorial terms, than by a literal presentation.

It has always attracted notice that Rembrandt also depicted Asenath, Joseph's wife, although she is not mentioned at this point in the biblical text. One explanation offered is that Rembrandt here adduces Jewish legends that speak of her presence. This argument has a certain justification in that Dutch history painters frequently drew on other sources apart from the Bible. All the same, this was probably not the real reason. Rembrandt was inclined, in biblical or mythological scenes referring expressly to the family as a unit — and they include death scenes — always to show husband

JACOB BLESSING THE SONS OF JOSEPH.
Faked signature: 'Rimbran(dt) f. 1656'.
Canvas 175 × 210.5 cm.
Cassel, Gemäldegalerie.
Cat. 26 / Bredius 525.

JOSEPH ACCUSED BY POTIPHAR'S WIFE.
Signed: 'Rembrandt f. 1655'.
Canvas 113.5 × 90 cm.
Berlin-Dahlem, Staatliche Museen Preussischer Kulturbesitz, Gemäldegalerie.
Cat. 25 / Bredius 524.

JACOB WRESTLING WITH THE ANGEL. About 1659.
Signed: 'Rembrandt f.'.
Canvas 137 × 116 cm.
Berlin-Dahlem, Staatliche Museen Preussischer Kulturbesitz, Gemäldegalerie.
Cat. 29 / Bredius 528.

and wife together, even if one of them was not mentioned in the written source.[304]

The composition of the painting is magnificient, in structure as in the disposition of colour. Through the overlapping of figures, the painting, concentrated on gestures and glances, conveys an immensely intimate and intense impression. The brown curtains and the red bed-cover act as a frame, the background as a foil that causes the main figures to stand out in proportion to their significance through their brighter colours. The composition seems so deliberate that the slight error in perspective of the bed-posts is not noticed.

It was only at the end of the decade that Rembrandt again produced a number of biblical histories. Amsterdam history painting was at that time given a new impulse by the fitting-out of the town hall.[305] As early as 1655, Vondel described the whole town hall plan as if the decorations for the monumental building were already complete. This only happened, however, in the course of the next decade. No doubt, the large pictures that were commissioned, for which many of Rembrandt's pupils made sketches, provided an impulse not only for the painters but for the citizens, who desired similarly imposing pieces for the fireplaces of their own palaces.

Rembrandt does not appear to have entered the competitions for the town hall fireplace pictures, but his pupils, who had good connections from painting numerous influential patricians, certainly did so. Rembrandt or his client was, however, inspired by the Moses themes to concern himself with the figure of the Old Testament hero who was commanded by God to lead the Israelites out of Egypt. The town hall plan included MOSES DISPLAYS THE TABLETS OF THE LAW. 286 Rembrandt chooses a different moment, when Moses comes down the mountain with the tablets to find that the people have defected from Jehovah. Moses is shown frontally as a slightly over-life-size three-quarter-length figure lifting up the tablets in order to smash them in his anger at the worship of the golden calf by the Israelites. We see his head, bent slightly to one side, framed by his arms. He does not conceal his disappointment. He wears a light garment which reflects the colours of the mountains, which are painted in warm brown and umber tones. Only the sleeves and the face are touched by a light shining from the left and glow brightly. In the later story, when Moses had received the tablets from God a second time and was showing them to the people, Moses's head is said to have shone. In Hebrew the word for 'shine' is related to the word for 'horns', giving rise to a misunderstanding that Moses had horns. In the picture tradition, horns became an attribute of Moses; however, in Rembrandt's model, an engraving by Fontana after Parmigianino, these are replaced by two locks of hair and by beams of light.[306] Rembrandt takes over the realistic motif of the locks of hair at the temples and also suggests the shining of the face. He has detached the figure of Moses from its narrative context.[307] The scene of MOSES SMASHES THE TABLETS OF THE LAW is often represented as taking place on a path cut into Mount Sinai, which Moses is descending. Rembrandt suggests this by the rocks in front of Moses. He has also taken over another motif, though in intensified form. In the older tradition of this scene, most of the Commandments, indicated by numbers, can be read. As a learned artist interested in the Old Testament, Rembrandt shows the Commandments in Hebrew script. Apart from a minor error, the last five Commandments are reproduced quite correctly.[308]

Heppner's theory dash that the painting was originally intended as a monumental fireplace piece for the lay assessors' chamber in the Amsterdam Town Hall, and was withdrawn by Rembrandt after being refused by the client and reduced to its present dimensions — was refuted by me in 1968.[309] Rembrandt depicts a scene different from that of Bol. In the meantime my objections have been confirmed by X-ray investigations. The canvas shows the stretch marks of the original frame all around. Heppner's surmise that the rock motif with the signature and date in the bottom right corner was added by Rembrandt after the supposed reduction in size is also invalidated by the X-ray pictures, for the cloak is not continued under the rock.[310]

In a second painting from the same year, JACOB WRESTLING 292 WITH THE ANGEL, Rembrandt has likewise consciously moderated everything that invited dramatic heightening and that he would have accentuated to the utmost in his youth.

The fight is only hinted at. While Jacob, who is shown from the back, holds the angel tightly clasped, the angel braces his right knee against his side and puts his left hand on his hip. Jacob's contorted body, which is bent at the hips, prefigures the outcome of the struggle: his hip was dislocated, causing him to limp throughout his life.

In the case of the angel, too, it is not only the fight that is suggested by the gestures and individual motifs (his garment is pushed up in the struggle; his foot is braced against the bank of the ford across the Jabbok River: the kindly expression of the face of the angel and the glow emanating from him make it clear that Jacob's wish has been fulfilled. When the angel had revealed himself as a man of God, Jacob said: 'I will not let thee go, except thou bless me'.[311] And as in the picture of Abraham, Rembrandt shows this pictorially 248 by the outstretched wings of the angel. So the biblical words: 'beneath the shadow of thy wings I have refuge' are made visual.[312] In this painting also — in a way suggested by the half-length-figure pictures on which he was working — Rembrandt has isolated the group of figures from the landscape. Working in large formats left its imprint on Rembrandt's style and that of his pupils. The small, full-length-figure history pictures produced at the same time show a similar summary treatment stressing only the essential motifs.

THE LANGUAGE OF PICTURES: ELIMINATION

GETHSEMANE. About 1652.
Pen drawing with bistre, white heightening. 184 × 301 mm.
Hamburg, Kunsthalle.
Benesch 899.

In one of the best and most influential works on Rembrandt, an essay published in 1854 and still worth reading, Eduard Koloff interprets a number of Rembrandt's histories and adds the following criticism of scholarship at the time:

> The whole action is treated so clearly that I am at a loss to explain how the contents of the picture have been so generally misunderstood until now. The chief reason may be the odd 'subjective tendency' and hidden intention always attributed to Rembrandt, whereas one seldom finds so 'objective' an artist — that is, one who thinks himself so totally into his object and becomes so uncompromisingly one with it.[313]

Despite all the progress scholarship had made, these words, which take issue with the classicist interpretation of Rembrandt, might still be used to preface an interpretation of Rembrandt's history pictures.

For a long time it was believed that Rembrandt often took liberties with the pictorial tradition, omitting important iconographic motifs at whim. The elimination of iconographic motifs[314] was first analysed by the well-known art historian F. Schmidt-Degener in his book on Rembrandt and the Dutch Baroque, using the small etching GETHSEMANE as his example.

> In Rembrandt's treatment we are struck by the absence of the traditional cup of suffering, the symbolic chalice taken from the imagery of the Gospel itself. The significance of this chalice was sometimes made all too obvious by artists who showed a cross growing from it. One of the two small preliminary studies for the etching (in Hamburg) contains a rough indication of the chalice. The hand-wringing Saviour recalled to Rembrandt a composition in which the chalice has great prominence, Dürer's GETHSEMANE from the Small Passion. In the Gethsemane scene from the Great Passion, a woodcut that Rembrandt knew as well as we do, the angel brings Christ a cross instead of the chalice. But Rembrandt seeks no symbol for the coming horror. His conception is new. Christ despairs in the darkness of his Gethsemane like someone who no longer understands anything except that his soul is wretched to the point of death. Rembrandt's compassionate angel knows of neither cross nor chalice. He has no other thought than to bring comfort to the haggard figure and to support one who is broken and despairing of himself.[315]

8, 295

In subsequent criticism this hypothesis was adopted and further examples were found, where Rembrandt was supposed to have proceeded in a similar way. A broad area of

GETHSEMANE. About 1653. [enlarged; see also p. 297]
Etching 129 × 83 mm. Only one state.
Hamburg, Kunsthalle.
Bartsch 75.

critical opinion is summed up and systematised by J. Bialostocki in an important essay of 1957. Rembrandt, he argues, frequently acted high-handedly with regard to the pictorial tradition, arbitrarily omitting iconographic motifs that by tradition were constituent parts of particular themes. This made his subjects, particularly in the late works, difficult to recognise, or the works even had several meanings. Perhaps this possibility of different interpretations is precisely the reason for the depth and richness we feel in the late works. Therefore, he concludes, the correct identification of the subject is not really necessary in interpreting the works. Since then, Bialostocki has rightly corrected this view[316] and defined it more precisely, for the hypotheses do not stand up to critical examination. They are sometimes developed in relation to histories that are unmistakably by pupils and follow different iconographic principles from those of Rembrandt's work.[317] They often rest simply on deficient knowledge of the broad iconographic currents which could impinge on different themes at the end of the 16th century. In the depiction of Christ in the Garden of Gethsemane, for example, in addition to the traditional type with the goblet or cross, established since the 14th century, or with both in the last third of the 16th, two new iconographic solutions now emerged. In a type which was modern at the end of the 16th and the beginning of the 17th century, the angel is replaced by a beam of light, and the chalice and cross are absent. In a more recent type the angel supports the exhausted Saviour, and chalice and cross are not shown.[318]

To understand this development of the Gethsemane theme, one must call to mind the general development of iconographic style in the 16th century. Up to the beginning of the 16th century, the iconography of the biblical history was governed both in the choice of subjects and in the manner of presentation by the medieval typological and symbolic interpretation. In the Reformation an interest in the literal meaning of texts arose. The typological interpretation was replaced by an historical and moral one. The new interpretation had a remarkable effect on the choice and treatment of subjects. In many cases the symbolic motifs receded, as the typological principle of selection was no longer decisive and the history itself was studied. In Germany and the Netherlands new iconographic solutions were found and new subjects treated which were of interest for the story and its moral implications. Vosmaer aptly characterised the preferred themes and manner of narrating them as follows:

> Instead of the visionary, prophetic parts of the Bible, it is the part concerned with the histories and the patriarchs that attracted these painters. Moving scenes were preferred to terrifying ones, the moral side to the dogmatic. Art had clearly drawn closer to life, to human feelings...these motifs are found in them all and later in the work of Rembrandt.[319]

The progression sketched very briefly here explains the development of the iconography of the Gethsemane theme and thus Rembrandt's decision in favour of a particular solution. The older Gethsemane type, in stressing symbolic and liturgical motifs (cross or chalice), deviates from the text of the Gospel. The synoptic Gospels tell of Christ's prayer, only Luke also mentioning the angel that comforts Christ. If, nevertheless, the angel in pictorial tradition holds the chalice or the cross, his appearance has been reinterpreted to enhance the symbolic or liturgical meaning. In the two later types of presentation, the picture is realigned with the text, and the chalice, which is only a metaphor in the text, is usually omitted, the angel is either replaced by a beam of light — only Christ's despairing prayer being shown — or he is seen comforting Christ.

Rembrandt possessed works showing all three solutions. He chose the most moving type, which he probably knew from a painting by Orazio Borgianni, since in both the Hamburg drawing and the etching he took over the main group almost unaltered and hardly changed the postures of the sleeping disciples. But in formal and iconographic terms he transformed the scene. Borgianni presents the scene as Luke tells it; contrary to the pictorial tradition, which follows Mark and Matthew, he shows all the disciples. Rembrandt, however, here follows the custom of showing only three favorite disciples, sleeping. As was usual, he depicts the scene in the Garden of Gethsemane. The persecutors with Judas are coming through the gate of the garden. This motif, not mentioned in the Gospels, is also absent in Borgianni; it was probably suggested by older Bible illustrations. In the etching Rembrandt has concentrated the scene on Christ and the angel. The flickering illumination of the main group makes clear Christ's inner struggle. The light that enters with the angel emphasizes the sleeping disciples and also falls on the group of soldiers with Pilate in the background, who are coming into the garden to arrest Christ.

295, 294

A study of the origin of the theme's iconography refutes the traditional judgement. The chalice is not a constituent motif of the pictorial tradition. It is not, therefore, the elimination of the chalice that is characteristic of Rembrandt's iconographic style, but his choice of the most moving type, in which Christ's suffering is made visible through the scenic arrangement.

Through the iconographic development in the 16th and 17th centuries many subjects underwent a new interpretation to which traditional motifs were no longer appropriate and so were discarded. In pictures of the crucifixion even before Rembrandt, the soldiers throwing dice for Christ's garment are often no longer shown; instead, the depiction is concentrated on the reactions of the spectators, the rejection by the Pharisees, the grief of the apostles, and the compassion of Mary.[320] The case is similar to the iconography of the Raising of Lazarus. In John, to make clear that Lazarus was really dead, Martha says to Jesus: 'Lord, by this time he stinketh: for he hath been dead four days'. Accordingly, spectators are often shown holding their noses while Lazarus rises from his grave.[321] An artist like Caravaggio has no need of this motif. He shows the body still rigid in death and reflects the miracle of the Resurrection in the shocked gestures and expressions of the spectators.[322] Rembrandt, too, decides on the type which eliminates the traditional motifs.[323] How unprogrammatically he proceeds, however, is demonstrated by many subjects that he treated several times. Christ appearing to Mary Magdalen is shown in the London painting with a spade, in keeping with the most common type, but in the Braunschweig picture he follows the type

162

279

without a spade, which adheres to the text. Before Rembrandt, the ladder was sometimes omitted in depictions of Jacob's dream, for example, a painting by François Venant.[324] Rembrandt follows this tradition in one drawing, but 147 shows the ladder in the late etching, perhaps at the desire of 297 his client.[325] The case is similar with the Hamburg drawing of Gethsemane. Rembrandt attempts to combine the modern iconographic version with the traditional motif of the chalice; since Christ does not look at the chalice as in the earlier version but is occupied with the angel who supports him, the inclusion of the chalice seems unmotivated. Rembrandt therefore omitted it from the etching.

These examples show that it was not his concern to eliminate the traditional iconographic or even symbolic motifs; rather, he aimed at a modern use of iconography which produced an emotive response.

GETHSEMANE. About 1653.
Etching 129 × 83 mm. Only one state.
Hamburg, Kunsthalle.
Bartsch 75.

AN OLD WOMAN READING.
Signed: 'Rembrandt f. 1655'.
Canvas 80 × 66 cm.
Drumlanrig Castle, Scotland, Collection of the Duke of Buccleuch and Queensberry, K.T.
Cat. 152 / Bredius 385.

Joachim von Sandrart, a contemporary of Rembrandt, wrote on the artist in his *Teutsche Akademie der edlen Bau-, Bild- und Malereikunst,* published in 1675 in Nuremberg: 'In the depiction of old people, particularly their skin and hair, he showed great diligence, patience and practice, so that he came very close to these humble lives'. This apparent commendation contains more censure than approval, for Sandrart goes on: 'But he painted few ancient poesies or allusions, or unusual histories, preferring simple subjects that do not lead to profound reflections, but which could be readily turned into pictures and were full of pretty things culled from nature'. These simple subjects, according to Sandrart, included the studies of heads and half-length figure portraits, of old people. In concerning himself with these studies from nature, in this painter's view, Rembrandt was abdicating from the true task of the erudite Classicist artist, which was to present histories and allegories while observing strict Classicist rules. These required that ancient statues should be used as the models for figures in histories. In addition, artists were to school themselves on Raphael's compositions with their strict and clearly legible structures and to master the rendering of anatomy, proportion and perspective.

Naturally, the Classicist adherent of Raphael's style could not tolerate Rembrandt's deference as a colourist to Titian and Caravaggio, and he comments censoriously:

> Because clear outlines have to be in their correct places, to avoid the danger of error he obliterates them with blackness, from which he seems to expect the maintenance of universal harmony. And in its use he indeed excels, not only grandly rendering the simplicity of nature but using natural forces to colour, heighten, and embellish it, particularly in half-length pictures or [studies of] old heads, as well as in small pieces, ornate clothing and other pretty effects.[326]

For Sandrart such studies were imperfect in that they did not take art but deformed nature as their model, and showed no clear 'disegno'.

However, in the 1650s and 1660s these picturesque studies of heads and historical figures by Rembrandt were in great demand. There is no other explanation why Rembrandt and his workshop produced them in such numbers. The studies of heads had long since lost their original function as preparatory material for history paintings, becoming a genre in their own right. As in the histories, in the late heads and historical figures Rembrandt reverts to the subjects chosen in his Leyden period. He is again concerned with the seers of the Old and New Testaments. They are pensive figures, seeing with their inner eye what is invisible to others. While many artists in the 16th and 17th centuries depict old people as decrepit, childish, miserly, and foolish, Rembrandt portrays them as waiting, hoping, meditating, and reading, taking on a profound human dignity through their faith and hope. His pupils were deeply impressed by these figures, painting many heads and historical figures according to Rembrandt's conception, which are often difficult to distinguish from his own.

Rembrandt's workshop.
AN OLD WOMAN SEATED, WITH A SATIN CAP AND FOLDED HANDS.
Signed: 'Rembrandt f. 165(.)'.
Canvas 82 × 72 cm.
Moscow, Pushkin Museum.
Cat. A115 / Bredius 371.

Rembrandt's workshop. AN OLD MAN IN AN ARMCHAIR.
Signed: 'Rembrandt f. 1652' (?). Canvas 111 × 88 cm.
London, National Gallery. Cat. A47 / Bredius 267.

Rembrandt's workshop.
AN OLD MAN IN A LINEN HEADBAND.
Signed: 'Rembrandt f' and dated 1651. Canvas 77 × 66 cm.
Wanås, Sweden, Collection of Count Wachtmeister.
Cat. A45 / Bredius 263.

Rembrandt circle. A BEARDED OLD MAN IN A CAP. About 1657.
Canvas 82 × 65 cm. Cambridge (Mass.), Fogg Art Museum.
Cat. A52 / Bredius 282.

A BEARDED OLD MAN IN A CAP. About 1657.
Signed: 'Rembrandt f 165(.)'. Canvas 78 × 66.7 cm.
London, National Gallery. Cat. 142 / Bredius 283.

School of Rembrandt
A BEARDED MAN. About 1657. Canvas 70.8 × 58.4 cm.
Berlin-Dahlem, Staatliche Museen Preussischer Kulturbesitz, Gemäldegalerie. Cat. A53 / Bredius 284.

Rembrandt's workshop.
AN OLD WOMAN IN AN ARMCHAIR.
Signed: 'Rembrandt f. 1654' (genuine?).
Canvas 109 × 84.5 cm.
Leningrad, Hermitage. Cat. A60 / Bredius 381.

Pupil of Rembrandt
OLD WOMAN. Signed: 'Rembrandt f. 1654'. Canvas 74 × 63 cm.
Moscow, Pushkin Museum. Cat. A61/Bredius 383.

P. 302 above:
Pupil of Rembrandt.
MARS (THE MAN WITH THE GOLDEN HELMET). About 1650.
Canvas 67 × 50 cm.
Berlin-Dahlem, Staatliche Museen Preussischer Kulturbesitz, Gemäldegalerie. Cat. A44 / Bredius 128.

School of Rembrandt.
OLD MAN.
Signed: 'Rembrandt f. 1650'.
Canvas 79.5 × 66 cm.
The Hague, Mauritshuis. Cat. A43 / Bredius 130.

Page 302 below:
Pupil of Rembrandt.
BIBLICAL OLD MAN SITTING IN AN ARMCHAIR (THE PATRIARCH JACOB OR THE PRIEST ELI). About 1652.
Canvas 51 × 37 cm.
Berlin-Dahlem, Staatliche Museen Preussischer Kulturbesitz, Gemäldegalerie. Cat. A48 / Bredius 269.

School of Rembrandt.
AN OLD MAN.
Signed: 'Rembrandt f. 1654'.
Canvas 74 × 63 cm.
Moscow, Pushkin Museum. Cat. A49 / Bredius 131.

OLD MAN IN AN ARMCHAIR.
Signed: 'Rembrandt f. 1654'. Canvas 109 × 84.8 cm.
Leningrad, Hermitage. Cat. 141 / Bredius 270.

THE SO-CALLED POLISH RIDER. About 1655.
Signed: 'Re' (cut off).
Canvas 116.8 × 134.9 cm.
New York, The Frick Collection.
Cat. 123 / Bredius 279.

Rembrandt (?).
ATHENA. About 1655.
Canvas 118 × 91 cm.
Lisbon, Museu Calouste Gulbenkian.
Cat. 110 / Bredius 479.

◀ SELF-PORTRAIT.
Signed: '...dt f. 1652'.
Canvas 112 × 81.5 cm.
Vienna, Kunsthistorisches Museum.
Cat. 169 / Bredius 42.

Rembrandt (?)
REMBRANDT ('SELF-PORTRAIT'). About 1645.
Signed: 'Re...'.
Wood 69 × 56 cm.
Karlsruhe, Staatliche Kunsthalle.
Cat. A70 / Bredius 38.

SELF-PORTRAIT.
Signed: 'Rembrandt f. 1657'.
Canvas 53 × 44 cm.
Edinburgh, National Gallery of Scotland (on loan from the Duke of Sutherland).
Cat. 170 / Bredius 48.

Imitator of Rembrandt.
REMBRANDT ('SELF-PORTRAIT').
Signed: 'Rembrandt f 1655'. Wood 66 × 53 cm.
Vienna, Kunsthistorisches Museum. Cat. A71 / Bredius 44.

REMBRANDT'S BANKRUPTCY AND THE SALE OF HIS ENCYCLOPAEDIC COLLECTION

When Rembrandt bought his house in the Jodenbreestraat in 1639, he promised the seller that he would pay the entire amount within five or six years. After fourteen years, about one-third of the price had been paid, so that Christoffel Tysz, the seller's heir, sent Rembrandt first an invoice for the outstanding sum of 8,470.16 guilders and then a lawyer. At that point Rembrandt clearly lost his head, and his unrealistic business transactions in the period that followed drove him towards bankruptcy. Difficult as his position was at that time, with more reflection he could have found a solution by disposing of his house, if at a loss. But instead of making a cool evaluation of his predicament, he entered into financial obligations which he could not meet and embarked on adventurous contracts. So, in the spring of 1653, he borrowed a total of 9,180 guilders from respected citizens who had a high regard for him. (Cornelis Witsen, a burgomaster, lent him 4,180 guilders without interest, Isaac van Haarsbeeck 4,000 guilders at five per cent interest, and Jan Six 1,000 guilders.) However, Rembrandt did not use these funds to clear his debt completely but left over 1,000 guilders owing, and kept for his own use a sum of almost 2,000 guilders, more than the annual salary of a professor. He undertook to repay his creditors within a year. Such empty promises were bound to discredit him, for even in his best times he never earned so much in a year. Jan Six soon lost faith in him and sold his promissory note. But worse was to come, for he fell further into debt with each year. In 1655, when he was up to his ears in debt, he tried to buy a new house for 7,000 guilders. He wanted to pay 4,000 guilders in cash and supply works of art worth 3,000 guilders. This contract does not seem to have been concluded, probably because of Rembrandt's looming bankruptcy. Even the voluntary sale of part of his collection in the winter of 1655 did not significantly relieve his financial situation.[327]

As disaster was in any case inevitable, Rembrandt gambled his reputation as an honest businessman by transferring his house into Titus's name at the Orphans' Board to exclude it from his assets. This manoeuvre probably induced his creditors to threaten him with legal action. He then had no alternative but to appeal to the High Court at The Hague for an honourable settlement of his hopeless situation. This *cessio bonorum* was permitted to citizens of good reputation who got into financial difficulties through no fault of their own.

From his assertion that he had sustained losses on land and sea, it appears that he had invested part of his capital in maritime trade or shipping. As the first naval war between

ABRAHAM SERVING THE THREE ANGELS.
Signed: 'Rembrandt f.' and dated 1656.
Etching 160 × 131 mm. Only one state.
Hamburg, Kunsthalle.
Bartsch 29.

FOUR ORIENTALS SITTING UNDER A TREE. Copy from an Indian miniature.
About 1656.
Pen drawing with bistre, 194 × 125 mm.
London, British Museum.
Benesch 1187.

PIETER HAERINGH (1609-1685).
Signed: 'Rembran f.' and dated 1655.
Etching 199 × 147 mm. 2nd state.
Hamburg, Kunsthalle.
Bartsch 275.

England and Holland took place in 1652-54, he may well have lost a substantial part of his capital. But he probably felt the economic effects of the war in his art business as well. However, reference to these circumstances certainly cannot hide the fact that the main causes of his bankruptcy were the decline in his productivity in the 1640s and his unrealistic business conduct.

Nevertheless, the High Court granted Rembrandt's request for settlement; he was spared the debtor's prison. His property was put up for auction so that his creditors could be paid off from the proceeds, and it is likely that Rembrandt himself collaborated. Ths inventory is therefore one of the best sources we have, for it tells us of his private preferences and his artistic and social criteria.[328] As his possessions were listed in order of the rooms, the document also gives us an idea of the arrangement of the house, which has since been rebuilt.

On the ground floor were the spacious living rooms. The furnishings and valuables were those of a well-to-do burgher. All the walls were covered with paintings; for the four rooms on this floor over 120 paintings are listed. Rembrandt's studio and his collection were on the next floor, and above it, in the attic, were his students' workrooms, separated by movable partitions. His collection was so large that the special art room provided for it was not sufficient, and the adjoining side rooms and the studio were also used to store art treasures. Of course, much of what was kept there was intended for sale, but the artist had also built up his collection with a view to his own studies and as a source of inspiration. As well as graphic works and paintings, it contained objects from the plant and animal realms, exotica from foreign lands, and objects of historical importance; in short, it was an encyclopaedic collection such as was common at that time among aristocratic and wealthy lovers of art. No doubt it also illustrated Rembrandt's social status, for he was able to assemble this collection only because he and Saskia were 'rich and endowed *ex superabundantia* (to excess) with property (for which they could not thank God enough)', as Saskia's brother Ulricus declared in another context in 1638.

The natural science section of his collection included different kinds of shells, land and sea plants, and stuffed animals. In the 17th century, fine shells were considered works of art which symbolised the transition from nature to art. For instance, the description of a similar collection in Rembrandt's time reads:

> We behold with pleasure in our collection the empty conches and houses of the most beautiful and rarest shellfish as they are found in nature, their beauty and wondrous forms fashioned as if by art, and rejoicing in them we praise the Lord.[329]

This is followed by the observation that neither the greatest artists of antiquity nor those of the present day could match the magnificent colours of the shells.

The United East India Company brought back costumes, weapons, and works of art from its travels to the countries of the East. Rembrandt wished to obtain an idea of the Oriental world through these exotic objects, so that his collection was rich in such folk art.

Rembrandt also had a considerable number of Greek and

Roman sculptures and plaster casts made from them. He owned 21 original pieces, most of which were probably from Hellenistic, Roman, or later times, as classical Greek art was hardly known in the 17th century. Among them were portrait busts of the three great Greek philosophers, Socrates, Plato, and Aristotle, the poet Homer, and the first twelve emperors, the latter in chronological order. What a thirst for culture underlies such a collection!

The largest part of the collection, of course, was made up of the works of art, which Rembrandt himself classified into paintings, paper works (these included drawings, miniatures and watercolours), copperplate works, and woodcuts. Among 17th-century Dutch artists, he collected, in particular, paintings by those masters who had influenced him substantially during his life, such as Hercules Seghers, Pieter Lastman, and their circle, or those to whom he was nearest stylistically, such as Jan Lievens, or to whom he was bound by friendship. But his desire for excellence is also shown by the fact that he owned works by such famous masters as Raphael, Palma Vecchio, Lucas van Leyden, and Rubens. His graphic collection was truly princely, although it is doubtful whether all the works would be accepted as authentic today. Even the auction notice admired and praised it as 'paper art by a number of the most famous Italian, French, German, and Dutch masters, brought together by Rembrandt van Rijn with great curiosity'. Among the engravings, works by the great German engravers of the 15th and 16th centuries, such as Martin Schongauer and Hans Holbein the Younger, deserve particular mention. One album was filled with engravings and woodcuts by Lucas Cranach. The great Italian masters of the Renaissance such as Mantegna, Titian, Raphael, and Michelangelo, the Mannerists Barocci and Tempesta, and the great Baroque painters such as the Carracci brothers and Reni were also represented. Naturally Rembrandt owned prints after the works of the Flemings Rubens, van Dyck, and Jordaens. The albums in which the works were kept were arranged partly by artists and countries and partly by iconographic subjects. The majority of the books contained histories and genre, but there were also volumes of portraits, landscapes, architecture, and erotica. It is significant that Rembrandt's own drawings — which filled no less than 26 books — were also arranged by subjects, because they were not generally intended as finished works of art to be sold. They were studies, preparatory drawings, sketches, or memory aids, or were drawn after other works, and were meant mainly for use in the studio.

We can hardly overestimate the importance of this collection for Rembrandt's work. I know of no other Dutch artist who made such extensive use, in copies, new creations, and borrowings, of impressions gathered from his own and other collections and from exhibitions and auctions. He chose subjects from nature, ethnography, classical antiquity, and the Bible. His work includes drawings of shells and birds of 308 paradise, copies of Indian miniatures and ancient busts, and many pieces based on Bible illustrations. In his collection there were often several depictions of the same biblical or mythological history, so that in his own work he could choose between various formal and iconographic solutions. Time and again he was fascinated by illustrations of unusual

THOMAS JACOBSZ. HAERINGH. About 1655.
Etching 196 × 149 mm. 2nd state.
Hamburg, Kunsthalle.
Bartsch 274.

histories whose subjects had not previously been treated by an artist in a single painting. When painting the face of a figure from antiquity, he could base the features on 'authentic' portraits in his collection. He could use books with representations of Indian and Turkish life to inform himself on milieu and local colour for his biblical histories. As already mentioned, he believed that the habits and costumes of these ancient peoples of the Middle East and Asia resembled those of biblical times. So he used his own copy of an Indian miniature as a model for his etching THE THREE ARCHANGELS VISITING ABRAHAM.[330] Yet despite all his studies, his paintings are not archeological reconstructions. Rembrandt never lost sight of his aim to produce, through assimilating the works of great artists, new masterpieces which were both moving and psychologically true.

308 309

On 14 November 1657, Thomas Jacobsz. Haeringh, the 'concierge' of the Town Hall, was commissioned to conduct the sale of the collection. The first auction took place in December of that year at an inn, the 'Emperor's Crown'. The result was in every respect disappointing: a grand total of 3,094 guilders and 10 stuiver! One cannot escape the impression that in view of the large volume of works on offer, the dealers and collectors had agreed among themselves to buy the goods at prices below their value. When other collections in Amsterdam were valued or sold between 1657 and 1660, Rembrandt's works were always assigned high values. Had his own works realised remotely similar prices at the auction, they alone would have brought in more than 20,000 guilders.

311

Because the proceeds from the auction were so meagre, Rembrandt's house had to be sold as well. This sale, on 1 February, brought 11,218 guilders, 2,000 less than he himself had paid. In the autumn of 1658 his graphic collection was also sold. The total sum realised by the auctions (about 15,000 guilders) was still not sufficient to pay Rembrandt's creditors, to say nothing of paying Titus his inheritance, which in 1647 had been valued at over 40,000 guilders. For this reason numerous court cases followed the auction. Louys Crayers, who had become Titus's guardian in 1658, worked tirelessly on his ward's behalf. With the aid of many statements certified by notaries, Rembrandt was able to prove what he had inherited, earned, and owned. Finally, half the proceeds of the auctions were awarded to Titus in 1665, and the creditor Isaac van Haarsbeeck had to repay the sum which the administrators of the bankruptcy had allocated to him. Naturally, these protracted legal arguments were far from helpful to Rembrandt's work, and it was only after the worst disputes were over in 1660 that the artist found any peace.

Rembrandt was forced to leave his home in the Breestraat after the auction in 1658.[331] In the last decade of his life he lived on the Rosengracht. It was situated in the Jordan quarter of the city, which had been built after 1613 for the more disadvantaged section of the population, above all, craftsmen and petty traders, and consisted of small houses crowded together. When the plague was rife in Amsterdam in 1663 and 1664, it claimed most of its victims in this quarter. In view of Rembrandt's incapacity for business, Titus and Hendrickje had rented the house. To protect him from his creditors, at the end of 1660 they founded a commercial art gallery, by which he was employed in exchange for board and lodging and on condition that he repaid the debts he had incurred with them. As security he pledged to them in advance all income he would derive from the sale of his pictures. This legal arrangement proved its worth. Under its protection Rembrandt could renew his activity as an art-dealer and again acquired a considerable collection, which *de jure* belonged to Titus and Hendrickje. Moreover, after his bankruptcy he again entered into contracts he could not keep and had to compensate his business partners for their lost interest.

Time and again his creditors called him up before a lawyer. He then undertook to pay off his debts from before the bankruptcy by instalments or with pictures, but usually defaulted. He was simply not able to shake off his burden of debt by the rapid production of pictures.

SHAH JAHAN AND HIS SON. About 1656.
Pen and brush in bistre, on light-brown japan paper. 94 × 88 mm.
Amsterdam, Rijksprentenkabinet.
Benesh 1196.

In the last decade of his life Rembrandt was active almost exclusively as a painter and draughtsman. The management of his business affairs by Titus and Hendrickje was clearly beneficial, Titus successfully securing commissions for his father. So, in the 1660s, Rembrandt painted more portraits than in the preceding two decades. He was asked to paint a 316, 317 large group portrait, the STAALMEESTERS, and was even involved in producing work for the Amsterdam Town Hall. Unfortunately, we know in only a few cases who commissioned the marvellous late portraits. Among them are the 318, 319 portraits of JACOB TRIP AND HIS WIFE MARGARETHA DE GEER, of 321, 327 JEREMIAS DE DECKER, and GÉRARD DE LAIRESSE. Jacob Trip and his wife, both of whom came from Dordrecht, were related by marriage to one of the leading arms dealers and metal magnates of the time, and from 1626 they had been partners in his business. In 1661, Trip's son commissioned the building of a palatial residence, the Trippenhuis, not far from the Breestraat. Rembrandt had already received commissions from the family at the end of the 1630s, so that they now turned to him, shortly before or just after the death of Jacob Trip in 1661, to paint portraits of the couple as 319 pendants. While Margaretha de Geer is shown in a strictly 318 frontal view in old-fashioned costume, Jacob Trip is depicted in a somewhat different manner that reflects Rembrandt's portrayal of old men in biblical scenes. As in several figures in his series of apostles, the dignity and wisdom of age are movingly caught. The unusual dress of the old man is perhaps an indication that the portraits were painted after his death.

In the 1660s, as in the previous decade, Rembrandt still preferred the large format, in which the figures usually appear life size. The models for his works at this time, particularly the half-length pictures, were compositions of the Venetian Renaissance and of Caravaggism. In 1661, through his studies of older art, he produced series of 338-343 evangelists and apostles. Some figures are shown sunk in meditation or prayer, and others are pictured composing their writings. They seem immersed in a kind of soliloquy or listening to Divine Inspiration. In these contexts the ancient attributes posed particular difficulties, as the artist was trying to make the pictures resemble portraits or histories with a single figure. How was he to include in the action a bull, a lion, an eagle, or even an angel, a saw, or a knife? The 340 depiction of the evangelist Matthew is particularly fine. He is listening to the voice of the angel, who has placed his right hand on Matthew's shoulder and is dictating the words of the Gospel. The painting is done in subdued colours; only

Philip GALLE after Maerten van Heemskerck.
AHASUERUS COMMANDING HAMAN TO HONOUR MORDECAI.
Engraving 190 × 243 mm.
Hollstein VIII, Nos. 248-255 (7).

HAMAN RECOGNISING HIS FATE.
Signed: 'Rembrandt f.'.
Canvas 127 × 117 cm.
Leningrad, Hermitage.
Cat. 31 / Bredius 531.

AN OFFICIAL OF THE DRAPERS' GUILD.
Study for the painting of 1662 (Cat. 256).
Pen, brush, and wash drawing on a lenghtwise fold paper.
195 × 160 mm.
Amsterdam, Rijksprentenkabinet.
Benesch 1179.

the faces and hands are emphasized through light. The strongest glow is on the face of the evangelist, as if he were illuminated by the words of the Gospel.

Rembrandt also preferred half-length figures in his histories, and here too the whole emphasis is on the faces and the extremely expressive gestures. The composition of the moving painting HAMAN AND AHASUERUS AT THE FEAST OF ESTHER 314 is concentrated on three people. Here Rembrandt dispenses with all the archaic iconographic attributes and instead portrays the spiritual condition of the three people. We see Haman, who by his boundlessly evil action has brought upon himself guilt and disgrace. He had planned to have all the Jews in the Persian kingdom killed in one night, not knowing that Esther, the wife of Ahasuerus, King of Persia, was a Jewess. The plan was foiled, and the painting shows Ahasuerus commanding Haman to put royal robes on Mordecai, the old Jew who had told the Queen about Haman's plan. Rembrandt has caught the moment in which Haman foresees his downfall. Yet Rembrandt shows this man, not as a despicable courtier, as in his earlier works, but rather as a 256 man fated to incur guilt, who moves us to pity even though we cannot condone his plan. Theology at that time included as an important tenet the doctrine of predestination, according to which a man's ruin was preordained. A man so damned could be saved only if he recognised God's decision and hoped for His mercy. Haman does not rebel against his fate. His gaze seems turned inwards, and the faces of the others convey a similar reflective gravity. The aim of the painting is not to inspire contempt and hatred, but fear and sympathy. By focusing on only a few figures and sharply reducing the narrative motifs, Rembrandt achieves an impressive concentration. The choice of subject in this and many other works shows Rembrandt's predilection for treating themes he has already painted, but which, in his old age, he tries to interpret in a new and often more compassionate way. Among these paintings are CHRIST AND THE WOMAN OF SAMARIA AT THE WELL, THE RETURN OF THE PRODIGAL SON, 359 and THE SONG OF PRAISE OF SIMEON — paintings which deal 358 with accusation and guilt, denial, forgiveness, and recognition. They bear witness to a deep and bitter experience of life.

THREE OFFICIALS OF THE DRAPERS' GUILD.
Pen and wash drawing. 173 × 205 mm.
Berlin-Dahlem, Staatliche Museen Preussischer Kulturbesitz, Kupferstichkabinett.
Benesch 1178.

THE BOARD OF THE DRAPERS' GUILD (DE STAALMEESTERS).
Signed: 'Rembrandt f. 1662'.
Canvas 191.5 × 279 cm.
Amsterdam, Rijksmuseum.
Cat. 256 / Bredius 415.

Page 318:
THE DORDRECHT MERCHANT JACOB TRIP (1575-1661). About 1661.
Signed: 'Rembr...'.
Canvas 130.5 × 97 cm.
London, National Gallery.
Cat. 214 / Bredius 314.

Page 319:
MARGARETHA DE GEER, WIFE OF JACOB TRIP. About 1661.
Canvas 130.5 × 97.5 cm.
London, National Gallery.
Cat. 245 / Bredius 394.

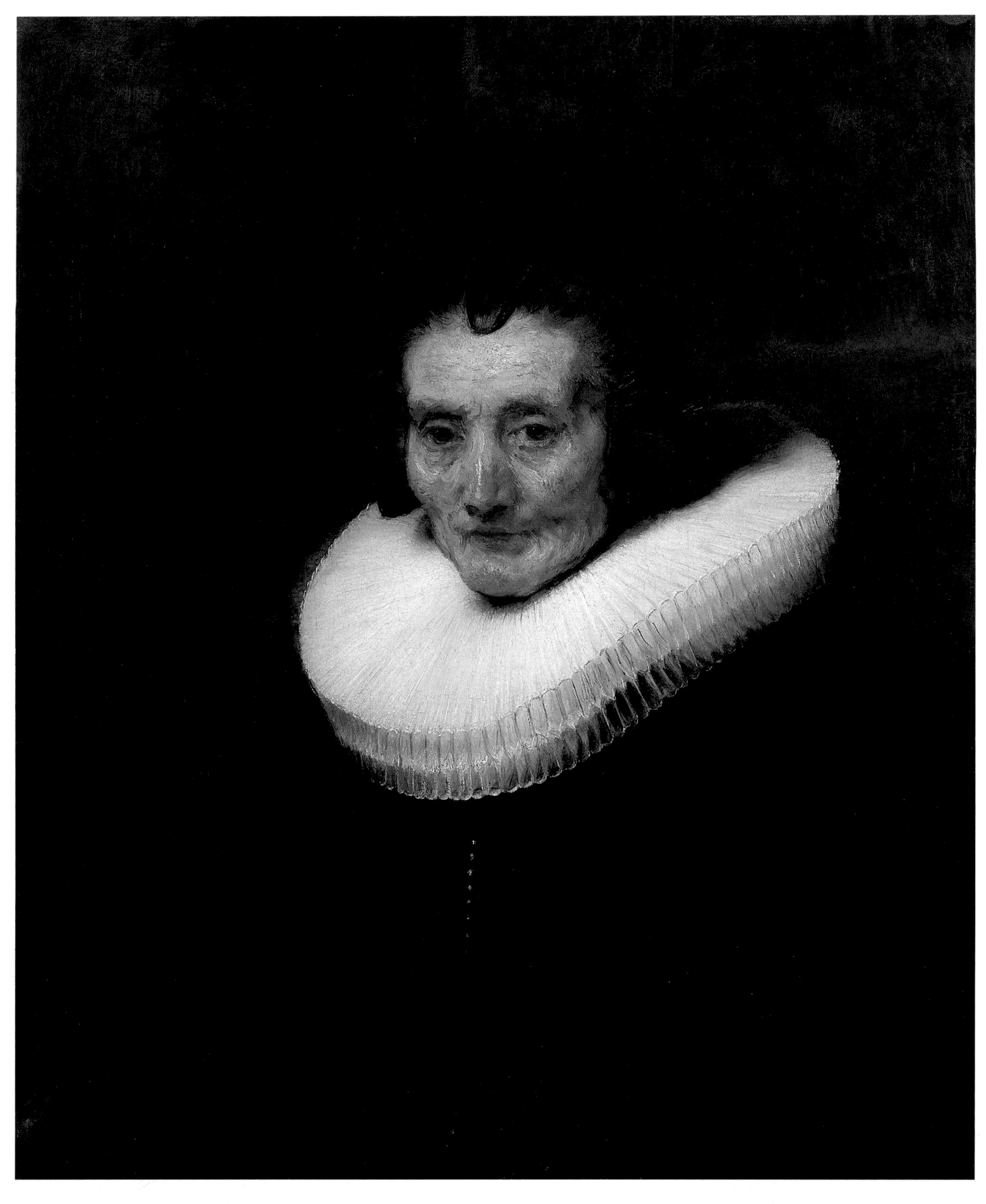

MARGARETHA DE GEER (1583-1672).
Signed: 'Rembrandt f. 1661'.
Canvas 75.3 × 63.8 cm.
London, National Gallery.
Cat. 246 / Bredius 395.

THE POET JEREMIAS DE DECKER (1609-1666).
Signed: 'Rembrandt f. 1666'.
Wood 71 × 56 cm.
Leningrad, Hermitage.
Cat. 225 / Bredius 320.

A YOUNG JEW WITH A BLACK CAP.
Signed: 'Rembrandt f. 1663'.
Canvas 65.8 × 57.5 cm.
Fort Worth, Texas, Kimbell Art Museum.
Cat. 146 / Bredius 300.

HENDRICKJE STOFFELS.
Signed: 'Rembrandt f. 1660'.
Canvas 78.4 × 68.9 cm.
New York, Metropolitan Museum of Art.
Cat. 189 / Bredius 118.

PORTAIT OF A MAN WITH A TALL HAT. About 1662/63.
Canvas 121 × 94 cm.
Washington DC, National Gallery of Art.
Cat. 219 / Bredius 313.

FREDERICK RIHEL ON HORSEBACK (1625/26-1681).
Signed: 'R...brandt 1633'. Canvas 294.5 × 241 cm.
London, National Gallery.
Cat. 220 / Bredius 255.

PORTRAIT OF A YOUNG MAN. About 1660.
Canvas 110 × 90 cm.
Washington DC, National Gallery of Art. Cat. 217 / Bredius 312.

GERARD DE LAIRESSE (1640-1711)
Signed: 'Rembrandt f. 1665'. Canvas 112.4 × 87.6 cm.
New York, Metropolitan Museum. Cat. 222 / Bredius 321.

Rembrandt (?)
PORTRAIT OF A MAN HOLDING GLOVES. About 1664.
Canvas 99.5 × 82.6 cm.
Washington DC, National Gallery of Art. Cat. 221 / Bredius 327.

Rembrandt (?)
A LADY WITH A FAN OF OSTRICH FEATHERS.
Signed: 'Rembrandt f. 166(.)'.
Canvas 99.5 × 83 cm.
Washington DC, National Gallery of Art. Cat. 250 / Bredius 402.

A MAN WITH A MAGNIFYING GLASS IN HIS RIGHT HAND. About 1665.
Canvas 91.4 × 74.3 cm.
New York, Metropolitan Museum of Art. Cat. 223 / Bredius 326.

A WOMAN WITH A RED CARNATION IN HER RIGHT HAND. About 1665.
Canvas 91 × 73.5 cm.
New York, Metropolitan Museum of Art.
Cat. 249 / Bredius 401.

PORTRAIT OF A YOUNG MAN.
Signed: 'Rembrandt f. 1666'.
Canvas 80.6 × 64.8 cm.
Kansas City Missouri, Nelson-Atkins Museum of Art (Nelson Fund).
Cat. 224 / Bredius 322.

PORTRAIT OF A FAIR-HAIRED MAN.
Signed: 'Rembrandt f. 1667'.
Canvas 108.9 × 92.7 cm.
Melbourne, National Gallery of Victoria (Felton Bequest 1951).
Cat. 226 / Bredius 323.

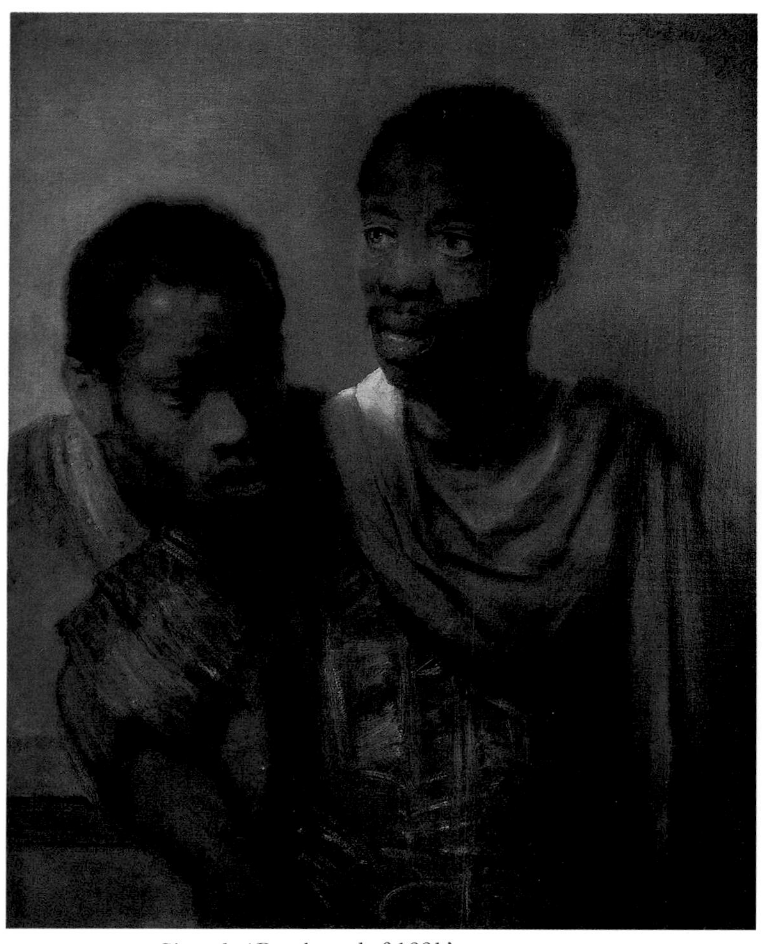

TWO NEGROES. Signed: 'Rembrandt f 1661'.
Canvas 77.8 × 64.5 cm. The Hague, Mauritshuis.
Cat. 145 / Bredius 310.

MAN WITH A BEARD.
Indistinctly signed: 'Rembrandt f. 1661' (?). Canvas 71 × 61 cm.
Leningrad, Hermitage. Cat. 144 / Bredius 309.

PORTRAIT OF A LADY WITH A LAP DOG. Canvas 81 × 64 cm.
Toronto, Art Gallery of Ontario. Cat. 247 / Bredius 398.

Rembrandt circle. PORTRAIT OF A YOUNG MAN.
Signed: 'Re(mbrandt) f. (1633)'. Canvas 78.6 × 64.2 cm.
London, Dulwich Picture Gallery. Cat. A97 / Bredius 289.

Rembrandt's workshop.
PORTRAIT OF A YOUNG MAN.
Signed: 'Rembrandt f. 1662'.
Canvas 89.9 × 70.8 cm.
St. Louis, St. Louis Art Museum. Cat. A101 / Bredius 311.

A YOUNG WOMAN. About 1665.
Canvas 56.3 × 47.5 cm.
Montreal, Museum of Fine Arts. Cat. 248 / Bredius 400.

Pupil of Rembrandt. DIRK VAN OS (1591-1666). About 1660-1665.
Canvas 103.5 × 86.4 cm. Omaha, Joslyn Art Museum.
Cat. A100 / Bredius 315.

Rembrandt's workshop. PORTRAIT OF A YOUNG MAN SEATED.
Signed: 'Rembrandt f. 1660'. Canvas 92.7 × 82.5 cm.
Rochester, NY, Memorial Art Gallery of the University of Rochester.
Cat. A98 / Bredius 299.

Rembrandt circle.
HENDRICKJE IN A WHITE GOWN. Signed: 'Rembrandt f. 166(.)'.
Canvas 100 × 83.5 cm.
London, National Gallery.
Cat. A77 / Bredius 113.

AN OLD MAN.
Signed: 'Rembrandt f. 1667'. Canvas 78.7 × 66 cm.
Cowdray Park, England, Collection of Lord Cowdray.
Cat. 147 / Bredius - Gerson 323A.

A FAMILY PORTRAIT. About 1668/69.
Signed: 'Rembrandt f.'.
Canvas 126 × 167 cm.
Brunswick, Herzog Anton Ulrich Museum.
Cat. 257 / Bredius 417.

◀◀ Rembrandt circle.
PORTRAIT OF A MAN HOLDING A MANUSCRIPT.
Signed: 'Rembrandt f. 1658'.
Canvas 109 × 86 cm.
New York, Metropolitan Museum of Art.
Cat. A94 / Bredius 294.

◀ Pupil of Rembrandt.
PORTRAIT OF A MAN. About 1660.
Canvas 83.5 × 64.5 cm.
New York, Metropolitan Museum of Art.
Cat. A96 / Bredius 277.

AN EVANGELIST (LUKE?). About 1661.
Canvas 102 × 80 cm.
Rotterdam, Boymans-van Beuningen Museum.
Cat. 89 / Bredius 618.

In an important essay of 1921 the eminent art historian Wilhelm R. Valentiner reconstructed from the surviving pictures of biblical figures of the same size a series of evangelists and a series of apostles.[332] The hypothesis was not generally accepted by scholars, perhaps partly because the series compiled by Valentiner were incomplete and in some cases incorrectly linked together. But many years after the appearance of the essay, to widespread surprise, a further apostle picture of the same size came to light and fitted into the series. In addition, I was able to interpret a number of single historical figures on the basis of their attributes as evangelists or apostles and so to reduce the gaps. Of the evangelist series, three of the four paintings are now known, as are nine of the fourteen apostles (in the pictorial tradition Mary and Christ are included as well as the twelve apostles).

338, 339, 340
341, 342, 343

The great engravers of the 16th and 17th centuries had produced series of apostles and evangelists with especial frequency. They had a great influence on the Baroque artists. For example, Rubens produced a series of twelve apostles for the Duke of Lerma, with an additional half-length figure of Christ. It is now in the Prado. In 1618 Rubens offered the collector Carleton a copy of the series executed by one of his pupils, which is now kept in the gallery of the Palazzo Rospigliosi in Rome. Guido Reni, Frans Hals, Hendrick Terbruggen, Jan Lievens, and Barent Fabritius, to name only a few important Baroque artists, produced pictures of evangelists. Clearly, Rembrandt or his unknown client was influenced by these models when producing entire series against his normal practice.

It is understandable that for such a large series Rembrandt would have made use of other members of his workshop, so that the works vary considerably in quality.

In his late works he no longer aims at historical realism in the apostle pictures, using the same extensive impasto as in the freer portraits and pictures of individual historical figures. The background is usually in brown tones without clear definition. The figure, draped in a heavy cloak, stands out against it. Sometimes the transition between cloak and background is blurred by shadow. The faces of the apostles and evangelists are deeply lined. They are shown in exalted moods. Some are depicted as old men. But despite their age and physical frailty, the emotion radiating from them makes them powerful witnesses of the Gospel.

Rembrandt's workshop (or a follower of Rembrandt).
THE EVANGELIST JOHN. About 1661.
Faked signature: 'Rembrandt f. 16(..)'.
Canvas 102.2 × 83.8 cm.
Boston, Museum of Fine Arts.
Cat. A24 / Bredius 619.

THE EVANGELIST MATTHEW.
Signed: 'Rembrandt f. 1661'.
Canvas 96 × 81 cm.
Paris, Louvre.
Cat. 88 / Bredius 614.

MARY, THE MOTHER OF SORROW.
Signed: 'Rembrandt f 1661'. Canvas 107 × 81 cm.
Epinal, France, Musée des Vosges.
Cat. 85 / Bredius 397.

THE APOSTLE BARTHOLOMEW.
Signed: 'Rembrandt f. 1661'.
Canvas 87.5 × 75 cm.
Malibu, The Paul Getty Museum.
Cat. 83 / Bredius 615.

THE APOSTLE BARTHOLOMEW.
Signed: 'Rembrandt f. 1657'.
Canvas 122.7 × 99.5 cm.
San Diego, Timken Art Gallery.
Cat. 80 / Bredius 613.

THE APOSTLE JAMES. Signed: 'Rembrandt f 1661'.
Canvas 90 × 78 cm.
Jerusalem, The Israel Museum (in loan). Cat. 82 / Bredius 617.

Rembrandt (?).
AN OLD MAN WITH CLASPED HANDS IN AN ARMCHAIR. About 1660.
Signed: 'Rembrandt f. 166.'(?).
Canvas 104.7 × 86 cm.
Florence, Uffizi.
Cat. 143 / Bredius 285.

Rembrandt (?).
AN OLD MAN AS ST. PAUL.
Signed: 'Rembrandt f. 165(9?)'.
Canvas 102 × 85.5 cm.
London, National Gallery.
Cat. 81 / Bredius 297.

◀◀ THE APOSTLE SIMON.
Signed: 'Rembrandt f 1661'.
Canvas 98.3 × 79 cm.
Zürich, Kunsthaus (Ruzicka Foundation).
Cat. 84 / Bredius 616A.

◀ JAMES THE YOUNGER.
Signed: 'Rembrandt f. 1661'.
Canvas 94.5 × 81.5 cm.
New York, Metropolitan Museum of Art.
Cat. 86 / Bredius 629.

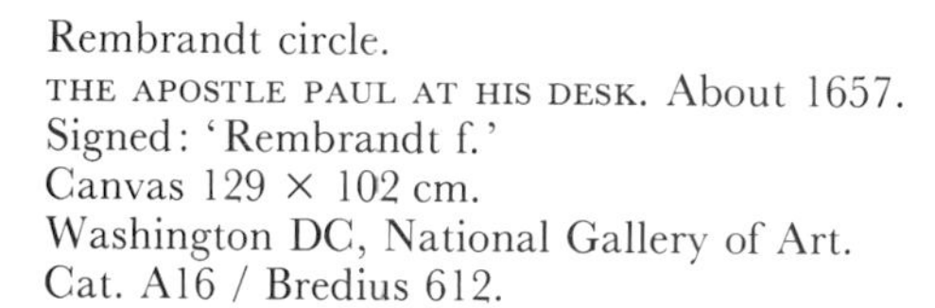

Rembrandt circle.
THE APOSTLE PAUL AT HIS DESK. About 1657.
Signed: 'Rembrandt f.'
Canvas 129 × 102 cm.
Washington DC, National Gallery of Art.
Cat. A16 / Bredius 612.

Rembrandt's workshop.
THE APOSTLE MATTHEW.
Signed: 'Rembrand(t) 166.' (?)
Canvas 87.6 × 72.4 cm.
Cleveland, Ohio, Museum of Arts.
Cat. A23 / Bredius 616.

CHRIST.
Signed: 'Rembrandt f. 1661'.
Canvas 78.5 × 63 cm.
Munich, Alte Pinakothek.
Cat. 87 / Bredius 630.

A BUST OF CHRIST FROM LIFE. About 1656. ►►
Wood 25 × 20 cm.
Berlin-Dahlem, Staatliche Museen Preussischer Kulturbesitz, Gemäldegalerie.
Cat. 78 / Bredius 622.

Rembrandt circle. ►
CHRIST. About 1665.
Canvas 47 × 37 cm.
New York, Metropolitan Museum of Art.
Cat. A20 / Bredius 626.

CHRIST. About 1656.
Wood 25.2 × 19.9 cm.
Cambridge, Mass., Fogg Art Museum.
Cat. 79 / Bredius[3] 624A.

Rembrandt's workshop.
CHRIST. About 1660/61.
Canvas 109.2 × 90.2 m.
Glenns Falls (N.Y.), The Hyde Collection.
Cat. A22 / Bredius 628.

Rembrandt circle.
CHRIST.
Signed: 'Rembrandt f. 1655'. Wood 25.5 × 22 cm.
Detroit, Institute of Arts.
Cat. A17 / Bredius 621.

Rembrandt's workshop.
CHRIST.
Faked signature: 'Rembrandt f. 1656'. Wood 24.7 × 20 cm.
Philadelphia, Museum of Art (John G. Johnson Collection)
Cat. A19 / Bredius 624.

Rembrandt (?)
ST. FRANCIS (or ST. ANTHONY?).
Signed: 'Rembrandt f. 165(.)'.
Canvas 89 × 66.5 cm.
London, National Gallery.
Cat. 90 / Bredius 308.

Rembrandt (?).
ST. FRANCIS.
Signed: 'Rembrandt f. 1661'.
Canvas 82 × 66 cm.
Helsinki, Sinebrychoff Art Museum.
Cat. 92 / Bredius 307.

Rembrandt (?).
ST. BAVO. About 1661.
Canvas 98.5 × 79 cm.
Gothenburg, Konstmuseum.
Cat. 93 / Bredius 319.

TITUS AS ST. FRANCIS.
Signed: 'Rembrandt f. 166(0)'.
Canvas 79.5 × 67.5 cm.
Amsterdam, Rijksmuseum.
Cat. 91 / Bredius 306.

THE SUICIDE OF LUCRETIA.
Signed: 'Rembrandt f. 1666'
Canvas 105.1 × 92.3 cm.
Minneapolis, The Minneapolis Institute of Arts.
Cat. 115 / Bredius 485.

THE SUICIDE OF LUCRETIA.
Signed: 'Rembrandt f. 1664'.
Canvas 120 × 101 cm.
Washington DC, National Gallery of Art.
Cat. 114 / Bredius 484.

In the last decade of his life Rembrandt's painting shows a grandiose increase in depth. This is connected, in my view, with the gigantic painting CLAUDIUS CIVILIS, which was commissioned from Rembrandt after the death of Govert Flinck in early 1660. This, the largest picture Rembrandt ever painted, was over six metres wide and over five metres high. It hung at a dizzy height in the gallery of the Amsterdam Town Hall. To make the painting effective when seen from below, Rembrandt had to build up the composition from large, luminous areas. The distance also imposed a summary mode of presentation. Schooled by Titian's late style, he had no difficulty in justifying his conception and in applying the paint with the spatula and the palette knife. The city councillors did not accept the painting, and Rembrandt had to take it back to be repainted. It was not rehung in its original position. Rembrandt then made the composition smaller.

The bold, monumental style of this painting had an extraordinarily liberating and invigorating effect on the later works. The first picture after 1660, THE APOSTLE PETER DENYING CHRIST, had clearly been finished, in essence, before this commission, so that in style it resembles the works of the 1650s. But the next picture, the FEAST OF ESTHER, is painted with the new freedom, so that anyone looking at a reproduction forgets that this work, which seems so monumental in its structure and brushwork, is a small painting, smaller than JOSEPH ACCUSED BY POTIPHAR'S WIFE.

But let us return to THE APOSTLE PETER DENYING CHRIST. Rembrandt based the painting on compositions in the manner of Caravaggio, which he boldly heightened by transferring his motif of disclosure and concealment to this scene for the first time. Peter is dressed in a thick cloak or blanket and has covered his head with a hood. It is the only history scene with more than one figure in which one of the apostles conceals his head with a cloth, and this motif does not occur in the pictorial tradition. Peter protects himself from the cold night. But Rembrandt uses this motif with a further meaning; he wishes to show by this concealment why Peter feels so safe, despite the great peril in the proximity of his Lord, who has been taken captive, accused, and interrogated. But Peter is mistaken, for he is recognised by a maid.

> And when she saw Peter warming himself, she looked upon him, and said: And thou also wast with Jesus of Nazareth. But he denied, saying: I know him not, neither understand I what thou sayest.[333]

To make certain, she shines a candle on him. Through her

354 352 353 291 352

Crispijn DE PASSE the Elder.
ISAAC AND REBECCA OBSERVED BY ABIMELECH.
Engraving c. 85 × 127 mm.
In *Liber Genesis, continens originem...* 1612.

ISAAC AND REBECCA (THE JEWISH BRIDE). About 1666. Detail.
Signed: 'Rembrandt f 16(..)'.
Canvas 121.5 × 166.5 cm.
Amsterdam, Rijksmuseum.
Cat. 32 / Bredius 416.

ISAAC AND REBECCA OVERHEARD BY ABIMELECH.
Pen and bistre. 145 × 185 mm.
New York, Kramarsky Coll.
Benesch 988.

THE APOSTLE PETER DENYING CHRIST.
Signed: 'Rembrandt 1660'.
Canvas 154 × 169 cm.
Amsterdam, Rijksmuseum.
Cat. 71 / Bredius 594.

action and the exchange of words she draws the attention of others to the apostle, whom she shows in the true light. This middle group is the centre of lighting in the picture. An armed man sitting spread-legged on an armchair pauses as he is about to lift a huge calabash to his mouth and looks mistrustfully at Peter. Another soldier also looks at the disciple. Rembrandt stresses the seated soldier's metal armour, which reflects the light, so drawing attention to the contrast between martial power, the tender maid, and the powerless disciple, who beats his breast with his right hand and emphasizes his words with his left. Behind this left hand we see Jesus , surrounded by soldiers and priests. 'And the Lord turned and looked upon Peter. And Peter remembered the word of the Lord, how he had said unto him: Before the cock crow, thou shalt deny me thrice'.[334]

In the foreground Rembrandt depicts a large table on which lie the sword and helmet of the soldier. This blocks

AHASUERUS AND HAMAN AT THE FEAST OF ESTHER.
Signed: 'Rembrandt f. 1660'.
Canvas 73 × 94 cm.
Moscow, Pushkin Museum.
Cat. 30 / Bredius 530.

Rembrandt (?).
OLD TOBIAS AND HIS WIFE WAITING FOR THE RETURN OF THEIR SON.
Signed: 'Rembrandt f. 1659'.
Wood 40.3 × 54 cm.
Rotterdam, Boymans-van Beuningen Museum.
Cat. 28 / Bredius 520.

Peter's way forward. He finds himself at the parting of the ways, between the threat from power and the fate of Christ. The only clear path is the one his left hand shows: he is still denying, but when he turns around, he will meet Christ's gaze and repent.

From the same year, 1660, is the picture already mentioned, THE FEAST OF ESTHER, which also takes its vitality from the tension between the 'not yet' and the 'but soon'.

The picture positively glows with colour. Nevertheless, it is built up mainly from three tones, brown, red, and gold. Against the brownish, almost black background the relatively colourful figures stand out like silhouettes. The foreground with the cushions and jug in red and brown forms a kind of colourful pedestal on which the three people — Esther in the most beautiful colours — can rise. In this composition Rembrandt was influenced by Persian miniatures.

THE CONSPIRACY OF CLAUDIUS CIVILIS. About 1661/62.
Canvas 196 × 309 cm.
Stockholm, National Museum.
Cat. 101 / Bredius 482.

ISAAC AND REBECCA (THE JEWISH BRIDE). About 1666.
Signed: 'Rembrandt f 16(..)'.
Canvas 121.5 × 166.5 cm.
Amsterdam, Rijksmuseum.
Cat. 32 / Bredius 416.

BADALOCCHIO.
ISAAC AND REBECCA OBSERVED BY ABIMELECH.
Reproduction engraving (after Raphael's fresco in the 5th transom of the Vatican loggias) 132 × 178 mm.
In *Historia del Testamento vecchio*... 1607. Sheet 22.

The moment portrayed is the one in which the Queen, Esther, voices her charge against Haman, accusing him of wanting to destroy the whole Jewish people including her, since she is Jewish. Her husband, King Ahasuerus, has not yet pronounced judgement. But he is already looking at Haman, whose fall is imminent. So a part of the story is anticipated. Esther's dignity as Queen is preserved, and the Jewish people are saved, but Haman will receive his punishment. Rembrandt has moved Haman, who was just now at the centre of power, to the far left of the picture, where he is in shadow. Esther, his antagonist, sits close to Ahasuerus, her husband. She emphasizes her words with outstretched arms (which seem originally to have held a cloth for her tears or the document ordering the annihilation). The dignity of the ruling couple is stressed by their magnificent, glowing robes. Ahasuerus wears a precious-looking royal mantle with a broad fur collar. Esther is dressed in a wide purple garment ornamented with sumptuous embroidery. Her golden train, spreading on the cushions, extends across the whole right quarter of the picture. She is luxuriously adorned with pearl necklaces and ear-rings. With her beauty and splendour she

attracts Ahasuerus's attention and benevolence, and her moving words frustrate Haman's attack on her people, and so on her own person.

The tension before the decisive moment of the king's judgement constitutes the drama of the outwardly tranquil picture. The composition radiates calm and dramatic tension at once. The impression of calm is achieved by the restrained gesture of the figures seen as surfaces, the tension by the emphatic spatial structure and the impressive imagery.

Among the most magnificent of all paintings I place the late works ISAAC AND REBECCA and the Brunswick FAMILY GROUP. We shall look here at the Amsterdam painting. The picture's harmony stems from the 'colour interval' of gold-yellow and purple-red against brown. The warm, prominent red and the solemn yellow underline the gestures of the couple. Isaac has put his arm around Rebecca and placed his right hand lovingly on her heart, tenderly embracing her. She concurs in this intimate gesture by lightly touching his hand with her left hand, pressing it more firmly to her breast.

350, 355
337

This picture has become known as THE JEWISH BRIDE. The

Rembrandt's workshop.
THE CIRCUMCISION OF CHRIST IN THE STABLE.
Signed: 'Rembrandt f. 1661'. Canvas 56.5 × 75 cm.
Washington DC, National Gallery of Art. Cat. A12 / Bredius 596.

JUNO. About 1660-1665.
Canvas 127 × 108 cm.
Los Angeles, The Armand Hammer Collection.
Cat. 113 / Bredius 639.

intimate act between man and wife could hardly have been more gravely misunderstood, for the woman was taken to be a daughter who is taking her leave from her father and her parental home to join her husband.[335] But such a leavetaking would have been portrayed quite differently by Rembrandt, not as an erotic act but as a chaste embrace. A preliminary drawing explains the context from which Rembrandt chose the story. It shows Isaac embracing Rebecca on his lap. If, in the Baroque pictorial language, one wished to show decently that a man and his wife have sexual community, the leg of one would be placed across that of the other. This is the way they are depicted here. But in their love act Isaac and Rebecca are observed by Abimelech, whom it angers, for in the land of the Philistines, Isaac had presented his beautiful wife as his sister, fearing that he might be murdered on her account. When Abimelech observed the act of love, he recognised the two as a married couple and censured Isaac for his lie, since a Philistine might easily have put himself at fault with the supposed sister. In the drawing Rembrandt took an etching after a fresco by Raphael on this theme as his starting point, but entirely transformed the composition. Isaac and Rebecca are turned to a more directly frontal view and shown partially, as three-quarter-length figures, the architectural motifs being simplified and reduced. In the painting Rembrandt has concentrated the composition entirely on Isaac and Rebecca. The observing Abimelech is no longer considered worthy of depiction.

351 354

Through the isolation of the figures from the historical scene, their presentation as three-quarter-length figures, and the use of models, Rembrandt's painting becomes indistinguishable from a historical portrait. Many historical single figures were earlier mistaken for portraits. Since Rembrandt adhered closely to his models — even though transfiguring and heightening them — many figures in his late histories seem very much like portraits, for example, Asenath in JACOB BLESSING THE CHILDREN OF JOSEPH or the figure of ARISTOTLE. They are hardly to be distinguished from portraits of subjects posing in historical roles.[336] When Rembrandt used models in histories, his intention was to show the significance of the stories for the present, and for the same reason he used models in the history portraits. Conversely, he wanted to show that contemporaries reappear in the biblical story. In the case of an artist like Rembrandt, the two meanings were bound to come close together to a point where the two types of picture cannot be distinguished and only documentary evidence or preliminary studies can tell us of Rembrandt's starting-point.

290 360

In the painting, as in the drawing, Rebecca sits on Isaac's lap. Since in his later work Rembrandt reduces the spatial element and depicts everything as a kind of relief on one picture plane, this position is only hinted at. Isaac's cloak lies on the bench; his right leg is bent forward, Rebecca's dress delineating the knee.

What is only lightly indicated in the painting was depicted very clearly in a version underlying it, as the X-ray photograph shows. Rembrandt then reduced the over-insistent and undignified pose, indicating the perspectives of the bodies in a more restrained way, so that at first glance Rebecca seems to be standing, in a reversion to the formal model which Rembrandt used.

In the impressive late painting THE RETURN OF THE PRODIGAL SON, Rembrandt makes the return of one who has incurred guilt and the forgiving, encompassing love of the father the real subject. The aged father, whom we see from the front, bends over the son, puts his hands lightly on his back, and presses him gently to him. We see the Prodigal Son from the back. He has fallen to his knees, his arms lifted in entreaty. He rests his head, which is turned to the right, gently on his father. The father's glowing red cloak, with its tassels of the same colour, and his arms and hands enclose the son's head in a rhomboid shape. So his acceptance is made visible. The group of the father and the Prodigal Son is portrayed on the left of the picture without being overlapped. The moment of welcoming and forgiveness is extended into infinity by the calmness of the depiction. There is nothing momentary, only an enduring quality, in the movements of father and son.

359

He has returned home in a ragged garment; tears and holes are to be seen everywhere. Yet the Prodigal Son still bears one attribute of his status, the short sword characterising him as the son of a noble landowner. His undergarment is painted in a warm brown tone similar to that of his father's, so that in terms of colour, a large, harmonious form is produced. We see the soles of the man who has returned.

Rembrandt circle.
CHRIST AND THE WOMAN OF SAMARIA AT THE WELL.
Signed: 'Rembrandt f. 1665'.
Wood 63.5 × 48.9 cm.
New York, Metropolitan Museum of Art.
Cat. A13 / Bredius 589.

Rembrandt and follower.
THE SONG OF PRAISE OF SIMEON. About 1666/69.
Canvas 98 × 79 cm.
Stockholm, Nationalmuseum.
Cat. 73 / Bredius 600.

His left foot has slipped from the sandal. The foot is bare, marked with scars. On his journey in foreign lands the Prodigal Son has received wounds. His other foot is still in a worn and dilapidated shoe.

Spectators on the right of the group and in the doorway witness the unusual event and react in different ways: quietly, meditatively, or questioningly.[337] The man at the front on the right is probably the elder brother. He wears a glowing, colourful cloak, leans on a stick, and looks at the group of father and son from above. Behind him a young man sits on a chair, beats his breast, and has his legs crossed. In the background two women appear. Are they the mother and sister, or simply maids who are following the unexpected event? In the pictorial tradition, too, these secondary figures are often not specified.

The model for Rembrandt's composition was obviously a painting by Maerten van Heemskerck which had been adapted in an engraving. Rembrandt, however, has turned the main group frontally towards us, so that we experience the story from the Prodigal Son's standpoint. Since the father is bending down, he is also near us.

Rembrandt's last depiction of the SIMEON theme is also the 358 most moving. The aged Simeon holds the Christ child in his feeble arms. His hands are stiff. They can no longer enclose the child and remain outstretched. In this way Rembrandt expresses Simeon's longing. He characterises him as the old man who sees with his inner eye that Christ is the Saviour of the World. Simeon's eyes are almost closed. But his face shines, and with deep emotion he speaks the words: 'Mine eyes have beheld thy Saviour'. Rembrandt has again made use of isolation. As in his late paintings ISAAC AND REBECCA 355 and MOSES SMASHING THE TABLETS OF THE LAW, he shows only 286 the main figures: Simeon and the Christ child.[338] Rembrandt probably also drew in the figure of Mary, who was then painted by a successor.

Rembrandt also treated this subject in an earlier drawing.[339] As compared to the etching B. 50, it is concentrated on the main figures. Here too he deliberately makes use of the incomplete, the unfinished. The vision is only hinted at. The state of suspension and the lack of firm contours convey the rapt, transcendental quality of the scene.[340] Simeon is scarcely distinct from the space around him; space and figure interpenetrate. Light falls on Simeon and the child. They are open to it.

Maerten VAN HEEMSKERCK.
THE RETURN OF THE PRODIGAL SON.
Signed and dated 1559.
Wood 67 × 85 cm.
Fürstenberg, Schloss Hugenpoet.

Rembrandt and workshop.
THE RETURN OF THE PRODIGAL SON. About 1666/69.
Faked signature: 'Rf Rynf'.
Canvas 262 × 206 cm.
Leningrad, Hermitage.
Cat. 72 / Bredius 598.

Rembrandt's fame had by now spread to Italy, and his pictures were compared to those of the Italian masters. A 321 poet who was a friend of Rembrandt's, Jeremias de Decker, wrote at that time an acknowledgement:

> Rhyming to extol your famous name would be to carry water to the sea, or to the forest, wood...This artful brush...is famous for itself, and has perhaps not borne its master's name less far abroad than Holland's vessels sail. His fame has crossed the Alpine peaks as far as famous Rome, and Italy itself looks up in wonder by the Tiber's stream. Thousands he has made to dip their flags; with Raphael's and Michelangelo's his brush-stroke can compare, and even oversoar.[341]

From the correspondence of the Italian collector Don Antonio Ruffo, we know that Rembrandt's work was indeed talked about in Italy in the 1660s. The Sicilian aristocrat had embellished his family palace in Messina, where he had lived since 1646, with paintings, sculptures, and valuable *objets d'art*.[342] He was a passionate collector, procuring works by the most important artists of past and present. In the inventories we find such names as Dürer, Titian, Lucas van Leyden, Jordaens, Ribera, van Dyck, and Poussin, to mention only a few. He corresponded with numerous contemporary painters about their works and gave them commissions.

So, by 1653 at the latest, he had commissioned an historical half-length figure from Rembrandt through a middle-man, and in 1654 he received the marvellous picture 360 of ARISTOTLE. Enthusiastic about the painting, he commissioned Rembrandt to paint two further half-length figures. As Rembrandt, on account of his bankruptcy, does not seem to have executed the commission at once, Ruffo wrote in 1660 to the distinguished Italian painter Guercino, asking him to paint a pendant for it in his earlier, expansive manner. In his letter he must have referred approvingly to Rembrandt. Guercino replies:

> Concerning, in particular, the half-length figure by Rembrandt which is in your possession, it must surely be of utmost perfecton, for I have seen many of his works which have reached us in the form of engavings, and all were very beautifully executed, engraved with much art, and well presented, and I believe him in all honesty to be a great artist.[343]

Guercino is even willing to adapt himself to Rembrandt's style and to paint a pendant in the manner desired. It reached Messina in early 1661. From an invoice of July in the same year, it emerges that Rembrandt had in the meantime

HOMER DECLAIMING VERSES.
Signed: 'Rembrandt aen Joannus Sicx 1652'.
Pen and bistre 255 × 180 mm.
Amsterdam, Six Foundation.
Benesch 913.

ARISTOTLE WITH THE BUST OF HOMER.
Signed: 'Rembrandt f. 1653'.
Canvas 143.5 × 136.5 cm.
New York, Metropolitan Museum of Art.
Cat. 108 / Bredius 478.

painted an ALEXANDER THE GREAT as a pendant to the ARISTOTLE, and had already bought the canvas for a third 362 painting, a HOMER.

Rembrandt seems to have chosen the subjects of the three pictures himself. The ARISTOTLE picture contains the programme uniting the three works. In Rembrandt's picture the Greek philosopher rests his right hand pensively on a bust of Homer, while his left touches a gold chain to which a likeness of Alexander the Great is attached. This presentation reveals an exact knowledge of historical connections. Aristotle was a great interpreter of Homer, making his pupil Alexander familiar with his works. Alexander is said to have had Homer's works constantly with him on his military campaigns. When Rembrandt was asked to create two further half-length figures, he decided to paint, beside the greatest philosopher, the greatest poet and the greatest military commander of antiquity. In the winter of 1661, Ruffo wrote enthusiastically about the ALEXANDER. However he later noticed that the canvas had been extended on three sides to enlarge the half-length figure picture and complained about this to Rembrandt. The artist reacted with undiplomatic vehemence, sending — in Italian — the following irate reply: 'I am astonished at what has been written about the Alexander, which is so extraordinarily well painted. There are, I believe, few art connoisseurs in Messina'.[344] Rembrandt then explains to Ruffo that as he painted he had felt the canvas to be too small and had therefore extended it. If the picture were hung in the correct light, the seams would not be visible. He often enlarged or reduced compositions to improve them or to adjust them to other works. He was 218 adept at painting over seams. The so-called NIGHT WATCH, too, on account of its unusual format, is made of three pieces of canvas which were joined. He had also enlarged the 157 famous ST JOHN THE BAPTIST PREACHING, which was earlier in the collection of the art amateur Jan Six. His concern was with artistic quality and a balanced composition, not with technical details.

On the high price Rembrandt was adamant. He would take the picture back, if Ruffo met the costs, and paint another, rather than give way here. In 1662, Rembrandt sent Ruffo the HOMER. But the client was not satisfied with this either. When the Dutch consul in Messina travelled to Amsterdam at the end of 1662, Ruffo gave him a memorandum for the art-dealer Isaac Just. He was to make clear to Rembrandt how dissatisfied he was with the unbelievably ugly seams. Moreover, Rembrandt's price was too high; he was demanding ten times the amount accepted by famous painters in Italy. Ruffo could really only accept the head, and would therefore only pay half. He was returning the HOMER as it was only half finished. Rembrandt would have to do much work on it to complete it to his satisfaction. If he did not fulfil this obligation, he would return the ALEXANDER as well and demand the refund of his fee. If the HOMER met his expectations, however, he would commission more pictures. He therefore requested some sketches from which he could choose the best. Rembrandt gave way and overpainted the picture. In the final version, as we know from the descriptions in Ruffo's inventory, two scribes were shown recording the blind poet's words.[345] The picture was later partly damaged by fire, and these secondary figures were destroyed.

HOMER DICTATING TO A SCRIBE.
Pen and bistre in Indian ink, white heightening with brush. 145 × 167 mm.
Stockholm, Nationalmuseum.
Benesch 1066.

HOMER.
Signed: '(Rembr)andt f. 1663'.
Canvas 108 × 82.4 cm.
The Hague, Mauritshuis.
Cat. 112 / Bredius 483.

With this version, which Rembrandt dated 1663, Ruffo was satisfied.

362 Rembrandt's painting HOMER, which is magnificent even as a fragment, departs from tradition in that the poet's physiognomy is made to resemble that of the famous marble bust at Naples, which he had already portrayed in the ARISTOTLE picture. In converting the idealised head of the old man of the ancient sculpture into a figure endowed with individuality, Rembrandt undoubtedly drew on his own experience of ageing. He had seen how in old age frailty and decrepitude can afflict a person whose activity is unimpaired. New paths and insights are opened to the aged even if, with diminishing vision and a reduction in the overall power of perception, the main outlines grow more prominent and the details recede. This is true of Rembrandt's own late work, above all, in the painting technique. Rembrandt's expressionist late style, the application of colour in large areas, and the coarse texture of the paint, put on with a palette knife, gave many contemporaries the impression that the late pictures were unfinished. Time and again he had to over-paint them, which, no doubt, went against his better judgement, for the impasto application was intended to give lustre to the colours.

ALEXANDER THE GREAT.
Signed: 'Rembrandt f. 1655'.
Canvas 137.5 × 104.5 cm.
Glasgow, Art Gallery and Museum.
Cat. 109 / Bredius 480.

THE LATE SELF-PORTRAITS

In his youth Rembrandt had often portrayed old people marked by life, on whose faces and hands the years had left their traces, who suffered under the increasing burden of illness and frailty and yet radiated the wisdom and dignity of 59 age. For this reason the prophetess Hannah, the wise 51, 28 Simeon, the mourning Jeremiah, the ancient witnesses of the Old and New Testaments, and the Early Fathers occupied him especially. After the mid-1650s — when he had clearly passed the peak of his success — he became increasingly 9, 306 aware of himself as an old man. A series of self-portraits from 307, 366-374 the last two decades of his life shows his hair growing thinner and his skin slackening. His face is lined and slightly puffed. How much these marks of age must have occupied an artist so prone to reflecting on himself, who worked again and again at his self-portrait! He nevertheless attained an attitude of affirmation and produced two portraits of himself in historical roles which convey something fundamental about 368 his understanding of himself. The famous self-portrait in Amsterdam depicts him as the Apostle Paul, and the no less 371 important painting in Cologne portrays him in the role of the ancient philosopher Democritus. Paul was the most important of the apostles, and it was owing to him that Christianity remained a joyful message. He constantly stressed that people could not be happy through the formal observance of the law. This too often concealed suppressed immoral and selfish thoughts. The only true liberation was the love of God, which again and again turns us into new people and makes us act compassionately. This teaching of Paul had been brought back into prominence by Luther's Reformation. In Rembrandt's thinking also it played an important 32 role. In one of his earliest paintings, PETER AND PAUL IN DISCUSSION, he showed these two important apostles in a study. It is known that they had agreed on a conception of Christianity which was not subservient to laws, and later, too, Rembrandt portrayed several scenes from the New Testament in which Jesus placed love and compassion above the Pharisees' inhuman observance of the law. In his own life Rembrandt had learned how little a human being can achieve by his own will and good intentions. If he represents himself in his late picture as the Apostle Paul, he thereby acknowledges how imperfect his own life has been and how much he depends on the grace of God. In his hand he holds the writings of the Old Testament, in quasi-Hebraic script. Of the apostle's sword, only the pommel is visible. It is the traditional attribute of Paul, who was put to death by the sword and who had propounded his teaching with militant zeal.

SELF-PORTRAIT. About 1668.
Canvas 85 × 61 cm.
Florence, Uffizi.
Cat. 176 / Bredius 60.

SELF-PORTRAIT.
Signed: 'Rembrandt f. 1658'.
Canvas 133.7 × 103.8 cm.
New York, The Frick Collection.
Cat. 172 / Bredius 50.

SELF-PORTRAIT AS THE APOSTLE PAUL.
Signed: 'Rembrandt f. 1661'.
Canvas 91 × 77 cm.
Amsterdam, Rijksmuseum.
Cat. 175 / Bredius 59.

In 1667/68, in the Cologne SELF-PORTRAIT, Rembrandt 371 presents himself as a laughing artist at his easel, painting the portrait of a grim-faced man. In Baroque art a famous pair of philosophers, one laughing and the other weeping, was painted again and again. Their busts had prominent places in the Amsterdam theatre. They were the laughing Democritus and the weeping Heraclitus, both in old age. The ageing artist alludes to these Greek philosophers in his self-portrait. He depicts himself as Democritus, a philosopher from Abdera, an Ionian colony in Thrace. His contemporaries called him 'the laughing philosopher', not only because his Abderite fellow-citizens gave him abundant reasons to mock, but mainly because his teaching on the nature of things is marked by a serene and equable temper that led to a feeling which he called cheerfulness, and which he described as the highest good. In contrast, Heraclitus, from Ephesus, was called the dark one (*skoteinos*) because his teaching culminated in nihilism; he was termed the weeping philospher on account of his sombre disposition. Before Rembrandt, the two philosophers had been depicted as old men contemplating the transitory nature of the world, one serene and happy, the other weeping and bitter. For this reason, a globe was usually included. However, in Rembrandt and his contemporaries even before the late 1660s, we can observe a tendency to show such attributes only in a hidden or less emphatic way. Sometimes they are even omitted altogether, the figures being characterised by their actions or facial expression, or by their relation to other people. This is particularly noticeable in the famous painting of ARISTOTLE, 360 where we look in vain for the attribute of teaching. Despite his age and his increasing awareness of the transitoriness of all life, and particularly of worldly goods, Rembrandt depicts himself in cheerful spirits.

Hendrickje, who with Titus had sheltered and tended him through all his tribulations, died in 1663. Titus, who in 1665 was paid his inheritance (6,952 guilders) from the proceeds of his father's bankruptcy, came of age in the same year, and on 1 February married Magdalena van Loo. He died in September 1668. His wife was expecting his child, who was baptised Titia, with her grandfather as her godfather.

So the old artist was left behind with his fifteen-year-old daughter Cornelia and an elderly housekeeper. Even in his

Rembrandt circle.
REMBRANDT ('SELF-PORTRAIT').
Signed: 'Rembrandt f. 1660'.
Canvas 80.3 × 67.3 cm.
New York, Metropolitan Museum of Art.
Cat. A73 / Bredius 54.

Rembrandt's workshop. ►
REMBRANDT ('SELF-PORTRAIT').
Signed: 'Rembrandt f. 1659'.
Canvas 84 × 66 cm.
Washington DC, National Gallery of Art (Andrew W. Mellon Collection).
Cat. A72 / Bredius 51.

SELF-PORTRAIT.
Signed (by a later hand): 'Rem... F. 1660'.
Canvas 111 × 90 cm.
Paris, Louvre.
Cat. 173 / Bredius 53.

old age he had not learned how to handle money; once he had to break open his daughter's money-box in order to buy food. Yet, as we know from notarial papers, he had again acquired a large and valuable collection. In his encyclopaedic urge to explore all things, he had assembled 'paintings, drawings, rarities, and antiquities'. The collector and firm-owner Pieter van Brederode visited him on 2 October 1669 and recorded some of the unusual objects in his notebook, among them a helmet of which he made a sketch with explanatory notes, a bust of a philosopher, and the four models of arms and legs already mentioned, which had been dissected by Vesalius. Rembrandt's interests had not changed in the last years of his life.[346]

Rembrandt died on 4 October 1669. One day later a notary made an inventory of his possessions. The household effects were very modest in comparison with those at the time of his bankruptcy, yet his extensive collection filled three rooms, which were sealed. Rembrandt was buried in the Westerkerk on 8 October. Official Amsterdam seems to have taken no notice of his death, but one member of the Painter's Guild stood at his grave, on which he placed a metal plaque as a mark of respect.[347]

At the time of his death his work was known to many European artists and collectors. In Italy his portrait hung in a 'Gallery of Great Painters'. For the generations of artists who followed, however, Rembrandt was the first heretic of painting, who had dared to break free from classical rules and go his own way as an individual. It was not until a century later that the value of Rembrandt's stubborn inclination to seek new possibilities of expression based on tradition was again appreciated; and since then Rembrandt's name has been symbolic of the modern painter.

SELF-PORTRAIT AS DEMOCRITUS. About 1668.
Canvas 82.5 × 65 cm.
Cologne, Wallraf-Richartz Museum.
Cat. 177 / Bredius 61.

SELF-PORTRAIT.
Signed: 'Rembrandt f. 1669'.
Canvas 63.5 × 57.8 cm.
The Hague, Mauritshuis.
Cat. 179 / Bredius 62.

SELF-PORTRAIT. About 1661.
Canvas 114.3 × 94 cm.
London, Kenwood House, Iveagh Bequest.
Cat. 174 / Bredius 52.

SELF-PORTRAIT.
Signed: '...f 1669'. Canvas 86 × 70.5 cm.
London, National Gallery.
Cat. 178 / Bredius 55.

THE MYTH OF THE MISJUDGED AND FORGOTTEN ARTIST

In the literature on Rembrandt we often come across the notion that the artist was forgotten and rejected for two hundred years after his death. This is far from the truth. What can be said is that as the Classical movement in art gathered strength, opinions on Rembrandt became divided. Many collectors and the colourists among painters revered him, while artists and theoreticians of the Classical movement rejected his work. These two attitudes existed side by side for almost 150 years without being reconciled.[348]

An early expression of this divergence of views is to be found in the correspondence of the Sicilian nobleman Ruffo, who owned three half-length portraits by Rembrandt which he valued above all the works of Italian masters. Ruffo wrote to this effect to Abraham Bruyghel, his Dutch art-dealer in Rome, who himself painted in the Classical style. Bruyghel replied in a didactic tone:

360, 362

> From your esteemed letter I note that your Highness has commissioned various half-length figures from the best masters in Italy, and that none of these can compare with those of Rembrandt. That is correct, and I share your opinion. However, we must bear in mind that these great masters do not readily condescend to paint anything as insignificant as a clothed half-length figure, where the light falls on just one point of the nose, and where you do not see whence the light comes because all else is dark. The great painters are interested in showing a beautiful nude figure, from which one can see that they know how to draw. Only an uneducated person tries to clothe his figure with a clumsy dark garment, and these artists compose the surroundings in such a way that we cannot make head or tail of them.[349]

Bruyghel's objections are not particularly original. He is merely repeating what the Roman artists trained in the school of Raphael and Michelangelo had been saying against colourist and realist artists since the middle of the 17th century. Titian and Caravaggio had been condemned in similar terms earlier. Since Classicist teaching was to dominate art theory for more than a century, Rembrandt, the most famous of the modern colourists, remained an object of criticism. Joachim von Sandrart, a German artist and theoretician, was the first to publish the damning Classicist judgement on Rembrandt; it appeared in 1675 in his *Teutsche Akademie*. He accused Rembrandt of disregarding the rules of art — anatomy, proportion, perspective, the standards of antiquity, and Raphael's skill in drawing — and of having opposed sensible teaching in the academies. As might be expected, he praised merely the overall harmony of the

TWO SLAUGHTERERS AT WORK. About 1635. Pen drawing with bistre 149 × 200 mm. Frankfurt, Städelsches Kunstinstitut. Benesch 400.

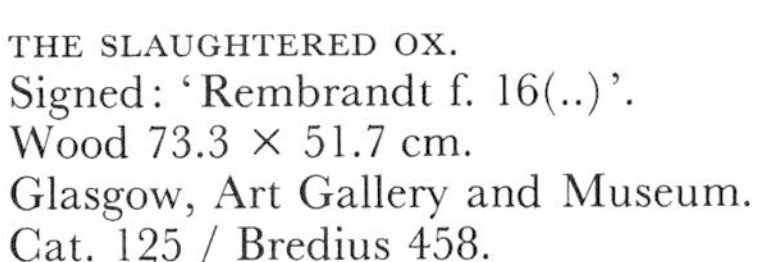

THE SLAUGHTERED OX.
Signed: 'Rembrandt f. 16(..)'.
Wood 73.3 × 51.7 cm.
Glasgow, Art Gallery and Museum.
Cat. 125 / Bredius 458.

THE SLAUGHTERED OX.
Signed: 'Rembrandt f. 1655'.
Wood 94 × 69 cm.
Paris, Louvre.
Cat. 124 / Bredius 457.

paintings, the use of chiaroscuro and colour, and a mode of representation modelled on nature. Sandrart's way of thinking led him to dismiss Rembrandt as an uneducated painter because, in his view, anyone who did not follow the rules of art could only be an ignoramus of low origin. Sandrart placed particular stress on Rembrandt's encyclopaedic collection, which he presents as an accumulation of junk. Arnold Houbraken, in his *Groote Schouburgh*, which appeared in 1718, advances his criticism of Rembrandt in the guise of alleged statements by the artist, and by passing on incorrect biographical facts and legends. As little was known about the actual course of Rembrandt's life at that time, a lowly social standing and a poor character were deduced from his paintings, from which conclusions were then drawn about his artistic views. In this way a distorted and legendary image of Rembrandt was created, which dominated the literature on art until the middle of the 19th century.

The collector Ruffo was undeterred by Bruyghel's letter, which had referred to the 'realistic' Rembrandt as uneducated. Ruffo's inventory in 1673 included a special list of the hundred most beautiful paintings in his collection, which were to pass to the eldest son in each generation. All three paintings by Rembrandt were included, but none by the great Italian artists praised by Bruyghel. The difference of opinion between the collector and the Classicist art dealer might be seen as almost paradigmatic of the later evaluation of Rembrandt's art. From that time on, the judgement of collectors differed from that of theoreticians. Ruffo was not alone in his enthusiasm for Rembrandt. At the time when most French artists of the 17th century were creating smooth idealised compositions under the constraints of Classicist dogmas, there was an active art market in Paris which valued the Dutch realists and Rembrandt so highly that it was worthwhile to produce fakes purporting to be their works, and this predilection for Dutch painting continued into the 18th century. For this reason the French art dealer Gersaint produced the first catalogue of Rembrandt's etchings as early as 1751 — a pioneer act in art history. True, in

NOTES

Publications included in the Bibliography are referred to in abbreviated form in the Notes (name of author and year of publication). For periodicals, collections, and series, the name, the year of publications, and the volume number are given.

The abbreviations B. (= Bartsch), Benesch and Ben. (= Benesch I-IV, 1954ff), Bredius (= Bredius 1935), Bredius[2] (= Bredius 2nd edit. 1936), Bredius[3] (= Bredius 3rd edit., edited by H. Gerson, 1969), Gerson (= Gerson 1969), and RRP (= Rembrandt Research Project) refer to the generally used catalogues raisonnés of the etchings, drawings, and paintings. Von Seidlitz, White-Boon, and Kok adopt the numbering used by B. (= Bartsch) in their oeuvre-catalogues of the etchings.

All documentary information is based, unless otherwise stated, on the chronologically arranged source materials compiled by Hofstede de Groot, 1906 (= *Urkunden*) and by W. Strauss and M. van der Meulen, 1979 (= *Documents*).

The documentary part of the present study is indebted to these two works and to the scholars who brought the material published in them to light. The reader can find documents referred to under the relevant year, even when they are not quoted explicitly in the notes.

When literature is referred to in the text of the oeuvre-catalogue relating to a picture, it is generally not specified again in the Notes.

1 J.S. HELD, 'Das gesprochene Wort bei Rembrandt', *Neue Beiträge zur Rembrandt-Forschung*, ed. by O. von Simson and J. Kelch, Berlin 1973, p. 112.

2 I am indebted to S.A.C. Dudok van Heel for demonstrating that Rembrandt's forbears included patricians. On Rembrandt's origins, cf. F. WIJNMAN, note on C. WHITE, *Rembrandt*, The Hague 1964, pp. 140f; J.F. JACOBS, 'Rembrandt verwant met Philips van Leyden', *De Nederlandsche Leeuw* 112, no. 12, 1985, pp. 457-465.

3 J. ORLERS, Leyden 1641[2], 375. The passage on Rembrandt is printed in *Urkunden* 86; *Documents* 1641/3. It is not clear from the documents whether or not Rembrandt completed his studies at the Latin School. According to Orlers, Rembrandt's parents intended him to go to university, but Rembrandt cut short his studies at the Latin School. This appears at variance with the fact that Rembrandt enrolled at the university at exactly the age at which he would normally have left the Latin School. Haak, 1968, pp. 18f, and Schwartz, 1984, pp. 20f, surmise that Rembrandt only enrolled to secure the many advantages enjoyed by students.
The question is left open here, needing further investigation.

4 W.R. VALENTINER, 1906; E.J. KUIPER, *De Hollandse 'schoolordre' van 1625*. Groningen 1958.

5 *Urkunden* 11; *Documents* 1620/1.

6 Cf. note 3.

7 K. BAUCH, 1960, pp. 45f. On Lastman, cf. K. FRIESE, 1911; K. BAUCH, *Münchner Jahrbuch der bildenden Kunst* N.S., 1955, pp. 213-221; same, 1960, pp. 51ff; A. TÜMPEL, *The Pre-Rembrandtists*. Exhibition catalogue Sacramento 1974, pp. 16ff and p. 47; same, *Oud Holland* 88, 1974, pp. 35ff; same, *Niederdeutsche Beiträge zur Kunstgeschichte* 17, 1978, pp. 87-101; same, *Gods, Saints and Heroes*, exhibition catalogue Washington-Detroit-Amsterdam 1980 and 1981, p. 126ff. Astrid Tümpel has written a monograph on Pieter Lastman. I was able to make use of this still unpublished work with oeuvre-catalogue in my discussion of the painter. On the other pre-Rembrandtists, cf. K. BAUCH, *Oud Holland* 52, 1935, pp. 145-158, 193-204; 53, 1936, pp. 79-88; 54, 1937, pp. 241-252; 55, 1938, pp. 254-265; same, 1960, pp. 60f; A. TÜMPEL, *The Pre-Rembrandtists*, 1974, pp. 15f and 21ff, and same, *Oud Holland* 88, 1974, pp. 1ff and 56ff; cf. the literature cited there.

8 Cf. note 3.

9 Rembrandt copied the main group — Abraham, Issac, and Hagar — in the drawing BENESCH 447 / Fig. II, 506 (Vienna, Albertina).

10 On the low viewpoint, cf. H. GURATZSCH, *Oud Holland* 89, 1975, pp. 243-265.

11 Joost van den Vondel's poem is printed in K. FRIESE, *Kunstwissenschaftliche Studien* Vol. 5, 1911, pp. 273f. It is quoted in part and discussed by K. BAUCH, 1960, pp. 66ff, and by A. TÜMPEL, *Oud Holland* 88, 1974, p. 54 and n. 207.

12 Cf. C. TÜMPEL. In: A. TÜMPEL, *The Pre-Rembrandtists*. Exhibition catalogue Sacramento 1974, p. 135 and Plate 79, and same, *Vestigia Bibliae* 2, 1980, pp. 137f.

13 On Lastman's Balaam painting, cf. A. TÜMPEL, *The Pre-Rembrandtists*, exh. cat. Sacramento 1974, no. 3 and the literature referred to there.

14 Cf. C. TÜMPEL. In: TÜMPEL, *The Pre-Rembrandtists*, exh. cat. Sacramento 1974, p. 140; same, *Vestigia Bibliae* 2, 1980, pp. 142f.

15 C. TÜMPEL. In: *Wort und Bild* ed. by H. VEKEMAN and J. MÜLLER HOFSTEDE, 1984, pp. 183ff and Fig. 15ff.

16 Lastman produced the paintings in Berlin-Dahlem (Gemäldegalerie), Paris (Fondation Custodia), Munich (Alte Pinakothek) and Karlsruhe (Kunsthalle). Rembrandt produced the etchings B. 98, an early painting, the composition of which is known only through a reproduction etching by Van Vliet (BAUCH A 16) and the early picture now in Utrecht (no. 35), as well as the workshop picture LANDSCAPE WITH THE BAPTISM OF THE CHAMBERLAIN (No. A 120).

17 On the other pre-Rembrandtists, see the literature in note.

18 On this commission, cf. H. GERSON, *Ausbreitung und Nachwirkung der holländischen Malerei des 17. Jahrhunderts*, Haarlem 1942. Photomechanical reprint, ed. by B.W. Meijer, Amsterdam 1983[2], p. 456.

19 Cf. A. TÜMPEL, *Oud Holland* 88, 1974, pp. 56ff.

20 The section on Rembrandt is printed in *Urkunden* 407.

21 New York, Metropolitan Museum. Cf. A. TÜMPEL, *The Pre-Rembrandtists*, exh. cat. Sacramento 1974, cat. no. 10.

22 Paris, Fondation Custodia. Cf. A. TÜMPEL, *Oud Holland* 88, 1974, p. 66 and Fig. 93.

23 Cf. A. TÜMPEL, *Oud Holland* 88, 1974, cat. no. 3 and pp. 72, 76f. W. Bode's judgement (1905, vol. 8, p. 3) is typical: 'Rembrandt stayed with Lastman for only six months; his art and teaching do not seem to have been congenial'. Most of the publications up to now confine themselves to noting Rembrandt's borrowings. In A. TÜMPEL's exhibition catalogue *The Pre-Rembrandtists*, Sacramento 1974, pp. 127ff, I examined Lastman's encyclopaedic style, showing its derivation. Rembrandt took it over and modified it.

24 On Jan Lievens, cf. H. SCHNEIDER, 1932; BAUCH 1960, cf. esp. pp. 208ff. The earlier view that Lievens became artistically dependent on Rembrandt immediately after the latter's return from Amsterdam was rightly corrected in *Jan Lievens, ein Maler im Schatten Rembrandts*, exh. cat. Brunswick, Herzog Anton Ulrich Museum 1979. The passage by Constantine Huygens on Lievens is taken from H. SCHNEIDER, 1923, pp. 290-292; the Brunswick exhibition catalogue gives a translation on pp. 33f. Orlers's comments on Jan Lievens are to be found in H. SCHNEIDER, 1932, pp. 293f, a translation being in the Brunswick exhibition catalogue, p. 35.

25 On the Utrecht Caravaggians, cf. B. NICOLSON, *Hendrick Terbrugghen*, The Hague 1958; J.R. JUDSON, 'Gerrit van Honthorst: a discussion of his position in Dutch Art', *Utrechtse bijdragen tot de kunstgeschiedenis* 6, The Hague 1970. L.J. SLATKES, 'Dirck van Baburen, C. 1592-1624. A Dutch Painter in Utrecht and Rome', *Utrechtse bijdragen tot de kunstgeschiedenis* 5, Utrecht 1965. A. VON SCHNEIDER, *Caravaggio und die Niederländer*, Marburg 1933 (reprinted Amsterdam 1967).

26 *Jan Lievens, ein Maler im Schatten Rembrandts*, 1979, nos. 2-5 and U 9. The Brunswick exhibition catalogue mentions Hendrick Terbrugghen's painting GIRL LIGHTING A CANDLE as the closest model (repr. in B. NICOLSON, 'Second Thoughts about Terbrugghen', *Burlington Magazine* 102, 1960, p. 466, Fig. 3).

27 Repr.: K. BAUCH, 1960, pp. 114f, Fig. 78.

28 B. NICOLSON, 1958 (ref. in n. 25), no. A13, Fig. 12.

29 J. BIALOSTOCKI, 'Lievens und Rembrandt', in: *Jan Lievens, ein Maler im Schatten Rembrandts*, exh. cat. Brunswick 1979, pp. 13-20, cf. esp. p. 14.

30 Lievens's drawing MUCIUS SCAEVOLA AND PORSENNA (Leyden, Prentenkabinet der Rijksuniversiteit) is reproduced in *Jan Lievens, ein Maler im Schatten Rembrandts*, exh. cat. Brunswick 1979, no. 49.

31 Berlin-Dahlem, Kupferstichkabinett, as a Lastman. Repr.: C. MÜLLER-HOFSTEDE, 1929, p. 62, Fig. 12 on Lastman.

32 K. BAUCH, 1960, p. 143.

33 P. SCHUBING, *Christliches Kunstblatt* 48, 1906, p. 227-234, quotation pp. 227f.

34 W. WEISBACH, 1926, p. 494.

35 Cf. C. TÜMPEL, in: A. TÜMPEL, *The Pre-Rembrandtists*, exh. cat. Sacramento 1974, pp. 146f; same, *Vestigia Bibliae. Jahrbuch des Deutschen Bibel-Archive Hamburg* 2, 1980, pp. 152ff.

36 Cf. C. TÜMPEL, in: *Wort und Bild in der niederländischen Kunst und Literatur des 16. und 17. Jahrhunderts*, ed. by H. Vekeman and J. Müller-Hofstede 1984, 173-204.

37 *Urkunden* 14; *Documents* 1628/1.

38 Cf. R.E.O. EKKART in the Supplement to the reprint by H. SCHNEIDER, *Jan Lievens* (Haarlem 1932) Amsterdam 1973, pp. 310f and n. 19.

39 On Huygens, cf. e.g. C. NEUMANN, 1924[4], pp. 89f.

40 The manuscript of the autobiographical fragment, written in Latin, is kept in the Royal Library at The Hague. The original text was published by J.A. WORP, *Bijdragen en Mededeelingen van het Historisch Genootschap* 18, 1897, pp. 1-121, and in 1946 by A.H. KAN in a Dutch translation.

41 The passages on Rembrandt and Lievens are in *Urkunden* 18 and quoted by H. SCHNEIDER, 1932, pp. 290f. Translation after B. HAAK, 1968, p. 42 (with changes).

42 German translation after B. HAAK, 1968, pp. 42f (with slight alterations).

43 Translation after B. HAAK, 1968 p. 44 (with slight alterations).

44 *Urkunden* 65; *Documents* 1639/2.

45 Jan Lievens, THE FOUR EVANGELISTS. Four wood panels, each 91 × 78 cm. Bamberg. Städtische Kunstsammlungen. Repr.: *Jan Lievens, ein Maler im Schatten Rembrandts*, exh. cat. Brunswick 1979, cat. nos. 10-13.

46 R. KLESSMANN in: *Jan Lievens, ein Maler im Schatten Rembrandts*, exh. cat. Brunswick 1979, cat. nos. 10-13, p. 56. For a characterisation of Lievens's style cf. K. BAUCH, 1960, pp. 208ff.

47 Jan Lievens, THE APOSTLE PAUL. Signed: 'Rembd.'. Canvas 110.5 × 101.5 cm. Bremen, Kunsthalle. SCHNEIDER-EKKART, 1973, p. 357.

48 Cf. R. KLESSMANN, in: *Jan Lievens, ein Maler im Schatten Rembrandts*, exh. cat. Brunswick 1979, cat. no. U2 (with fig.).

49 On Jan Lievens, cf. SCHNEIDER-EKKART, 1973, no. 13 and p. 347; may be same as 13 a).

50 R. KLESSMANN, *Jan Lievens, ein Maler im Schatten Rembrandts*, exh. cat. Brunswick, 1979, cat. no. U4.

51 Cf. R. KLESSMANN, in: *Jan Lievens, ein Maler im Schatten Rembrandts*, exh. cat. Brunswick 1979, cat. no. 19 (fig.). SCHNEIDER-EKKART, 1973, no. 264b p. 335.

52 Rembrandt produced at that time a painting (no. 42), an etching (repr. p. 45, B. 73), and a drawing, which he later converted into a BURIAL OF CHRIST (repr. p. 40; Ben. 17), while Jan Lievens produced the painting dated 1631 now in Brighton (SCHNEIDER-EKKART no. 31) and an etching (repr. 41; Rovinski 3).

53 Cf. A. TÜMPEL, *God en de Goden*, exh. cat. Washington-Detroit-Amsterdam 1980-1981, pp. 123ff.

54 On the pictorial tradition cf. H. GURATZSCH, 'Die Auferweckung des Lazarus in der niederländischen Kunst von 1400 bis 1700. Ikonographie und Ikonologie.' In: *Ars Neerlandica*, Vol. II, ed. by J. DESCHAMPS and P.J.J. VAN THIEL, Part If, Kortrijk 1980. As a result of the development of the picture tradition, the pre-Rembrandtists often showed the scene taking place in a cave.

55 Caravaggio, THE SACRIFICE OF ISAAC. About 1603. Florence, Galleria degli Uffizi.

56 Cf. H. GURATZSCH, *Oud Holland* 89, 1975, pp. 243-265, p. 252. The moral presentation of the story typical of its theological interpretation is also to be found in Baroque hymns: the hearer of the story is to be raised from the grave of sin. Cf., for example, the hymn by Jan Baptist Stalpaert van der Wiele, 'Lazarus, Vierden Vrijdach van de Vasten', printed in same, 'Gulde-Jaer Ons Heeren Jesu Christi op alle de zonnen-dagen des Jaers', in: *Zwolse Drukken en Herdrukken voor de Maatschappij der Nederlandse Letterkunde te Leiden* Vol. 61, Zwolle 1968, pp. 190ff. Verses 12 and 13 run:

12
O sondaer neemt hier spieghel aan.
Komt uyt het graf; 't en is geen rede
Dat ghy des Heeren roep versmaen
Sult boven de verrotte leden.

13
't Is meer als tijt dat ghy verrijst:
Wilt IESUS smarten niet verlengen.
Hy sucht, hy schreyt, hy knarst, hy brijst,
Om u we'er uyt het graf de brenghen.

57 Jan Lievens, THE RAISING OF LAZARUS. Signed IL 1631. Brighton, Art Gallery and Museum. (SCHNEIDER-EKKART, 1973, no. 31 and p. 322). See R. KLESSMANN's comments on the painting in *Jan Lievens, ein Maler im Schatten Rembrandts*, exh. cat. Brunswick 1979, no. 26.

58 A different view is expressed by R.E.O. EKKART in: *Jan Lievens, ein Maler im Schatten Rembrandts*, exh. cat. Brunswick 1979, no. 102.

59 Benesch 17.

60 On B. 73 and the models used cf. A. and C. TÜMPEL, 1971, no. 73.

61 Jacob Pynas, THE RAISING OF LAZARUS. Milwaukee, collection of Dr. and Mrs. A. Bader. Our mention of this painting was first followed up by M. Dierker, 'Rembrandt — ein protestantischer Künstler.' In: exhibition catalogue of the Hamburg Kunsthalle, *Luther und die Folgen für die Kunst*, ed. by Werner Hofmann, 1983, no. 209 (with fig.).

62 Jan Lievens, CHRIST ON THE CROSS. Signed IL 1631. Canvas 129 × 84 cm. Nancy, Musée des Beaux-Arts (SCHNEIDER-EKKART, 1973, no. 35 and p. 323). On Lievens's painting cf. R. KLESSMANN, *Jan Lievens, ein Maler im Schatten Rembrandts*, exh. cat. Brunswick 1979, no. 27 (with fig.).

63 The engraving copy is reproduced in RRP A9 (Fig. 7, p. 136).

64 To denote exalted rank, Rembrandt used the formula of children holding the hero's train in, for example, the painting SAMSON THREATENING HIS FATHER-IN-LAW (no. 10) and in the drawing THE ADORATION OF THE KINGS (Ben. 160).

65 As I have only later become aware, the Rembrandt Research Project has also noticed the significance of this play on words. It could not be represented literally. Rembrandt had to fall back on other biblical synonyms for baptism that could be represented. The engraved copy by Claes Jansz. Visscher which I mentioned is reproduced by the Rembrandt Research Project in Vol. I, p. 38, Fig. 5.

66 R. HAMANN, 1969[2], p. 250. See also Exh. Cat. Bielefeld 1969, no. 19; the author, H.G. GMELIN, makes use of similar formulations by C. NEUMANN and W. VON SEIDLITZ, quoted by GURATZSCH on p. 216. We owe the elucidation of these motifs to H. GURATZSCH I, 1980, pp. 215-221, in his excellent discussion *Lazarus und die 'militia'*.

67 K. VAN MANDER, *Het Schilder-Boeck waer in Voor eerst de leerlustighe jueght den grondt der Edel Vry Schilder const in verscheyden deelen Wort voorghedraghen*, Haarlem 1604, ch. 6 (ser. 22, v ff). This didactic poem has been edited, annotated, and translated into German by R. HOECKER, 'Das Lehrgedicht des Karel van Mander', *Quellenstudien zur Holländischen Kunstgeschichte*, ed. by C. HOFSTEDE DE GROOT, vol. VIII, The Hague 1916. The current standard edition, with commentary and translation into modern Dutch, is by H. MIEDEMA (ed.), *Karel van Mander, Den grondt der edel vry schilder-const.*, Utrecht 1973, vol. 1f. The section quoted in the text is in ch. VI, §1,2 and 5. Our quotation follows the translation by R. HOECKER. The RRP rightly supposes that Rembrandt took Tobias's gesture from a depiction of a sinner's repentance. G. SCHWARTZ, 1984, p. 45 and Fig. 28, has pointed out that Rembrandt's starting-point was Willem van Swanenburgh's engraving after Abrahaam Bloemaert's ST. PETER REPENTING.

68 Cf. the brilliant and seminal essay by J. HELD, *Neue Beiträge zur Rembrandt-Forschung*, ed. by O. von Simson and J. Kelch, 1973, pp. 111ff.

69 VAN MANDER, 1604, *Grondt*, ch. 6, §62 (ser. 28); quoted here from R. HOECKER's translation (ref. n. 67). On Plempius's poem cf. Cat. no. 5. The poem is printed and translated into English in RRP A25.

70 Cf. M. DIERKER (ref. in n. 61), no. 208.

71 *Urkunden* 18; *Documents* 1630/5.

72 Cf. the fundamental discussions by K. BAUCH, 1933, pp. 55-62 and 128-150; same, 1960, pp. 168-181.

73 KAN, 1946, p. 81.

74 The inventory of Lambert Jacobsz. includes '*Noch een cleine oostersche vrouwen troni, het conterfei(t)sel van H. Ulenburgs huysvrouwe nae Rembrandt*' (*Documents* 1637/4).

75 F. LABAN, *Zeitschrift für Bildende Kunst*, N.S. 9 (1897/8), p. 75.

76 Cf. L. MÜNZ, *Jahrbuch der kunsthistorischen Sammlungen in Wien* 50, 1953, pp. 141ff., esp. p. 143, where there is a reference to *Urkunden* 346, no. 10). However, Münz did not recognise the one certain portrait of Rembrandt's father (repr. p. 13; Ben. 56).

77 BAUCH, 1960, pp. 171ff.

78 On Frans Floris, cf. VAN MANDER, 1604 (ref. in n. 67), v. 242.

79 J. HELD, 'The Oil Sketches of Peter Paul Rubens.' *Kress Foundation Studies in the History of European Art 7*, Princeton, vol. 1f, 1980, cf. I, pp. 595ff.

80 On the type of the old woman, cf. C. Bloemaert's engraving after A. Bloemaert AN OLD WOMAN WITH A ROSARY (Fig. 2 in RRP A27).

81 B. 51.

82 The best study of the early self-portraits is by K. BAUCH, 1960, pp. 180f. A comprehensive examination of the self-portraits and role-portraits, making use of the secondary literature, is a desideratum of art history. Of the earlier (largely obsolete) studies, the monograph by F. ERPEL (1967) should be mentioned.

83 Cf. the translation by H. FLOERKE (1906), VOL. II, pp. 405f.

84 Cf. K. BAUCH, 1960, p. 176, who bases himself primarily on K. van Mander.

85 SANDRART (1675). The passage on Rembrandt is printed in *Urkunden* 329, the modern version being based on L. GOLDSCHEIDER (1963) 12f.

86 Cf. n. 41.

87 BAUCH, 1960, p. 140.

88 On Rembrandt as etcher cf. the catalogues raisonnés by A. BARTSCH (vol. If 1797); A.M. HIND (1923); W.V. SEIDLITZ (1922); G. BJÖRKLUND (1955); MÜNZ (vol. 1f 1952); K.G. BOON (1963), CHR. WHITE, and K.G. BOON (1969). Of especial value is the monograph by C. WHITE (1969). Very informative on Rembrandt the etcher is the catalogue of the Rembrandt House by J.P. FILEDT KOK 1972, and the exhibition catalogue *Rembrandt. Eaux-Fortes*, Musée du Petit Palais, Paris 1986 is also useful. A study of the iconography of the etchings with biblical themes is to be found in A. and C. TÜMPEL, 1971.

89 On the history of Amsterdam, cf. M. CARASSO-KOK, *Amsterdam Historisch*, Bussum 1975.

90 Apart from the histories of Amsterdam, biographies of families of burgomasters indicate the influence of the latter. Reference is made here to J.F.L. DE BALBIAN VERSTER, *Burgemeesters van Amsterdam in de 17e en 18e eeuw*, Amsterdam 1932 and 1970[2] (photomechanical reprint).

91 On Joan Huydecoper, cf. the biography by J.F.L. DE BALBIAN VERSTER, 1932 (ref. n. 90), pp. 36-50.

93 Cf. A. TÜMPEL, *Gods, Saints and Heroes*, exh. cat. Washington-Detroit-Amsterdam, 1980-81, pp. 45-53, cf. esp. pp. 45ff; C. TÜMPEL, 'Die Reformation und die Kunst der Niederlande.' In: Exh. cat. Hamburg Kunsthalle, *Luther und die Folgen für die Kunst*, ed. by W. HOFMANN, Munich 1983, pp. 309-321, cf. esp. p. 313.

94 On Nicolaes Tulp, cf. J. WAGENAAR, III 1776, p. 239; H.C. ROGGE, 'Nicolaes Tulp', *De Gids*, 1880, Part III; J.F.L. DE BLABIAN VERSTER (ref. n. 90), pp. 51-65.

95 On the Synod of Dordrecht, cf. *Realenzyklopädie für protestantische Theologie und Kirche*, 3rd edit., Leipzig,

vol. IV, 1898, pp. 798ff.
96 *Urkunden* 34; *Documents* 1634/2.
97 *Urkunden* 35; *Documents* 1634/3.
98 Rembrandt's church wedding took place on 2 July. In interpreting the marriage document (*Urkunden* 37; *Documents* 1634/5) it is often overlooked that up to 1700 in Friesland the Julian calendar was generally used, whereas the Gregorian was already adopted in Holland. Cf. C. HOFSTEDE DE GROOT, 1905, commentary on *Urkunden* 94.
99 Cf. C. TÜMPEL, 1975, p. 15.
100 Cf. C. NEUMANN, 1924[4], pp. 101f.
101 Cf. I. BERGSTRÖM, *Nederlands Kunsthistorisch Jaarboek* 17, 1966, pp. 143-169 and C. TÜMPEL, *Kunstchronik* 19, 1966, pp. 302; same, 1968, pp. 90ff; same, *Jahrbuch der Hamburger Kunstsammlungen* 13, 1968, pp. 116ff. B. HAEGER, 1983, has devoted a very careful monograph with numerous important new insights to the theme of the Prodigal Son.
102 F. BALDINUCCI, 1686, pp. 78ff, the passage on Rembrandt's links to the Mennonites in §4. Cf. *Urkunden* 360. L. GOLDSCHEIDER, 1960, pp. 13ff reproduces a German translation of this text.
103 HOFSTEDE DE GROOT (1906), in his commentary on *Urkunden* 157, concludes from the fact that on the third or fourth summons only Hendrickje was called before the Reformed Church Court, when she was expecting Cornelia, that Baldinucci's information on Rembrandt's being a member of the Mennonites must be correct. When the Court realised that Rembrandt was no longer a member of the Reformed Church, he supposes, only she was summoned to be excluded from communion. W. STRAUSS and W. VAN DER MEULEN accept this argument (*Documents* 1654/11). G.A.: Nederduitse hervormde gemeente, Protokol 9, PA 376, ser. 53v. Numerous art historians since then have assumed that Rembrandt was a Mennonite, explaining his themes and iconographic style on the basis of this alleged belief, for example, C. NEUMANN, J. ROSENBERG, and J. HELD. H.M. ROTERMUND, *Nederlands Kunsthistorisch Jaarboek* 4, 1952/3, pp. 104-192, in an otherwise informative study of the sources, themes and iconographic style of Rembrandt, has attempted to show that he did indeed belong to a Mennonite community. The interpretation of the documents is unfortunately very defective. The 17th century had its special rites and customs, ignorance of which leads to incorrect interpretations. Rotermund's attempt to deduce Rembrandt's religious views from his iconographic style and choice of themes was bound to fail since painters could, in Holland, have different religious affiliations but the same style and subjects, and even portray subjects typical of an opposed denomination. Useful clarification is brought to the discussion by the study by S.A.C. DUDOK VAN HEEL, *Doopsgezinde Bijdragen,* Nieuwe reeks 6, 1980, pp. 105-123.
104 On Rembrandt and Hendrick Uylenburgh cf. H.F. WIJNMAN, 'Rembrandt en Hendrick Uylenburgh te Amsterdam.' *Maandblad Amstelodamum* 43, pp. 94-104.
105 Inventories of Mennonites also mention: '*Een conterfeijtsel van Jan Pietersz. Bryningh ende sijn huysvrouwe zal: van Rembrandt*', and '*Een conterfeijtsel van Pieter Jansz. Moutmaker mede van Rembrandt*'. Cf. *Documents* 1647/1a; S.A.C. DUDOK VAN HEEL, *Doopsgezinde Bijdragen,* Nieuwe reeks 6, 1980, p. 117.
106 Cf. S.A.C. DUDOK VAN HEEL, *Doopsgezinde Bijdragen,* Nieuwe reeks 6, 1980, p. 117.
107 *Documents* 1637/4. Cf. S.A.C. DUDOK VAN HEEL, *Doopsgezinde Bijdragen,* Nieuwe reeks 6, 1980, p. 108.
108 S.A.C. DUDOK VAN HEEL, *op. cit.* p. 112.
109 K. BAUCH, 1960, p. 200, clearly influenced by liberal religious sympathies, assigned Rembrandt to this confession. 'One would most readily count Rembrandt among the moderate Arminians, whose clergy at that time were being expelled from the country in the hundreds' (sic!). G. SCHWARTZ, 1984, in a book which in many chapters is highly meritorious, makes Rembrandt a victim of the various religious-political groupings, to which he was particularly exposed as a Remonstrant sympathiser. In these sections, despite many useful suggestions, his book often resembles a detective novel. On Rembrandt and the Remonstrants, cf. particularly S.A.C. DUDOK VAN HEEL, 'Abraham Anthonisz. Recht (1588-1664), een Remonstrants opdrachtgever van Rembrandt', *Maandblad Amstelodamum* 65, 1978, pp. 81ff; same, 'Mr. Joannes Wtenbogaert (1608-1680), een man uit Remonstrants milieu en Rembrandt van Rijn', *Jaarboek Amstelodamum,* 70, 1978, 146-169. B. TIDEMAN, 'Portretten van Johannes Wtenbogaert', *Oud Holland* 21, 1903, pp. 125-128.
110 *Urkunden; Documents.*
111 E. HAVERKAMP-BEGEMANN, *The Art Bulletin* 54, 1971, p. 96, rightly emphasises 'that we have to incorporate into our image of the artist the knowledge that both were Catholic'. It is typical of leading Dutch artists of the 17th century that they worked for clients of different denominations. This phenomenon has long been overlooked.
112 Dutch art history has been so dominated by the notion of a strict separation between denominations (which was actually the case in the 19th and early 20th centuries), that Rembrandt scholars paid no attention to the balanced account given by Neumann, 1924[4], II, pp. 640ff.
113 The Institute of Art History at the University of Nijmegen plans to make an inventory of the concealed Catholic and Lutheran churches.
114 C. NEUMANN, 1924[4], p. 640.
115 Unknown Dutch master. REPRESENTATIVES OF DENOMINATIONS AS MEMBERS OF A DEBATING CHAMBER. 1659. Wood. Haarlem, Frans Hals Museum. Cf. C. TÜMPEL, 'Die Reformation und die Kunst der Niederlande', *Luther und die Folgen für die Kunst,* exh. cat. Hamburg Kunsthalle, Munich 1983, pp. 309-321, cf. pp. 319f and Fig. 31.
116 I have pointed out in various places that the different denominations did not generally portray biblical scenes differently. Rather, there was a lively exchange of ideas among artists of different denominations in precisely this area; cf. my notes on this in: A TÜMPEL, *The Pre-Rembrandtists,* exh. cat. Sacramento 1974, pp. 146f; in *Gods, Saints and Heroes,* exh. cat. Washington-Detroit-Amsterdam 1980/81, pp. 51 and 52, n. 24; same, 1983 (ref. n. 115), p. 317. J. BRUYN, 1959, p. 6, first drew attention to this, giving a number of telling examples.
117 *Documents* 1633/1.
118 *Documents* 1641/1.
119 *Documents* 1633/1.
120 In *Documents* 1633/1 there is a reference to a poem by Huygens on this portrait, which does not include the burlesque poem mentioned in *Documents* 1633/1 itself, but seven variations on it. Rembrandt's name is not mentioned. G. SCHWARTZ, 1984, p. 97, prints the whole poem. In his interpretation he overlooks the neo-platonic attitude of the poem and the special nature of Baroque poems. Huygens does not formulate his personal opinion of the portrait here, but simply writes variations on the neo-platonic theme of 'primal image and likeness'. How much the poem is a literary exercise is clear from the fact that in one verse the picture can be censured and in the next praised as 'beautiful'. The idea that this poem expresses a breach between Huygens and Rembrandt is wrongly imported into the poem by SCHWARTZ through lack of knowledge of Baroque poetry.
121 Cf. H. GERSON 112 and B. HAAK, 1968, pp. 84f. *Documents* 1632/3 (no. 79).
122 A careful investigation of Frederick Hendrick's commissions to Rembrandt from the sources is lacking. The list compiled by G. SCHWARTZ, 1984, p. 69, contains too many hypotheses.
123 Rembrandt's letters have been newly edited by H. GERSON, 1961. They can be found in *Urkunden* 47f, 65-69; *Documents* 1636/1-2, 1639/2-6. Cf. E. BROCHHAGEN, 'Beobachtungen zu den Passionsbildern Rembrandts', *Minuscula discipulorum. Kunsthistorische Studien für H. Kauffmann zum 70. Geburtstag,* Berlin 1968, pp. 37ff. Because Rembrandt writes in the first letter of 'three Passion pictures... which Your Excellence has himself commissioned from me.... These accord with the Raising of the Cross and the Descent from the Cross' in the first letter, recent scholarship has mistakenly assumed that the Raising and the Descent were ordered first, and the three other Passion pictures only later. Rembrandt is referring to what he has already delivered and what still has to be completed. Thus he writes in the third letter of 'these two pictures which Your Highness has commissioned from me'.
124 Letter from DR. A. HÜBNER.
125 Cf. J. BRUYN, 1959, p. 8.
126 BENESCH 152 (Amsterdam).
127 Revius wrote about that time: *Hy droech onse Smerten,* which contains the lines:
T'en zijn de Joden niet, Heer Jesu, die u cruysten.
Noch die verraderlijck u togen voort gericht.
Nich die versmadelick u spogen int gesicht
Noch die u knevelden, en stieten u vol puysten.
T'en sijn de crijchs-luy niet die met haer felle vuysten
Den rietstock hebben of den hamer obgelicht,
Of het vervloecte hout op Golgotha gesticht,
Of over uwen rock tsaem dobbelden en tuyschten:
Ick ben, ô Heer, ick ben die u dit heb gedaen,
Ick ben den swaren boom die u had overlaen
Ick ben de taeye streng daermee ghy ginct gebonden,
De nagel, en de speer, de geessel die u sloech,
De bloet-bedropen croon die uwen schedel droech:
Want dit is al geschiet, eylaes! om mijne sonden.
128 1st letter. *Urkunden* 47; *Documents* 1636/1. Cf. n. 123.
129 H. GERSON, 1961, p. 31.
130 2nd letter. *Urkunden* 48; *Documents* 1636/2. Cf. n. 123.
131 Cf. E. BROCHHAGEN, 1968 (ref. n. 123), pp. 40f and Fig. 24f.
132 3rd letter. *Urkunden* 65; *Documents* 1639/2. Cf. n. 123.
133 Cf. W. SUMOWSKI, *Wissenschaftliche Zeitschrift der Humboldt-Universität zu Berlin. Gesellschafts- und sprachwissenschaftliche Reihe* 7, 1957f, p. 225 and Figs, 21-24; E. BROCHHAGEN, 1968, (ref. n. 123), pp. 41f and C. TÜMPEL, 1968, pp. 196f, same, *Ars Auro Prior. Studia Joanni Bialstocki Sexagenario Dicata,* 1981, pp. 429ff.
134 Cf. H. GERSON, 1961, pp. 39f.
135 Cat. no 12, Frankfurt, Städelsches Kunstinstitut.
136 4th letter. *Urkunden* 66; *Documents* 1639/3. Cf. n. 123.
137 5th letter. *Urkunden* 67; *Documents* 1639/4. Cf. n. 123.
138 6th letter. *Urkunden* 68; *Documents* 1639/5. Cf. n. 123.
139 7th letter. *Urkunden* 69; *Documents* 1639/6. Cf. n 123.
140 B. 281. On the etching, cf. W.L. STRAUSS, 'Rembrandt: de koperen slang'. *De kroniek van het Rembrandthuis* 36, 1984, pp. 24-35.
141 Munich, Alte Pinakothek. THE CIRCUMCISION has been lost. There is a copy in Brunswick, Herzog Anton Ulrich Museum, cf. cat. no. K3.
142 On this chapter, cf. esp. N. REILING (Anna Seghers), 1924; H. VAN DE WAAL, 'Rembrandts Radierungen zur Piedra Gloriosa des Menasseh ben Israël'. In: *Imprimatur, ein Jahrbuch für Bücherfreunde* 12, 1954/55, pp. 51-56; R.H. FUCHS, 1968, pp. 40ff, and E. PANOFSKY, *Jahrbuch der Hamburger Kunstsammlungen* 18, 1973, pp. 75-108.
143 E. KOLLOFF, 1854, pp. 497f.
144 E. PANOFSKY, *Jahrbuch der Hamburger Kunstsammlungen* 18, 1973, p. 78.
145 By word of mouth from Mr. S.A.C. DUDOK VAN HEEL.
146 Cf. C. TÜMPEL, 'The iconography of the Pre-Rembrandtists', in: A. TÜMPEL, *The Pre-Rembrandtists,* exh. cat. Sacramento 1974, pp. 127f.

147 B.77.
148 Cf. J. DYSERINCK, 'Eene Hebreeuwsche inscriptie op een schilderij van Rembrandt', *De Nederlandsche Spectator* 1904, p. 160; R. HAUSHERR, *Oud Holland* 78, 1963, pp. 142ff; E. PANOFSKY, *Jahrbuch der Hamburger Kunstsammlungen* 18, 1973, pp. 87f.
149 Cat. no. 11.
150 B. 77.
151 The section on Rembrandt's life in HOUBRAKEN, 1718, I, pp. 254-274 is reproduced in *Urkunden* 407. Rembrandt's saying is in *Urkunden* 407 §35.
152 Cf. H. VAN DE WAAL, *Imprimatur, ein Jahrbuch für Bücherfreunde* 12, 1954/55, pp. 53ff; C. TÜMPEL, 1970, no. 39.
153 Reproductions of the copies are in H. VAN DE WAAL, *Imprimatur, ein Jahrbuch für Bücherfreunde* 12, 1954/55 (following p. 58), Figs. 9-12.
154 In 1678 Rembrandt's pupil Samuel van Hoogstraten complains 'dat de konst sedert de Beeltstorming in den voorgaende eeuw, in Holland niet geheel vernietigt is, schoon ons de beste loopbaenen, naementlijk de kerken, daer door geslooten zijn, en de meeste schilders zich deshalven tot geringe zaeken, jae zelfs tot beuzelingen te schilderen geheelijck begeeven', HOOGSTRATEN, 1678, p. 257. Cf. TÜMPEL, in *Gods, Saints and Heroes,* exh. cat. Washington-Detroit-Amsterdam 1980-81, pp. 45-53, and same, exh. cat. Hamburg Kunsthalle, *Luther und die Folgen für die Kunst,* Munich 1983, pp. 309-321.
155 A compilation of these paintings is still lacking. Many examples are to be found in the award-winning work by H. GERSON, *Ausbreitung und Nachwirkung der holländischen Malerei des 17. Jahrhunderts,* Haarlem 1942 and Amsterdam 1983[2], cf. e.g. the commission for the chapel at Frederiksborg, to the decoration of which *'Werner van den Valckert, Everard Crynsz, v.d. Maes, Pieter Lastman and Adriaen van Nieuwland'* (p. 456) also contributed (A. TÜMPEL, *Oud Holland* 88, p. 47; Fig. 60 shows a copy of Lastman's lost painting from this commission). The problem of artists working for churches of denomination to which they did not themselves belong was first raised by J. BRUYN, 1959, p. 6 and n. 3. Some examples of church decorations are in C. TÜMPEL, exh. cat. Hamburg Kunsthalle, *Luther und die Folgen für die Kunst,* Munich 1983, pp. 317f. Gerard de Lairesse painted the organ screen for the Amsterdam Westerkerk.
156 *Urkunden* 54; *Documents* 1637/6.
157 Cf. the 4th chapter, 'Die Andeutung des Erzählungszusammenhanges' in C. TÜMPEL, 1968, pp. 137-160.
158 From Bel to Babel 4.
159 From Bel to Babel 7f.
160 John 20:27.
161 Cf. the paintings CHRIST APPEARING TO THE DOUBTING THOMAS by Rubens (about 1613/5, Antwerp, Koninklijk Museum voor Schone Kunsten) and by Caravaggio (1599, Potsdam, Sanssouci).
162 Cf. the fundamental essay by J. HELD, *Neue Beiträge zur Rembrandt-Forschung*, ed. by O. v. Simson and J. Kelch, 1973, pp. 111-125.
163 John 19:7.
164 Rembrandt's portrayal of this group was probably suggested by Jan Swart van Groningen's woodcut JESUS PREACHING FROM THE SHIP (B. VII, § 494, no. 1), for it shows a similar group of orientals in discussion in the foreground. Rembrandt 'reformulated' this group in the Berlin drawing Ben. 141 for the scene of St. John preaching, as his concern was to show the reaction of the Pharisees.
165 Matthew 3:7f.
166 B. 208.
167 S. VAN HOOGSTRATEN, 1678, V, I, p. 183; *Urkunden* 339.
168 Judges 15:3.
169 G. SCHWARTZ, 1984, p. 138 quotes from the inventory without noticing this connection.
170 Genesis 22:11f.
171 Caravaggio, THE SACRIFICE OF ISAAC, about 1603, Florence, Galleria degli Uffizi.
172 J. BRUYN, *Simiolus* 4, 1970, p. 39, Fig. 12ff.
173 Cf. the history of the picture's interpretation in C. TÜMPEL, 1967, no. 3.
174 C. HOFSTEDE DE GROOT, *Repertorium für Kunstwissenschaft* 22, 1899, p. 163.
175 C. NEUMANN, I, 1922, p. 219.
176 W. WEISBACH, 1926, pp. 218f.
177 R. HAMANN, 1948, pp. 278f.
178 My investigations have attempted to demonstrate this. G. SCHWARTZ, 1984, reverts to a prescholarly mode when, in his own interpretation, he fails to take account of the iconographic derivation of Rembrandt's works, interpreting on a basis of free association.
179 Cf. C. TÜMPEL, in: A. TÜMPEL, *The Pre-Rembrandtists,* exh. cat. Sacramento 1974, p. 128, and same, *Vestigia Bibliae* 2, 1980, pp. 127ff, esp. p. 130.
180 On the history of history bibles and their interpretation, cf. H. VOLLMER, *Materialien zur Bibelgeschichte und religiösen Volkskunde*, vols. 1-4, 1912-1929, and the various series of publications by the Deutsches Bibel-Archiv, Hamburg.
181 The information is passed down by von Sandrart, cf. the introduction by Adolf Rosenberg to R. OLDENBOURG, 'P.P. Rubens. Des Meisters Gemälde', *Klassiker der Kunst* vol. 5, Stuttgart and Berlin 1921, p. XV.
182 There is much evidence of this tradition, e.g. the catalogue of the exhibition by the Deutsches Bibel-Archiv in the Staats- und Universitätsbibliothek Hamburg, *Schrift, Bild und Druck der Bibel,* Hamburg 1955, no. 119.
183 Cf. the excellent section 'Originaliteit en ontlening in de 17de eeuw' in J.A. EMMENS, 1968, pp. 111-115.
184 Cf. R.W. LEE, *Ut pictura poesis: The Humanistic Theory of Painting*, New York 1967 (previously published in *Art Bulletin* 22, 1940); cf. esp. ch. II, 'Invention', pp. 16ff.
185 *Ibid.* p. 17.
185 *Ibid.* p. 17.
186 The encyclopaedic interests of the 17th century are generally underestimated by many art historians who interpret the pictures of the 17th century typologically, emblematically, or symbolically. On the uncommon theme, cf. my observations in the *Jahrbuch der Hamburger Kunstsammlungen* 16, 1971, pp. 20ff, cf. esp. pp. 24f.
187 Cf. Pieter Lastman, ELISHA AND THE SHUNAMMITE WIFE. About 1616 (?). Moscow, Pushkin Museum (repr. p. 169). The second painting, the attribution of which to Pieter Lastman is disputed, is monogrammed PL and dated 1626 (auct. Amsterdam 13.4.1920, lot 111).
188 A. PIGLER (*Barockthemen,* Budapest and Berlin 1956, I, p. 180; same, 2nd edit. Budapest 1974, p. 182) has compiled a list of Dutch depictions of the subject. It would need to be completed by, among others, the paintings reproduced by A. TÜMPEL (*Oud Holland* 88, 1974, cat. nos. 84 and 86).
189 Jacob Pynas, THE PROPHET ELISHA SENDING HIS SERVANT TO THE SHUNAMMITE WIFE. Kurhessische Hausstiftung, Kronberg. Repr. in C. TÜMPEL (*Vestigia Bibliae* 2, 1980, pp. 150f).
190 Eeckhout painted the subject twice (Warsaw and Budapest), cf. W. SUMOWSKI, 1983ff, cf. II, 1983, Fig. 407 (Warsaw) and 440 (Budapest). The Warsaw picture was still regarded by J. BIALOSTOCKI and M. WALICKI (*Europäische Malerei in polnischen Sammlungen, 1300-1800* Warsaw 1957, text on Fig. 248) as an EXPULSION OF HAGAR; in the Corrigenda and Addenda the misinterpretation is corrected.
191 Cf. R. Earlom after anonymous member of the Rembrandt school (Smith 1028). Repr. in W.R. VALENTINER (*Oud Holland* 50, 1933, 241 as W. Horst).
192 Rembrandt followed his learned teacher Pieter Lastman in this encyclopaedic discovery of numerous unknown histories, treating subjects previously found only in printed graphics for the first time as isolated scenes in a drawing or a painting. In the late drawing THE MESSENGER BRINGING ELI THE NEWS OF THE DEATH OF HIS SONGS AND OF THE LOSS OF THE ARK (repr. p. 171), Rembrandt used a woodcut from his edition of Josephus. Whereas the previous pictorial tradition only showed Eli, after receiving the news of the loss of the ark, falling dead from his seat, Tobias Stimmer also shows the preceding scene in the background of his woodcut. It was this background scene which inspired Rembrandt to give an impressive form to the uncommon theme. (cf. C. TÜMPEL, *Nederlandse Kunsthistorisch Jaarboek* 20, 1969, pp. 125ff). Of course, literary sources might also suggest to Rembrandt the treatment of a somewhat earlier, or later, especially emotive moment. As M. DIERKER, *(Luther und die Folgen für die Kunst,* exh. cat. Hamburg Kunsthalle, ed. by W. HOFFMANN, no. 196) observed, in creating the drawing NATHAN ADMONISHING DAVID (repr. p. 171; Berlin-Dahlem), Rembrandt drew not only on the Bible but on Flavius Josephus's *Jewish Antiquities.* As an example of the treatment of uncommon themes in Rembrandt's circle I would mention the painting by J.A. Backer, THE ANGEL APPEARING TO CORNELIUS, THE CENTURION OF CAESAREA, AS HE PRAYS AND FASTS (Milwaukee, Collection of Dr. and Mrs. A. Bader, repr. p. 169). The iconographic treatment is based on an engraving by Philipp Galle after Johannes Stradanus's series on the acts of the apostles (repr. p. 169; Hollstein VIII, 306-340). In the formal composition Backer is influenced by treatments of the Annunciation.
193 Cf. E. KIESER (*Zeitschrift für Kunstgeschichte* 10, 1941/42, pp. 129-162, esp. p. 129); E.J. SLUIJTER ('De uitbeelding van mythologische thema's', *God en de Goden.* exh. cat. Washington-Detroit-Amsterdam 1980-81, pp. 55-63). In this chapter I summarise results which I set out in my dissertation 1968 (cf, esp. § 27 'Die Bedeutung der literarischen Quellen und der Bildtradition für die Themen aus der Heiligengeschichte, der Mythologie and Profangeschichte', pp. 222ff, and in the essay 'Bild und Text: Zur Rezeption antiker Autoren in der europäischen Kunst der Neuzeit (Livius, Valerius Maximus)', *Forma et subtilitas. Festschrift für Wolfgang Schöne zum 75. Geburtstag,* ed. by W. SCHLINK and M. SPERLICH, Berlin/New York 1986, pp. 198-218).
194 G. SCHWARTZ, 1984, p. 119: 'Rembrandt, de jongen, die de Latijnse school niet had afgemaakt, hield zich ver van klassieke onderwerpen'.
195 Attention was first drawn to this passage by M. DIERKER, *Die Bedeutung der jüdischen Altertümer für die holländische Historienmalerei des 16. und 17. Jahrhunderts,* (seminar paper for my course on 'Dutch history-painting in the 17th century', Berlin, Free University, winter term 1980/81).
196 W. KRAUS, article 'P. Ovidius Naso', *Der kleine Pauly, Lexikon der Antike,* Munich, vol. IV, 1979, col. 383ff, cf. esp. col. 387. The best account of the mythological subjects is by E.J. SLUIJTER, *God en de Goden* exh. cat. Washington-Detroit-Amsterdam 1980-81, pp. 55-63. On the Ovid editions, cf. *ibid.*, p. 55 and n. 3 and 4.
197 M. FUHRMANN, article 'Livius', *Der kleine Pauly, Lexikon der Antike,* Munich, vol. III, 1979, col. 689ff, cf. esp. col. 698.
198 In the account of Valerius Maximus, I follow, among others, P.L. SCHMIDT, article 'V. Maximus', *Der kleine Pauly, Lexikon der Antike,* Munich, vol. V, 1979, col. 1117f.
199 P.L. SCHMIDT (ref. n. 198) col. 1118. (Abbreviated words completed).
200 On Rembrandt's library cf. C. TÜMPEL, *Nederlands Kunsthistorisch Jaarboek* 20, 1969, pp. 109ff.
201 Cf. E. KIESER, *Zeitschrift für Kunstgeschichte* 10, 1941/42, pp. 129f.
202 Cf. E. KIESER, *Zeitschrift für Kunstgeschichte* 10, 1941/42, pp. 130f.
203 Adapted from the translation by R. SUCHIER, Ovid, 'Metamorphosen', *Goldmanns Gelbe Taschenbücher,* Vol. 583f, Munich 1959.

204 Cf. n. 203.

205 *Urkunden* 65; *Documents* 1639/2.

206 K. CLARK, 1966, p. 13. P. SCHATBORN, *De Kroniek van het Rembrandthuis* 27, 1975, pp. 8-19, has convincingly demonstrated that Rembrandt's treatment of Ganymede is by no means anti-classical, but strongly influenced by models from the Renaissance and the Baroque. J. BRUYN, ('On Rembrandt's Use of Studio-Props and Model Drawings during the 1630's', *Essays in Northern European Art Presented to Egbert Haverkamp Begemann,* Doornspijk 1983, pp. 52-60, cf. pp. 52f) has supported Schatborn's arguments.

207 H. VON EINEM, 'Michelangelo', *Urban-Bücher. Die wissenschaftliche Taschenbuchreihe* Vol. 42, ed. by F. ERNST, Stuttgart 1959, pp. 108f. Quoted by C. TÜMPEL, 1968, pp. 223f.

208 Cf. M. RUSSELL (*Simiolus* 9, 1977, pp. 5-18, cf. pp. 9f), who independently advances a similar interpretation to that of TÜMPEL, 1968, pp. 224f. Her interpretation omits to mention that the symbolic meanings are 'embedded' in the primitive reactions, that Rembrandt develops a 'disguised symbolism' in GANYMEDE as in DANAË.

209 Cf. the catalogue text in VALENTINER II, 609, and the title in Benesch I, 1954 on Ben. 92.

210 C. TÜMPEL, 1968, pp. 224f.

211 Cf. M. RUSSELL, *Simiolus* 9, 1977, p. 12 (quotation van Mander) and pp. 14f (Duquesnoy).

212 C. TÜMPEL, 1968, pp. 224f and n. 649.

213 Cf. C. TÜMPEL, *Nederlands Kunsthistorisch Jaarboek* 20, 1969, p. 158.

214 E. PANOFSKY, *Oud Holland* 50, 1933, pp. 209f.

215 E. FECHNER, 1964, pp. 72, 74.

216 To E. PANOFSKY, *Oud Holland* 50, 1933, pp. 193ff) we owe the interpretation of the fettered Eros.

217 E. KIESER, *Zeitschrift für Kunstgeschichte* 10, 1941-42, p. 154, n. 7.

218 G. SCHWARTZ, 1984, pp. 129f.

219 In the text on ARTEMISIA, I summarise conclusions argued in detail in the essay mentioned in n. 192.

220 Repr. in C. TÜMPEL, 1984 (ref. n. 192), Plate XLII, Fig. 97.

221 *Ibid.*, Pl. XLV, Fig. 107.

222 Cf. the paintings by Fetti (Vienna, Kunsthistorisches Museum) and by F. Furini (formerly Augsburg, Royal Gallery), repr. in C. TÜMPEL, 1984, (ref. n. 192), Pl. XLV, Figs. 108, 109.

223 C. NEUMANN, 3rd edit. 1922, I, p. 204.

224 W. WEISBACH, 1926, p. 237.

225 On the literature on the self-portraits cf. n. 82.

226 On the significance of the gold chain cf. the section on 'The Chain' in the brilliant essay by J. HELD, *Rembrandt's 'Aristotle'*, and same, 1969, pp. 3-44, esp. pp. 32-41.

227 B. HAEGER in a letter has rightly stressed the importance of the lyrical 'I' for interpretation.

228 O. BENESCH, 1958, p. 61.

229 Ben. 451.

230 B. HAAK, 1968, p. 163.

231 BALDINUCCI, 1686, pp. 78ff, writes on Rembrandt. Printed in *Urkunden* 360. A German translation of his text on Rembrandt is in L. GOLDSCHEIDER, 2nd edit., 1963, pp. 13ff. My translation is based on that of Goldscheider, *ibid.*, p. 14.

232 On Andries de Graef cf. J.F.L. DE BALBIAN VERSIER, 'Andries de Graef', in same, 1970[2], pp. 59-65.

233 K. VAN BAERLE (alias C. Barlaeus), *Blyde Inkomst der allerdoorluchtighste Koninginne, Maria de Medicis, t'Amsterdam,* Amsterdam (Johan en Cornelis Blaeu) 1639; a detailed analysis of the programme in D.P. SNOEP, *Praal en Propaganda, Triumfalia in de Noordelijke Nederlanden in de 16de en 17de eeuw*. Alphen aan den Rijn 1975, pp. 39-64; A. TÜMPEL, *Oud Holland* 88, 1974, 22-26.

234 In Bibliography cf. articles by I.H. VAN EEGHEN. The article on the couple is mentioned in Catalogue nos. 208 and 243.

235 *Urkunden* 208; *Documents* 1659/21.

236 Trompe-l'œil effects were already regarded in antiquity as proof of especial artistic skill (rivalry between Apelles and Zeuxis). In Dutch painting in the 17th century such effects (partly to revive ancient motifs passed down only in literature) were familiar. In 1626 Frans Hals in his portrait of PETRUS SCRIVERIUS (New York, Metropolitan Museum of Art) had shown the scholar's right hand projecting outside the picture frame and holding a pair of gloves.

237 S. SLIVE (1953), pp. 83ff, and J. EMMENS (1968), pp. 63ff, date the classicist criticism of Rembrandt too late. It does not start only when manifested in literature; it is already apparent earlier in the works of Rembrandt's pupils and circle.

238 Sandrart's biography of Rembrandt is printed in *Urkunden* 329.

239 *Urkunden* 208; *Documents* 1659/21.

240 Ben. A35a, New York, Metropolitan Museum of Art (Robert Lehman Collection).

241 In 1712 the so-called NIGHT WATCH was removed from the meeting-house of the guardsmen to the Amsterdam town hall, and was at that time recklessly cut on all sides to fit it between two doors. The most important literature used here: F. SCHMIDT-DEGENER, *Onze Kunst* 26, 1914, 1-17; 29, 1916, 61-84; 30, 1916, 29-56; 31, 1917, 1-32; D. WIJNBEEK, 1944; V. MARTIN, 1947; same, *Miscellanea Leo van Puyvelde*, 1949, 225-228; same, *Oud Holland* 66, 1951, 1-9; A. VAN SCHENDEL and H.H. MERTENS, *Oud Holland* 62, 1947, 1-52; W. GS. HELLINGA, 1956; K. BAUCH, *Werkmonographien zur bildenden Kunst in Reclams Universal-Bibliothek,* ed. by C.G. HEISE, no. 20, 1957; M. KOK, *Bulletin van het Rijksmuseum* 15, 1967, 116-121; C. TÜMPEL, *Neue Beiträge zur Rembrandt-Forschung,* ed. by O. VON SIMSON and J. KELCH, Berlin 1973, pp. 162-175.
The most comprehensive account, which, with the exception of the female symbolic figures, agrees with my interpretation, is by HAVERKAMP BEGEMANN (1982).

242 My study of the Dutch group portrait, the first volume of which is complete, is to appear after this book. It contains a lengthy account of the Amsterdam guardsmen's guilds.

243 In this way the three cloveniers embody by their activity the quite specific guild together with its use of weapons and their function. To this end Rembrandt has given the shooting guardsman a helmet wreathed in fresh oak leaves. Oak leaves were the symbol of civic virtue and strength, and also appeared in the cloveniers' chain as an emblematic motif in silver. On this too Rembrandt informed himself from a specialist work, a graphics series by Jakob de Gheyn showing the individual actions when shooting in approx. 120 sheets. The rifleman blowing the powder from the pan is taken over almost exactly, as also is the man shooting. However, the one loading his weapon has been turned to a frontal position (cf. the illustrations in C. TÜMPEL, 1973 [ref. n. 241, pp. 125-127).

244 Illustrations of the claw as symbol of the cloveniers in C. TÜMPEL, 1973 (ref. n. 241), Figs. 121-124, 128-131.

245 Cf. the examples in C. TÜMPEL, 1973 (ref. n. 241), Figs. 108 and 117f.

246 Cf. the painting by Bartholomeus van der Helst, THE WARDENS OF THE ST. SEBASTIAN'S OR BOWMEN'S GUILD, 1656, Amsterdam, Rijksmuseum. Repr. in C. TÜMPEL, 1973 (ref. n. 241), Fig. 119.

247 W. GS. HELLINGA, 1956, p. 24; cf. the critical observations of W.M.H. HUMMELEN, 'Rembrandt und Gijsbrecht', *Neue Beiträge zur Rembrandtforschung,* ed. by O. VON SIMSON and J. KELCH, Berlin 1973, pp. 151-161, esp. 160f. On the officers' custom of wearing gloves, cf. the portraits of guardsmen reproduced in this chapter.

248 *Urkunden* 206; *Documents* 1659/19.

249 S. VAN HOOGSTRATEN (1678), quoted *Urkunden* 338.

250 W. SCHÖNE, *Jahrbuch der Akademie der Wissenschaften in Göttingen 1972*, 1973, pp. 33-39. The quotations are condensed from the following pages: 48, 49, 51, 52, 53. The last quotation in the chapter comes from p. 56.

251 Ben. 413.

252 B. 359.

253 H. GERSON, *Ausbreitung und Nachwirkung der holländischen Malerei des 17. Jahrhunderts,* Haarlem 1942. Cf. e.g. the altar painting in the castle chapel at Eutin.

254 Ben. 345.

255 On this subject, which cannot be discussed in more detail here, cf. esp. F. LUGT, *Mit Rembrandt un Amsterdam*, Berlin 1920.

256 Ben. 1047.

257 *Urkunden* 163; *Documents* 1655/8.

258 Cf. the chapter 'Rembrandt and Antiquity'. E. PANOFSKY was the first to draw attention to the 'disguised symbolism' of the early Dutch painters. E. PANOFSKY (*Oud Holland* 50, 1933, 193-217) was also the first to decipher the 'disguised symbolism' of Rembrandt's Danaë painting. Curiously, few later studies have investigated whether Rembrandt incorporates 'coded' symbolic meanings in other biblical histories (Egbert Haverkamp Begemann has rightly pointed out to me that the term 'disguised symbolism' is not quite appropriate, since an open symbolism is usually involved.) Only C. TÜMPEL, 1968, p. 224f, and same, *Neue Beiträge zur Rembrandt-Forschung,* ed. by O. VON SIMSON and J. KELCH, 1973, pp. 162-175, follwed up Panofsky suggestion in his interpretation of Rembrandt's GANYMEDE and the so-called NIGHT WATCH

259 According to the biblical text: 'And entered into the house of Zacharia, and saluted Elizabeth' (Luke 1:40) Mary and Elizabeth greet each other in Elizabeth's house.

260 On the various real and symbolic meanings of animals cf. HERMANN HEINRICH FREY, Therobiblia. Biblisch Thier-, Vogel- und Fischbuch (Leipzig 1595). Photomechanical reprint in: *Naturalis historia bibliae* vol. I, ed. by H. REINITZER, Graz 1978. On the peacock, cf. in this work the 'Biblisch Vogelbuch', ser. 86bff.

261 In Luke 1, 45 Elizabeth tells Mary of what the Lord has said to her. The promise of the angel is in Luke 1:32f, Mary's reply in Luke 1:46ff, the passage quoted, 48f.

262 The same motif is used in the ANNUNCIATION of Rubens.

263 In the 19th century the painting THE HOLY FAMILY (no. 61) bore the title 'LE MÉNAGE DU MENUISIER'.

264 In early Dutch painting we frequently find in depictions of the birth reference to Christ's Passion. So, with portrayals of Mary with the child, Old Testament scenes are often shown, pre-figuring the Passion. Sometimes, however, a crucifix is simply shown in the stable. Rembrandt prefers to allude to the Passion by an apparently 'realistic' action, an attitude recalling that of Jesus on the Cross. Such allusions are typical of Baroque art. Mattia Preti, in the scene of the 'DOUBTING THOMAS' (Vienna, Kunsthistorisches Museum), shows Christ with outstretched arms recalling the attitude of the crucifixion.

265 Joseph is shown still more often as a marginal figure, a figure in the shadows, excluded from the redeeming event. Cf. A. and C. TÜMPEL, 1970, no 64.

266 Ezekiel 34:27.

267 2 Corinthians 3:14ff.

268 For a brilliant interpretation of this picture cf. E. PANOFSKY, *Early Netherlandish Painting,* New York-Hagerstown-San Francisco-London, vol. If, 1971, cf. vol. I, p. 337: 'Two gloomy, hortatory Prophets draw semi-transparent curtains...as in boldly literal illustration of their function 'to reveal', that is,

'to unveil', the New Dispensation: Vetus testamentum velatum, novum testamentum revelatum'.
269 Cf. previous note.
270 Translation from the Latin, quoted from *Adam Eisheimer. Werk, künstlerische Herkunft und Nachfolge*, exh. cat. Städelsches Kunstinstitut, Frankfurt/M, 1966-67, no. 275.
271 Quoted from W. SCHÖNE, *Über das Licht in der Malerei*, Berlin 1954, p. 158.
272 Cf. the excellent analysis by W. SCHÖNE (ref. n. 271), p. 158.
273 Cf. A. and C. TÜMPEL, 1970, no. 4, on the Berlin drawing copied from the painting.
274 J. KELCH in: *Katalog der Gemäldegalerie der Staatlichen Museum Preussischer Kulturbesitz Berlin*, 1975, p. 349, no. 828E.
275 Cf. cat. no. 23.
276 Cf. n. 307.
277 A. JORDAN, 'Bemerkungen zu Rembrandts Radierungen', in: *Repertorium für Kunstwissenschaft*, 16, 1893, pp. 296-302, cf. pp. 299-301. R. SCHREY, *Kunstchronik*, N.S. 18, 1906/7, pp. 854-86; H.A.F. KEUTNER, 1950; C. TÜMPEL, 1968, pp. 137-160, 'Die Andeutung des Erzählungszusammenhanges', esp. § 18, pp. 150-155; same, 1969, pp. 149-152; A. and C. TÜMPEL, 1970, (ref. n. 265), no. 86.
278 The etching fulfils all of Karel van Mander's expectations of a composition. However, if Rembrandt knew his book, which I think probable, he read it with eyes newly schooled by the European tradition and understood it differently from the author himself.
279 On the essay by JORDAN, cf. n. 277; the research history of THE HUNDRED-GUILDER PRINT is in TÜMPEL, 1968, pp. 150ff.
280 H.F. WATERLOOS's poem is quoted in *Urkunden* 266.
282 MATTHÄUS MERIAN, *Icones biblicae praecipuas S. Sctipturae historias eleganter et graphice repraesentantes. Biblische Figuren etc. mit Versen und Reymen in dreyen Sprachen*, Strasbourg, Zetzner, Part I, 1625, Part II, 1627, Part III, 1630, Part IV, 1629. The illustration on the blessing of children is in Part IV, 1629, p. 69.
283 A. and C. TÜMPEL, 1970, (ref. n. 265), no. 86.
284 In earlier depictions of this scene the Pharisees are characterised as adversaries of Jesus and as critical listeners. What is typical of Rembrandt's work is that in all his history scenes with multiple figures he sets them clearly apart from the group of the other listeners. His comments on the drawing CHRIST AND THE WOMAN TAKEN IN ADULTERY (cf. p. 237) are very characteristic. In Rembrandt's late work this crass antithesis between Jesus and the Pharisees is less prominent, firstly because he often isolates the main figures from their scenic context, and secondly because he is now more concerned to show deep emotion than opposition between figures.
285 Matthew 19, 24.
286 R. SCHREY, 1906/7 (ref. n. 277), col. 85.
287 J. BREYN, 1959, p. 22 and Fig. 23: 'De verschijning van dit dier, hoe realistisch en onopvallend ook, schijnt een zinspeling te bevatten op de door Christus gebruikte beeldspraak'.
288 In Rembrandt's so-called NIGHT WATCH the shadow of Captain Frans Banning Cocq's hand, extended in a rhetorical gesture, falls on the uniform of Lieutenant van Ruytenburgh, thus emphasising the embroidered coat-of-arms of Amsterdam.
289 Cf. e.g. the illustrations in *Evangelicae Historiae Imagines. Ex ordine Evangeliorum, atque toto anno in Missae sacrificio recitantur. In Ordinem temporis vitae Christi digestae.* Auctore Hieronymo Natali Societatis Jesu Theologo. Antwerp 1593.
290 On Geertghe Dircx, cf. D. VIS, 1965 (thorough interpretation of the facts, combined with a faulty interpretation of two paintings by Frans Hals); H.F. WIJNMAN in his note 40 (p. 147) in: CHR. WHITE, *Rembrandt*, The Hague 1964; H.F. WIJNMAN, *Jaarboek Amstelodamum* 60, 1968, pp. 103f.
291 Cf. the systematising summary of this interpretation in J. BIALOSTOCKI, *Münchner Jahrbuch der bildende Kunst* 3, S. 8, 1957, pp. 195-210. A critical standpoint was adopted by C. TÜMPEL, *Kunstchronik* 19, 1966, pp. 300-302 and K. BAUCH, 'Ikonographischer Stil', in: same, *Studien zur Kunstgeschichte*, Berlin 1967, pp. 123-151. In the meantime J. BIALOSTOCKI has modified his position in the important essay 'Der Sünder als tragischer Held bei Rembrandt', *Neue Beiträge zur Rembrandt-Forschung*, ed. by O. VON SIMSON and J. KELCH, Berlin 1973, pp. 137f.
292 On the pictorial sources used by Rembrandt cf. A. and C. TÜMPEL, 1970, (ref. n. 265), no. 103.
293 On Rembrandt's pictorial sources, cf. A. and C. TÜMPEL, 1970, (ref. n. 265), no. 97.
294 B. 45, 47, 55, 60, 63, 64.
295 Cf. C. TÜMPEL, 1968, pp. 202ff and A. and C. TÜMPEL, 1970 (ref. n. 265), no. 46.
296 H. AURENHAMMER, *Lexikon der christlichen Ikonographie* vol. 1f, Vienna 1959, p. 356.
297 Ben. 1175.
298 ANDREAS VESALIUS, *De Humani corporis fabrica*, Basle 1555. The woodcut is reproduced in W.S. HECKSCHER, 1958, p. 71, Fig. 12, and in R.H. FUCHS, 1968, Fig. 41.
299 Cf. W. STECHOW, *Art Quarterly* 5, 1942, pp. 135-146.
300 Cf. J. EMMENS, 1968, who puts the date of the start of classicist criticism too late because he refers only to written sources. In artistic discussion it began much earlier, in the 1640s at the latest.
301 Rembrandt's contemporaries and pupils of his pupils already saw the change in style quite clearly. Cf. HOUBRAKEN (1718). His observations on Rembrandt's pupils are reproduced in *Urkunden* 412, 414, 419, 423. The stylistic change is documented admirably in W. SUMOWSKI's monumental works (1ff 1979ff; I-IV 1983ff) on the drawings and paintings of the Rembrandt school.
302 H. JANTZEN, 1923², pp. 60 and 62.
303 H. BRAMSEN, *The Burlington Magazine* 92, 1950, p. 131, n. 6 and Figs. 15f.
304 Cf. C. TÜMPEL, *Koninklijke Nederlandse Akademie van Wetenschappen, Sonderdruck der Bijzondere Bijeenkomst der Afdeling Letterkunde*, 13.3.1972, pp. 16f.
305 Cf. A. BLANKERT, *Kunst als regeringszaak in Amsterdam in de 17de eeuw, Rondom schilderijen van Ferdinand Bol*, Lochem 1975.
306 C. TÜMPEL, *Nederlands Kunsthistorisch Jaarboek* 20, 1969, pp. 171 and 173, Fig. 53.
307 Cf. the chapters on the isolation of figures in C. TÜMPEL, 1968, pp. 85ff; same, *Jahrbuch der Hamburger Kunstsammlungen* 13, 1968, pp. 113ff; same, *Nederlands Kunsthistorisch Jaarboek* 20, 1969, pp. 160ff.
308 One letter is omitted.
309 C. TÜMPEL, 1968, pp. 107ff; same, *Nederlands Kunsthistorisch Jaarboek* 20, 1969, pp. 169ff.
310 J. KELCH, in: *Katalog der Gemäldegalerie der Staatlichen Museen Preussischer Kulturbesitz Berlin*, 1975, no. 811, cf. p. 341.
311 Genesis 32:26.
312 Psalm 57:2.
313 E. KOLLOFF, 1854, pp. 445f.
314 The subject treated in this chapter has been discussed in detail in the third part of my dissertation, 1968, pp. 178-194 and in *Jahrbuch der Hamburger Kunstsammlungen* 13, 1968, pp. 96-102.
315 F. SCHMIDT-DEGENER, *Studien der Bibliothek Warburg* 9, 1928, p. 18.
316 J. BIALOSTOCKI, *Münchner Jahrbuch der bildenden Kunst* 3, S. 8, 1957, p. 201.
317 Same, *Beiträge zur Rembrandt-Forschung*, ed. by O. VON SIMSON and J. KELCH, Berlin 1973, pp. 137ff.
318 Cf. C. TÜMPEL, *Jahrbuch der Hamburger Kunstsammlungen* 13, 1968, pp. 99ff and Figs. 4ff.
319 C. VOSMAER, 1877², p. 63 (quotation translated in the text).
320 Cf. the Rembrandt etchings B. 79, 80 and 81.
321 On the Lazarus theme, cf. H. GURATZSCH, 'Die Auferweckung des Lazarus in der niederländischen Kunst von 1400 bis 1700', in: *Ars Neerlandica* vol. II, ed. by J. DESCHAMPS and P.J.J. VAN THIEL, Kortrijk, Part 1f 1980.
322 Museo Nazionale Messina. Fig.: LIONELLO VENTURI, *Caravaggio*, Munich 1955, no. 47.
323 Cf. etchings B. 72 and 73 and painting no. 42.
324 François Venant, signed and dated 1617. Stockholm, Coll. Gösta Stenemann (1936). Repr. in A. TÜMPEL, *Oud Holland* 88, 1974, p. 70, Fig. 95.
325 Cf. e.g. drawing Ben. 557. Cf. etching B. 36.
326 Cf. n. 85.
327 Cf. I.H. VAN EEGHEN, *Maandblad Amstelodamum* 56, 1969, pp. 162-168.
328 Cf. R.W. SCHELLER, *Oud Holland* 84, 1969, pp. 81-147.
329 R.W. SCHELLER, *Oud Holland* 84, p. 120.
330 B. 29.
331 I.H. VAN EEGHEN, *Maandblad Amstelodamum* 56, 1969, pp. 180-183.
332 W.R. VALENTINER, *Kunstchronik und Kunstmarkt* N.S. 32, 1920/21, pp. 219-222.
333 Mark 14:67 and 68.
334 Luke 22:61.
335 On the history of the work's interpretation, cf. C. TÜMPEL, 1967, no. 5f, pp. 36-53.
336 Albert Blankert has kindly pointed out to me that Rembrandt's pupil Ferdinand Bol painted a married couple in the role of Isaac and Rebecca. This role, portrait of Bol's second wife, Anna van Erckel, with her first husband, Erasmus Scharlaken, is mentioned in the inventory of Anna's legacy of 1681. Cf. A. BLANKERT, *Ferdinand Bol. 1616-1680.* Diss. Utrecht 1976, cat. no. A167. My interpretation has been critically discussed by R.H. FUCHS, *Tijdschrift voor geschiedenis* 82, 1969, pp. 482-493 and by A. SMITMANS, 'Probleme des Bildsinns bei Rembrandt', in: H. VEKEMAN and J. MÜLLER-HOFSTEDE (eds.), *Wort und Bild in der niederländischen Kunst und Literatur des 16. und 17. Jahrhunderts*, Erftstadt 1984, pp. 205-208, esp. pp. 206f.
337 In discussion Rembrandt scholars are divided as to whether the secondary figures are by Rembrandt himself. The Rembrandt Research Project considers them the work of a pupil who completed the unfinished painting on Rembrandt's death.
338 On the subject of the isolation of figures, cf. n. 307.
339 Ben. 1057/Fig. 1275.
340 Cf. M. BOCKMÜHL, 1981.
341 *Urkunden* 291; translation S. HEILAND and H. LÜDECKE, 1960, pp. 21f, esp. p. 22.
342 Cf. V. RUFFO, *Bolletino d'Arte* 10, 1916, pp. 21-192; G.J. HOOGEWERFF, *Oud Holland* 35, 1917, pp. 129-148; C. RICCI, 1918; H. VON EINEM, *Wallraf-Richartz-Jahrbuch* 14, 1952, pp. 182-205; J. HELD, 1969; B. HAAK, 1968, pp. 240-243, 265.
343 Translation by B. HAAK, 1968, p. 240.
344 Translation by B. HAAK, 1968, pp. 241f.
345 The Stockholm sketch Ben. 1066 (repr. p. 363) suggests that in an earlier version only one scribe was shown.
346 Cf. H. D[e] L[a] F[ONTAINE] V[ERWEY], *Maandblad Amstelodamum* 56, 1969, pp. 177-179.
347 Cf. E. HAVERKAMP BEGEMANN, *Art Bulletin* 53, 1971, p. 91 and I.H. VAN EEGHEN, *Jaarboek Amstelodamum* 61, 1969, pp. 67-70.
348 On this chapter cf. esp. HEILAND-LÜDECKE, 1960 and R.W. SCHELLER, *Nederlands Kunsthistorisch Jaarboek* 12, 1961, pp. 81ff.
349 V. RUFFO, *Bolletino d'Arte* 10, 1916, pp. 100ff, cf. esp. p. 186.
350 E. KOLLOFF, 1854, reprinted 1971.

BIBLIOGRAPHY

AGAFONOVA, K.A. Two Drawings by Rembrandt. *The Burlington Magazine* 107 (1966), 402-405.

AHBEL, F. *"Haman in Ungnade" oder "Urias und David". Zur Deutung des Gemäldes von Rembrandt in der Eremitage.* Universität Hamburg, seminar treatise under Prof. Schöne, 1964/65.

ALBACH, B. Rembrandt en het toneel. *Kresge Art Center Bulletin* 31/2 (1979), 2-32.

ALLEN, J.L. The Museum's Rembrandt. *Metropolitan Museum of Art Bulletin* N.S.5 (1945), 73-77.

ALTEN, W. von — Rembrandt. Zeichnungen. *Die Kunstbücher des Volkes* 45, Berlin 1947.

ALPATOW, M. Le Paysage avec le Pont en Pierre de Rembrandt à Amsterdam. In: *Ars Auro Prior. Studia Ioanni Bialostocki Sexagenario Dicata.* Warsaw 1981, 435-439.

ANGEL, Ph. *Lof der schilderkonst.* Leyden 1642.

ANONYMOUS
Het Sint Lucas Gilde te Amsterdam. *Obreen's Archief* 3 (1789), 89-196.
Early works by Rembrandt. *Art in America* 6 (1917/18), 118-123.
Rembrandt te Rotterdam. *Rotterdamsch Jaarboekje* 8 (1920), 126.
Rembrandt's Joodsche Buren. *Maandblad Amstelodamum* 17 (1930), 113-114.
Hoe lang heeft Rembrandt in de Breestraat gewoond? *Maandblad Amstelodamum* 17 (1930), 122.
Rembrandt en de Bruyninghs. *Maandblad Amstelodamum* 25 (1938), 76-77.
Marten Looten van Rembrandt. *Maandblad Amstelodamum* 25 (1938), 159-160.
In 't Huis van Rembrandt. Leiden 1938.

AUBURN, W. Rembrandt; Christ Driving the Money Changers from the Temple. *Auckland City Art Gallery Quarterly* 62/63 (1976), 2-3.

BACKER, J.F.
Een briefje van nichtje Anna de Witt. *Amsterdamsch Jaarboekje voor 1901* (1901), 16-24.
Rembrandt's Boedelafstand. *Elsevier's Geillustreerd Maandschrift* 57 (1919), 1-17; 97-112; 173-182.
Les tracas judiciaires de Rembrandt. *Gazette des Beaux-Arts* 66/1 (1924), 237-248; 66/2, 219-240; 66/3, 361-368; 67/1 (1925), 50-60.

BADER, A. *The Bible through Dutch Eyes.* Exhibition catalogue Milwaukee 1976.

BAILEY, A. *Rembrandt's House: Exploring the World of the Great Master.* Boston/London 1978.

BALDINUCCI, F. *Cominciamento e progresso dell'arte dell'intagliare in rame.* Florence 1686.

BANGS, J.D. Rembrandt's Le Petit Orfèvre, Possible Additional Sources. *Source* 1/4 (1982), 16-19.

BARTSCH, A. von — *Catalogue raisonné de toutes les estampes qui forment l'œuvre de Rembrandt, et ceux de ses principaux imitateurs.* Vienna 1797.
Le peintre graveur, Vienna 1803-21.

BARUCH, J.Z. Meester Rembrandt en zijn Buren. *Ons Amsterdam* 21 (1969), 27-72.

BAUCH, K.
Zur Kenntnis von Rembrandts Frühwerken. *Jahrbuch der Preußischen Kunstsammlungen* 45 (1924), 277-280.
Die Kunst des jungen Rembrandt. Heidelberg 1933.
Beiträge zum Werk der Vorläufer Rembrandts I-V. *Oud Holland* 52 (1935), 145-158; 193-204; 53 (1936), 79-88; 54 (1937), 241-252; 55 (1938), 254-265.
Rembrandt und Lievens. *Wallraf-Richartz-Jahrbuch* N.S. 11 (1939), 239-268.
Frühwerke Pieter Lastmans. *Münchner Jahrbuch der bildenden Kunst* 3rd S. 2 (1951), 225-237.
Entwurf und Komposition bei Pieter Lastman. *Münchner Jahrbuch der bildenden Kunst* N.S. (1955), 213-221.
Die Nachtwache. Stuttgart 1957.
A Portrait of Rembrandt's Last Period. *The Burlington Magazine* 101 (1959), 105-106.
Der frühe Rembrandt und seine Zeit. Studien zur geschichtlichen Bedeutung seines Frühstils. Berlin 1960.
Ein Selbstbildnis des frühen Rembrandt. *Wallraf-Richartz-Jahrbuch* 24 (1962), 321-332.
Rembrandts Christus am Kreuz. *Pantheon* 20 (1962), 137-144.
Rembrandt Gemälde. Berlin 1966.
Zum Werk des Jan Lievens. *Pantheon* 25 (1967), 160-170; 259-269.
Ikonographischer Stil. In: id., *Studien zur Kunstgeschichte.* Berlin 1967, 123-151.
Zu einem verschollenen Selbstbildnis Rembrandts. *Pantheon* 27 (1969), 224-26.

BAUDISSIN, K. von —
Rembrandt und Cats. *Repertorium für Kunstwissenschaft* 45 (1925), 148-179.
Anmerkungen zur Rembrandt-Erklärung. *Repertorium für Kunstwissenschaft* 46 (1925), 190-204.

BAUER, H. Rembrandt vor der Staffelei. In: *Festschrift Wolfgang Braunfels.* Tübingen 1977, 1-11.

BEAUFORT, H. Laman Trip de — *Rembrandt.* Haarlem 1957.

BECK, M.D. *Der junge Rembrandt und Italien. Zur Herleitung und Verarbeitung der italienischen Motive im Frühwerk Rembrandts.* Diss. Bonn 1949.

BEHLING, L. Rembrandts sog. "Dr. Faustus", Johann Baptista Portas Magia naturalis und Jacob Böhme. *Oud Holland* 79 (1964), 49-77.

BELONJE, J. Nog eens Jan Heykens. *Maandblad Amstelodamum* 57 (1970), 90-91.

BELONJE, J. & I.H. van EEGHEN
De familie van de drukker Jan Willemsz. (i.e. Willem Jansz.) Blaeu in Alkmaar en Amsterdam. *Jaarboek Amstelodamum* 64 (1972), 75-93.

BEMMELEN, J.F. van — Identificatie van familieportretten. *Jaarboek Amstelodamum* 26 (1929), 59-77.

BENESCH, O.
Rembrandts Falkenjäger. *Wiener Jahrbuch für Kunstgeschichte* 3 (1925), 115-118.
Rembrandt-Relicta aus der Münchner Graphischen Sammlung. *Mitteilungen der Gesellschaft für vervielfältigende Kunst. Beilage der "Graphischen Künste"* 2-2 (1925), 25-39.
Unbekanntes und Verkanntes von Rembrandt. *Wallraf-Richartz-Jahrbuch* N.S. 2/3 (1933/34), 295-309.
Rembrandt. Werk und Forschung, Vienna 1935.
Rembrandt Harmensz. van Rijn. In: *Allgemeines Lexikon der bildenden Künste von der Antike bis zur Gegenwart* 29, hrsg. von Hans VOLLMER. Leipzig 1935, 259-271.
Rembrandt. Zeichnungen. London 1947.
An Unknown Rembrandt Painting of the Leiden Period. *The Burlington Magazine* 96 (1954), 134-135.
The Drawings of Rembrandt. A Critical and Chronological Catalogue I-VI. London 1954-57.
Worldly and Religious Portraits in Rembrandt's Late Art. *Art Quarterly* 19 (1956), 335-354.
Rembrandt. Biographisch-kritische Studie. *Der Geschmack unserer Zeit.* Geneva 1957.
Rembrandt and Ancient History. *Art Quarterly* 22 (1959), 309-332.
Rembrandt als Zeichner. Cologne 1963.
Über den Werdegang einer Komposition Rembrandts. *Bulletin du Musée Hongrois des Beaux-Arts* 22 (1963), 71-87
Neuentdeckte Zeichnungen von Rembrandt. *Jahrbuch der Berliner Museen. Jahrbuch der Preußischen Kunstsammlungen* N.S. 6 (1964), 105-150.

BERGSTRÖM, I. Rembrandt's Double-Portrait of Himself and Saskia at the Dresden Gallery. A Tradition Transformed. *Nederlands Kunsthistorisch Jaarboek* 17 (1966), 143-169.
Œuvres de Jeunesse de Rembrandt. *L'Œil* 173 (Mai 1969), 2-8.

BERNHARD, M. *Rembrandt.* Vol. 1: *Druckgraphik.* Vol. 2: *Handzeichnungen.* Munich 1976.

BIALOSTOCKI, J.
Rembrandt et ses élèves: trois problèmes. *Biuletyne historii sztuki* 18 (1956), 349-369.
Ikonographische Forschungen zu Rembrandts Werk. *Münchner Jahrbuch der bildenden Kunst* 3d S. 8 (1957), 195-210.
Rembrandts "Terminus". *Westdeutsches Jahrbuch für Kunstgeschichte. Wallraf-Richartz-Jahrbuch* 28 (1966), 49-60.
Rembrandt's "Eques Polonus", *Oud Holland* 84 (1969), 163-176.
Rembrandt and Posterity, *Nederlands Kunsthistorisch Jaarboek* 23 (1972), 131-157.

BICKER, C.A. Rembrandt als Molenaarszoon. *Jaarboekje voor Geschiedenis en Oudheidkunde van Leiden en Omstreken* 48 (1956), 117-127; 49 (1957), 136.

BIE, C. de — *Het Gulden Cabinet van de edele vry Schilder-const.* Antwerp 1661.

BILLE, C.
Rembrandt's Claudius Civilis at Amsterdam in 1734. *Konsthistorisk Tidskrift* 25 (1956), 25-30.
Rembrandts Eendracht van het land en Starters "Wt-treckinge van de Borgery van Amsterdam". *Oud Holland* 71 (1956), 25-35.
Rembrandt's Claudius Civilis and its Owners in the 18th Century. *Oud Holland* 71 (1956), 54-58.
Oopjen Coppit en haar ring. *Maandblad Amstelodamum* 45 (1958), 186-187.
Rembrandt and Burgomaster Jan Six. *Apollo* 85 (1967), 160-165.

BINAI, P.F. Rembrandt's Etchings. *Carnegie Magazine* 50/9 (1976), 412-419.

BIÖRKLUND, G. *Rembrandt's Etchings. True and False.* London/Stockholm/New York 1955.

BLANC, C. le —
Manuel de l'Amateur d'Estampes I-IV. Paris Vol. 1 1854; Vol. 2 1856; Vol. 3 s.a.; Vol. 4 [1889].
L'Œuvre complet de Rembrandt... I-II. Paris 1859-61.

BLANKERT, A.
Rembrandt, Zeuxis and Ideal Beauty. In: *Album Amicorum J.G. van Gelder.* Ed. J. BRUYN et al. Den Haag 1973, 32-39.
Ferdinand Bol 1616-1680, een leerling van Rembrandt. Diss. Utrecht 1976, Doornspijk 1982.

BLOCH, E.M. Rembrandt and the Lopez Collection. *Gazette des Beaux-Arts* 88/1 (1946), 175-186.

BLOCH, V.
Zum frühen Rembrandt. *Oud Holland* 50 (1933), 97-102.
Musik im Hause Rembrandt. *Oud Holland* 54 (1937), 49-53.
The Problem of the Early Rembrandt. *The Burlington Magazine* 97 (1955), 259-260.

BLOTKAMP, C. A Tercentenary for Rembrandt, 1906. *Delta* 12/2 (1969), 96-101.

BOBER, H. *Jan van Vliet's Book of Crafts and Trades: with a reappraisal of his etchings.* Albany/New York 1981.

BOCK, E. & J. ROSENBERG Die niederländischen Meister. *Staatliche Museen zu Berlin. Die Zeichnungen im Kupferstichkabinett.* Ed. by M. FRIEDLÄNDER. If Berlin 1930.

BOCKEMÜHL, M. *Rembrandt: zum Wandel des Bildes und seiner Anschauung im Spätwerk.* Mittenwald 1981.

BODE, W. von —
Rembrandt's früheste Thätigkeit. Der Künstler in seiner Vaterstadt Leiden. *Die Graphischen Künste* 3 (1881), 49-72.
Studien zur Geschichte der holländischen Malerei. Braunschweig 1883.
Das Bildnis von Rembrandt's Bruder "Adriaen Harmensz. van Rijn" im Mauritshuis. *Oud Holland* 9 (1891), 1-6.
The Complete Works of Rembrandt I-VIII. Paris 1897-1906.
Rembrandt und seine Zeitgenossen. Charakterbilder der grossen Meister der holländischen und flämischen Malerschule im siebzehnten Jahrhundert. Leipzig 1906.
The Earliest Dated Paintings by Rembrandt, of the Year 1626. *Art in America* 1 (1913), 3-7.
Additional Notes on Early Paintings by Rembrandt. *Art in America* 1 (1913), 109-112.
Ein Studienkopf aus Rembrandts Spätzeit im Berliner Schloß und seine Beziehung zu den slawischen Pilger- und Mönchsbildnissen des Meisters aus dem Jahre 1661. *Jahrbuch der königlich Preußischen Kunstsammlungen* 38 (1917), 107-111.
Rembrandts Landschaft mit der Brücke. *Jahrbuch der Preußichen Kunstsammlungen* 46 (1929), 159-163.

BODE, W. & W. VALENTINER *Rembrandt in Bild und Wort.* Berlin [1907].

BOECK, W.
Rechts und links in Rembrandts Druckgraphik. *Westdeutsches Jahrbuch für Kunstgeschichte. Wallraf-Richartz-Jahrbuch* N.S. 15 (1953), 179-219.
Rembrandt. *Urban-Bücher* 66. Ed. by Fritz ERNST. Stuttgart 1962.

BOER, M.G. de — Vergeten leden van een bekend geslacht. *Jaarboek Amstelodamum* 42 (1948), 10-34.

BOJANOWSKI, M. Das Anagram in Rembrandts "Faust". *Deutsche Vierteljahrsschrift für Literaturwissenschaft und Geistesgeschichte* 16 (1938), 527ff.

BOL, L.J. Rembrandts Musicerend Gezelschap: een vanitas-allegorie. *Bulletin van het Rijksmuseum* 25/3 (1977), 95-96.

BOLTEN, J. *Rembrandt.* Wiesbaden 1977.

BOLTEN, J. & H. BOLTEN-REMPT *The Hidden Rembrandt.* Milan/Chicago 1977.

BOON, K.G.
"Rembrandt.f." Das graphische Werk. Munich-Vienna 1963.
De Toren "Swijgh Utrecht" door Rembrandt getekend. *Bulletin van het Rijksmuseum* 17 (1969), 119-125.
Rembrandt's laatste geëtste zelfportret. *De Kroniek van het Rembrandthuis* 23 (1969), 4-9.
Critici over de Rembrandt-Tentoonstelling. *De Kroniek van het Rembrandthuis* 24 (1969), 21-22.
Rembrandt de etser: het volledige werk. Amsterdam 1977.

BORENIUS, T. The new Rembrandt. *The Burlington Magazine* 57 (1930), 53-59.

BRAMSEN, H. The Classicism of Rembrandt's "Bathseba". *The Burlington Magazine* 92 (1950), 128-131.

BRAUNFELS, W. *Rembrandt. Leben und Werk.* Berlin/Darmstadt 1955.

BREDIUS, A.
Gemäldepreise in Holland um 1650. *Zeitschrift für bildende Kunst* 18 (1883), 228-230.
Catalogue des peintures du Musée de l'Etat à Amsterdam. Amsterdam 1888.
Kunstkritiek der XVIIe eeuw. *Oud Holland* 7 (1889), 41-44.
Nieuwe Rembrandtiana. *Oud Holland* 7 (1889), 1-5.
Rembrandt als verzamelaar. *Jaarboekje voor Geschiedenis en Oudheidkunde van Leiden* (1906), 85-97.
Eenige taxaties van schilderijen in de 17e en het begin der 18e eeuw. *Oud Holland* 24 (1906), 236-241.
Een schilderij van Rembrandt? op de kermis te Leiden 1641. *Oud Holland* 26 (1908), 68.
Rembrandtiana. *Oud Holland* 26 (1908), 219-224.
Rembrandt als plaatsnijder. *Oud Holland* 27 (1909), 111-114.
Uit Rembrandt's laatste levensjaar. *Oud Holland* 27 (1909), 238-240.
Bol's Kunstschatten. *Oud Holland* 28 (1910), 234-235.
Rembrandtiana. *Oud Holland* 28 (1910), 1-18.
Rembrandtiana. I. Rembrandt's zoogenaamde portret van Turene bij Lord Cowper te Panshanger; II. De nalatenschap van Harmen Becker. *Oud Holland* 28 (1910), 193-204.
Verdere bijdragen tot de geschiedenis van Rembrandt's broeders en zusters. *Oud Holland* 29 (1911), 49-56.
De nalatenschap van Rembrandt's schoondochter. *Oud Holland* 29 (1911), 112-118.
Rembrandtiana. *Oud Holland* 31 (1913), 71-73.
Bij Rembrandt's Portret van Jeremias de Decker. *Oud Holland* 31 (1913), 272.
Rembrandtiana. *Oud Holland* 32 (1914), 132-136; 260-261.
Iets over het Rembrandt-Huis. *Oud Holland* 32 (1914), 262.
Künstler-Inventare: Urkunden zur Geschichte der holländischen Kunst des XVI, XVII. und XVIII. Jahrhunderts I-VII. The Hague 1915-1922.
Rembrandtiana. *Oud Holland* 33 (1915), 126-128.
Wiedergefundene "Rembrandts" (Review: W.R. Valentiner. Rembrandt. Wiedergefundene Gemälde "1910-1920". Klassiker der Kunst in Gesamtausgaben 27. Stuttgart/Berlin 1921). *Zeitschrift für bildende Kunst* N.S. 32 (1921), 146-152.
Rembrandtiana. *Oud Holland* 42 (1925), 263-270.
Bol oder Backer. *Festschrift Max Friedländer zum 60. Geburtstag.* Leipzig 1927.
Over een Rembrandt. *Oud Holland* 48 (1931), 97-98.
Rembrandt Schilderijen. Utrecht 1935.
Rembrandt. Gemälde. Vienna 1935.
Ein wiedergefundener Rembrandt. *Pantheon* 18 (1936), 277.
The Paintings of Rembrandt. Vienna 1936^2.
The Complete Edition of the Paintings of Rembrandt, 3th edition revised by H. GERSON. London 1969.

BREDT, E.W. Rembrandt-Bibel. *Bilderschatz der Weltliteratur* IV. Munich 1921.

BRIÈRE-MISME, C.
Un portrait retrouvé de Constantin Huygens. *Oud Holland* 53 (1936), 193-201.
La Danaë de Rembrandt et son véritable sujet. *Gazette des Beaux-Arts* 6/39 (1952), 305-318.

BRION, M. *Rembrandt.* Paris 1940.

BROCHHAGEN, E.
Holländischen Malerei des 17. Jahrhunderts. Munich 1967.
Beobachtungen an den Passionsbildern Rembrandts in München. In: *Minuscula discipulorum. Kunsthistorische Studien für Hans Kauffmann zum 70. Geburtstag.* Berlin 1968.

BROM, G.
De traditie in Rembrandt's Dood van Maria. *Oud Holland* 43 (1926), 112-116.
Hollandse schilders en schrijvers in de vorige eeuw. Rotterdam 1927.
Rembrandt in de literatuur. Groningen 1936.

BROOS, B. P.J.
Rembrandt borrows from Altdorfer. *Simiolus* 4 (1970/71), 100-108.
The "O" of Rembrandt. *Simiolus* 4 (1971), 150-184.
Rembrandt en zijn eeuwige leermeester Lastman. *De Kroniek van het Rembrandthuis* 26/2 (1972), 76-96.
Rembrandt's portrait of a Pole and his horse. *Simiolus* 7 (1974), 192-218.
Rembrandt and Lastman's "Coriolanus", the History Piece in the 17th Century, Theory and Practice. *Simiolus* 8/4 (1975), 199-228.
Rembrandt Studies. Utrecht 1977.
Index to the Formal Sources of Rembrandt's Art. Maarssen 1977.
Review: W. STRAUSS et al. The Rembrandt Documents. New York 1979. *Simiolus* 12/4 (1981/82), 245-262.
Rembrandt en tekenaars uit zijn omgeving. *Oude tekeningen in het bezit van de Gemeentemusea van Amsterdam, waaronder de collectie Fodor* 3. Amsterdam 1981.

BROWN, C.
Rembrandt's Portrait of a Boy. *Connoisseur* 193/777 (1976), 217-219.
Titian "Portrait of a Man"; Rembrandt "Selfportrait at the Age of 34". Exhibition catalogue London National Gallery 1980.

BROWN, C. & J. PLESTERS Rembrandt's Portrait of Hendrickje Stoffels. *Apollo* 106/188 (1977), 286-291.

BROWNE, A. *Ars Pictoria: or an Academy Treating of Drawing, Painting, Limning, Etching, To Which Are Added XXXI. Copper Plates, Expressing the Choicest, Nearest, and Most Exact Grounds and Rules of Symmetry. Collected out of the Most Eminent Italian, German and Netherland Authors.* London 1675.

BRUIJN, I. de —
Rembrandt's portret van Abram Francen. *Oud Holland* 43 (1926), 39-44.
De staten van Rembrandt's ets van Jan Six. *Oud Holland* 56 (1939), 193-198.
Catalogus van de verzameling etsen van Rembrandt in het bezit van I. de Bruijn en J.G. de Bruijn-van der Leeuw. The Hague 1932.

BRUYN, J.
A Corpus of Rembrandt Paintings; cf.: RRP.
Het Claudius Civilis-nummer van het Konsthistorisk Tidskrift. *Oud Holland* 71 (1956), 49-54.
Rembrandt's keuze van Bijbelse onderwerpen. Utrecht 1959.
300 jaren Rembrandt, Rede uitgesproken op de Universiteitsdag van de Universiteit van Amsterdam. *De Kroniek van het Rembrandthuis* 23 (1969), 113-128.
Enige indrukken van het Rembrandt-symposium in Chicago. *De Kroniek van het Rembrandthuis* 24 (1970), 7-11.

BRUYN KOPS, C.J. de — De inlijsting van Rembrandt's "Nachtwacht" in het verleden en de nieuwe lijst. *Bulletin van het Rijksmuseum* 24/1-2 (1976), 99-119.

BURCKHARDT, J. *Rembrandt und Van Dyck. Zwei Vorträge.* Bern s.a.

BURNET, J. *Rembrandt and His Work, Comprising a Short Account of his Life with a Critical Examination into his Principles and Practise of Design, Light, Shade, and Colour.* London 1894.

BURROUGHS, A. New Illustrations of Rembrandt's Style. *The Burlington Magazine* 59 (1931), 3-10.

BUSCH, W. Zu Rembrandts Anslo-Radierung. *Oud Holland* 86 (1971), 196-199.

BUSKEN HUET, C. *Het leven van Rembrandt. Studien over de Noordnederlandse beschaving in de zeventiende eeuw.* The Hague 1974[2].

CAILLEUX, J. Esquisse d'une Etude sur le goût pour Rembrandt en France au XVIIIe siècle. *Nederlands Kunsthistorisch Jaarboek* 23 (1972), 159-166.

CAMON AZNAR, J. La Pintura de Rembrandt y su justificación religiosa. *Goya* 151 (1979), 2-6.

CAMPBELL, C.
Studies in the Formal Sources of Rembrandt's Figure Composition. Diss. London 1971.
De Reis van de Verloren Zoon. *De Kroniek van het Rembrandthuis* 26/3 (1972), 51-66.
Raphael door Rembrandts pen herschapen. *De Kroniek van het Rembrandthuis* 27 (1975), 20-37.
Portretten en Kaerteblaren. *De Kroniek van het Rembrandthuis* 30/2 (1978), 3-35.

CARASSO-KOK, M. *Amsterdam Historisch.* Bussum 1975.

CARPENTIER ALTING, M.P. & T.W. WATERBOLK Nieuw licht op de anatomie van de "Anatomische les van Dr. Nicolaas Tulp". *Oud Holland* 92 (1978), 43-48.

CARROLL, M. Deutsch —
Rembrandt and Tacitus. Adress at the College Art Association Meeting. New York 1978.
Rembrandt as Meditational Printmaker, *Art Bulletin* 63 (1981), 585-610.

CATALOGUES:
Amsterdam, Museum van der Hoop
Catalogus der schilderijen van het Museum van der Hoop te Amsterdam. 1855.
Amsterdam
Rembrandt. Au Musée de la Ville à Amsterdam. 1898.
Amsterdam, Rembrandthuis
Rembrandt, Etchings & Drawings in the Rembrandt House. Zie: Filedt Kok, J.P.
Work in Progress: Rembrandt Etchings in Different States. 11.4-31.5 1981.
Landscapes by Rembrandt and his Precursors, 1983.
Bij Rembrandt in de leer/Rembrandt as a Teacher, 1984-1985.
Amsterdam, Rijksmuseum
Catalogus van de tentoongestelde schilderijen, pastels en aquarellen. Rijksmuseum Amsterdam 1951.
Rembrandt. Schilderijen. Rijksmuseum Amsterdam — Museum Boymans Rotterdam. 1956.
Bijbelse Inspiratie. Tekeningen en prenten van Lucas van Leyden en Rembrandt. Rijksmuseum Amsterdam 1964/65.
Rembrandt 1669/1969, Paintings and Drawings from European and Other Collections. Rijksmuseum Amsterdam 1969.
Landscapes by Rembrandt and his precursors, 16.4.-26.6.1983.
All the paintings of the Rijksmuseum in Amsterdam. A completely illustrated catalogue. Amsterdam/Maarssen 1976.
Auckland, City Art Gallery
Still-life in the Age of Rembrandt. 1982.
Berlin (East), Bode Museum
Rembrandt-Graphik und Malerei der Rembrandt-Schule. 1969.
Berlin
Stiftung Preußischer Kulturbesitz, Staatliche Museen, Gemäldegalerie. Verzeichnis der ausgestellten Gemälde des 13.-18.Jahrhunderts im Museum Dahlem. Berlin 1964.
Kupferstichkabinett der Staatlichen Museen Berlin-Dahlem: Rembrandt zeichnet. 1968.
Katalog der Gemäldegalerie der Staatlichen Museen Preußischer Kulturbesitz. Berlin 1975. (Dutch painting by J. Kelch).
Bielefeld, Kunsthalle, Richard Kaselowsky Haus
Rembrandt van Rijn Radierungen, 17.4.-15.5.1969.
Boston, Museum of Fine Arts
Rembrandt: Experimental Etcher. Boston, Museum of Fine Arts and New York, The Pierpont Morgan Library. 1969.
Braunschweig, Herzog Anton Ulrich-Museum
Jan Lievens, ein Maler im Schatten Rembrandts, 6.9-11.11.1979.
Chicago, The Art Institute.
Rembrandt after Three Hundred Years, An Exhibition of Rembrandt and His Followers. Chicago, The Art Institute; Minneapolis, The Minneapolis Institute of Arts; Detroit, The Detroit Institute of Arts. 1969-1970.
Cincinnati, Institute of Fine Arts, Taft Museum
Dutch Couples; Rembrandt and his Contemporaries, 15.12.1973-3.3.1974.
Darmstadt, Landesmuseum
Rembrandt und seine Zeitgenossen, 11.10.--23.11.1969.
Dresden
Staatliche Kunstsammlungen Dresden. Gemäldegalerie Dresden. Alte Meister. Dresden 1961.
Kupferstichkabinett: Rembrandt, die Radierungen im Dresdner Kupferstich-Kabinett. 1969.
Edinburgh, National Gallery of Scotland.
Catalogue of Paintings and Sculpture. 1957.
Haarlem
Rembrandt. Zeichnungen und Radierungen. Haarlem. Vleeshal 1951.
The Hague
Musée Royal de La Haye (Mauritshuis): Catalogue raisonné des tableaux et des sculptures. 1958.
Museum Bredius: Catalogus van de schilderijen en tekeningen. 1978.
Karlsruhe
Altdeutsche Meister aus der Staatlichen Kunsthalle Karlsruhe. 1958.
Leyden, De Lakenhal
Stedelijk Museum "De Lakenhal". Catalogus van de schilderijen en tekeningen. Leyden 1983.
Leningrad, Hermitage
Musée de l'Ermitage. Département de l'art occidental. Catalogue des peintures I. Leningrad, Moscow 1958.
The Hermitage: Rembrandt, ego Predsjestvenniki i Posledovateli. 1969.
Londen, National Gallery
The Dutch School. Cf.: MACLAREN.
Madrid, Museo del Prado
Catalogo de las Pinturas. 1963.
Malibu, J. Paul Getty Museum
Masterpieces of Painting in the J. Paul Getty Museum. 1980.
Montreal, Museum of Fine Arts
Rembrandt and His Pupils. Montreal, Museum of Fine Arts and Toronto, Art Gallery of Ontario. Jan.-Apr. 1969.
Moscow, Pushkin Museum
Staatliches A.S. Puschkin-Museum der bildenden Künste. Moscow I. 1961.
Exhibition of the Works of Rembrandt, Paintings, Drawings, Etchings. 1969.
Munich
Katalog der Älteren Pinakothek zu München. 1925.
Nantes, Musée Dobrée
Eaux-fortes de Rembrandt, 1606-1669, de la collection Thomas Dobrée. 1976.
New York, Metropolitan Museum of Art
Rembrandt and the Bible. 5.4.-10.6.1979.
Nice, Musée national Message Biblique Marc Chagall
Rembrandt et la Bible. 12.7.-29.9.1975.
Oldenburg, Großherzogliche Sammlung
Verzeichnis der Gemälde, Gypsabgüsse, geschnitten Steine etc. in der Großherzoglichen Sammlung zu Oldenburg. 1875.
Verzeichnis der Gemälde Gypse und Bronzen in der Großherzoglichen Sammlung zu Oldenburg. 1890.
Paris, Musée du Louvre
Rembrandt et son temps; Dessins, des collections publiques et privées conservées en France. 3.2.-27.4.1970.
Paris, Musée du Petit Palais
Rembrandt: Eaux-Fortes. 6.2.-20.4.1986.
Rotterdam, Museum Boymans-van Beuningen
Catalogus schilderijen tot 1800. 1962.
Rembrandt, De Eendracht van het land. 1981.
Salzburg
Residenzgalerie Salzburg mit Sammlung Czernin und Sammlung Schönborn-Buchheim. 1962.
Utrecht, Centraal Museum
Catalogus der schilderijen. 1952.
Washington, National Gallery
Exhibition of Paintings and Drawings by and Attributed to Rembrandt, and Etchings, from the Museum's Collection. s.a.
Washington, National Gallery of Art
Gods, Saints & Heroes; Dutch Paintings in the Age of Rembrandt. Washington, National Gallery of Art; The Detroit Institute of Arts; Amsterdam, Rijksmuseum. 1980-81.
Vienna, Kunsthistorisches Museum
Gemäldegalerie. II: Flamen, Holländer, Deutsche, Franzosen. 1958.

CHARRINGTON, J. *A Catalogue of the Mezzotints after, or said to be after, Rembrandt.* Cambridge 1923.

CHROSCICKI, J.A. Rembrandt's Polish Rider. Allegory or portrait. In: *Ars Auro Prior. Studia Ioanni Bialostocki Sexagenario Dicata.* Warsaw 1981, 441-448.

CIECHANOWIECKI, A. Notes on the Ownership of Rembrandt's "Polish Rider". *Art Bulletin* 42 (1960), 294-296.

CLARK, K.
Rembrandt and the Italian Renaissance. London 1966.
Rembrandt's Good Samaritian in the Wallace Collection *The Burlington Magazine* 118/885 (1976), 806-809.
An Introduction to Rembrandt. London 1978.

CLAUSSIN, C. de — *Catalogue raisonné de toutes les estampes qui forment l'œuvre de Rembrandt, et des principales pièces de ses élèves.* Paris 1824. Supplement 1828.

COLLINS BAKER, C.H.
Rembrandt's "Painter in his Studio". *The Burlington Magazine* 48 (1926), 42.
Rembrandt's Thirty Pieces of Silver. *The Burlington Magazine* 75 (1939), 179-180; 235.

COMMELIN, C.
Beschryvinge van Amsterdam. Amsterdam 1691.
Vervolg van de Beschrijvinge der Stadt Amsterdam. Amsterdam 1693.

CONWAY, M. A Rembrandt Landscape in the Hermitage. *The Burlington Magazine* 46 (1925), 245; 322.

COPPIER, A.C.
Les eaux-fortes de Rembrandt. Paris 1917; 1922[2]; 1929[3].
Rembrandt Forschungen. *Kunst und Künstler* 15 (1917), 246-247.
De Koperen etsplaten van Rembrandt te Parijs. *Oude Kunst* 6 (1921), 239-300.

COPPLESTONE, T. *Rembrandt.* London 1974.

CORNELISSEN, J.D.M.
"De Eendracht Van Het Land". Nijmegen 1941.
Twee allegorische etsen van Rembrandt. I. Het scheepje van Fortuin. *Oud Holland* 58 (1941), 111-126.
Some Observations on Rembrandt and Lastman. *Oud Holland* 84 (1969), 148-162.

COUPRIE, L.D. A Statue for Rembrandt-Amsterdam, 1852. *Delta* 12/2 (1969), 89-95.

COURBOIN, F. *Bibliothèque Nationale, Catalogue Exposition d'œuvres de Rembrandt.* Paris 1908.

CRAIG, K.M. Rembrandt and "The Slaughtered Ox" *Journal of the Warburg and Courtauld Institutes* 46 (1983), 235-239.

CUNNINGHAM, C.C. "The Evangelist" by Rembrandt van Rijn. *Bulletin of the Museum of Fine Arts of Boston* 37 (1939), 56-57.

CURAKOV, S.S. & K.S. EGOROVA Restavracija kartiny Rembrandta Artakserks, "Aman in Esfir". *Reports of the Pushkin State Museum of Fine Arts* 6 (1980), 104-110.

CZOBOR, A. *Rembrandt et son cercle.* Budapest 1969.

DAULBY, D. *A Descriptive Catalogue of the Works of Rembrandt and of his Scholars, Bol, Livens, and van Vliet, Compiled from the Original Etchings and from the Catalogues of de Burgy, Gersaint, Helle and Glomy, Marcus and Yver.* Liverpool 1796.

DEFOER, H.L.M. Rembrandt van Rijn, De Doop van de Kamerling. Oud Holland 91 (1977), 3-26.

DIERKER, M. Rembrandt — ein protestantischer Künstler. In: *Luther und die Folgen für die Kunst.* Exhibition catalogue Hamburger Kunsthalle. Ed. by W. HOFMANN. Munich 1983, 322-347.

DILLEN, J.G. van —
De sergeants en schutters van Rembrandt's schuttersoptocht. *Jaarboek Amstelodamum* 31 (1934), 97-110.
Marten Looten en zijn portret. *Tijdschrift voor Geschiedenis* 54 (1939), 181-190.

DONAHUE KURETSKY, S. Rembrandt's Tree Stump: An Iconographic Attribute of St. Jerome. *Art Bulletin* 56 (1974), 571-580.

DROSSAERS, S.W.A., Inventaris van de meubelen van het Stadhouderlijk Kwartier met het Speelhuis en van het Huis in het Noordeinde te 's-Gravenhage (Annotated by C. HOFSTEDE de GROOT and C.H. de JONGE). *Oud Holland* 47 (1930), 193-236; 241-276.

DROSSAERS, S.W.A. & TH. H. LUNSINGH SCHEURLEER (ed.), *Inventarissen van de inboedels in de verblijven van de Oranjes en daarmede gelijk te stellen stukken, 1567-1795,* I. The Hague 1974 (Rijks Geschiedkundige Publicatien, grote reeks 147).

DUDOK VAN HEEL, S.A.C.
Het maecenaat De Graeff en Rembrandt. *Maandblad Amstelodamum* 16 (1969), 150-155; 249-253.
De Rembrandt's in de verzameling "Hinloopen". *Maandblad Amstelodamum* 16 (1969), 233-237.
Mr Joannes Wtenbogaert (1608-1680), een man uit remonstrants milieu en Rembrandt van Rijn. *Jaarboek Amstelodamum* 70 (1978), 146-169.
Willem Bartel(omeu)sz. Ruyters (1587-1639) Rembrandt's Bisschop Gosewijn. *Maandblad Amstelodamum* 66/4 (1979), 83-87.
Het maecenaat Trip; opdrachten aan Ferdinand Bol en Rembrandt van Rijn. *De Kroniek van het Rembrandthuis* 31/1 (1979), 14-26.
Enkele portretten à l'antique door Rembrandt, Bol, Flinck en Backer. *De Kroniek van het Rembrandthuis* 32/1 (1980), 2-9.
Schrijfoefeningen van Titus van Rijn (1641-1668). *Maandblad Amstelodamum* 67 (1980), 3-7.
Doopsgezinden en schilderkunst in de 17e eeuw. Leerlingen, opdrachtgevers en verzamelaars van Rembrandt, *Doopsgezinde Bijdragen* N.S. 6 (1980), 105-123.

DUTUIT, E. *L'Œuvre complet de Rembrandt.* Paris/London/Leipzig 1883, Supplement 1885.

DYSERINCK, J. Rembrandts Hanna en Samuel in de Eremitage te St.-Petersburg en de Bridgewatergallery te London. *Leidsch Jaarboekje* 3 (1906), 103-109.

EEGHEN, I.H. VAN —
De anatomische lessen van Rembrandt. *Maandblad Amstelodamum* 35 (1948), 34-36.
Rembrandt's Claudius Civilis and the Funeral Ticket. *Konsthistorisk Tidskrift* 25 (1956), 55-57.
Rembrandts portret van Salomon Walens. *Maandlad Amstelodamum* 43 (1956), 113.
Marten Soolmans en Oopjen Coppit. *Maandblad Amstelodamum* 43 (1956), 85-90.
De portretten van Philips Lucas en Petronella Buys. *Maandblad Amstelodamum* 43 (1956), 116.
De echtgenoot van Cornelia Pronck. *Maandblad Amstelodamum* 43 (1956), 111-112.
Maria Trip op een anoniem vrouwsportret van Rembrandt. *Maandblad Amstelodamum* 43 (1956), 166-169.
Baertjen Martens en Herman Doomer. *Maandblad Amstelodamum* 43 (1956), 133-137.
Toen de Rembrandts nog de Amsterdamsche woonkamers sierden. *Maandblad Amstelodamum* 43 (1956), 113.
Een Doodshoofd van Rembrandt bij het Amsterdamse Chirurgijnsgilde. *Oud Holland* 71 (1956), 34-40.
De Familie de la Tombe en Rembrandt. *Oud Holland* 71 (1956), 43-49.
De Staalmeesters. *Jaarboek Amstelodamum* 49 (1957), 65-80.
Frederick Rihel, een 17de eeuwse zakenman en paardenliefhebber. *Maandblad Amstelodamum* 45 (1958), 73-81.
Een Amsterdamse burgemeestersdochter van Rembrandt in Buckingham Palace. Amsterdam 1958.
De Staalmeesters. *Oud Holland* 73 (1958), 80-84.
Het begraafbriefje van de Claudius Civilis. *Maandblad Amstelodamum* 56 (1969), 149.
Cornelis Frisius, een imaginair persoon. *Maandblad Amstelodamum* 56 (1969), 1161.
Handboogstraat 5. *Maandblad Amstelodamum* 56 (1969), 169-176.
Het Pourtrait van mijn vaeder. *Maandblad Amstelodamum* 56 (1969), 244-248.
Rembrandt en de mensenvilders. *Maandblad Amstelodamum* 56 (1969), 1-11.
De Rembrandts van Josephus Deutz. *Maandblad Amstelodamum* 56 (1969), 211.
De restauratie van het voormalige Anslohofje. *Maandblad Amstelodamum* 56 (1969), 199-205.
Samuel Smijters. *Maandblad Amstelodamum* 56 (1969), 176.
Wat veroverde Rembrandt met zijn Claudius Civilis? *Maandblad Amstelodamum* 56 (1969), 145-149.
Een brief aan Jan Heykens. *Maandblad Amstelodamum* 56 (1969), 196-198.
Elsje Christiaens en de kunsthistorici. *Maandblad Amstelodamum* 56 (1969), 73-78.
Het huis op de Rozengracht. *Maandblad Amstelodamum* 56 (1969), 180-183.
"De Keizerskroon" een optisch bedrog. *Maandblad Amstelodamum* 56 (1969), 162-168
Abraham Wilmerdonx en Anna van Beaumont: een dubbelportret van Rembrandt. *Maandblad Amstelodamum* 56 (1969), 179.
Het Amsterdamse Sint Lucasgilde in de 17de eeuw. *Jaarboek Amstelodamum* 61 (1969), 65-102.
Jan Rijcksen en Griet Jans. *Maandblad Amstelodamum* 57 (1970), 121-127.
De vaandeldrager van Rembrandt. *Maandblad Amstelodamum* 58 (1971), 173-181.
Drie portretten van Rembrandt (Bruyningh, Cater, Moutmaker) Vondel en Blaeu. *Jaarboek Amstelodamum* 68 (1976), 55-72.

EEGHEN, I.H. van & H. de la FONTAINE VERWEY e.a. *Rembrandt aan de Amstel.* Amsterdam 1969.

EINEM H. von
Rembrandt und Homer. *Wallraf-Richartz-Jahrbuch* 14 (1952), 182-205.
Rembrandt: Der Segen Jakobs. *Werkmonographien zur bildenden Kunst 110.* Stuttgart 1965.
Bemerkungen zum Christusbild Rembrandts. *Das Münster* 25 (1972), 349-360.

EISLER, M. *Der alte Rembrandt.* Vienna 1927.

EMMENS, J.A.
Ay Rembrant, maal "Cornelis" stem. *Nederlands Kunsthistorisch Jaarboek* 7 (1956), 133-165.
Rembrandt en de regels van de kunst. *Utrechtse Kunsthistorische Studiën* 10. Utrecht 1968.
Reputation and Meaning of Rembrandt's 'Slaughtered Ox'. *Museumjournaal* 12 (1967), 112.
Rembrandt e sua concezione dell'arte. Florence 1978.
Kunsthistorische opstellen I-II. Amsterdam 1981.

ERPEL, F. *Die Selbstbildnisse Rembrandts.* Vienna 1967.

ESCHWEILER, J. *Katalog der Ausstellung: Handzeichnungen des 16.-18. Jahrhunderts aus dem Besitz der Stadt Konstanz a.B. im Wessenberghaus.* Konstanz 1951.

ESTEBAN, C. & J. RUDEL & S. MONNERET *Rembrandt.* New York 1980.

FALCK, G.
Über einige von Rembrandt übergangene Schülerzeichnungen. *Jahrbuch der Preußischen Kunstsammlungen* 45 (1924), 191-200.
Einige Bemerkungen über Ph. Konincks Tätigkeit als Zeichner. Ein Beitrag zur Echtheitskritik der Handzeichnungen Rembrandts. In: *Festschrift für Max. J. Friedländer.* Leipzig 1927, 168-180.

FECHNER, E. *Rembrandt.* Leningrad/Moscow 1964.

FEINBLATT, E. "Dido divides the ox-hid" by Rembrandt. *Master Drawings* 9 (1971), 39-42.

FILEDT KOK, J.P.
Rembrandt, Etchings & Drawings in the Rembrandt House, Amsterdam 1972.

FINKE, U. Venezianische Rembrandtstecher um 1800. *Oud Holland* 79 (1964), 49-77.

FONTAINE VERWEY, H. de la —
Antiquiteiten en rariteiten van Rembrandt. *Maandblad Amstelodamum* 56 (1969), 177-179.
Rembrandt as a Book-Illustrator. *Quaerendo* 3 (1973).

FORSSMAN, E. Rembrandts Radierung "Der Triumph des Mardochai". *Zeitschrift für Kunstgeschichte* 39 (1976), 297-311.

FOUCART, J. *Rembrandt au Louvre.* Paris 1982.

FOWKES, C. *The Life of Rembrandt.* London 1978.

FRANKL, P. Die Persephone-Bilder von Lambert, Sustris, Rubens und Rembrandt. *Oud Holland* 55 (1938), 156-171.

FREDERICKSEN, B.B. *Masterpieces of Painting in the J. Paul Getty Museum.* Malibu 1980.

FREISE, K. Rembrandt and Elsheimer. *The Burlington Magazine* 13 (1908), 38-39.

FREISE, K. & K. LILIENFELD & H. WICHMANN *Rembrandts Handzeichnungen.* I: *Rijksprentenkabinet zu Amsterdam;* II: *Kupferstichkabinett zu Berlin;* III: *Staatl. Kupferstich-Kabinett und Sammlung Friedrich August II. zu Dresden.* Parchim 1912-1925.

FRERICHS, L.C.J. De schetsbladen van Rembrandt voor het schilderij van het echtpaar Anslo. *Maandblad Amstelodamum* 56 (1969), 206-211.

FRIEDLÄNDER, M.J. *Von Kunst und Kennerschaft.* Oxford/Zurich 1946.

FROENTJES, W. Schilderde Rembrandt op goud? *Oud Holland* 84 (1969), 233-237.

FUCHS, R.H.
Rembrandt en Amsterdam. Rotterdam 1968.
Het zogenaamde "Joodse bruidje" en het probleem van de "voordracht" in Rembrandts werk. *Tijdschrift voor geschiedenis* 82 (1969), 482-493.

GAGE, J. A Note on Rembrandt's "Meeste Ende die Naetureelste Beweechgelickheijt". *The Burlington Magazine* 111 (1969), 381.

GANTNER, J.
Rembrandts "Falkenier" in Göteborg. In: *Festschrift Karl Swoboda.* Wien 1959, 97-102.
Rembrandt und die Verwandlung klassischer Formen. Bern 1964.

GELDER, H.E. van —
Marginalia bij Rembrandt. *Oud Holland* 60 (1943), 33-37.
Rembrandt's portretjes van M. Huygens en J. de Gheyn III. *Oud Holland* 68, (1953), 107.
Rembrandt. Amsterdam [1955][2].
Nederlands Rembrandtwaardering. *Maatstaf* 4 (1956), 186-201.
Const. Huygens en Rembrandt. *Oud Holland* 74 (1959), 174-179.

GELDER, J.G. van —
Rembrandt's philosophen in den kunsthandel D.A. Hoogendijk & Co. Amsterdam. *Elsevier's geillustreerd maandschrift* 45/89 (1935), 65-66.
The Rembrandt Exhibition at Edinburgh. *The Burlington Magazine* 92 (1950), 327-329.
Rembrandt's vroegste ontwikkeling. *Mededelingen der Koninklijke Nederlandse Akademie van Wetenschappen, afd. Letterkunde* N.S. 16 (1953), 273-300.
Rembrandt en de zeventiende eeuw. *De Gids* 119 (1956), 397-413.
Een Rembrandt van 1633. *Oud Holland* 75 (1960), 73-78.
Review: Otto Benesch. The Drawings of Rembrandt, dl. 1-6. Londen 1954-57. *The Burlington Magazine* 97 (1955), 395-396; 103 (1961), 149-151.
Rembrandt: "Jeremia treurende over de verwoesting van Jeruzalem". *Openbaar kunstbezit* 7 (1963), No. 15.
Rembrandt: "De Staalmeesters". *Openbaar kunstbezit* 8 (1964), No. 11.
Falconet op bezoek bij de Goll van Franckenstein's. *De Kroniek van het Rembrandthuis* 31/1 (1979), 2-8.

GERSAINT, G. & HELLE & GLOMY *Catalogue raisonné de toutes les pièces qui forment l'œuvre de Rembrandt.* Paris 1751.

GERSON, H.
Philips Koninck. Ein Beitrag zur Erforschung der holländischen Malerei des XVII. Jahrhunderts. Berlin 1936.
Het tijdperk van Rembrandt en Vermeer. De Nederlandse schilderkunst. *De schoonheid van ons land. Schilderkunst.* Amsterdam 1952.
Probleme der Rembrandtschule. *Kunstchronik* 10 (1957), 121-124.
Seven Letters by Rembrandt. *Publicaties van het Rijksbureau voor Kunsthistorische Documentatie te s'Gravenhage.* The Hague 1961.
"La Lapidation de Saint Etienne" par Rembrandt en 1625. *Bulletin des musées et monuments lyonnais* 3 (1962/6), 57-62.
A Rembrandt Discovery. *Apollo* 77 (1963), 371-372.
Review: Kurt Bauch, Rembrandt Gemälde. *Gazette des Beaux-Arts* 4/72 (1968), 207-208.
Rembrandt. Gemälde. Gütersloh 1969.
Rembrandt and the Flemish Baroque: His Dialogue with Rubens. *Delta* 12/2 (1969), 7-23.
Rembrandt's portret van Amalia van Solms. *Oud Holland* 84 (1969), 244-249.
The Rembrandt Exhibitions of 1969. *The Burlington Magazine* 111 (1969), 781-783.
Imitaties naar Rembrandt door Thomas Worlidge (1700-1766). *Nederlands Kunsthistorisch Jaarboek* 21 (1970), 301-307.
Rembrandt: oratio pro domo. *Gazette des Beaux-Arts* 77 (1971), 193-199.
Rembrandt: La ronde de nuit. Fribourg 1973.
Dutch and Flemish Painting. *Connoiseur* 193/777 (1976) 163-171.

GLÜCK, G. Rembrandts Selbstbildnis aus dem Jahre 1652. In: id., *Aus drei Jahrhunderten europäischer Malerei.* Vienna 1933, 294-312.

GOLDSCHEIDER, L. *Rembrandt. Gemälde und Graphik,* Cologne 1960.

GOUDSWAARD, J. & I.H. van EEGHEN Hendrickje Stoffels: jeugd en sterven. *Maandblad Amstelodamum* 43 (1956), 114-116.

GRAUL, R. Rembrandt. I: Die Radierungen. *Meister der Graphik* Vol. 8, ed. by P. VOSS. Leipzig 1923.

GRAVENKAMP, C. Rembrandt im Wandel seines Werks. In: *Gedenkbuch zu Georg Hartmanss 75. Geburtstag am 13. Juli 1945.* Frankfurt 1946, 75-90.

GREEFF, R. *Rembrandts Darstellungen der Tobiasheilung.* Stuttgart 1907.

GRIMME, E.G. Rembrandt-Zeichnungen im Suermondt-Museum. *Aachener Kunstblätter* 44 (1973), 323-327.

GROEN, K. Schildertechnische aspecten van Rembrandts vroegste schilderijen. *Oud Holland* 91 (1977), 66-74.

GÜNTHER, H. Damals oder heute unverstanden. *Weltkunst* 50/13 (1980), 1848-1850.

GURATZSCH, H.
Die Untersicht als ein Gestaltungsmittel in Rembrandts Frühwerk. *Oud Holland* 89 (1975), 243-265.
Die grosse Zeit der niederländischen Malerei. With the co-operation of G. BAUER, P. EIKEMEIER, C. GRIMM, E.W. HUBER, U.KREMPEL, G. LEINZ, G. UNVERFEHRT. Freiburg/Basel/Vienna 1979.

HAAK, B.
Rembrandt. Sein Leben, sein Werk, seine Zeit. New York/Cologne 1969.
Rembrandt anno 1969. *Antiek* 3 (1968/69), 537-547.
De nachtelijke samenzwering van Claudius Civilis in het Schakerbos op de Rembrandttentoonstelling te Amsterdam. *Antiek* 4 (1969/70), 136-148.
Rembrandt Zeichnungen. Cologne 1974.
Rembrandt: Leben und Werk. Cologne 1976.

HAEGER, B. *The Religious Significance of Rembrandt's Return of the Prodigal Son: an Examination of the Picture in the Context of the Visual and Iconographic Tradition.* Diss. Ann Arbor, The University of Michigan, 1983.

HALEWOOD, W.H. *Six Subjects of Reformation Art: a Preface to Rembrandt.* Toronto 1982.

HALL, H. van — *Repertorium voor de geschiedenis der Nederlandsche schilder- en graveerkunst.* The Hague 1936, 1949.

HAMANN, R.
Rembrandts Radierungen. Berlin 1906.
Hagars Abschied bei Rembrandt und im Rembrandt-Kreise. *Marburger Jahrbuch für Kunstwissenschaft* 8/9 (1936), 471-578.
Rembrandt. Berlin 1948.
Rembrandt. New edition by R. HAMANN-MAC LEAN, annotated by W. SUMOWSKI. Berlin 1969.

HAMEL, J.A. van — *De eendracht van het land.* Amsterdam 1945.

HANFSTAENGL, E. *Rembrandt Harmensz. van Rijn.* Munich 1947[2].

HARRIS, A. Rembrandt's Study for "The Lamentation for Christ". *Master Drawings* 7 (1969), 158-164.

HART, S.
Een trony van Rembrandt in 't groot gedaen. *Maandblad Amstelodamum* 56 (1969), 188.
De Pellicorne portretten van Rembrandt geveild: Bravo!. *Maandblad Amstelodamum* 56 (1969), 189.
Rembrandts geslachte os getaxeerd. *Maandblad Amstelodamum* 56 (1969), 161.

HAUSMANN, M. *Der Mensch vor Gottes Angesicht: Rembrandt-Bilder. Deutungsversuche.* Neukirchen-Vluyn 1976.

HAUSSHERR, R.
Zur Menetekel-Inschrift auf Rembrandts Belsazarbild. *Oud Holland* 78 (1963), 142-149.
Rembrandts Jacobssegen. Überlegungen zur Deutung des Gemäldes in der Kasseler Galerie. *Abhandlungen der rheinisch-westfälischen Akademie der Wissenschaften* 60 (1976).

HAVERKAMP BEGEMANN, E.
Hercules Seghers. Rotterdam 1954.
Tentoonstellingscatalogus: Rembrandt. Tekeningen. Museum Boymans-van Beuningen Rotterdam - Rijksmuseum Amsterdam. 1956.
Review: O. Benesch. The Drawings of Rembrandt, I-VI, Londen 1954-1957. *Kunstchronik* 14 (1961), 10-14, 19-28, 50-57 85-91.
Rembrandt backward and forward. *The Yale Review* 56 (1967), 301-309.
Rembrandt as Teacher. *Actes Congr. intern. Hist. Art, Budapest 1969* II (1972), 105-113.
Rembrandt und seine Schule; Zur Ausstellung in Kanada. *Kunstchronik* 22 (1969), 281-289.
The Present State of Rembrandt Studies. *Art Bulletin* 53 (1971), 88-104.
Creative Copies. *Print Collector's Newsletter* 11/5 (1980), 168-170.
Eine unbekannte Vorzeichnung zum Claudius Civilis. In: *Neue Beiträge zur Rembrandt-Forschung.* Ed. by O. von SIMSON and J. KELCH. Berlin 1973, 12-30.
The Nightwatch. Princeton 1982.

HAYES, C. *On Rembrandt's "The Woman Taken in Adultery".* London 1969.

HECKSCHER, W.S. *Rembrandt's Anatomy of Dr. Nicolaas Tulp.* New York 1958.

HEIL, W. Die Rembrandt-Ausstellung in Detroit. *Pantheon* 6 (1930), 380-383.

HEILAND, S. & H. LÜDECKE *Rembrandt und die Nachwelt.* Leipzig 1960.

HELD, J.S.
Rembrandt's "Polish Rider". *Art Bulletin* 26 (1944), 246-255.
Paintings by Rembrandt. New York 1956.
Flora, Goddess and Courtesan. In: *De artibus opuscula XL: Essays in honor of Erwin Panofsky.* New York 1961, 201-218.
Rembrandt and the Book of Tobit. *The Gehenna Essays in Art* II Northampton (Mass.) 1964.
Rembrandt's "Aristotle" and Other Rembrandt Studies. Princeton 1969.
De tentoonstelling "Rembrandt and his Pupils" te Montreal en Toronto. *Pantheon* 27 (1969), 384-388.
Das gesprochene Wort bei Rembrandt. In: *Neue Beiträge zur Rembrandt-Forschung.* Ed. by O. von SIMSON and J. KELCH. Berlin 1973, 111-125.
Rembrandt's "Juno". *Apollo* 105/184 (1977), 478-485.
Der Blinde Tobias und seine Heilung in Darstellungen Rembrandts. Heidelberg 1980.
Was Abraham lefthanded?. *Print Collector's Newsletter* 11/5 (1980), 161-164.
Rembrandt Studien. Leipzig 1983.

HELL, H. Die späten Handzeichnungen Rembrandts. *Repertorium für Kunstwissenschaft* 51 (1930), 4-43, 92-136.

HELL, J. Beobachtungen über Rembrandts Malweise und Probleme der Konservierung. Resumée des Vortrages auf der vom Zentralinstitut für Kunstgeschichte in München veranstalteten Arbeitstagung "Die Rembrandtforschung im Licht der Ausstellungen des Jahres 1956". *Kunstchronik* 10 (1957), 138-140; 140-141.

HELLINGA, W.G.
Rembrandt fecit 1642. Amsterdam 1956.
De bewogenheid der "Staalmeesters". *Nederlands Kunsthistorisch Jaarboek* 8 (1957), 151-184.

HELSDINGEN, H.W. van — Enkele opmerkingen over het Franse zeventiende-eeuwse Rembrandtbeeld. *Oud Holland* 84 (1969), 224-231.

HENKEL, M.D.
Nederlandsche Ovidius-Illustraties van de 15e tot de 18e eeuw. *Oud Holland* 39 (1921), 149-187.
"The denial of St. Peter" by Rembrandt. *The Burlington Magazine* 64 (1934), 153-159; 65 (1935), 187.
Teekeningen van Rembrandt en zijn school. *Catalogus van de Nederlandsche teekeningen in het Rijksmuseum te Amsterdam* I. The Hague 1942, 1943[2].

HEPPNER, A. "Moses zeigt die Gesetzestafeln" bei Rembrandt und Bol. *Oud Holland* 52 (1935), 241-251.

HIJMANS, W. & L. KUIPER & A. VELS HEIJN *Rembrandts Nachtwacht: het vendel van Frans Banning Cocq, de geschiedenis van een schilderij*. Leyden 1976.

HIND, A.M.
The Portraits of Rembrandt's father. *The Burlington Magazine* 8 (1905/6), 426-431.
Drawings by Rembrandt and his School. *Catalogue of Drawings by Dutch and Flemish Artists preserved in the Department of Prints and Drawings in the British Museum* I. London 1915.
A Catalogue of Rembrandt's Etchings. London 1923.
Rembrandt. Cambridge 1932, 1938[2].

HINZ, B. Studien zur Geschichte des Ehepaarbildnisses. *Marburger Jahrbuch für Kunstwissenschaft* 19 (1974), 139-218.

HIRST, M. Rembrandt and Italy. *Burlington Magazine* 110 (1968), 221.

HOETINK, H.R.
Tekeningen van Rembrandt en zijn school, Catalogus van de verzameling in het Museum Boymans-van Beuningen. Rotterdam 1969.
Nog een portret van Margaretha de Geer. *Miscellanea I.Q. van Regteren Altena*. Amsterdam 1969, 150-151.

HOFF, U.
Rembrandt und England. Diss. Hamburg 1935.
Dutch and Flemish Pictures in Melbourne. *Apollo* 79 (1964), 448-457.

HOFSTEDE DE GROOT, C.
Entlehnungen Rembrandts. *Jahrbuch der Königlich Preussischen Kunstsammlungen* 15 (1894), 175-181.
Review: Woldemar von Seidlitz. Kritisches Verzeichnis der Radierungen Rembrandt's, zugleich eine Anleitung zu deren Studium. Leipzig 1895. *Repertorium für Kunstwissenschaft* 19 (1896), 376-383.
Die Rembrandt-Ausstellung zu Amsterdam (September-Oktober 1898) und zu London (Januar-März 1899). *Repertorium für Kunstwissenschaft* 22 (1899), 159-164.
Varia omtrent Rembrandt. *Oud Holland* 19 (1901), 91-94.
Die Handzeichnungen Rembrandts. Versuch eines beschreibenden und kritischen Katalogs. Haarlem 1906.
Die Urkunden über Rembrandt (1575-1721) *Quellenstudium zur Holländischen Kunstgeschichte III*. The Hague 1906.
Rembrandts Bibel. Amsterdam [1911].
Rembrandt's portretten van Philips Lucasse en Petronella Buys. *Oud Holland* 31 (1913), 236-240.
Beschreibendes und kritisches Verzeichnis der Werke der hervorragendsten holländischen Maler des 17.Jahrhunderts VI. *Rembrandt-Maes*. Esslingen/Paris 1915.
Rembrandt's Bijbelsche en historische voorstellingen. *Oud Holland* 41 (1923-24), 49-59, 97-114.
Rembrandt's youthful works. *The Burlington Magazine* 44 (1924), 126.
Rembrandt's "Painter in His Studio". *The Burlington Magazine* 47 (1925), 265.
De portretten van het echtpaar Jacob Trip en Margaretha de Geer door de Cuyp's, N. Maes en Rembrandt. *Oud Holland* 45 (1928), 255-264.

HOLLSTEIN, F.W.H.
German Engravings, Etchings and Woodcuts, ca. 1400-1700. Amsterdam Iff 1949ff.
Dutch and Flemish Etchings, Engravings and Woodcuts, ca. 1450-1700. Iff Amsterdam 1949ff.

HOLMES, C.J. An Undescribed Panel by Rembrandt. *The Burlington Magazine* 31 (1917), 171-172.

HOOGEWERFF, G.J. Rembrandt en een italiaansche maecenas. *Oud Holland* 35 (1917), 129-148.

HOOGSTRATEN S. van —*Inleyding tot de hooge schoole der schilderkunst*. Rotterdam 1678.

HOUBRAKEN, A. *De groote schouburgh der nederlantsche konstschilders en schilderessen*. Amsterdam 1718-21.

HOURS, M. Rembrandt: Observations et présentations de radiographies... *Bulletin du laboratoire du musée du Louvre* 6 (1961), 3-43.

HUYGENS, C. *De jeugd van Constantijn Huygens door hemzelf beschreven*. Ed. by A.H. KAN. Rotterdam/Antwerp 1946.

JAHN, J. *Rembrandt*. Leipzig 1956.

JANSON, A.F. Rembrandt in the Indianapolis Museum of Art. *Perceptions* I (1981), 7-21.

JANTZEN, H. *Rembrandt*. Bielefeld/Leipzig 1923.

JOHNSON, B.B. Examinations and Treatment of Rembrandt's "Raising of Lazarus". *Los Angeles County Museum of Art Bulletin* 20/22 (1974), 18-35.

JONGH, E. de —
The Spur of Wit: Rembrandt's Response to an Italian Challenge. *Delta* 12/2 (1969), 49-67.
Portretten van echt en trouw. Huwelijk en gezin in de Nederlandse kunst van de zeventiende eeuw. Exhibition catalogue Frans Halsmuseum Haarlem. Zwolle/Haarlem 1986.

JORDAN, A. Bemerkungen zu einigen Bildern Rembrandt's. *Repertorium für Kunstwissenschaft* 7 (1884), 183-187.

JOSEPHUS, F.
Flavii Josephi/des Hochberühmten Jüdischen Geschichtsschreibers Historien und Bücher. Strasbourg (Rihel) 1574.
Flavius Josephus. Jüdische Altertümer, Cologne 1959.

JUDSON, R.J.
Review: William Heckscher. Rembrandt's Anatomy of Dr. Tulp, an Iconological Study. New York 1958. *Art Bulletin* 42 (1960), 305-310.
Pictorial Sources for Rembrandt's Denial of Saint Peter. *Oud Holland* 79 (1964), 141-151.
Rembrandt in Canada. *The Burlington Magazine* 111 (1969), 703-704.

KAHR, M. Millner
A Rembrandt Problem: Haman or Uriah?. *Journal of the Warburg and Courtauld Institutes* 28 (1965), 258-273.
Rembrandt's "Esther": A Painting and an Etching Newly Interpreted and Dated. *Oud Holland* 81 (1966), 228-244.
Danäe: Virtuous, Voluptuous, Venal Woman. *Art Bulletin* 60/1 (1978), 43-55.

KAUFFMANN, H.
Rembrandt und die Humanisten vom Muiderkring. *Jahrbuch der Preußischen Kunstsammlungen* 41 (1920), 46-81.
Rembrandts Berliner Susanna. *Jahrbuch der Preußischen Kunstsammlungen* 45 (1924), 72-80.
Zur Kritik der Rembrandtzeichnungen. *Repertorium für Kunstwissenschaft* 47 (1926), 157-178.
Die Fünfsinne in der niederländischen Malerei des 17.Jahrhunderts. In: *Kunstgeschichtliche Studien, Festschrift für Dagobert Frey*. Ed. by H. TINTELNOT. Breslau [1943], 133-157.
Die "Staalmeesters". Resumée des Vortrages auf der vom Zentralinstitut für Kunstgeschichte in München veranstalteten Arbeitstagung "Die Rembrandtforschung im Lichte der Ausstellungen des Jahres 1956". *Kunstchronik* 10 (1957), 125-127, 128-129.
Rembrandts "Belsazar". In: *Festschrift Wolfgang Braunfels*. Tübingen 1977, 167-176.

KELCH, J. Cf.: *Katalog der Gemäldegalerie der Staatlichen Museen Preussischer Kulturbesitz Berlin*. Berlin 1975.

KELLER, U. Knechtschaft und Freiheit: ein neutestamentliches Thema bei Rembrandt. *Jahrbuch der Hamburger Kunstsammlungen* 24 (1979), 77-112.

KETTERING, A. McNeil — Rembrandt's Flute Player: a unique Treatment of Pastoral. *Simiolus* 9 (1977), 19-44.

KEUTNER, H.A.F. *Rembrandts Hundertguldenblatt*. Diss. Cologne 1950.

KIESER, E. Über Rembrandts Verhältnis zur Antike. *Zeitschrift für Kunstgeschichte* 10 (1941/44), 129-162.

KITSON, M.
Rembrandt. London 1969.
Rembrandt. Oxford 1982.

KLAMT, J.C. Ut magis luceat: eine Miszelle zu Rembrandt's "Anslo". *Jahrbuch der Berliner Museen* 17 (1975), 155-165.

KLESSMANN, R.
Rembrandt und sein Kreis. *Bilderhefte des Herzog Anton Ulrich-Museums* 4. Brunswick 1973.
Die holländischen Gemälde, kritisches Verzeichnis. Brunswick 1983.

KLUCKERT, E. *Rembrandt. Von der Themenvielfalt der Kunst*. Pliezhausen 1982.

KNIPPING, J. B. *De iconografie van de contra-reformatie in de Nederlanden* If. Hilversum 1939-1942.

KNUTTEL, G.
Rembrandt's Earliest Works. *The Burlington Magazine* 97 (1955), 44-49.
On the "Bathseba" of Rembrandt in the Metropolitan Museum. *Actes du 17e congrès international d'histoire de l'art. Amsterdam 1952*. The Hague 1955, 421-424.
Rembrandt. De meester en zijn werk. Amsterdam 1956.

KOCK, E. *Dein Kleid ist Licht, Rembrandt malt das Glauben*. Limburg 1977.

KOK, M. Rembrandts "Nachtwacht": van feeststoet tot schuttersstuk. *Bulletin van het Rijksmuseum* 15 (1967), 116-121.

KOLLOFF, E.
Rembrandt's Leben und Werke. *Historisches Taschenbuch*. Ed. by F. von RAUMER. 3d S. 5 (1854), 401-582.
Photomechanical reprint with introduction and index, ed. by C. TÜMPEL, *Deutsches Bibelarchiv, Abhandlungen und Vorträge* IV. Hamburg 1971.

KONERDING, V. *"David und Jonathan" und "David und Absalom" bei Rembrandt und seinem Umkreis*. Lecture (No. 39) under Prof. Schöne. University Hamburg, 1964/65 (Manuscript).

KONSTAM, N. Rembrandt's Use of Models and Mirrors. *The Burlington Magazine* 119/887 (1977), 94-98.

KOOT, T.
Rembrandt's Nachtwacht in nieuwen luister. Amsterdam 1947.
Rembrandt's Night Watch: a Fascinating Story. Amsterdam 1969.

KRAFT, K. Der behelmte Alexander. *Jahrbuch für Numismatik und Geldgeschichte* 15 (1965), 7-32.

KÜHN, H. Untersuchungen zu den Pigmenten und Malgründen Rembrandts, durchgeführt an den Gemälden der Staatlichen Kunstsammlungen Dresden. *Maltechnik* 83 (1977), 223-233.

KUIPER, L. & W. HESTERMAN Restauratieverslag van Rembrandts "Nachtwacht". *Bulletin van het Rijksmuseum* 24/1-2 (1976), 14-51.

KUZNETSOV, Yu.
New Data on Rembrandt's "Danae". *Bulletin du musée de l'Ermitage* 27 (1966), 26-31.
Zagadki "Danai". Leningrad 1970.
Rembrandt Discoveries at the Hermitage. *Apollo* 100/154 (1974), 486-495.
Rembrandts Danae. *Kunstmuseets årsskrift* 62 (1975), 1-29.

KUZNETSOV, Yu. & I. LINNIK *Dutch Painting in Soviet Museums.* New York/Leningrad 1982.

LABAN, F. Rembrandt's Bildnis seines Bruders Adriaen Harmensz. van Rijn in der Berliner Galerie. *Zeitschrift für Bildende Kunst* N.S. 9 (1897/98), 74-78.

LANDSBERGER, F. *Rembrandt, the Jews, and the Bible.* Philadelphia 1946.

LAURIE, A.P. *The Brushwork of Rembrandt and His School.* London 1932.

LECALDANO, P. *The Complete Paintings of Rembrandt.* London 1973.

LEE, S.F. Rembrandt, "Old Man Praying". *The Bulletin of The Cleveland Museum of Art* 54 (1967), 295-301.

LENGL, G. Beiträge zu den Bildern Rembrandts in der Alten Pinakothek in München. Ein neu entdecktes Selbstbildnis Rembrandts. *Das Münster* 20 (1967), 52-59.

LEVIE, S.H.
The Fifth Rembrandt Exhibition at the Rijksmuseum. *The Connoisseur* 172 (1969), 2-7.
De Nachtwacht hersteld. *Bulletin van het Rijksmuseum* 24/1-2 (1976), 1-3.

LEVY, A. The Rembrandt Research Project: Old Myths, New Methods. *Art News* 75/7 (1976), 34-42.

LINDENBORG, I. Did the Execution of Charles the First Influence Rembrandt's "Ecce Homo"? A Tentative Investigation. *Print Review* 6 (1976), 19-26.

LINNIK, I.
Sur le sujet du tableau de Rembrandt dit "La Disgrâce d'Aman". *Bulletin du musée de l'Ermitage* 11 (1957), 8-12.
"Die Anbetung der Könige" von Rembrandt. *Pantheon* 27 (1969), 36-41.
A Picture by Jacob van Spreeuwen. *Soobscenija, Hermitage* 43 (1978), 11-12.

LOEWINSON-LESSING, V.
Sur l'histoire du tableau de Rembrandt "David et Jonathan". *Bulletin du musée de l'Ermitage* 11 (1957), 5-8.
Rembrandt Harmensz van Rijn, Paintings from Soviet Museums, ed. V. LOEWINSON-LESSING, Leningrad 1981[4].

LOUTTIT, M. The Romantic Dress of Saskia van Ulenborch: Its Pastoral and Theatrical Associations. *The Burlington Magazine* 115 (1973), 317-326.

LÜTJENS, H. *Untersuchungen zur Graphik des Rembrandtkreises.* Diss. Freiburg/B. 1921.

LUGT, F.
Mit Rembrandt in Amsterdam. Berlin 1920.
Beiträge zu dem Katalog der niederländischen Handzeichnungen in Berlin. *Jahrbuch der Preußischen Kunstsammlungen* 52 (1931), 36-80.
Rembrandt. Ses Elèves, ses Imitateurs, ses Copistes. *Musée du Louvre. Inventaire Général des Dessins des Ecoles du Nord. Ecole Hollandaise*, III. Paris 1933.
Italiaansche kunstwerken in Nederlandsche verzamelingen van vroeger tijden. *Oud Holland* 53 (1936), 97-135.
Rembrandt's "Man with the Magnifying Glass", a New Identification. *Art in America* 30 (1942), 174-178.
Ecole Hollandaise. *Ecole Nationale Supérieure des Beaux-Arts Paris. Inventaire Général des Dessins des Ecoles du Nord*, I. Paris 1950.

LUNSINGH SCHEURLEER, P. Mogol-miniaturen door Rembrandt nagetekend. *De Kroniek van het Rembrandthuis* 32/1 (1980), 10-40.

LURIE, A.T. Pictorial Ties between Rembrandt's "Danae" in the Hermitage and Orazio Gentileschi's "Danae" in the Cleveland Museum of Art. *Acta Historiae Artium* 21/1-2 (1975), 75-81.

LUTTERVELT, R. van —
Bij het portret van Oopje Coppit. *Maandblad Amstelodamum* 43 (1956), 93.
De Grote Ruiter van Rembrandt. *Nederlands Kunsthistorisch Jaarboek* 8 (1957), 185-219.
Frederick Rihel of Jacob de Graeff. *Maandblad Amstelodamum* 45 (1958), 147-150.

MacLAREN, N. *The Dutch School. National Gallery Catalogues.* London 1960.

MANDER, C. van —
Das Leben der niederländischen und deutschen Maler des Carel van Mander. Translated and commented by H. FLOERKE. *Kunstgeschichtliche Studien. Der Galleriestudien IV. Folge* I-II, ed. by Th. von FRIMMEL in co-operation with colleagues, Munich/Leipzig 1906.
Das Lehrgedicht des Karel van Mander, Text, Übersetzung und Kommentar, nebst Anhang über Manders Geschichtskonstruktion und Kunsttheorie von R. HOECKER, *Quellenstudien zur Holländischen Kunstgeschichte* VIII. Ed. under direction of C. HOFSTEDE DE GROOT, The Hague 1916.
Den grondt der edel vry schilder-const I-II, ed., transl. and comm. by H. MIEDEMA, Utrecht 1973.

MANKE, I. Zu Rembrandts "Jakobsegen" in der Kasseler Galerie. *Zeitschrift für Kunstgeschichte* 23 (1960), 252-260.

MAREL, A. van der — De kunstschilders de Bray en hun familie. *De Nederlandsche Leeuw* 81 (1964), 6-26.

MARTIN, G.
A Rembrandt Self-Portrait from his last year. *The Burlington Magazine* 109 (1967), 733.
The Death of a Myth. *Apollo* 90 (1969), 266-267.

MARTIN, W.
Rembrandts portretten van Herman Doomer en Baertjen Martens. *Bulletin van den Nederlandschen Oudheidkundigen Bond* 2/2 (1909), 126-129.
Rembrandt-Rätsel. II *[Der] Kunstwanderer* 3 (1921-22), 30-34.
Buytewech, Rembrandt en Frans Hals. *Oud Holland* 42 (1925), 48-51.
Uit Rembrandt's Leidsche jaren. *Jaarboek van de Maatschappij der Nederlandsche Letterkunde* (1936-37), 50-62.
De Hollandsche schilderkunst in de zeventiende eeuw. Rembrandt en zijn tijd. Amsterdam 1936, 1942[2].
Van Nachtwacht tot feeststoet. Amsterdam 1947.
Een sleutel voor Rembrandt's "Nachtwacht", in: *Miscellanea Leo van Puyvelde.* Brussels 1949, 225-228.
"Nachtwacht" overdenkingen. *Oud Holland* 66 (1951), 1-9.

MARX, C.R. *Rembrandt.* s.l. 1960.

MARZLUF, A. *Selbstbewußtsein als Bildkategorie: das Selbstbildnis bei Rembrandt.* Diss. Frankfurt 1978.

MAYER-MEINTSCHEL, A. Rembrandt und Saskia im Gleichnis vom verlorenen Sohn. *Staatliche Kunstsammlungen Dresden, Jahrbuch* 1970/71, 39-57.

MEYER, R. *Das Werk Rembrandts in Auffassung und Beurteilung von seinen Zeitgenossen bis heute.* Diss. Hamburg 1924.

MICHEL, E. *Rembrandt. Sa vie, son œuvre et son temps.* Paris 1893.

MIDDLETON, C.H. *A Descriptive Catalogue of the Etched Work of Rembrandt.* London 1878.

MIEDEMA, H. Review: J.A. Emmens. Rembrandt en de regels van de kunst. Utrecht 1968. *Oud Holland* 84 (1969), 249-256.

MILES, H. *Dutch and Flemish... Paintings.* Glasgow 1961.

MILLAR, O. Abraham van der Doort's Catalogue of the Collections of Charles I. *Walpole Society* 37 (1958/60).

MOES-VETH, A.J. Rembrandt's "Claudius Civilis" en de "Nachtwacht" van ter zijde beschouwd. *Oud Holland* 75 (1960), 143-156.

MOLSTER, H.C.
De Bedelaar. *De Kroniek van het Rembrandthuis* 26/3 (1972), 49.
Het Catalogusprobleem. *De Kroniek van het Rembrandthuis* 26/3 (1972), 50..

MOLTKE, J.W. von — *Govaert Flinck.* Amsterdam 1965.

MÜLLER, J. Rembrandts früheste Darstellung des Emmauswunders. *Nederlands Kunsthistorisch Jaarboek* 23 (1972), 113-120.

MÜLLER[-HOFSTEDE], C. *Beiträge zur Geschichte des biblischen Historienbildes im 16. und 17. Jahrhundert in Holland.* Diss. Berlin 1925.

MÜLLER-HOFSTEDE, C.
Studien zu Lastman und Rembrandt. *Jahrbuch der Preußischen Kunstsammlungen* 50 (1929), 45-83.
Rembrandts Familienbild und seine Restaurierung. *Kunsthefte des Herzog Anton Ulrich-Museums* 7. Brunswick 1952.
Die Rembrandt-Ausstellung in Stockholm. *Kunstchronik* 9 (1956), 89-96.
Das Stuttgarter Selbstbildnis von Rembrandt. *Pantheon* 21 (1963), 65-90.
Rembrandt und Amsterdam. *Pantheon* 28 (1970), 240-243.

MÜNZ, L.
Rembrandts Altersstil und die Barockklassik. Ein Beitrag zum Verstehen des Altersstiles Rembrandts. *Jahrbuch der kunsthistorischen Sammlungen in Wien* N.S.9 (1935), 183-222.
The Original Shape of Rembrandt's "Shipbuilder and His Wife". *Burlington Magazine* 89 (1947), 253-254.
A Newly Discovered Late Rembrandt. *Burlington Magazine* 90 (1948), 64-67.
Rembrandt's Etchings If. London 1952.
Rembrandts Bild von Mutter und Vater. *Jahrbuch der kunsthistorischen Sammlungen in Wien* 50 (1953), 141-190.
Claudius Civilis, sein Antlitz und seine äußere Erscheinung. *Konsthistorisk Tidskrift* 25 (1956), 58-69.
Rembrandts Vorstellung vom Antlitz Christi. In: *Festschrift Kurt Bauch* s.l. [1962], 205-226.
Rembrandt. Cologne 1967.

MUTHER, R. *Rembrandt. Ein Künstlerleben.* Berlin 1904[2].

NAGLER, G.K. *Leben und Werke des Malers und Radirers Rembrandt van Ryn.* Munich 1843.

NEUMANN, C.
Rembrandt. Handzeichnungen. Munich 1918.
Aus der Werkstatt Rembrandts. *Heidelberger Kunstgeschichtliche Abhandlungen.* Ed. by C. NEUMANN and K. LOHMEYER. Vol. 3. Heidelberg 1918.
Rembrandt. Munich 1924[4].

NICOLAUS, K. Makro- und Infrarotuntersuchungen der Signatur von Rembrandts "Männlichem Bildnis" in Braunschweig. *Maltechnik-Restauro* 1 (1973), 40-43.

NIEMEYER, W. Rembrandts "Danae" ist Hagar. *Repertorium für Kunstwissenschaft* 52 (1931), 58-65.

NIEUWSTRATEN, J.
Recensie: Hans Martin Rotermund: Rembrandts Handzeichnungen und Radierungen zur Bibel. Lahr/Stuttgart 1963. *Oud Holland* 80 (1965), 60-63.
Haman, Rembrandt und Michelangelo. *Oud Holland* 82 (1967), 61-63.

NISSEN, M. Rembrandt und Honthorst. *Oud Holland* 32 (1914), 73-80.

NORDENFALK, C.
Some Facts about Rembrandt's "Claudius Civilis". *Konsthistorisk Tidskrift* 25 (1956), 71-93.
The Batavians' Oath of Allegiance'. Rembrandt's only Monumental Painting. Stockholm 1982.

NYSTAD, S. Joseph and Mary Find their Son among the Doctors. *Burlington Magazine* 117 (1975), 140-147.

OLDEWELT, W.F.H. *Amsterdamsche archiefvondsten.* Amsterdam 1942.

ORLERS, J.J. *Beschrijvinge der stad Leyden.* Leyden 1641.

ORNSTEIN VAN SLOTEN, E. Het huis waar Rembrandt woonde. *De Kroniek van het Rembrandthuis* 27 (1975), 4-7.

PANOFSKY, E.
Der gefesselte Eros: Zur Genealogie von Rembrandts Danae. *Oud Holland* 50 (1933), 193-217.
Rembrandt und das Judentum. *Jahrbuch der Hamburger Kunstsammlungen* 18 (1973), 75-108.

PERRY, B.A.S. *The Eastern Motif in the Works of Rembrandt.* Diss. Syracuse 1980.

PHILLIPS, C. The New Rembrandt. *The Burlington Magazine* 15 (1909), 71-72.

PIGLER, A. *Barockthemen. Eine Auswahl von Verzeichnissen zur Ikonographie des 17. und 18. Jahrhunderts* II. Budapest/Berlin 1956.

PILES, R. de *Abregé de la vie des peintres.* Paris 1715.

PINDER, W. *Rembrandts Selbstbildnisse.* Königstein 1950.

POINDEXTER, J. The Rembrandt Print Market. *Art News* 73/3 (1974), 60-62.

QUERIDO, A. De anatomie van de "Anatomische Les". *Oud Holland* 82 (1967), 128-136.

RRP (= Stichting Foundation Rembrandt Research Project)
A Corpus of Rembrandt Paintings door J. BRUYN, B. HAAK, S.H. LEVIE, P.J.J. van THIEL and E. van de WETERING. The Hague/Boston/London vol. I 1982. Vol. II 1986.

RAAF, K.H. de —
Rembrandt's portret van Jeremias de Decker. *Oud Holland* 30 (1912), 1-5.
Rembrandt's Christus en Maria Magdalena. *Oud Holland* 30 (1912), 6-8.

REGTEREN ALTENA, J.Q. van —
Rembrandt's Way to Emmaus. *Kunstmuseets årsskrift* 35/6 (1948/9), 1-26.
De zogenaamde voorstudie voor de "Anatomische Les van Dr. Deyman". *Oud Holland* 65 (1950), 171-178.
Het genetische probleem van de "Eendracht van Het Land". *Oud Holland* 67 (1952), 30-50; 59-67.
Het "Landschap van de Goudweger". *Oud Holland* 69 (1954), 1-17.
Quelques remarques sur Rembrandt et "La Ronde De Nuit". *Actes du 17ème congrès international d'histoire de l'art, Amsterdam 1952.* The Hague 1955, 405-420.
Rembrandt und die Amsterdamer Bühne. *Kunstchronik* 10 (1957), 135-137.
Recensie: K. Bauch. Rembrandt Gemälde. Berlin 1966. *Oud Holland* 82, (1967), 69-71.
Het pontje van Rembrandt. *Nederlands Kunsthistorisch Jaarboek* 23 (1972), 121-125.

REILING, N. (= SEGHERS, A.)
Jude und Judentum im Werk Rembrandts. Diss. Heidelberg 1924, Leipzig 1981.

REMBRANDT RESEARCH PROJECT, zie: RRP

REZNICEK, E.K.J. Opmerkingen bij Rembrandt. *Oud Holland* 91 (1977), 75-107.

RICCI, C. *Rembrandt in Italia.* Milan 1918.

ROBB, D.M. Rembrandt's "Portrait of a Young Jew". *Apollo* 191 (1978), 44-47.

ROBERTS, K. *Rembrandt: Master Drawings.* Oxford 1976.

ROBINSON, F.W.
Rembrandt's Influence in 18th-Century Venice. *Nederlands Kunsthistorisch Jaarboek* 18 (1967), 167-196.
A Note on the Visual Tradition of Balaam and his Ass. *Oud Holland* 84 (1969), 238-244.

ROOSEN-RUNGE, H. Zur Rembrandt-Forschung. Literaturbericht und Bibliographie. *Zeitschrift für Kunstgeschichte* 13 (1950), 140-151.

ROSAND, D. Rembrandt's "Presentation in the Temple". *Art News* 79/4 (1980), 136-137.

ROSENBERG, A. Rembrandt. Des Meisters Gemälde. *Klassiker der Kunst in Gesamtausgaben* II. Stuttgart/Leipzig 1906.

ROSENBERG, J.
Rembrandt's Technical Means and their Stylistic Significance. *Technical Studies in the Field of the Fine Arts* 8 (1940), 193-206.
Rembrandt I. Cambridge/Mass. 1948.
Notes on Old and Modern Drawings. Rembrandt and Mantegna. *Art Quarterly* 19 (1956), 153-161.
Die Rembrandt-Ausstellungen in Holland. *Kunstchronik* 9 (1956), 345-354.
Recensie: Otto Benesch. The Drawings of Rembrandt I-VI. London 1954-1957. *Art Bulletin* 38 (1956), 63-70; 41 (1959), 108-119.
Rembrandt. London 1964.
Rembrandt, Life and Work. New York 1980.

ROSENTHAL, S. Neue Deutungen von Historienbildern aus dem Rembrandtkreis. *Jahrbuch für Kunstwissenschaft* 5 (1928), 105-110.

ROTERMUND, H.M.
Rembrandt und die religiösen Laienbewegungen in den Niederlanden seiner Zeit. *Nederlands Kunsthistorisch Jaarboek* 4 (1952/53), 104-192.
Wandlungen des Christus-Typus bei Rembrandt. *Wallraf-Richartz-Jahrbuch* 18 (1956), 197-237.
Rembrandts Bibel. *Nederlands Kunsthistorisch Jaarboek* 8 (1957), 123-150.
Rembrandts Handzeichnungen und Radierungen zur Bibel. Lahr/Stuttgart 1963.

ROUIR, E. *Europäische Graphik im 17. Jahrhundert: Rembrandt und seine Zeitgenossen.* Stuttgart 1974.

ROUSSEAU, T. Aristotle Contemplating the Bust of Homer. *Metropolitan Museum of Art Bulletin* 20 (1961/62), 149-156.

ROVINSKI, D. *L'œuvre gravé de Rembrandt.* St. Petersburg 1890, Supplement 1914.

RUFFO, V. Galleria Ruffo nel secolo XVII in Messina. *Bollettino d'Arte* 10 (1916), 21-192.

RUSSELL, M. The Iconography of Rembrandt's "Rape of Ganymede". *Simiolus* 9/1 (1977), 5-18.

RYCKEVORSEL, J.L.A.A.M. van —
Rembrandt en de traditie. Rotterdam 1932.
The recovered "Juno" of Rembrandt. *Oud Holland* 53 (1936), 271-274.

SALOMON, H. *Catalogo completo dell'opera grafica di Rembrandt* I. Milan 1972.

SANDRART, J. von —
Teutsche Academie der Edlen Bau-, Bild- und Mahlerey-Künste. Nuremberg 1675/79.
New edition commented by A.R. PELZER. Munich 1925.

SASS, E.K. Comments on Rembrandt's Passion Paintings and Constantijn Huygens's Iconography. *Det Kongelige Danske Videnskabernes Selskab. Historisk-Filosofiske Skrifter* 5/3. Kopenhagen 1971.

SAXL. F.
Eine unbekannte Entlehnung Rembrandts. *Zeitschrift für bildende Kunst* N.S. 19 (1908), 224.
Rembrandt und Italien. *Oud Holland* 41 (1923/24), 145-160.
Rembrandt's "Sacrifice of Manoah". London 1939.
Rembrandt and Classical Antiquity. In: *Lectures.* London 1957.

SCHATBORN, P.
De iconografie bij Rembrandt. *De Kroniek van het Rembrandthuis* 24 (1970), 29-30.
Twee Aanbiddingen van de Koningen. *De Kroniek van het Rembrandthuis* 26/3 (1972), 98-106. Review: Otto Benesch. The Drawings of Rembrandt: Complete Edition. *Simiolus* 8 (1974/75), 34-39.
Over Rembrandt en kinderen. *De Kroniek van het Rembrandthuis* 27 (1975), 8-19.
De geschiedenis van een tekening. *De Kroniek van het Rembrandthuis* 28/1 (1976), 19-27.
Beesten nae't leven. *De Kroniek van het Rembrandthuis* 29/2 (1977), 3-31.
Figuurstudies, Nederlandse tekeningen uit de 17de eeuw. The Hague 1981.
Tekeningen van Rembrandt, zijn onbekende leerlingen en navolgers. *Catalogus van de Nederlandse Tekeningen in het Rijksprentenkabinet, Rijksmuseum, Amsterdam* IV. The Hague 1985.

SCHEIDEGG, W. *Rembrandt und seine Werke in der Dresdner Galerie.* Dresden 1958.

SCHELLER, R.W.
Rembrandt's Reputatie van Houbraken tot Scheltema. *Nederlands Kunsthistorisch Jaarboek* 12 (1961), 81-118.
Rembrandt en de encyclopedische verzameling. *Oud Holland* 84 (1969), 81-147.

SCHENDEL, A. van —
Some Comments on the Cleaning of the "Nightwatch". *Museum* 3 (1950), 220-222.
De schimmen van de "Staalmeesters". *Oud Holland* 71 (1956), 1-23.
Het portret van Constantijn Huygens door Jan Lievens. *Bulletin van het Rijksmuseum* 11 (1963), 5-10.

SCHENDEL, A. van & H.H. MERTENS
De restauraties van Rembrandt's "Nachtwacht". *Oud Holland* 62 (1947), 1-52.

SCHEPELERN, H.D. Engelen forlader Tobias. Omkring Rembrandts Maleri fra 1637. In: *En bog om kunst til Else Kai Sass.* S.l., s.d., 193-206.

SCHMID, M. Das Hundertguldenblatt. *Kunstchronik* N.S. 6 (1894-95), 161-165.

SCHMIDT-DEGENER, F.
Rembrandt. Een beschrijving van zijn leven en zijn werk. *Wereld Bibliotheek* 28/29. Amsterdam 1906.
Een voorstudie voor de Nachtwacht: De Eendracht van het Land. *Onze Kunst* 21 (1912), 1-20.
Rembrandt's portret van Gerard de Lairesse. *Onze Kunst* 23 (1913), 117-129.
Portretten door Rembrandt. *Oud Holland* 32 (1914), 217-224.
Het genetische probleem van de "Nachtwacht". *Onze Kunst* 26 (1914), 1-17; 29 (1916), 61-84; 30 (1916), 29-56; 31 (1917), 1-32.
De ringkraag van Ruytenburch. *Onze Kunst* 33 (1918), 91-94.
Rembrandt en Vondel. *De Gids* 83 (1919), 222-275.
Rembrandt und der holländische Barock. *Studien der Bibliothek Warburg,* Ed. by F. SAXL, 9. Leipzig/Berlin 1928.
Tentoonstellingscatalogus: Rembrandt. Rijksmuseum Amsterdam 1935.
Rembrandt's "Eendracht van Het Land" opnieuw beschouwd. *Maandblad voor beeldende kunst* 18 (1941), 161-172.
Rembrandt's "Clementie van Keizer Titus". *Oud Holland* 58 (1941), 106-111.
Compositie-problemen in verband met Rembrandt's Schutteroptocht. *Verhandelingen der Nederlandsche Akademie van Wetenschappen, Afdeeling letterkunde* N.S. 47/1, Amsterdam 1943².
Verzamelde studiën en essays II, Rembrandt. Amsterdam 1950.

SCHNEIDER, H.
Rembrandt in Italien. *Kunstchronik und Kunstmarkt* 54 (1918), 69-73.
Jan Lievens. Sein Leben und seine Werke. Haarlem 1932. Photographical Reprint with a suppelement by R.E.O. EKKART, Amsterdam 1973.

SCHNITZLER, J.H. *Notice sur les principaux tableaux du Musée Impérial de l'Ermitage à Saint-Pétersbourg.* St.-Petersburg/Berlin 1828.

SCHÖNE, W.
Rembrandt. *Berühmte Gemälde alter Meister.* [Hamburg 1964], 4-34.

Rembrandts "Mann mit dem Goldhelm". *Jahrbuch der Akademie der Wissenschaften in Göttingen 1972* (1973), 33-99.

SCHRADE, H. Rembrandts "Anatomie des Dr. Tulp". *Das Werk des Künstlers* 1 (1939/40), 60-100.

SCHREY, R. Zu Rembrandt. *Kunstchronik* N.F. 18 (1906-07), 84-86.

SCHUBRING, P. Rembrandt und das Alte Testament. *Christliches Kunstblatt* 48 (1906), 227-234.

SCHULTE NORDHOLT, H. Rembrandt: "Simeon in de Tempel". *Openbaar kunstbezit* 4 (1960), No. 40.

SCHUPBACH, W. The Paradox of Rembrandt's "Anatomy of Dr. Tulp". *Medical History,* Supplement 2, London 1982.

SCHUT, P.H. *Toneel ofte Vertooch der Bybelsche Historien, Cierlyck in 't Koper gemaeckt door Pieter H. Schut.* Amsterdam (Nicolaes Visscher) 1659.

SCHWARTZ, G.
Rembrandt: all the Etchings Reproduced in True Size. Maarssen 1977.
Rembrandt: "Connoisseurship" et érudition. *Revue de l'art* 42 (1978), 100-106.
Rembrandt; zijn leven, zijn schilderijen. Maarssen 1984.

SCIOLLA, G.C. *Rembrandt: disegni scelti e annotati.* Florence 1976.

SEGHERS, A., zie REILING, N. *Jude und Judentum im Werk Rembrandts.* Leipzig 1981.

SEIDLITZ, W. von —
Kritisches Verzeichnis der Radierungen Rembrandts. Leipzig 1895.
Die Radierungen Rembrandts. Leipzig 1922.

SIMMEL, G. *Rembrandt, ein kunstphilosophischer Versuch.* Leipzig 1919².

SIMSON, O. von & J. KELCH (Hrsg.) *Neue Beiträge zur Rembrandt-Forschung.* Berlin 1973.

SINGER, H.W. Rembrandt. Des Meisters Radierungen. *Klassiker der Kunst* 8. Stuttgart/Leipzig 1906.

SIX, J.
De Homerus van Rembrandt. *Oud Holland* 15 (1897), 1-10.
Rembrandt en Lastman. *Bulletin uitgegeven door den Nederlandschen Oudheidkundigen Bond* 8 (1907), 141-146; 148.
Gersaints lijst van Rembrandts prenten. *Oud Holland* 27 (1909), 65-110.

SIX, J.
Jan Six aan het venster. *De Kroniek van het Rembrandthuis* 23 (1969), 34-52.

SLATKES, L.J.
Review: C. White and K.G. Boon. Rembrandt's Etchings. Rembrandt as an Etcher. *Art Quarterly* 36 (1973), 250-261.
Rembrandt's Elephant. *Simiolus* 11 (1980), 7-13.
Rembrandt and Persia. New York 1983.

SLIVE, S.
Rembrandt and His Critics, 1630-1730. The Hague 1953.
The Young Rembrandt. *Allen Memorial Art Museum Bulletin* 20 (1962), 120-149.
Rembrandt's "Self-Portrait in a Studio". *The Burlington Magazine* 106 (1964), 483-486.
Drawings of Rembrandt. With a Selection of Drawings by His Pupils and Followers If. New York 1965.
An Unpublished "Head of Christ" by Rembrandt. *Art Bulletin* 47 (1965), 407-417.
Rembrandt at Harvard. *Apollo* 107/196 (1978), 452-463.

SMIDT-DÖRRENBERG, I. *David und Saul, Variationen über ein Thema von Rembrandt.* Vienna 1969.

SMITH, J. *A catalogue raisonné of the Works of the Most Eminent Dutch, Flemish and French Painters* VII. *Rembrandt van Rhyn.* London 1836.

SMITH, D.R.
The Dutch Double and Pair Portrait: Studies in the Imagery of Marriage in the Seventeenth Century. Diss. Columbia University 1978.
Rembrandt's Early Double Portraits and the Dutch Conversation Piece. *Art Bulletin* 64 (1982), 259-288.

SOMOF, A. *Eremitage Impérial. Catalogue de la galerie des tableaux. II: Ecoles néerlandaises et école allemande.* St.-Petersburg 1895.

SONNENBURG, H. von —
Maltechnische Gesichtspunkte zur Rembrandtforschung. *Maltechnik* 82 (1976), 9-24.
Rembrandts "Segen Jakobs". *Maltechnik* 84 (1978), 217-241.

STARING, A. Vraagstukken der Oranje-Iconographie. III: Conterfeitte Rembrandt Frederik Hendrick en Amalia? *Oud Holland* 68 (1953), 12-24.

STECHOW, W.
Römische Gerichtsdarstellungen von Rembrandt und Bol. *Oud Holland* 46 (1929), 134-139.
Rembrandts Darstellungen der Kreuzabnahme. *Jahrbuch der Preußischen Kunstsammlungen* 50 (1929), 217-232.
Rembrandts Darstellungen des Emmausmahles. *Zeitschrift für Kunstgeschichte* 3 (1934), 329-341.
Rembrandt's "Presentation in the Dark Manner". *Print Collectors Quarterly* 27 (1940), 365-379.
The Myth of Philemon and Baucis in Art. *Journal of the Warburg and Courtauld Institutes* 4 (1940/41), 103-113.
Rembrandt and Titian. *Art Quarterly* 5 (1942), 135-146.
"Jacob Blessing the Sons of Joseph", from Early Christian Times to Rembrandt. *Gazette des Beaux-Arts* 85/1 (1943), 193-208.
Rembrandt-Democritus. *Art Quarterly* 7 (1944), 233-238.
Dutch Landscape Painting of the 17th Century. London 1966.
"Jacob Blessing the Sons of Joseph", from Rembrandt to Cornelius. *Festschrift Ulrich Middeldorf.* Berlin 1968, 460-465.
Rembrandt's Representations of the "Raising of Lazarus". *Bulletin of the Los Angeles County Museum of Art* 19/2 (1973), 7-11.
The Crisis in Rembrandt Research. In: *Essays in Memory of Milton S. Fox.* New York 1975, 235-244

STRAUSS, W. & M. van der MEULEN *The Rembrandt Documents.* New York 1979.

SULLIVAN, S.A. Rembrandt's "Self-Portrait with a Dead Bittern". *The Art Bulletin* 62 (1980), 236-243.

SUMOWSKI, W.
Eine Anmerkung zu Rembrandts Gastmahl des Belsazar. *Oud Holland* 71 (1956), 233.
Einige frühe Entlehnungen Rembrandts. *Oud Holland* 71 (1956), 109-113.
Nachträge zum Rembrandtjahr 1956. *Wissenschaftliche Zeitschrift der Humboldt-Universität zu Berlin, Gesellschafts- und sprachwissenschaftliche Reihe* 7 (1957-58), 223-278.
Bemerkungen zu Otto Beneschs Corpus der Rembrandt-Zeichnungen I, *Wissenschaftliche Zeitschrift der Humboldt-Universität zu Berlin, Gesellschafts- und sprachwissenschaftliche Reihe* 6 (1956-57), 255-266.
Bemerkungen zu Otto Beneschs Corpus der Rembrandtzeichnungen II. Bad Pyrmont 1961.
Das Leben Jesu in Bildern. Handzeichnungen. Radierungen von Rembrandt. Witten/Berlin 1963.
Rembrandt 1669/1969. Zur Amsterdamer Ausstellung. *Pantheon* 271 (1969), 464-469.
Rembrandtzeichnungen. *Pantheon* 29 (1971), 125-138.
Gemälde der Rembrandt-Schüler I-IV, Landau (Pfalz) 1983ff.
Drawings of the Rembrandt School Iff. Edited and translated by W.L. STRAUSS. New York 1979ff.

THIEL, P.J.J van — Beschadiging en herstel van Rembrandts "Nachtwacht". *Bulletin van het Rijksmuseum* 24/1-2 (1976), 4-13.

THIELE, R. *Rembrandt. Eine Einführung in Leben und Werk.* Leipzig 1982.

TIETZE, H. Rembrandt. Die Judenbraut. *Meisterwerke der Kunst in Holland.* Vienna 1922.

TOLNAY, C. de —
The Syndics of the Draper's Guild by Rembrandt. An Interpretation. *Gazette des Beaux-Arts* 85, 6ᵉ. série 23 (1943), 31-38.
A Note on the "Staalmeesters". *Oud Holland* 73 (1958), 85-86.

TRIVAS, N.S. New Light on Rembrandt's so-called "Hendrickje" at Edinburgh. *The Burlington Magazine* 70 (1937), 252.

TÜMPEL, A.
The Pre-Rembrandtists. Exhibition catalogue Sacramento, 1974.
Claes Cornelisz. Moeyaert. *Oud Holland* 89 (1974), 1-163, 245-290.
"Ruth erklärt Naemi die Treue" von Pieter Lastman. Zur Genese eines typischen Barockthemas. *Niederdeutsche Beiträge zur Kunstgeschichte* 17 (1978), 87-101.

TÜMPEL, C.
Ikonographische Beiträge zu Rembrandt. *Kunstchronik* 19 (1966), 300-302.
Katalog zur Geschichte der Rembrandtforschung. Hamburg 1967.
Ikonographische Beiträge zu Rembrandt I und II. *Jahrbuch der Hamburger Kunstsammlungen* 13 (1968), 95-126; 16 (1971), 20-38.
Studien zur Ikonographie der Historien Rembrandts. Diss. Hamburg 1968; in: *Nederlands Kunsthistorisch Jaarboek* 20 (1969), 107-198.
Rembrandt legt die Bibel aus. Berlin 1970.
Iconografische verklaring van de voorstelling op twee tekeningen van Rembrandt. *De Kroniek van het Rembrandthuis* 26/3 (1972), 67-75.
Beobachtungen zur "Nachtwache". In: *Neue Beiträge zur Rembrandtforschung.* Ed. by O. von SIMSON and J. KELCH. Berlin 1973, 162-175.
Rembrandt, *De grote Meesters.* Amsterdam 1975.
Rembrandt mit Selbstzeugnissen und Bilddokumenten, *Rowohlts Monographien* 251, ed. by K. KUSENBERG, Reinbek bei Hamburg 1977, 1984⁴.
Die Ikonographie der Amsterdamer Historienmalerei in der ersten Hälfte des 17. Jahrhunderts und die Reformation. Litteratura Laicorum. Beiträge zur christlichen Kunst. *Vestigia Bibliae. Jahrbuch des Deutschen Bibel-Archives Hamburg* 2 (1980), 127-158.
Beweeglijke historie. *Kunstschrift. Openbaar Kunstbezit* 25/2 (1981), 64-70.
Rembrandt, die Bildtradition und der Text. In: *Ars Auro Prior. Studia Ioanni Bialostocki Sexagenario Dicata.* Warsaw 1981, 429-434.
Die Reformation und die Kunst der Niederlande. In: *Luther und die Folgen für die Kunst.* Ausstellungskatalog Hamburger Kunsthalle. Ed. by W. HOFMANN. Munich 1983, 309-321.
Die Rezeption der Jüdischen Altertümer des Flavius Josephus in den holländischen Historiendarstellungen des 16. und 17. Jahrhunderts. In: H. VEKEMAN and J. MÜLLER HOFSTEDE, *Wort und Bild in der niederländischen Kunst und Literatur des 16. und 17. Jahrhunderts.* Erftstadt 1984, 173-204.
Bild und Text: Zur Rezeption antiker Autoren in der europäischen Kunst der Neuzeit (Livius, Valerius Maximus). In: *Forma et subtilitas. Festschrift für Wolfgang Schöne.* Ed. by W. SCHLINK and M. SPERLICH. Berlin/New York 1986, 198-218.

UNVERFEHRT, G. *Rembrandt als Radierer. Die Bestände der Universitäts-Kunstsammlung Göttingen.* Hannover 1982.

VALENTINER, W.R.
Rembrandt und seine Umgebung. *Zur Kunstgeschichte des Auslands.* Vol. 29. Strasbourg 1905.
Rembrandt auf der Lateinschule. *Jahrbuch der Preußischen Kunstsammlungen* 27 (1906), 118-128.
Rembrandt. Des Meisters Gemälde. *Klassiker der Kunst.*

Stuttgart/Leipzig [1908].
Rembrandts Gemälde. *Klassiker der Kunst.* Stuttgart/Berlin [1909].
Die vier Evangelisten Rembrandts. *Kunstchronik und Kunstmarkt* N.S. 32 (1920/21), 219-222.
Wiedergefundene Gemälde. *Klassiker der Kunst.* Stuttgart/Berlin 1921.
Deutung der Judenbraut. *Kunst und Künstler* 22 (1923-24), 17-22.
Komödiantendarstellungen Rembrandts. *Zeitschrift für bildende Kunst* N.S. 59 (1925/26), 265-277.
Two Early Self-Portraits by Rembrandt. *Art in America* 14 (1926), 116-119.
Rediscovered Rembrandt Paintings. *The Burlington Magazine* 57 (1930), 259-271.
A Bust of Christ by Rembrandt. *Bulletin of the Detroit Institute of Arts of the City of Detroit* 12 (1930), 2-3.
Rembrandt Paintings in America. New York 1931.
Rembrandt. Des Meisters Handzeichnungen. *Klassiker der Kunst in Gesamtausgaben* XXXI f. I: Stuttgart/Berlin/Leipzig [1925], II: Stuttgart/Berlin 1934.
Rembrandt's Conception of Historical Portraiture. *Art Quarterly* 11 (1948), 117-135.
Rembrandt's "Landscape with a Country House". *Art Quarterly* 14 (1951), 341-347.
Exhibition catalogue: Rembrandt and His Pupils. The North Carolina Museum of Art. Raleigh 1956.
The Rembrandt Exhibitions in Holland. *The Art Quarterly* 19 (1956), 390-404.
Noch einmal "Die Judenbraut". In: *Festschrift Kurt Bauch* s.l. [1957], 227-237.

VELS HEIJN, A.A.E.
Rembrandt 1606-1669. Amsterdam 1969.
Eerbetoon aan Rembrandt 1852-1956. *Spiegel Historiael* 4 (1969), 450-457.

VETH, J.
Rembrandt's wijze van adapteeren. *Onze Kunst* 4 (1905), 79-90.
Rembrandt's vroegste werk. *Onze Kunst* 4 (1905), 133-148.
Rembrandts zoogenaamde Jodenbruid uit de kollektie van der Hoop. *Oud Holland* 24 (1906), 41-44.
Rembrandt's leven en kunst. Amsterdam 1941.

VETTER, E. Der verlorene Sohn. *Lukas Bücherei zur christlichen Ikonographie* 7. Düsseldorf 1955.

VIKTURINA, M.P. & A.L. DUB & K.S. EGORDVA Issledovanie kartin Rembrandta. *Pamjatniki kultury. Novye otkrytija* URSS 1975, 388-414.

VIS, D. *Rembrandt en Geertje Dircx.* Haarlem 1965.

VISSER 'T HOOFT, W.A. *Rembrandts Weg zum Evangelium.* Zurich 1955.

VOGEL KÖHN, D. *Rembrandts Kinderzeichnungen.* Diss. Würzburg 1974, Cologne 1981.

VOORDE, G. van de — De radiografie van Rembrandts "Nachtwacht". *Bulletin van het Rijksmuseum* 24/1-2 (1976), 52-67.

VOSMAER, C. *Rembrandt. Sa vie et ses œuvres.* The Hague 1877.

VRIES, A.B. de — *Rembrandt.* Cologne [1956].

VRIES, A.B. de & M. TÓTH-UBBENS & W. FROENTJES *Rembrandt in the Mauritshuis: an Interdisciplinary Study.* Alphen aan de Rijn 1978.

VRIES, J. de — Archiefsprokkelingen. Een Rembrandt-Acte uit 1667. *Oud Holland* 71 (1956), 40-43.

WAAL, H. van de —
"Hagar in de Woestijn" door Rembrandt en zijn School. *Nederlands Kunsthistorisch Jaarboek* 1 (1947), 145-159.
Rembrandt 1956. *Museum* 61 (1956), 193-209.
The Mood of "The Staalmeesters". *Oud Holland* 73 (1958), 86-89.
Rembrandt: "Landschap met Stenen Brug". *Openbaar Kunstbezit* 2 (1958), No. 26.
Rembrandt: "Portret van zijn Zoon Titus". *Openbaar Kunstbezit* 9 (1965), No. 9.
Light and Dark: Rembrandt and Chiaroscuro. *Delta* 12/2 (1969), 74-88.
Rembrandt and the Feast of Purim. *Oud Holland* 84 (1969), 199-223.
Steps towards Rembrandt: Collected Articles 1937-1972. Ed. R.H. FUCHS. Amsterdam/London 1974.

WEGNER, W. Symposium und Ausstellung "Rembrandt after Three Hundred Years in Chicago". *Kunstchronik* 22 (1970), 29-34; 41-44.

WEHLTE, K. Gemäldeuntersuchung mit Röntgenstrahlen. *Verhandlungen der deutschen Röntgengesellschaft* 25 (1932), 12-18.

WEISBACH, W.
Rembrandt. Berlin 1926.
Rembrandt's Allegorical Subjects I. *Apollo* 4 (1926), 47-52; 101-104.
Review: W.R. Valentiner. Rembrandt. Des Meisters Handzeichnungen I. Klassiker der Kunst in Gesamtausgaben 31. Stuttgart/Berlin/Leipzig [1925]. *Jahrbuch für Kunstwissenschaft* 5 (1928), 53-56.

WETERING, E. van de —
De jonge Rembrandt aan het werk. *Oud Holland* 91 (1977), 27-65.
Studies in the workshop practice of the early Rembrandt, Diss. Amsterdam 1986.

WETERING, E. van de & C.M. GROEN & J.A. MOSK. Beknopt verslag van de resultaten van het technisch onderzoek van Rembrandts "Nachtwacht". *Bulletin van het Rijksmuseum* 24/1-2 (1976), 68-98.

WESSEM, J. van — *Rembrandt als leermeester.* Exhibition catalogue. Leyden 1956.

WHEELOCK, A.K. De geschiedenis en bekoring van De Molen. *De Kroniek van het Rembrandthuis* 29/1 (1977), 20-32; 31/1 (1979), 9.

WHITE, C.
Rembrandt Exhibitions in Holland. *The Burlington Magazine* 98 (1956), 321-324.
Rembrandt. Two Recently Discovered Drawings. *The Burlington Magazine* 103 (1961), 278-279.
Did Rembrandt ever visit England? *Apollo* 76 (1962), 177-184.
Rembrandt and his World. London 1964.
Rembrandt as an Etcher; A Study of the Artist at Work I, II. London 1969.
A Rembrandt Copy after a Titian Landscape. *Master Drawings* 13/4 (1975), 375-379.

WIJNBEEK, D.
De Nachtwacht. De historie van een meesterwerk. Amsterdam 1944.

WIJNMAN, H.F.
Een drietal portretten van Rembrandt. *Jaarboek Amstelodamum* 31 (1934), 81-96.
Rembrandt en Hendrick Uylenburgh te Amsterdam. *Maandblad Amstelodamum* 43 (1956), 94-103.
Rembrandts portretten van Joannes Elison en zijn vrouw Maria Bockenolle naar Amerika verkocht. *Maandblad Amstelodamum* 44 (1957), 65-72.
Een episode uit het leven van Rembrandt: De geschiedenis van Geertje Dircx. *Jaarboek Amstelodamum* 60 (1968), 103-104.
Rembrandt en Saskia wisselen trouwbeloften. *Maandblad Amstelodamum* 56 (1969), 156.

WINKLER, F. Echt, falsch, verfälscht. Resumée des Vortrages auf der vom Zentralinstitut für Kunstgeschichte in München veranstalteten Arbeitstagung "Die Rembrandtforschung im Lichte der Ausstellungen des Jahres 1956". *Kunstchronik* 10 (1957), 141-144, 144-147.

WINTERNITZ, E. Rembrandt's "Christ Presented to the People" — 1655. A Meditation on Justice and Collective Guilt. *Oud Holland* 84 (1969), 177-198.

WISCHNITZER, R. Rembrandt, Callot, and Tobias Stimmer. *Art Bulletin* 39 (1957), 224-230.

WOLTERS, C. *Die Bedeutung der Gemäldedurchleuchtung mit Röntgenstrahlen für die Kunstgeschichte.* Frankfurt 1938.

WRIGHT, C. *Rembrandt and his Art.* London 1975.

WURZBACH, A. von — *Niederländisches Künstler-Lexikon.* Vienna 1906-10; supplement, Vienna 1911.

WUSTMANN, R. Die Josephgeschichte bei Vondel und Rembrandt. *Kunstchronik* N.S. 18 (1906-07), 81-84.

ZALUSKI, A. Le paysage avec le bon samaritain de Rembrandt. *Biuletyn historii sztuki* 18 (1956), 370-383.

ZWARTS, J.
Haham Saul Levy Monteyra en zijn portret door Rembrandt. *Oud Holland* 43 (1926), 1-17.
The Significance of Rembrandt's "The Jewish Bride". Amersfoort 1929.
Het echtpaar van "Het Joodsche Bruidje" van Rembrandt. *Onze Kunst* 46 (1929), 11-42.

ZYGULSKI, Z. Rembrandt's "Lisowczyk": A study of costume and weapons. *Bulletin du musée national de Varsovie* 6 (1965), 43-67.

ACKNOWLEDGEMENTS

The author wishes to thank all persons who have contributed by their co-operation and sympathy to the realisation of this book:

Dr. Alfred and Isabel Bader (Milwaukee, Wisconsin); Mrs. Katharine Baetjer (New York); P. M. Bardi (Sao Paulo); J. Benington (Glasgow); Mr. M.E. Bishop (London); Dr. Paul Boerlin (Basel); Dr. Hans-Olof Boström (Göteborg); Mr. Christopher Brown (London); Prof. Joos Bruyn (Amsterdam); Cynthia Burt (Los Angeles); Sara Campbell (Pasadena); Görel Cavalli-Björkman (Stockholm); Herrn Daan Cevat (St. Martin's, Guernsey); Lord Chamberlain (London); Janice L. Collins (Washington, D.C.); Herrn Hans Max Cramer (Den Haag); Herrn Peter Day (Chatsworth); Dr. Günther Dankl (Innsbrück); Dorota Dec (Krakow); Dr. Klaus Demus (Wien); Cecilia M. Esposito (Glenns Falls, New York); Mr. and Mrs. Richard Feigen (New York); M. Jacques Foucart (Paris); Dr. Jeroen Giltaij (Rotterdam); Mrs. Frances Gillespie (Dublin); Cheryl Harvey (San Diego); Prof. Egbert Haverkamp Begemann (New York); Prof. Werner Hofmann (Hamburg); Mr. Martin Hopkinson (Glasgow); Mr. Arthur A. Houghton Jr. (Queenstown, Maryland); Frau Dr. Annemarie Hübner (Hamburg); Monsieur B. Huin (Epinal); Rosamund Hurrel (Minneapolis); John Ingamells (London); Philip Jago (Melbourne); David Torbet Johnson (Cincinnati, Ohio); Dr. Roswitha Juffinger (Salzburg); Dr. Jan Kelch (Berlin); Dr. Christian Klemm (Zürich); Dr. Rüdiger Klessmann (Braunschweig); Daniel L. Knerr (Rochester, New York); Olaf Koester (Kopenhagen); Herrn Vladimir Korolev, Brüssel; Jiri Kotouc (Prag); Dr. Boris Kutkov, Aurora Verlag, Leningrad; Dr. Anette Kruszynski (Stuttgart); Dr. Juy Kusnetzow † (Leningrad); Mary Kuzniar (Chicago); Lionel Lambourne (London); Daphna Lapidot (Jeruzalem); Dr. Helmuth R. Leppien (Hamburg); Dr. Walter Liedtke (New York); Dr Irena Linnik (Leningrad); Iva Lisikewyck (Detroit); Dr. Kurt Löcher (Nürnberg); Dr. Dietmar Lüdke (Karlsruhe); Hugh Macandrew (Edinburgh); Dr. Maek-Gérard (Frankfurt); Herrn Dr. Mielke (Berlin); Dr. Anneliese Mayer-Meintschel (Dresden); Herrn Dr. Mielke (Berlin); Edward Morris (Liverpool); Jacques Nicourt (Tours); Miss Gil Nock (London); S. Nystad (Den Haag); Frau Eva Ornstein van Slooten (Amsterdam); Dr. Lynn Federle Orr (San Francisco); Mrs. Phoebe Peebles (Cambridge, Massachusetts); M. Pierre Rosenberg (Paris); Mr. Willem M.J. Russel (Amsterdam); Fürst zu Salm-Salm (Anholt); Elsie Y. Sakuma (Kansas City, Missouri); Dr. Eckart Schaar (Hamburg); Peter Schatborn (Amsterdam); Dr. Bernhard Schnackenburg (Kassel); Prof. Dr. Wolfgang Schöne (Hamburg); C.J.F. van Schooten (Utrecht); Herrn Dr. Albert Schug (Köln); Gary Schwartz (Maarssen); Mr. Stephen Sommerville (London); Maria Helena Soares Costa (Lissabon); Carl Strehlke (Philadelphia); Dr. Margret Stuffmann (Frankfurt); Marja Supinen (Helsinki); Dr. V. Suslow (Leningrad); Dr. Peter C. Sutton (Boston); Dr. Georg Syamken (Hamburg); Rosalba Tardito (Mailand); Dr. P.J.J. van Thiel (Amsterdam); Earl C. Townsend Jr. (Indianapolis); Dr. Michail Yu. Treister (Moskau); Dr. Renate Trnek (Wien); Dr. Meinolf Trudzinski (Hannover); Mrs. Ann Tzeutschler Lurie (Cleveland); Pascal de La Vaissiere (Paris); Prof. Dr. Martin Warnke; G.A. Waterfield MA (London); Miss Lavinia Wellicome (Woburn Abbey); The Duke of Westminster DL; Patricia J. Whitesides (Toledo, Ohio); Herrn M.L. Wurfbain (Leiden).

PHOTOGRAPHIC ACKNOWLEDGEMENTS

ALLSCHWIL, Colorphoto Hinz SWB — AMSTERDAM, Het Rembrandthuis — AMSTERDAM, Rijksdienst Beeldende Kunst — AMSTERDAM, Rijksmuseum-Stichting — AMSTERDAM, Mr Willem J.J. Russell — AMSTERDAM, Collectie Six — ATAMI, Japan, MOA Museum — BARCELONA, Ampliaciones Reproducciones MAS — BASEL, Kunstmuseum/ Öffentliche Kunstsammlung — BERLIN, Jörg P. Anders — BERLIN, Bildarchiv Preussischer Kulturbesitz — BOSTON, Museum of Fine Arts — BOSTON, The Isabella Stewart Gardner Museum — BRAUNSCHWEIG, Herzog Anton Ulrich-Museum — BRUGGE, Hugo Maertens fotograaf — BRUSSEL, Patrimonium van de Koninklijke Musea voor Schone Kunsten van België — BRUSSEL, Jean Jacques Rousseau — CAMBRIDGE, Fogg Art Museum — CARDIFF, National Museum of Wales — CHESTER, By kind permission of His Grace, The Duke of Westminster DL — CHICAGO, The Art Institute of Chicago — CINCINNATI, The Taft Museum — CLEVELAND, The Cleveland Museum of Art — COLUMBUS, Ohio, Columbus Museum of Art (Museum Purchase, Derby Fund) — COPENHAGEN, The Royal Museum of Fine Arts — DEN HAAG, Hans M. Cramer — DEN HAAG, Stichting Johan Maurits Van Nassau, Mauritshuis — DETROIT, Detroit Institute of Arts Founders Society Purchase — CHATSWORTH, Devonshire Collection (Reproduced by permission of the Chatsworth Trustees) — DRESDEN, Staatliche Kunstsammlungen Dresden — DUBLIN, The National Gallery of Ireland — DUMFRIESSHIRE, Collection of The Duke of Buccleuch and Queensberry, K.T., at Drumlanrig Castle — EDINBURGH, National Gallery of Scotland — EDINBURGH, Antonia Reeve Photography — EDINBURGH, South Queensferry, The Earl of Rosebery, Dalmeny House — EPINAL, Musée Départemental des Vosges et Musée International de l'Imagerie — EPINAL, Photo C. Pernot — FARINGDON, The Faringdon Collection Trust — FORT WORTH, Texas, Kimbell Art Museum — HEADINGTON, Thomas Photos — FIRENZE, Scala Instituto Fotografico Editoriale S.p.A. — FRANKFURT AM MAIN, Kurt Haase Fotograf — FRANKFURT AM MAIN, Städelsches Kunstinstitut und Städtische Galerie — GLASGOW, Glasgow Museums & Art Galleries — GLASGOW, Hunterian Art Gallery — GÖTEBORG, Göteborgs Konstmuseum — GUERNSEY, Daan Cevat M.B.E. — HAARLEM, Teylers Museum — HAMBURG, Fotostudios Ralph Kleinhempel — HAMBURG, Hamburger Kunsthalle — HAMBURG, Kunstbildarchiv Aline Lenz — HANNOVER, Niedersächsisches Landesmuseum Hannover — HELSINKI, Sinebrychoff Art Museum — HORNBAEK, Hans Petersen Photographer — INDIANAPOLIS, Earl C. Townsend jr. — INNSBRUCK, Tiroler Landesmuseum Ferdinandeum — ISSELBURG-ANHOLT, Museum Wasserburg Anholt — JERUSALEM, Israel Museum — KANSAS CITY, The Nelson-Atkins Museum of Art — KARLSRUHE, Staatliche Kunsthalle Karlsruhe — KASSEL, Staatliche Kunstsammlungen Kassel — KÖLN, Museum der Stadt Köln — KRAKOW, Museum Narodowo Krakowie — KREFELD, Kaiser Wilhelm Museum Krefeld — LEIDEN, Gemeentearchief — LEIDEN, Museum de Lakenhal — LEIPZIG-MÖLKAU, Gerhard Reinhold Farbenfotografie — LENINGRAD, Aurora Art Publishers — LENINGRAD, Ermitage — LISBOA, Calouste Gulbenkian Foundation — LIVERPOOL, Walker Art Gallery — LONDON, The British Museum — LONDON, Sally Chappell Photographer — LONDON, Courtauld Institute of Art — LONDON, Dulwich Picture Gallery — LONDON, Greater London Council — LONDON, National Gallery — LONDON, Photographic Records Limited — LONDON, Victoria & Albert Museum — LONDON, The Wallace Collection — LOS ANGELES, Los Angeles County Museum of Art — LOS ANGELES, The Armand Hammer Foundation — LOUISVILLE, The JB Speed Art Museum — LYON, Studio Bernard Lontin — LYON, Musée des Beaux-Arts — MADRID, Museo del Prado — MALIBU, The J. Paul Getty Museum — MELBOURNE, National Gallery of Victoria — MILANO, Pinacoteca di Brera — MILWAUKEE, Collection of Dr and Mr Alfred Bader — MINNEAPOLIS, The Minneapolis Institute of Arts — MONTRÉAL, Musée des Beaux-Arts de Montréal — MOSKOW, Puschkin Museum — NANCY, Musée des Beaux-Arts — NEW YORK, Art Resource — NEW YORK, Richard L. Feigen & Co — NEW YORK, The Frick Collection — NEW YORK, The Hyde Collection — NEW YORK, The Metropolitan Museum of Art — NÜRNBERG, Germanisches Nationalmuseum — OMAHA, Joslyn Art Museum — ONTARIO, Art Gallery of Ontario — OTTAWA, National Gallery of Canada — PARIS, R.M. Jourdan — PARIS, Musée National du Louvre — PARIS, Photographie Bulloz — PARIS, Musée Cognacq-Jay — PARIS, Musée Jacquemart-André — PARIS, Service Photographiquue de la Réunion des Musées Nationaux — PASADENA, Norton Simon Museum of Art — PENRHYN CASTLE, Wales, lady Janet Douglas Pennant — PHILADELPHIA, Philadelphia Museum of Art — PHILADELPHIA, John G. Johnson Collection at Philadelphia Museum of Art — PLANEGG, Artothek — PRAHA, Nârodnî Galerie V Praze — QUEENSTOWN, Maryland, Arthur A. Houghton jr. — ROCHESTER, New York, Memorial Art Gallery — ROTTERDAM, Museum Boymans-van Beuningen — ROXBURGHSHIRE, Duke of Sutherland Collection — ST. JAMES'S PALACE, Lord Chamberlain's Office — SAINT LOUIS (Missouri), The Saint Louis Art Museum — SALISBURY, Wiltshire, Little Durnford Manor — SAN DIEGO, Timken Art Gallery. Courtesy of the Putnam Foundation, Timken Art Gallery, San Diego California — SAN FRANCISCO, The Fine Arts Museums of San Francisco — SAO PAULO, Musea de Arte de São Paulo (photo: Luiz Hossaka) — SALTASH, Cornwall, Port Eliot Estate Office — SALZBURG, Salzburger Landessammlungen — STOCKHOLM, Nationalmuseum — STUTTGART, Staatsgalerie Stuttgart — TEL AVIV, Israël, Private Collection — TOLEDO, Ohio, The Toledo Museum of Art — TORINO, Chomon-Perino Fotografie — TOURS, Photographies J.J. Moreau — TOURS, Musées de la Ville de Tours — UTRECHT, Stichting Het Catharijneconvent — WANAS, Sweden, Graf Wachtmeister — WASHINGTON, D.C., National Gallery of Art — WIEN, Graphische Sammlung Albertina — WIEN, Gemäldegalerie der Akademie der bildenden Künste in Wien — WIEN, Kunsthistorisches Museum — ZÜRICH, Kunsthaus Zürich, Stiftung Prof. dr. L. Ruzicka — WILTSHIRE, David Robson — WOBURN, Bedfordshire, Woburn Abbey

PUBLISHED IN 1986 BY FONDS MERCATOR ANTWERP
AT THE INITIATIVE OF THE BANQUE PARIBAS BELGIUM AND
THE PARIBAS GROUP. TYPESETTING BY PHOTOCOMPO CENTER, BRUSSELS.
LITOGRAPHY BY SCAN 2000, BILBAO.
PRINTED BY DRUKKERIJ LANNOO, TIELT. BOUND BY
BOEKBINDERIJ SPLICHAL, TURNHOUT. DESIGN BY MARK VERSTOCKT.